VIZ GRAPHIC

# Descendants of Darkness

## Yami no Matsuei

**Story & Art by Yoko Matsushita**

1

# Descendants of Darkness
## Yami no Matsuei
Vol. 1
Shôjo Edition

**Story & Art by**
**Yoko Matsushita**

English Adaptation/Kelly Sue DeConnick
Translation/David Ury
Touch-Up & Lettering/Gia Cam Luc
Graphics & Cover Design/Hidemi Sahara
Editor/Eric Searleman

Managing Editor/Annette Roman
Director of Production/Noboru Watanabe
VP of Publishing/Alvin Lu
Sr. Director of Acquisitions/Rika Inouye
VP of Sales & Marketing/Liza Coppola
Publisher/Hyoe Narita

DESCENDANTS OF DARKNESS, Yami no Matsuei, is rated T+ and is recommended for readers who are age 13 and older. This book contains violence and mature situations.

Printed in the U.S.A.

Published by VIZ Media, LLC
P.O. Box 77064
San Francisco, CA 94107

Shôjo Edition
10 9 8 7 6 5 4 3
First printing, August 2004
Second printing, June 2005
Third printing, October 2005

For advertising rates or media kit, e-mail advertising@viz.com

store.viz.com

www.viz.com

# Two on the River's Edge

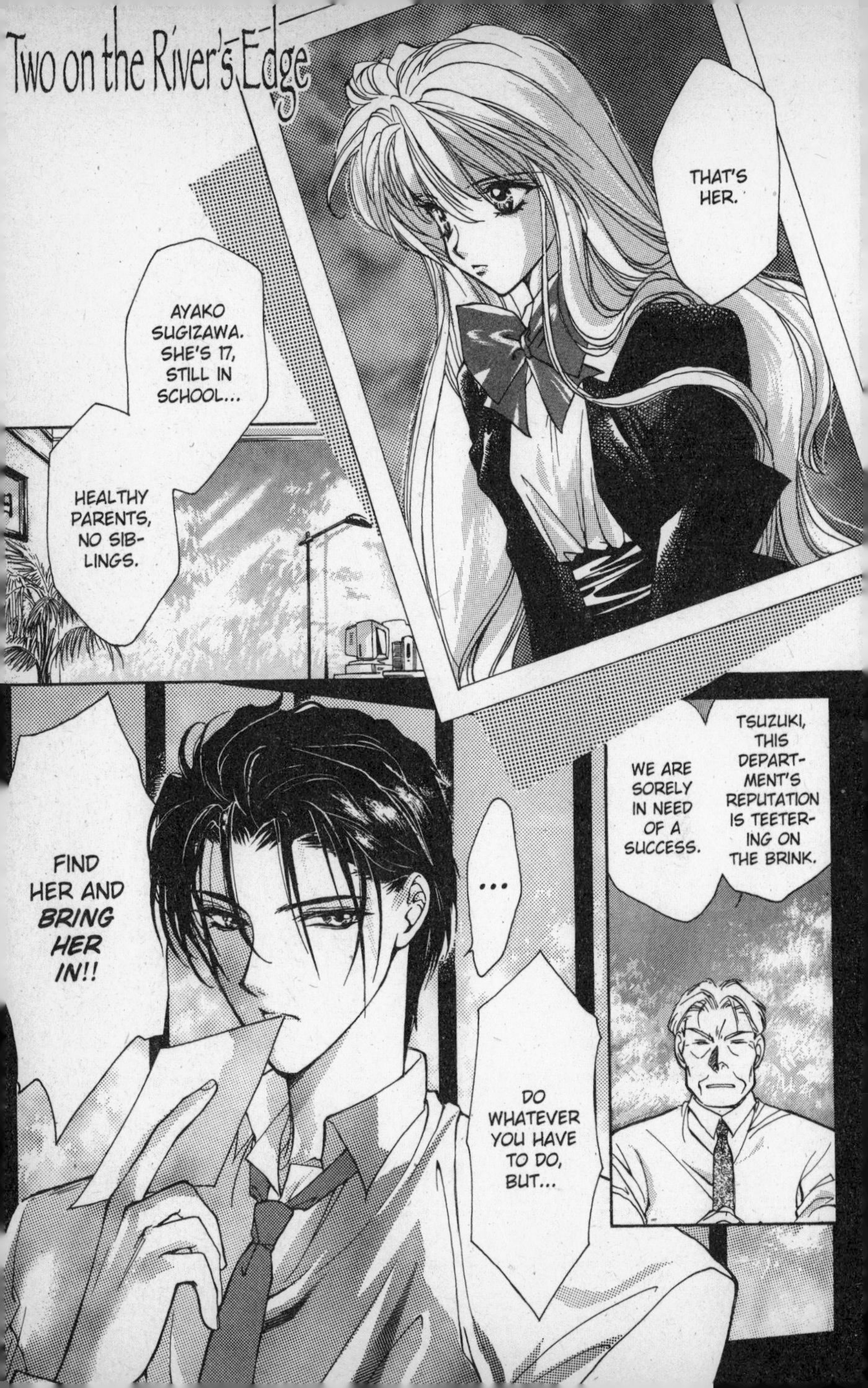
THAT'S HER.
AYAKO SUGIZAWA. SHE'S 17, STILL IN SCHOOL...
HEALTHY PARENTS, NO SIB-LINGS.
TSUZUKI, THIS DEPART-MENT'S REPUTATION IS TEETER-ING ON THE BRINK.
WE ARE SORELY IN NEED OF A SUCCESS.
...
DO WHATEVER YOU HAVE TO DO, BUT...
FIND HER AND ***BRING HER IN!!***

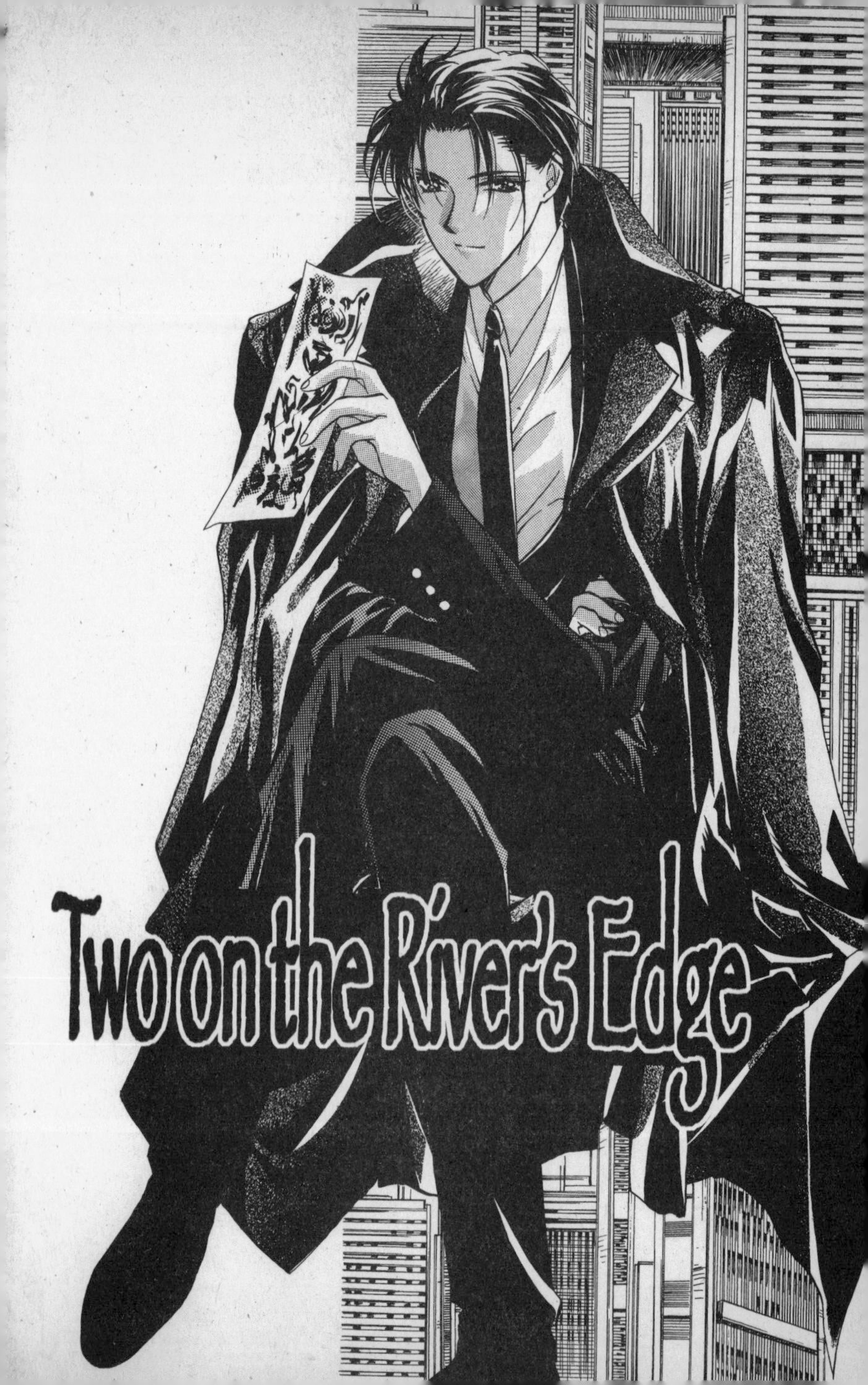
Two on the River's Edge

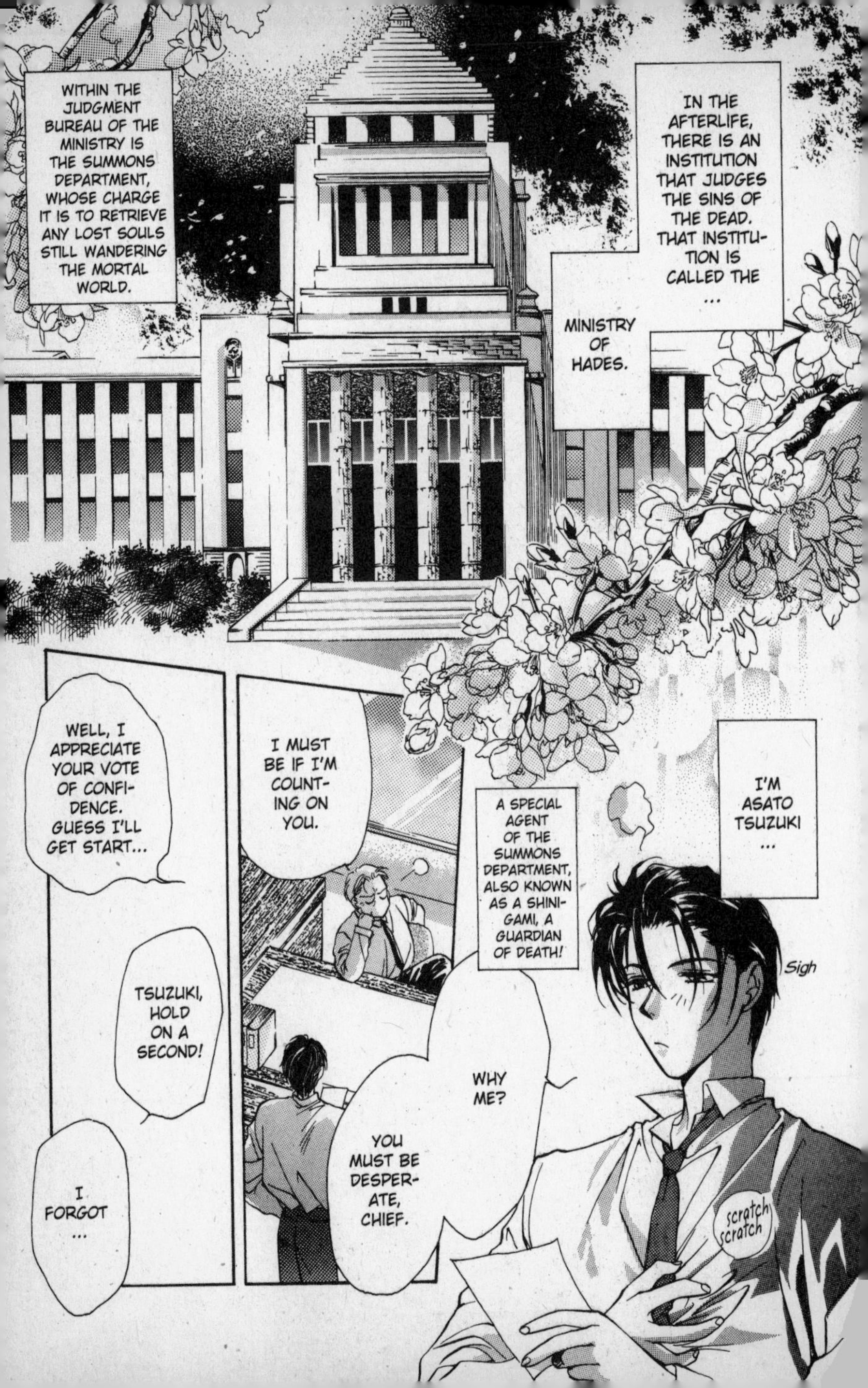
IN THE AFTERLIFE, THERE IS AN INSTITUTION THAT JUDGES THE SINS OF THE DEAD. THAT INSTITUTION IS CALLED THE ...
MINISTRY OF HADES.
WITHIN THE JUDGMENT BUREAU OF THE MINISTRY IS THE SUMMONS DEPARTMENT, WHOSE CHARGE IT IS TO RETRIEVE ANY LOST SOULS STILL WANDERING THE MORTAL WORLD.
I'M ASATO TSUZUKI ...
A SPECIAL AGENT OF THE SUMMONS DEPARTMENT, ALSO KNOWN AS A SHINIGAMI, A GUARDIAN OF DEATH!
Sigh
WHY ME?
YOU MUST BE DESPERATE, CHIEF.
scratch scratch
I MUST BE IF I'M COUNTING ON YOU.
WELL, I APPRECIATE YOUR VOTE OF CONFIDENCE. GUESS I'LL GET START...
TSUZUKI, HOLD ON A SECOND!
I FORGOT ...

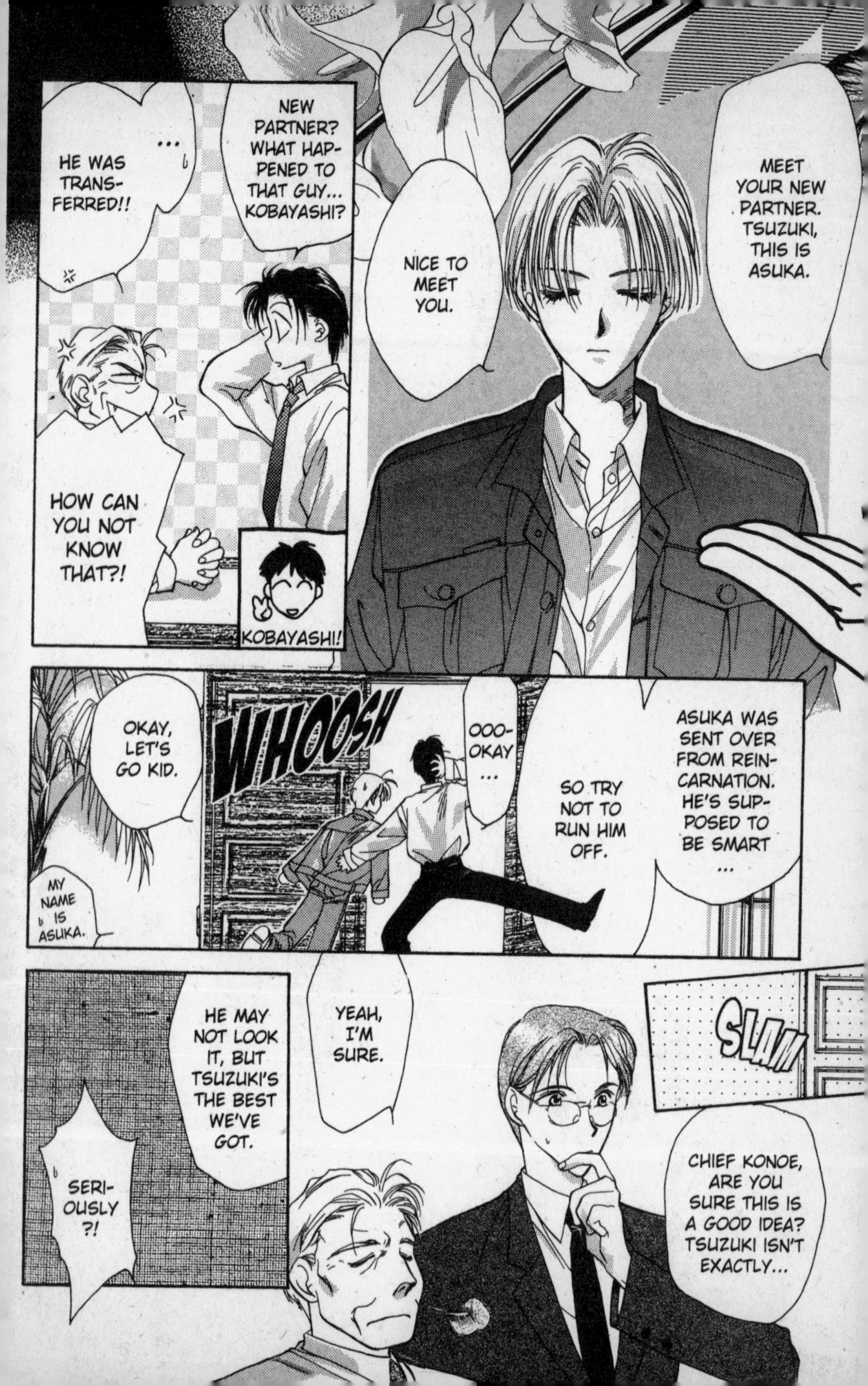
MEET YOUR NEW PARTNER. TSUZUKI, THIS IS ASUKA.
NICE TO MEET YOU.
NEW PARTNER? WHAT HAPPENED TO THAT GUY... KOBAYASHI?
...
HE WAS TRANSFERRED!!
HOW CAN YOU NOT KNOW THAT?!
KOBAYASHI!
ASUKA WAS SENT OVER FROM REINCARNATION. HE'S SUPPOSED TO BE SMART ...
SO TRY NOT TO RUN HIM OFF.
OOO-OKAY ...
WHOOSH
OKAY, LET'S GO KID.
MY NAME IS ASUKA.
SLAM
CHIEF KONOE, ARE YOU SURE THIS IS A GOOD IDEA? TSUZUKI ISN'T EXACTLY...
YEAH, I'M SURE.
HE MAY NOT LOOK IT, BUT TSUZUKI'S THE BEST WE'VE GOT.
SERIOUSLY?!

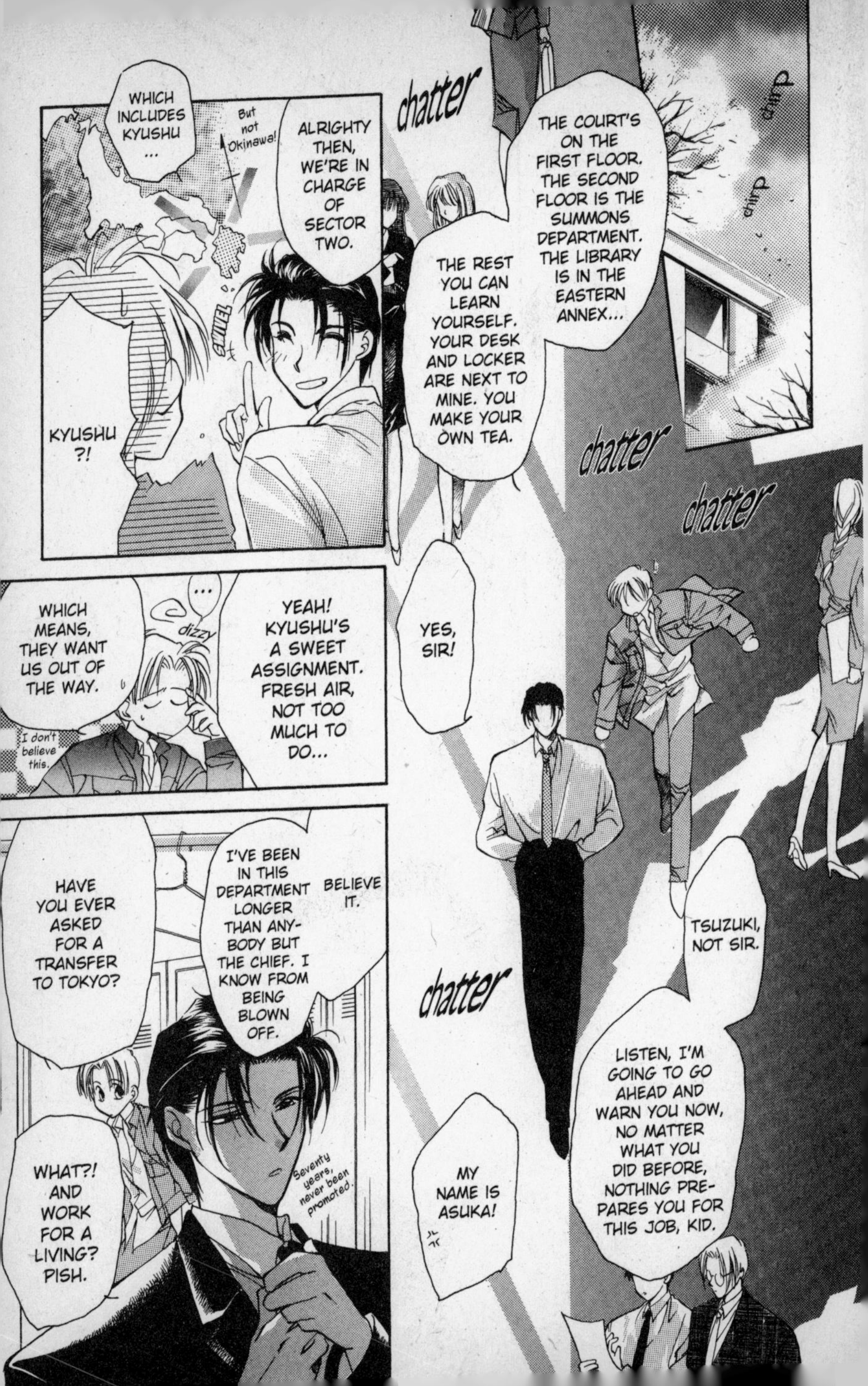
chirp
chirp
chatter
THE COURT'S ON THE FIRST FLOOR. THE SECOND FLOOR IS THE SUMMONS DEPARTMENT. THE LIBRARY IS IN THE EASTERN ANNEX...
THE REST YOU CAN LEARN YOURSELF. YOUR DESK AND LOCKER ARE NEXT TO MINE. YOU MAKE YOUR OWN TEA.
chatter
chatter
YES, SIR!
TSUZUKI, NOT SIR.
chatter
LISTEN, I'M GOING TO GO AHEAD AND WARN YOU NOW, NO MATTER WHAT YOU DID BEFORE, NOTHING PREPARES YOU FOR THIS JOB, KID.
MY NAME IS ASUKA!
ALRIGHTY THEN, WE'RE IN CHARGE OF SECTOR TWO.
But not Okinawa!
WHICH INCLUDES KYUSHU...
SWIVEL
KYUSHU?!
YEAH! KYUSHU'S A SWEET ASSIGNMENT. FRESH AIR, NOT TOO MUCH TO DO...
...
dizzy
WHICH MEANS, THEY WANT US OUT OF THE WAY.
I don't believe this.
BELIEVE IT.
I'VE BEEN IN THIS DEPARTMENT LONGER THAN ANY-BODY BUT THE CHIEF. I KNOW FROM BEING BLOWN OFF.
HAVE YOU EVER ASKED FOR A TRANSFER TO TOKYO?
Seventy years, never been promoted.
WHAT?! AND WORK FOR A LIVING? PISH.

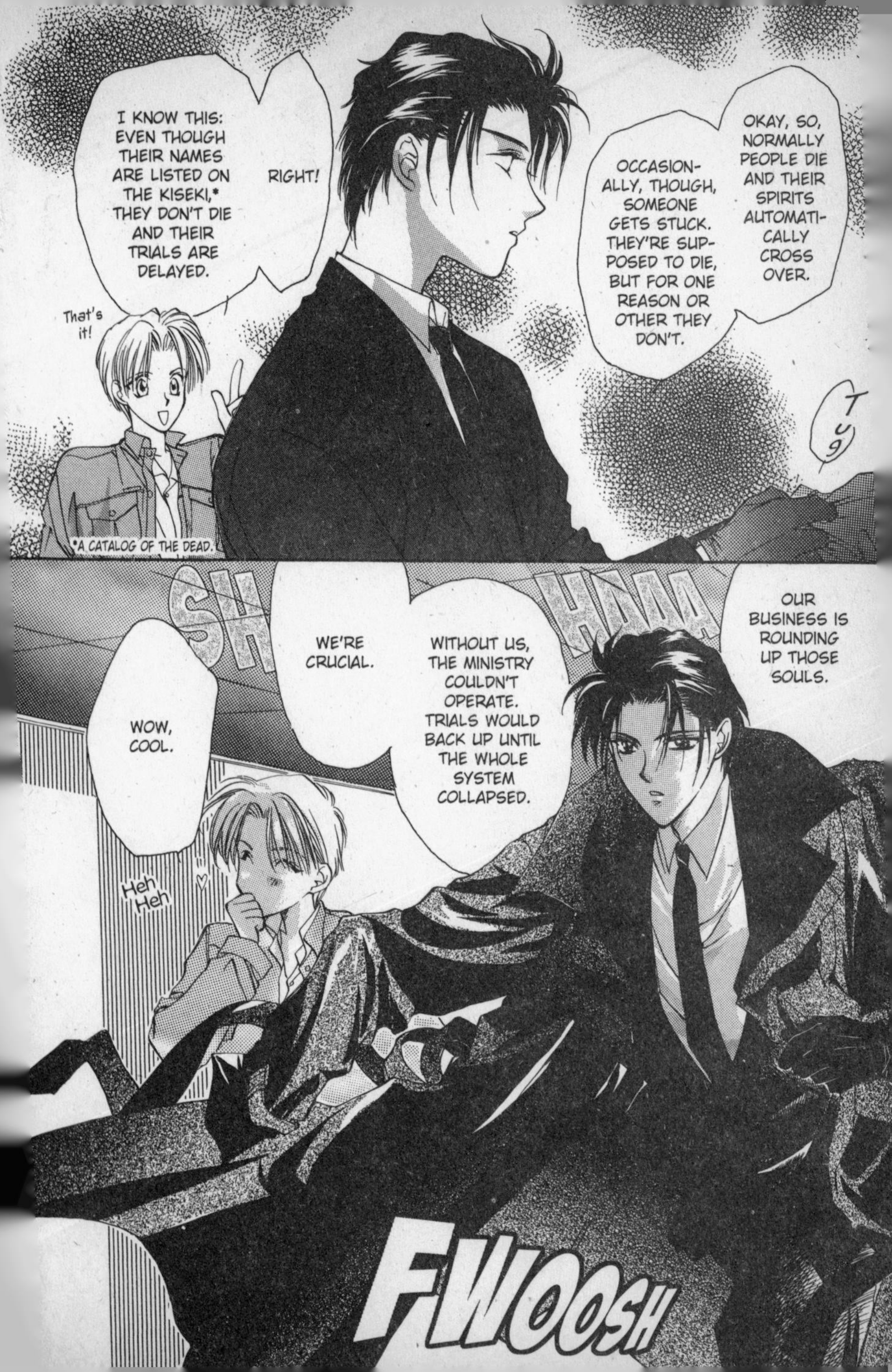
OKAY, SO, NORMALLY PEOPLE DIE AND THEIR SPIRITS AUTOMATICALLY CROSS OVER.
OCCASIONALLY, THOUGH, SOMEONE GETS STUCK. THEY'RE SUPPOSED TO DIE, BUT FOR ONE REASON OR OTHER THEY DON'T.
Tug
RIGHT!
I KNOW THIS: EVEN THOUGH THEIR NAMES ARE LISTED ON THE KISEKI,* THEY DON'T DIE AND THEIR TRIALS ARE DELAYED.
That's it!
*A CATALOG OF THE DEAD.
OUR BUSINESS IS ROUNDING UP THOSE SOULS.
SHHAAA
WITHOUT US, THE MINISTRY COULDN'T OPERATE. TRIALS WOULD BACK UP UNTIL THE WHOLE SYSTEM COLLAPSED.
WE'RE CRUCIAL.
WOW, COOL.
Heh Heh
FWOOSH

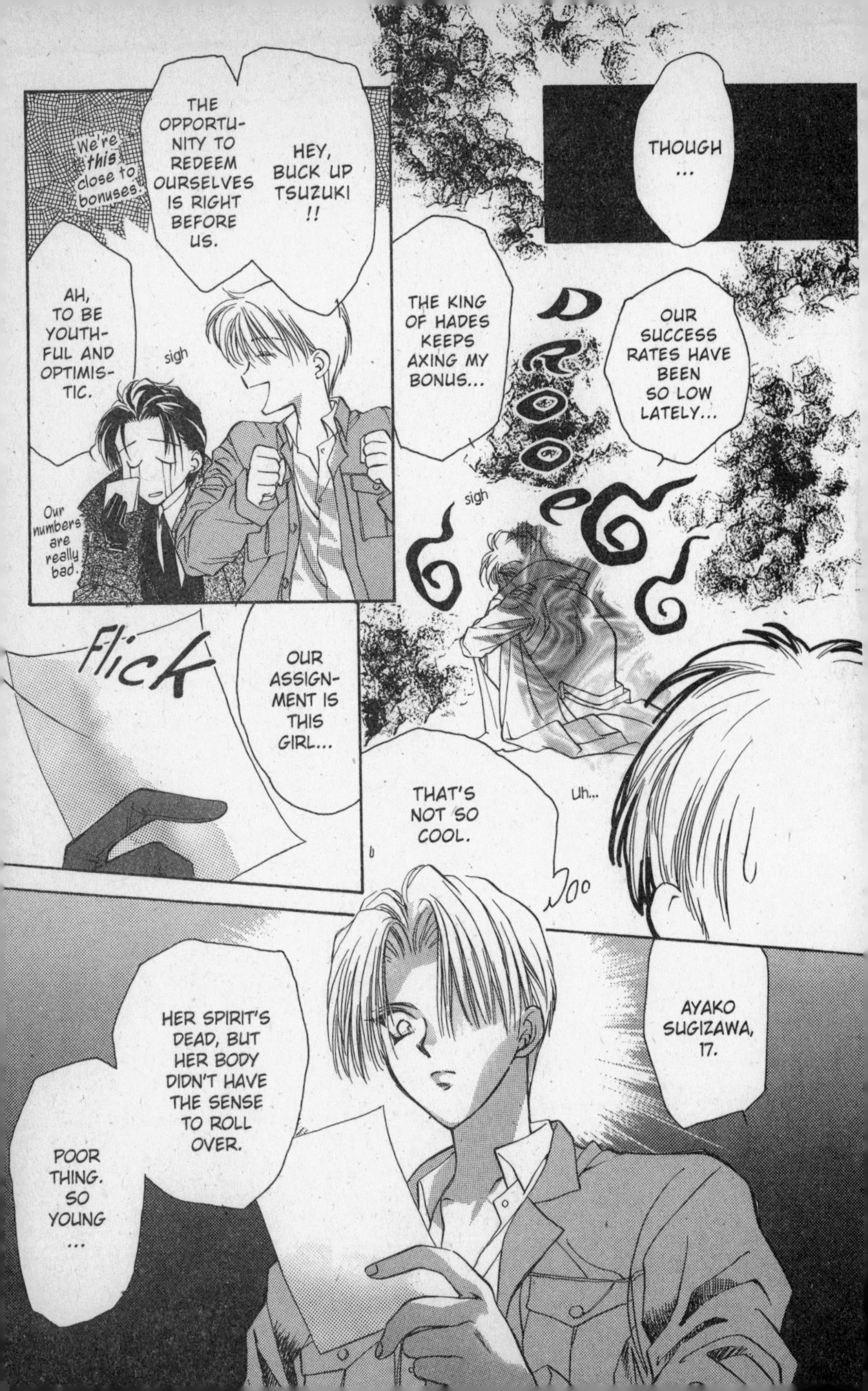

THOUGH...
OUR SUCCESS RATES HAVE BEEN SO LOW LATELY...
THE KING OF HADES KEEPS AXING MY BONUS...
DROOOOP
sigh
HEY, BUCK UP TSUZUKI!!
THE OPPORTUNITY TO REDEEM OURSELVES IS RIGHT BEFORE US.
We're this close to bonuses.
AH, TO BE YOUTHFUL AND OPTIMISTIC.
sigh
Our numbers are really bad.
uh...
THAT'S NOT SO COOL.
OUR ASSIGNMENT IS THIS GIRL...
Flick
AYAKO SUGIZAWA, 17.
HER SPIRIT'S DEAD, BUT HER BODY DIDN'T HAVE THE SENSE TO ROLL OVER.
POOR THING. SO YOUNG...

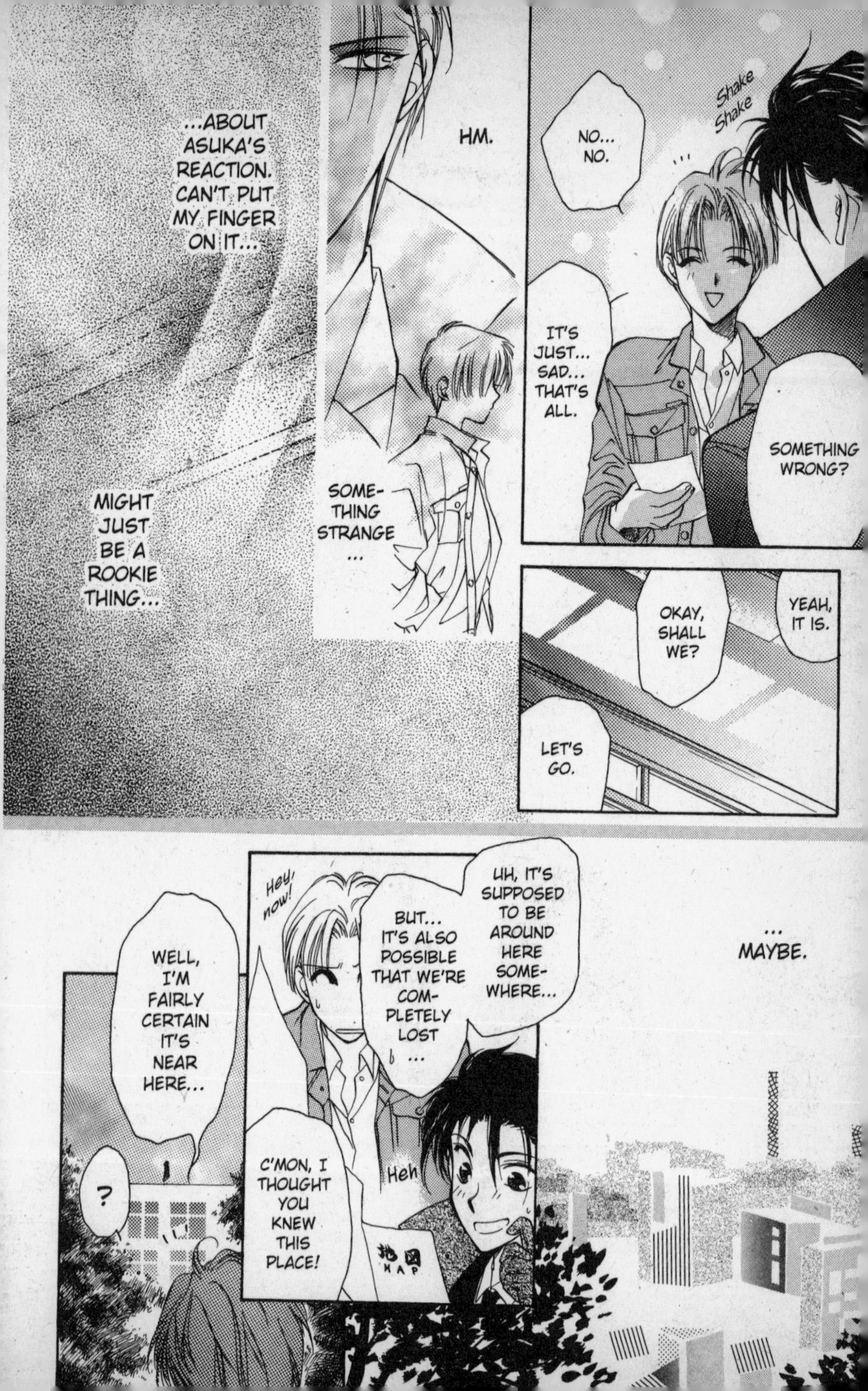
Shake Shake
NO... NO.
...
IT'S JUST... SAD... THAT'S ALL.
SOMETHING WRONG?
YEAH, IT IS.
OKAY, SHALL WE?
LET'S GO.
HM.
SOME-THING STRANGE ...
...ABOUT ASUKA'S REACTION. CAN'T PUT MY FINGER ON IT...
MIGHT JUST BE A ROOKIE THING...
... MAYBE.
UH, IT'S SUPPOSED TO BE AROUND HERE SOME-WHERE...
Hey, now!
BUT... IT'S ALSO POSSIBLE THAT WE'RE COM-PLETELY LOST ...
Heh
C'MON, I THOUGHT YOU KNEW THIS PLACE!
地図 MAP
WELL, I'M FAIRLY CERTAIN IT'S NEAR HERE...
?

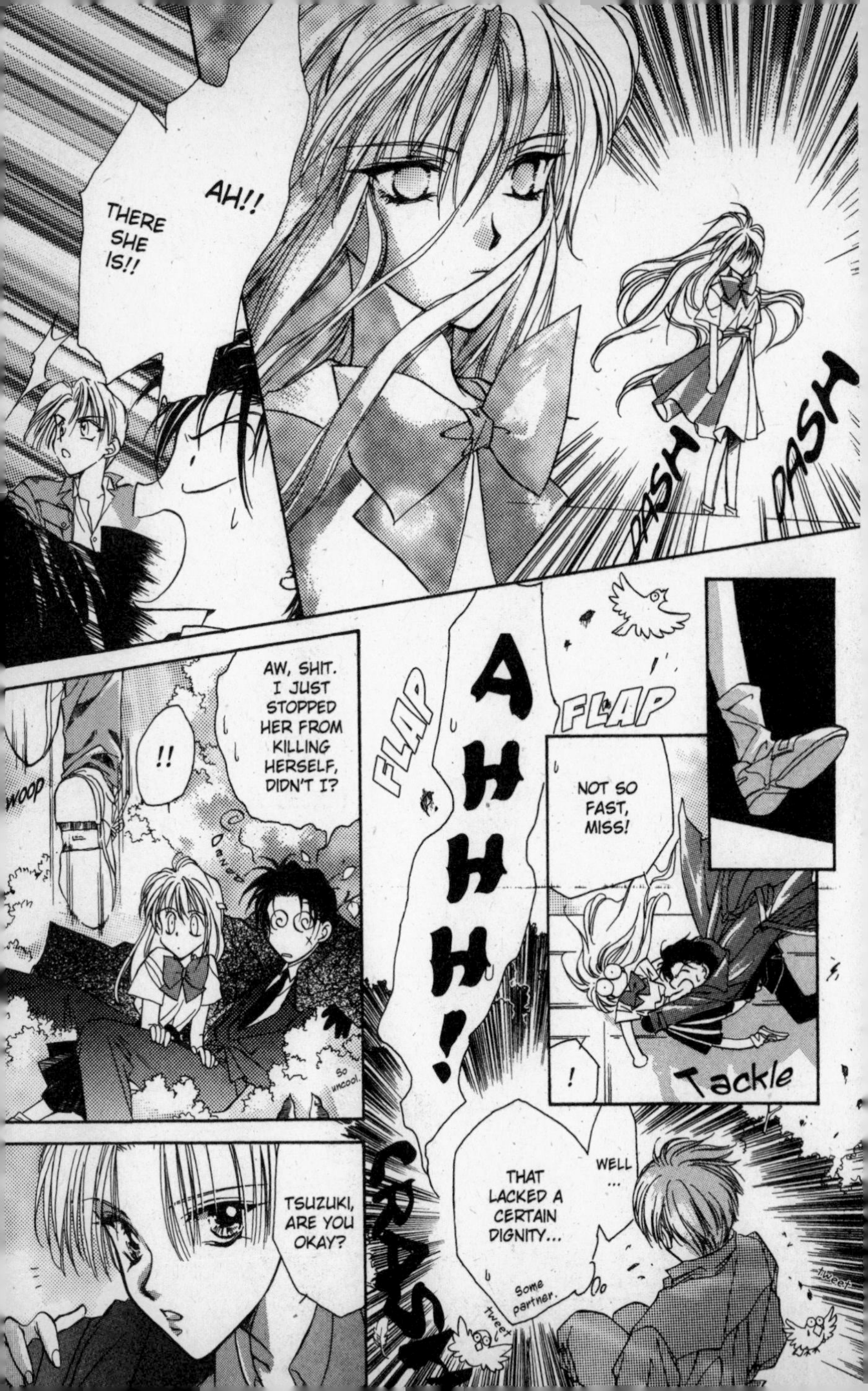
DASH
DASH
AH!!
THERE SHE IS!!
NOT SO FAST, MISS!
!
Tackle
FLAP
FLAP
AHHHH!
AW, SHIT. I JUST STOPPED HER FROM KILLING HERSELF, DIDN'T I?
!!
woop
So uncool.
WELL...
THAT LACKED A CERTAIN DIGNITY...
Some partner.
tweet
tweet
CRAS
TSUZUKI, ARE YOU OKAY?

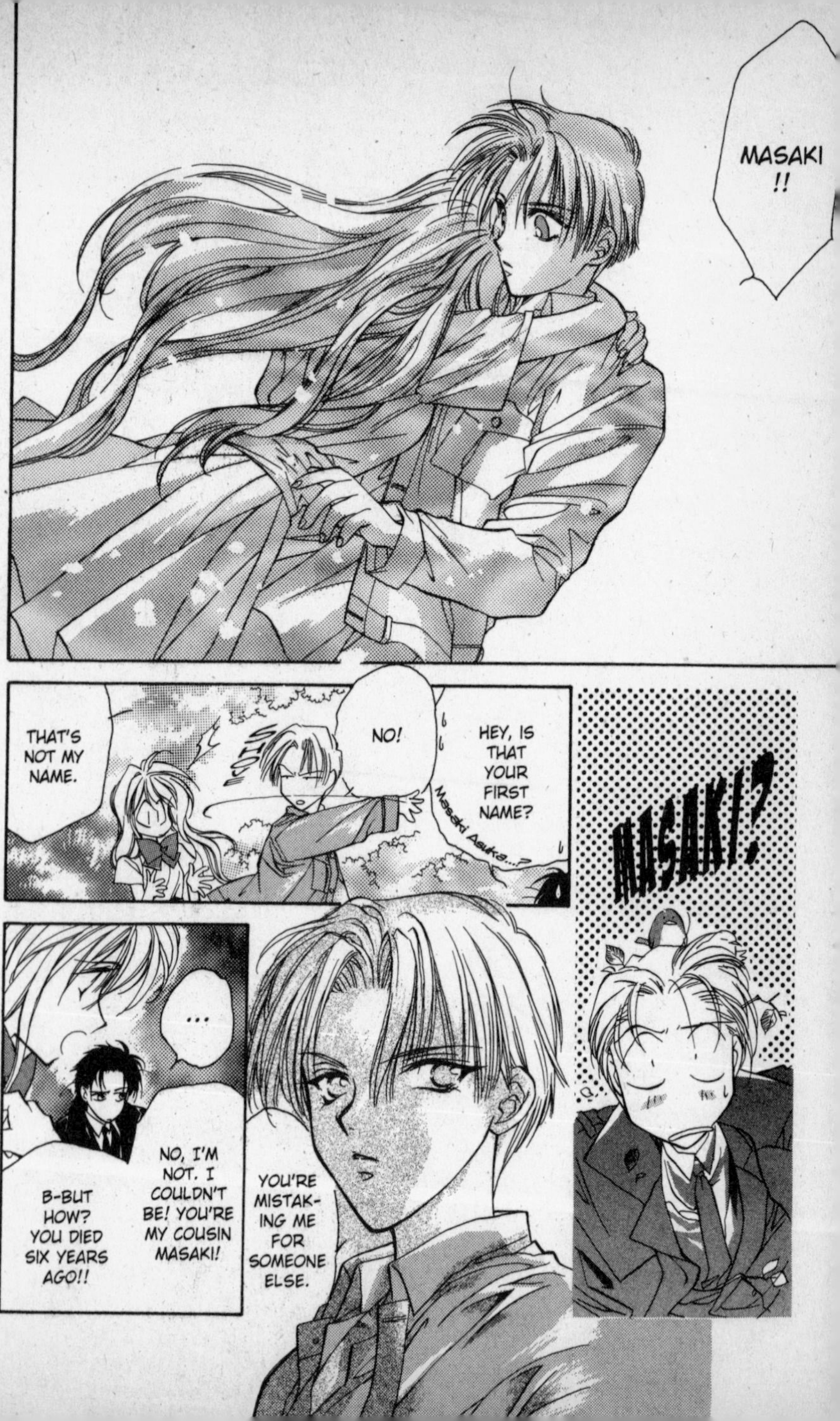
MASAKI !!
MASAKI!?
HEY, IS THAT YOUR FIRST NAME?
Masaki Asuka...?
NO!
THAT'S NOT MY NAME.
YOU'RE MISTAKING ME FOR SOMEONE ELSE.
...
NO, I'M NOT. I COULDN'T BE! YOU'RE MY COUSIN MASAKI!
B-BUT HOW? YOU DIED SIX YEARS AGO!!

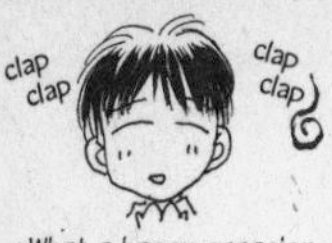
clap clap
clap clap

What a happy occasion.

# Huzzah!

My first comic is finally out!! Thank you so much for all of your support. I'm Yoko Matsushita (yes, that's my real name). I first wrote Tsuzuki's story as a one-shot comic I had no idea it would catch on like this! Really. In fact, when I was developing the story, I thought Masaki was going to be the main character. But then Tsuzuki kind of took over and... well, here we are! I like the way it turned out.

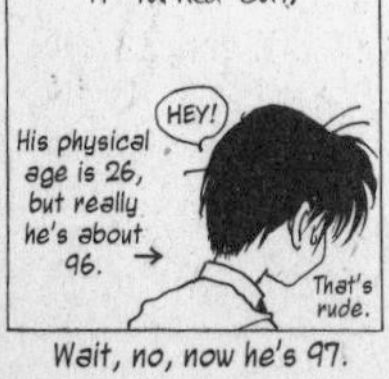
HEY!
His physical age is 26, but really he's about 96.
That's rude.

Wait, no, now he's 97.

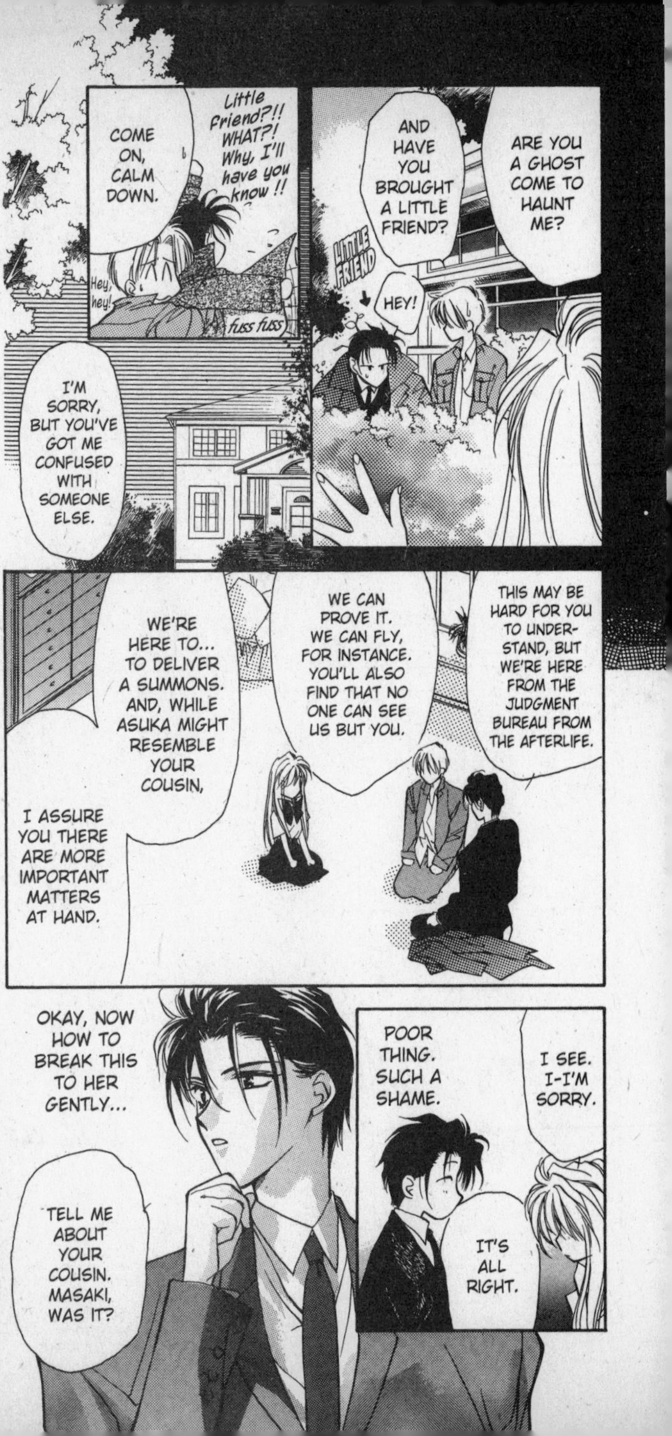
ARE YOU A GHOST COME TO HAUNT ME?
AND HAVE YOU BROUGHT A LITTLE FRIEND?
LITTLE FRIEND
HEY!
Little friend?!! WHAT?! Why, I'll have you know !!
COME ON, CALM DOWN.
Hey, hey!
fuss fuss
I'M SORRY, BUT YOU'VE GOT ME CONFUSED WITH SOMEONE ELSE.
THIS MAY BE HARD FOR YOU TO UNDERSTAND, BUT WE'RE HERE FROM THE JUDGMENT BUREAU FROM THE AFTERLIFE.
WE CAN PROVE IT. WE CAN FLY, FOR INSTANCE. YOU'LL ALSO FIND THAT NO ONE CAN SEE US BUT YOU.
WE'RE HERE TO... TO DELIVER A SUMMONS. AND, WHILE ASUKA MIGHT RESEMBLE YOUR COUSIN,
I ASSURE YOU THERE ARE MORE IMPORTANT MATTERS AT HAND.
I SEE. I-I'M SORRY.
POOR THING. SUCH A SHAME.
IT'S ALL RIGHT.
OKAY, NOW HOW TO BREAK THIS TO HER GENTLY...
TELL ME ABOUT YOUR COUSIN. MASAKI, WAS IT?

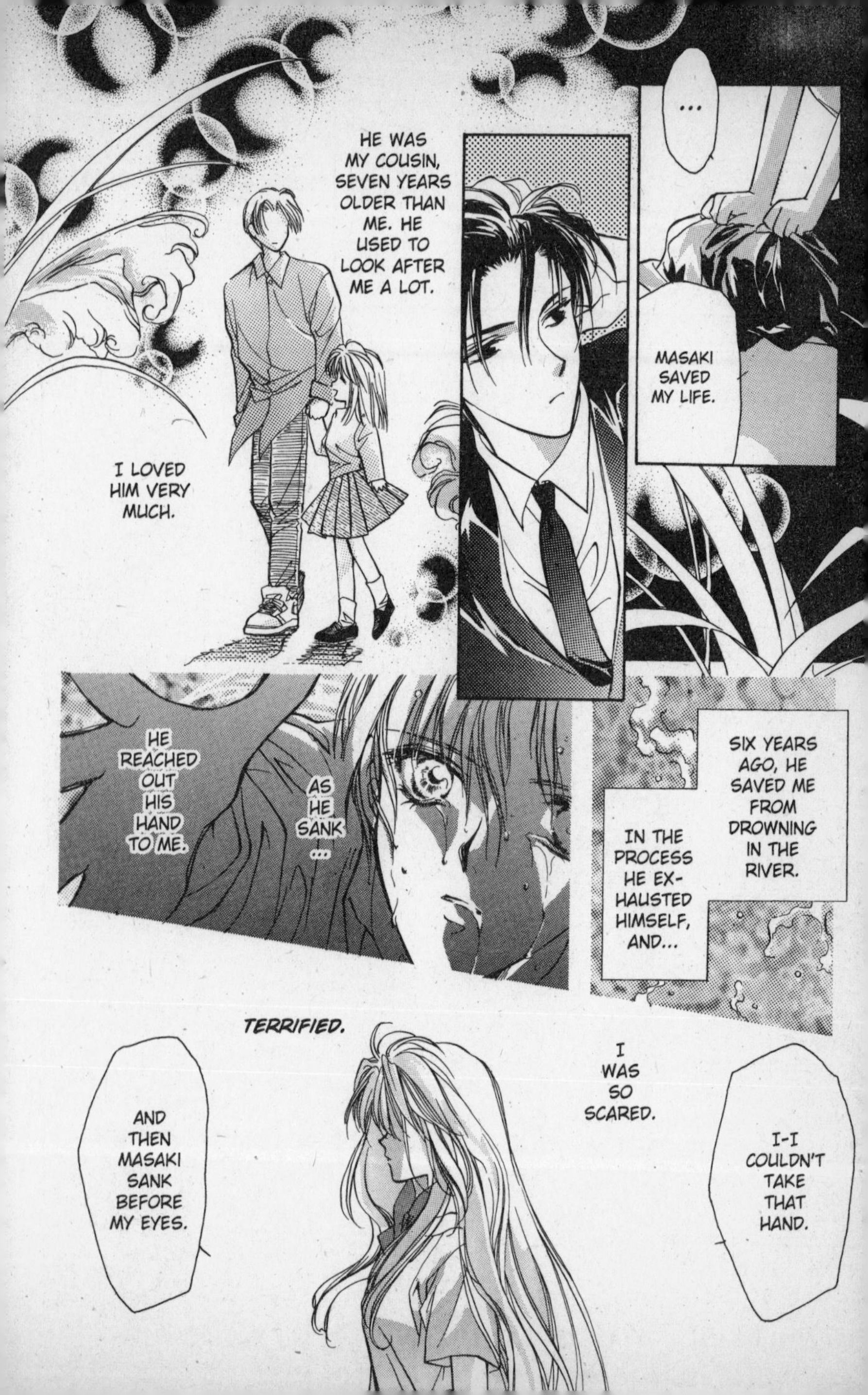
...
MASAKI SAVED MY LIFE.
HE WAS MY COUSIN, SEVEN YEARS OLDER THAN ME. HE USED TO LOOK AFTER ME A LOT.
I LOVED HIM VERY MUCH.
SIX YEARS AGO, HE SAVED ME FROM DROWNING IN THE RIVER.
IN THE PROCESS HE EX-HAUSTED HIMSELF, AND...
AS HE SANK ...
HE REACHED OUT HIS HAND TO ME.
I-I COULDN'T TAKE THAT HAND.
I WAS SO SCARED.
TERRIFIED.
AND THEN MASAKI SANK BEFORE MY EYES.

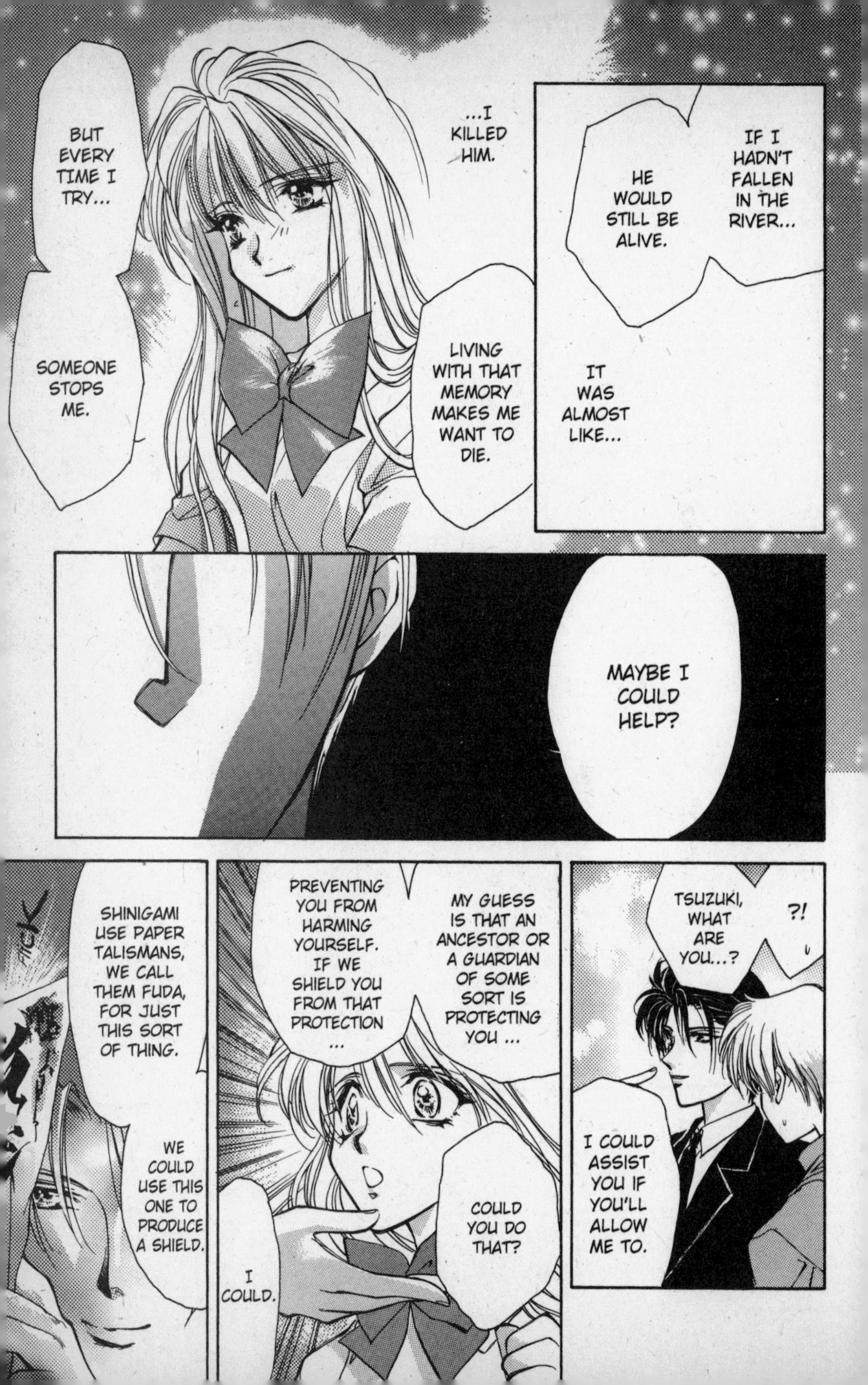
IF I HADN'T FALLEN IN THE RIVER...
HE WOULD STILL BE ALIVE.
IT WAS ALMOST LIKE...
...I KILLED HIM.
LIVING WITH THAT MEMORY MAKES ME WANT TO DIE.
BUT EVERY TIME I TRY...
SOMEONE STOPS ME.
MAYBE I COULD HELP?
?!
TSUZUKI, WHAT ARE YOU...?
I COULD ASSIST YOU IF YOU'LL ALLOW ME TO.
MY GUESS IS THAT AN ANCESTOR OR A GUARDIAN OF SOME SORT IS PROTECTING YOU ...
PREVENTING YOU FROM HARMING YOURSELF. IF WE SHIELD YOU FROM THAT PROTECTION ...
COULD YOU DO THAT?
I COULD.
FLICK
SHINIGAMI USE PAPER TALISMANS, WE CALL THEM FUDA, FOR JUST THIS SORT OF THING.
WE COULD USE THIS ONE TO PRODUCE A SHIELD.

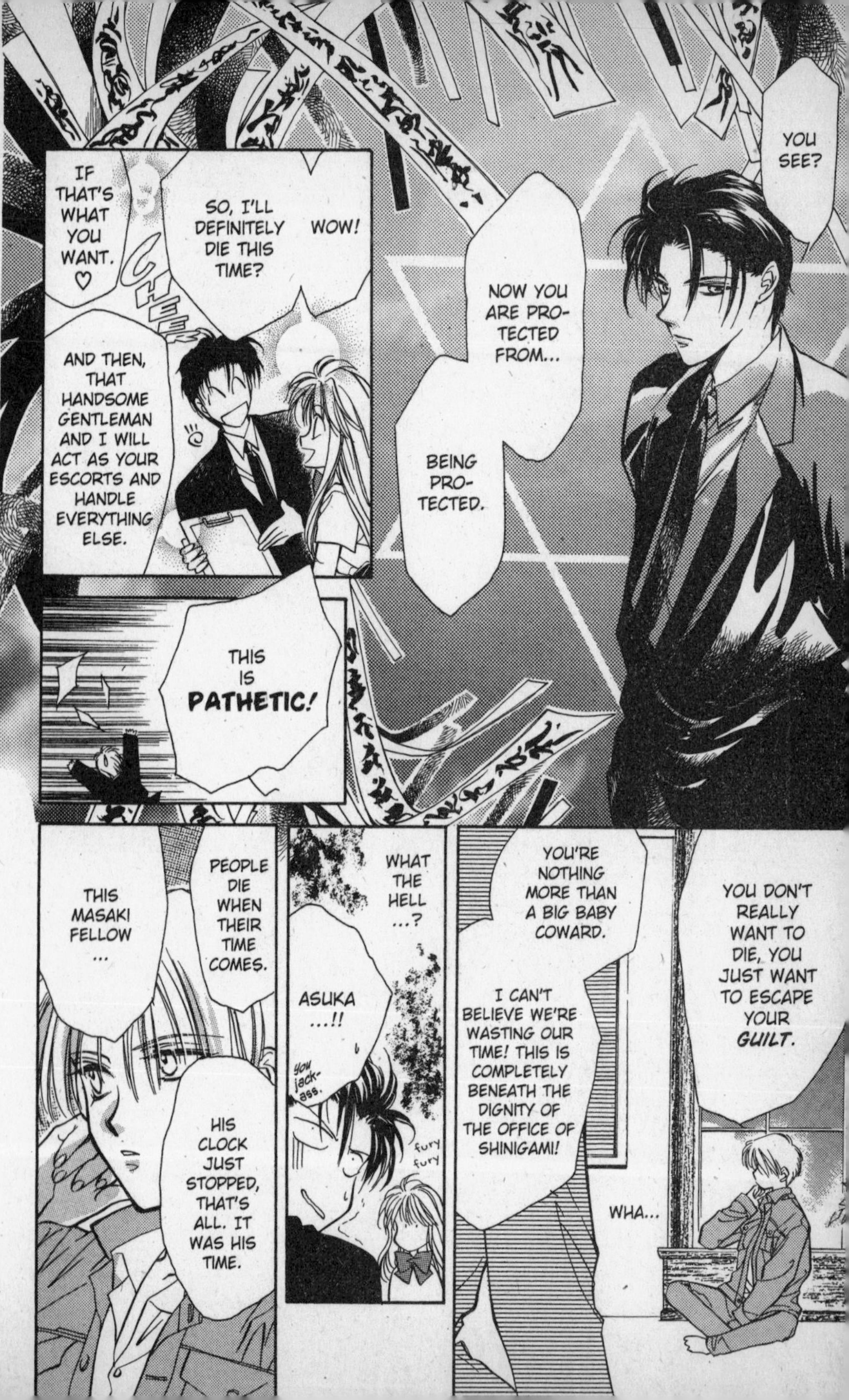
YOU SEE?
NOW YOU ARE PRO-TECTED FROM...
BEING PRO-TECTED.
WOW!
SO, I'LL DEFINITELY DIE THIS TIME?
IF THAT'S WHAT YOU WANT. ♡
AND THEN, THAT HANDSOME GENTLEMAN AND I WILL ACT AS YOUR ESCORTS AND HANDLE EVERYTHING ELSE.
THIS IS **PATHETIC!**
YOU DON'T REALLY WANT TO DIE, YOU JUST WANT TO ESCAPE YOUR ***GUILT***.
YOU'RE NOTHING MORE THAN A BIG BABY COWARD.
I CAN'T BELIEVE WE'RE WASTING OUR TIME! THIS IS COMPLETELY BENEATH THE DIGNITY OF THE OFFICE OF SHINIGAMI!
WHA...
WHAT THE HELL ...?
ASUKA ...!!
you jack-ass.
fury fury
PEOPLE DIE WHEN THEIR TIME COMES.
THIS MASAKI FELLOW ...
HIS CLOCK JUST STOPPED, THAT'S ALL. IT WAS HIS TIME.

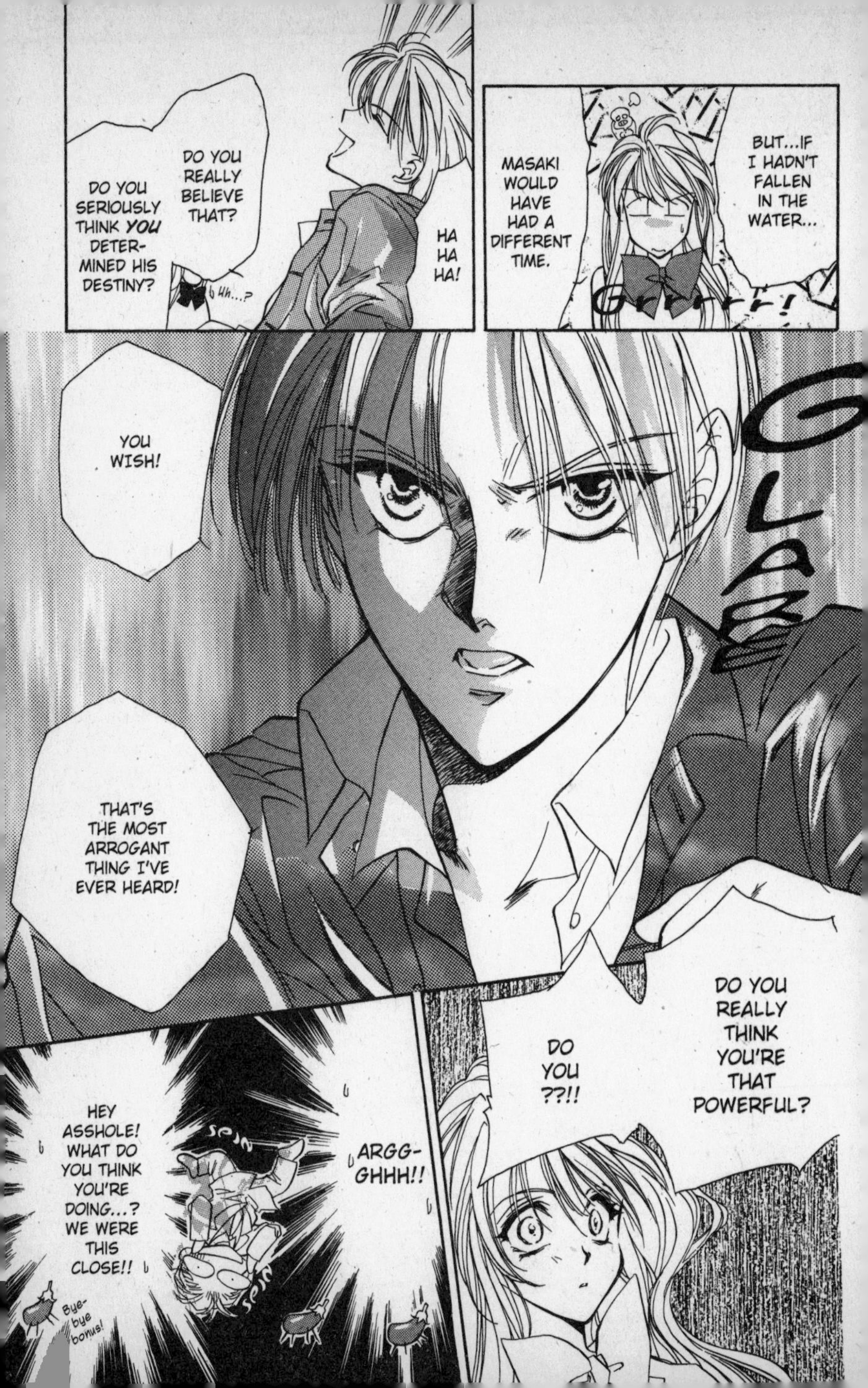
BUT...IF I HADN'T FALLEN IN THE WATER...
MASAKI WOULD HAVE HAD A DIFFERENT TIME.
Grrrrr!
HA HA HA!
DO YOU REALLY BELIEVE THAT?
DO YOU SERIOUSLY THINK YOU DETERMINED HIS DESTINY?
Uh...?
GLARE
YOU WISH!
THAT'S THE MOST ARROGANT THING I'VE EVER HEARD!
DO YOU REALLY THINK YOU'RE THAT POWERFUL?
DO YOU ??!!
ARGG-GHHH!!
HEY ASSHOLE! WHAT DO YOU THINK YOU'RE DOING...? WE WERE THIS CLOSE!!
Bye-bye bonus!

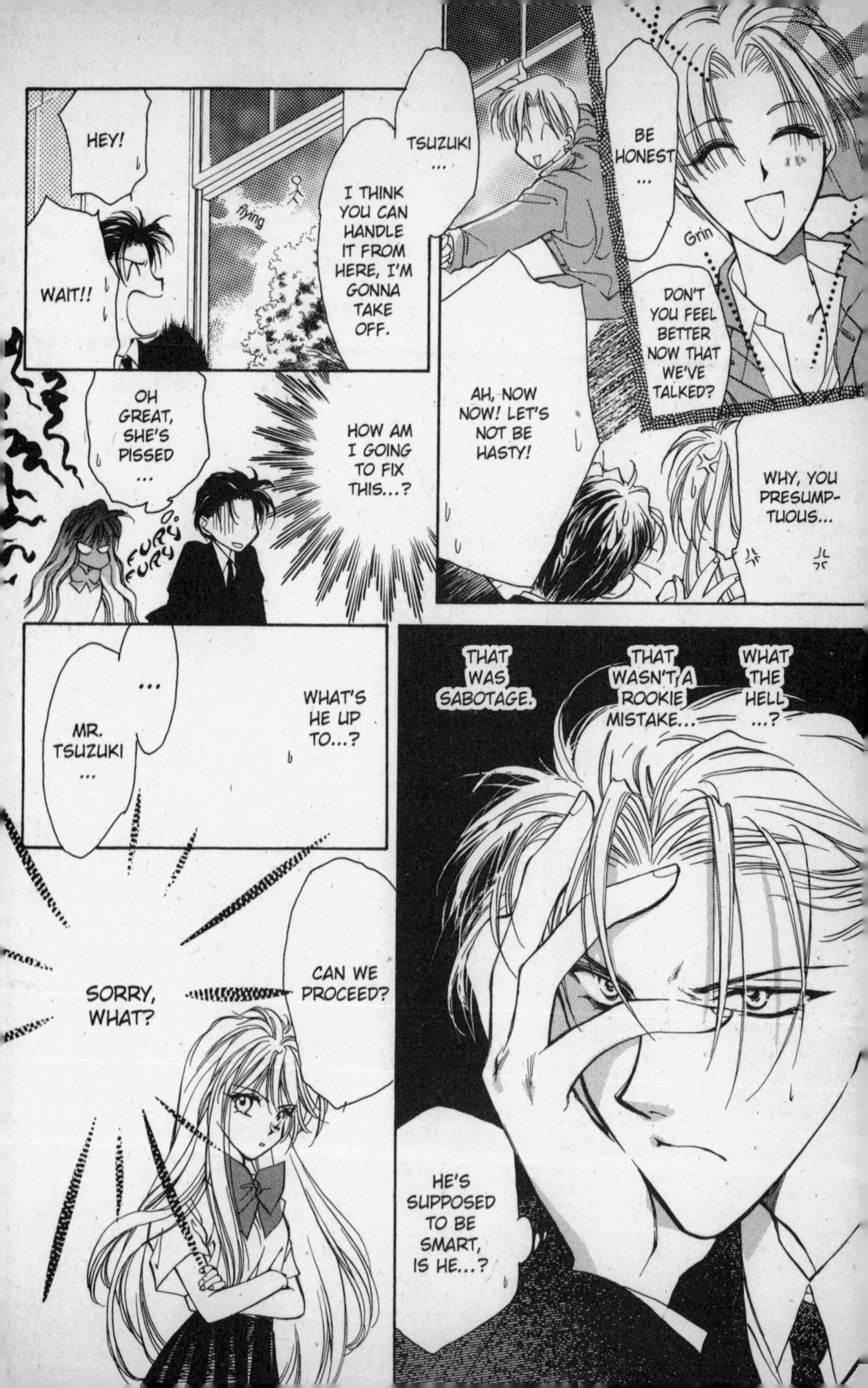
BE HONEST ...
Grin
DON'T YOU FEEL BETTER NOW THAT WE'VE TALKED?
WHY, YOU PRESUMPTUOUS...
AH, NOW NOW! LET'S NOT BE HASTY!
TSUZUKI ... I THINK YOU CAN HANDLE IT FROM HERE, I'M GONNA TAKE OFF.
HEY!
flying
WAIT!!
HOW AM I GOING TO FIX THIS...?
OH GREAT, SHE'S PISSED ...
FURY FURY
WHAT THE HELL ...?
THAT WASN'T A ROOKIE MISTAKE...
THAT WAS SABOTAGE.
HE'S SUPPOSED TO BE SMART, IS HE...?
WHAT'S HE UP TO...?
... MR. TSUZUKI ...
CAN WE PROCEED?
SORRY, WHAT?

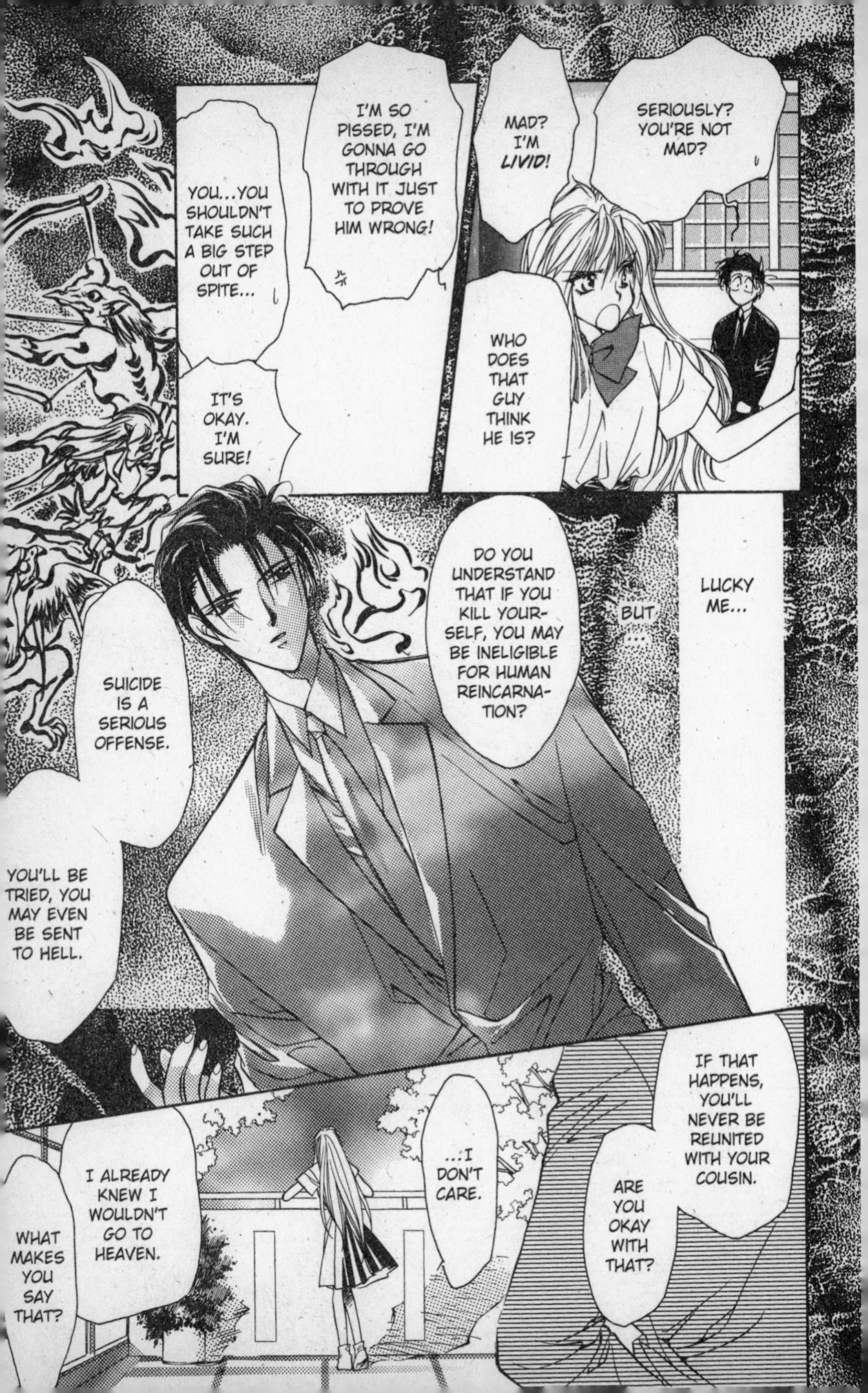
SERIOUSLY? YOU'RE NOT MAD?
MAD? I'M *LIVID!*
WHO DOES THAT GUY THINK HE IS?
I'M SO PISSED, I'M GONNA GO THROUGH WITH IT JUST TO PROVE HIM WRONG!
YOU...YOU SHOULDN'T TAKE SUCH A BIG STEP OUT OF SPITE...
IT'S OKAY. I'M SURE!
LUCKY ME...
BUT...
DO YOU UNDERSTAND THAT IF YOU KILL YOURSELF, YOU MAY BE INELIGIBLE FOR HUMAN REINCARNATION?
SUICIDE IS A SERIOUS OFFENSE.
YOU'LL BE TRIED, YOU MAY EVEN BE SENT TO HELL.
IF THAT HAPPENS, YOU'LL NEVER BE REUNITED WITH YOUR COUSIN.
ARE YOU OKAY WITH THAT?
...I DON'T CARE.
I ALREADY KNEW I WOULDN'T GO TO HEAVEN.
WHAT MAKES YOU SAY THAT?

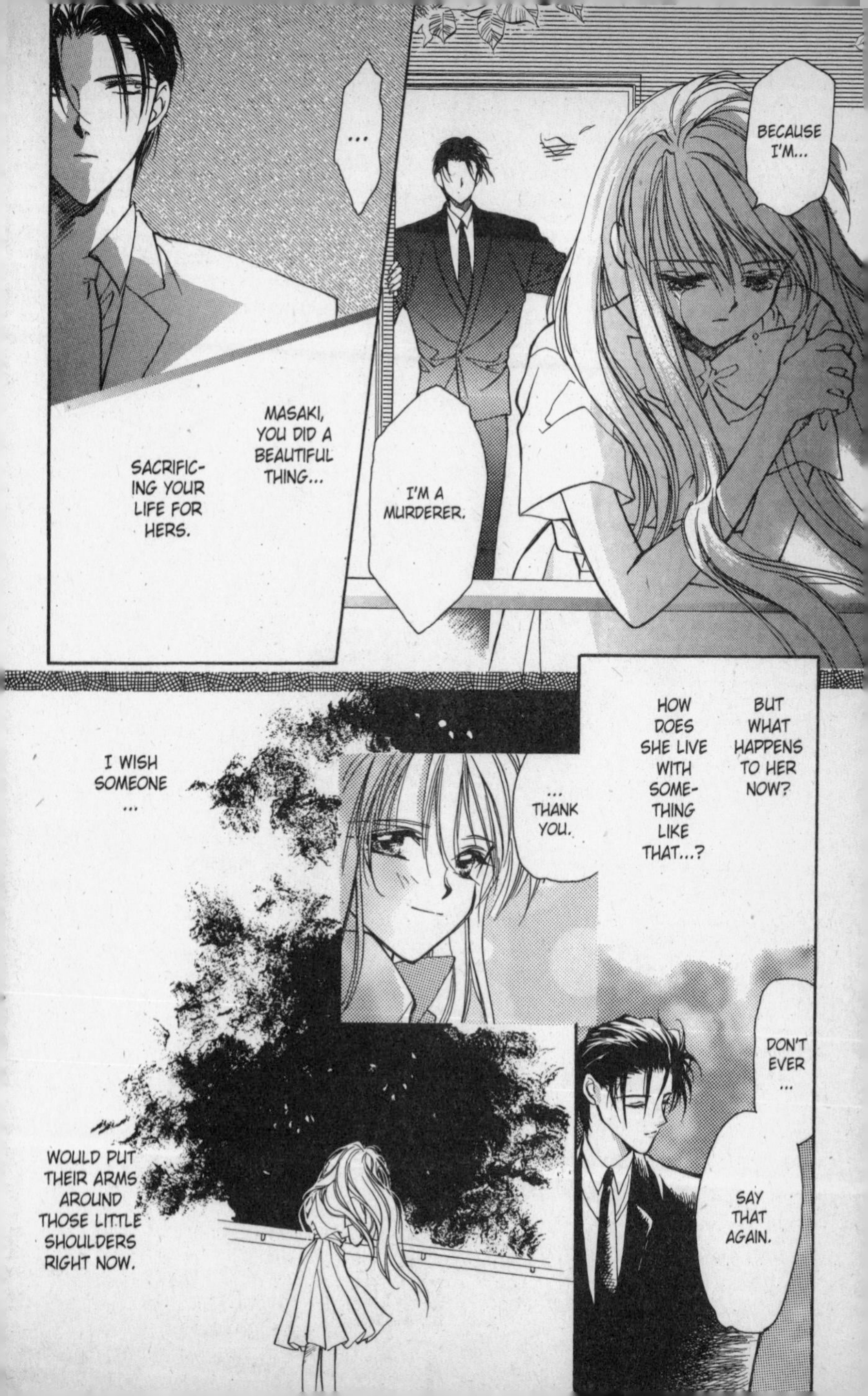
BECAUSE I'M...
I'M A MURDERER.
...
MASAKI, YOU DID A BEAUTIFUL THING...
SACRIFICING YOUR LIFE FOR HERS.
BUT WHAT HAPPENS TO HER NOW?
HOW DOES SHE LIVE WITH SOMETHING LIKE THAT...?
... THANK YOU.
DON'T EVER ...
SAY THAT AGAIN.
I WISH SOMEONE ...
WOULD PUT THEIR ARMS AROUND THOSE LITTLE SHOULDERS RIGHT NOW.

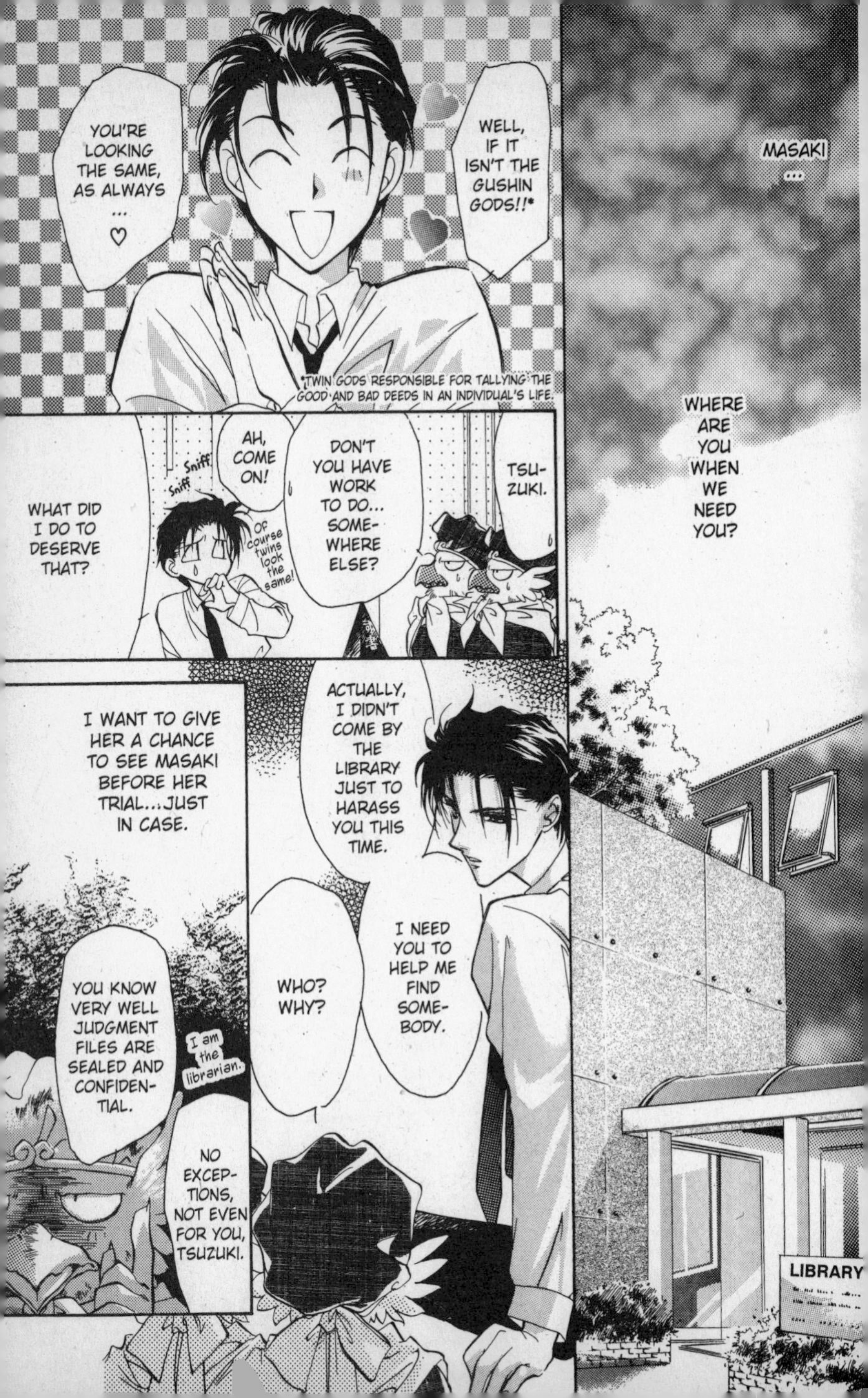
MASAKI ...
WHERE ARE YOU WHEN WE NEED YOU?
LIBRARY
WELL, IF IT ISN'T THE GUSHIN GODS!!*
YOU'RE LOOKING THE SAME, AS ALWAYS ... ♡
*TWIN GODS RESPONSIBLE FOR TALLYING THE GOOD AND BAD DEEDS IN AN INDIVIDUAL'S LIFE.
TSU-ZUKI.
DON'T YOU HAVE WORK TO DO... SOME-WHERE ELSE?
AH, COME ON!
Sniff Sniff
Of course twins look the same!
WHAT DID I DO TO DESERVE THAT?
ACTUALLY, I DIDN'T COME BY THE LIBRARY JUST TO HARASS YOU THIS TIME.
I WANT TO GIVE HER A CHANCE TO SEE MASAKI BEFORE HER TRIAL...JUST IN CASE.
I NEED YOU TO HELP ME FIND SOME-BODY.
WHO? WHY?
YOU KNOW VERY WELL JUDGMENT FILES ARE SEALED AND CONFIDEN-TIAL.
I am the librarian.
NO EXCEP-TIONS, NOT EVEN FOR YOU, TSUZUKI.

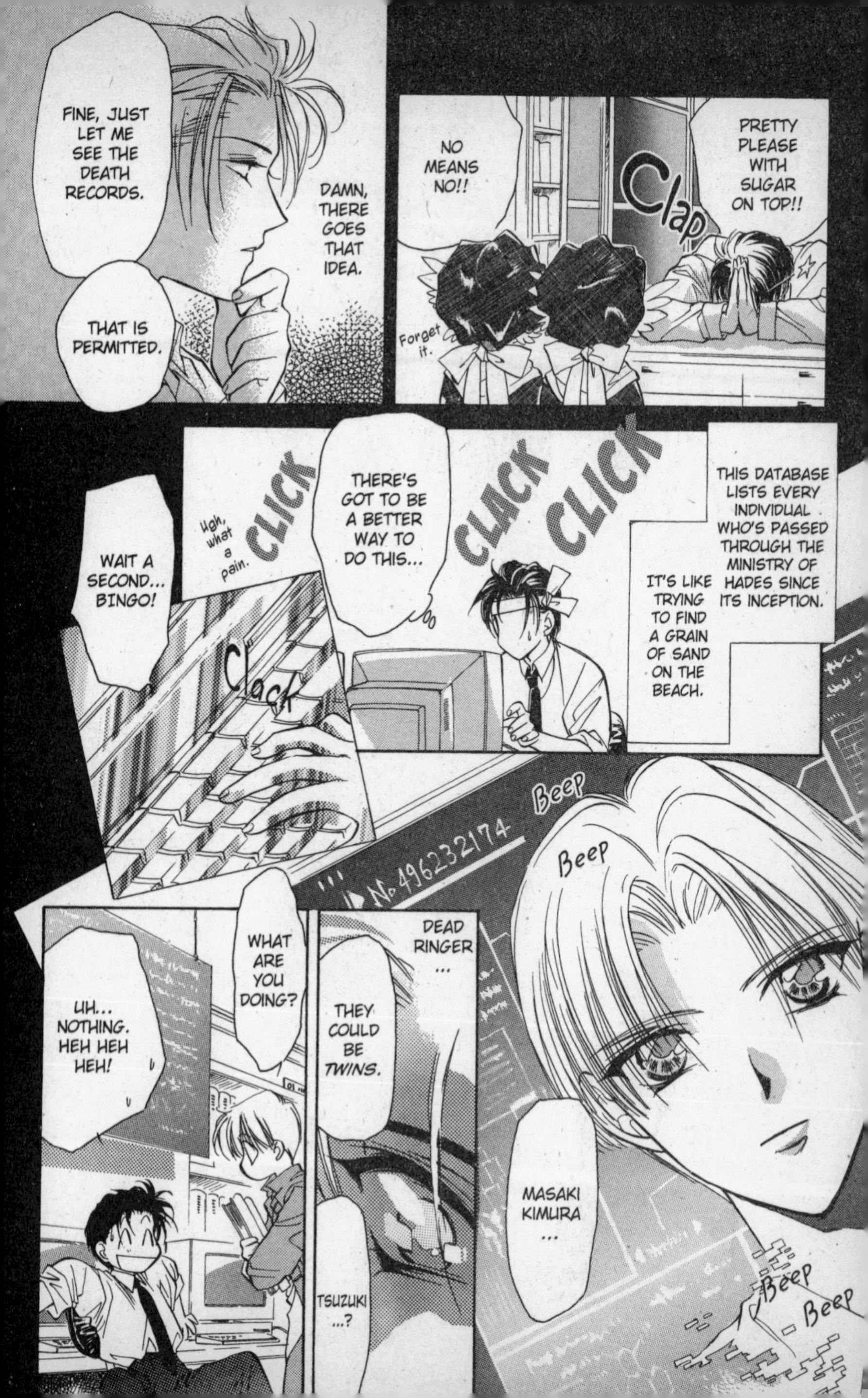
PRETTY PLEASE WITH SUGAR ON TOP!!
Clap
NO MEANS NO!!
Forget it.
DAMN, THERE GOES THAT IDEA.
FINE, JUST LET ME SEE THE DEATH RECORDS.
THAT IS PERMITTED.
THIS DATABASE LISTS EVERY INDIVIDUAL WHO'S PASSED THROUGH THE MINISTRY OF HADES SINCE ITS INCEPTION.
IT'S LIKE TRYING TO FIND A GRAIN OF SAND ON THE BEACH.
CLICK
CLACK
THERE'S GOT TO BE A BETTER WAY TO DO THIS...
CLICK
Ugh, what a pain.
WAIT A SECOND... BINGO!
Clack
Beep
No.496232174
Beep
Beep
Beep
MASAKI KIMURA ...
DEAD RINGER ...
THEY COULD BE TWINS.
TSUZUKI ...?
WHAT ARE YOU DOING?
UH... NOTHING. HEH HEH HEH!

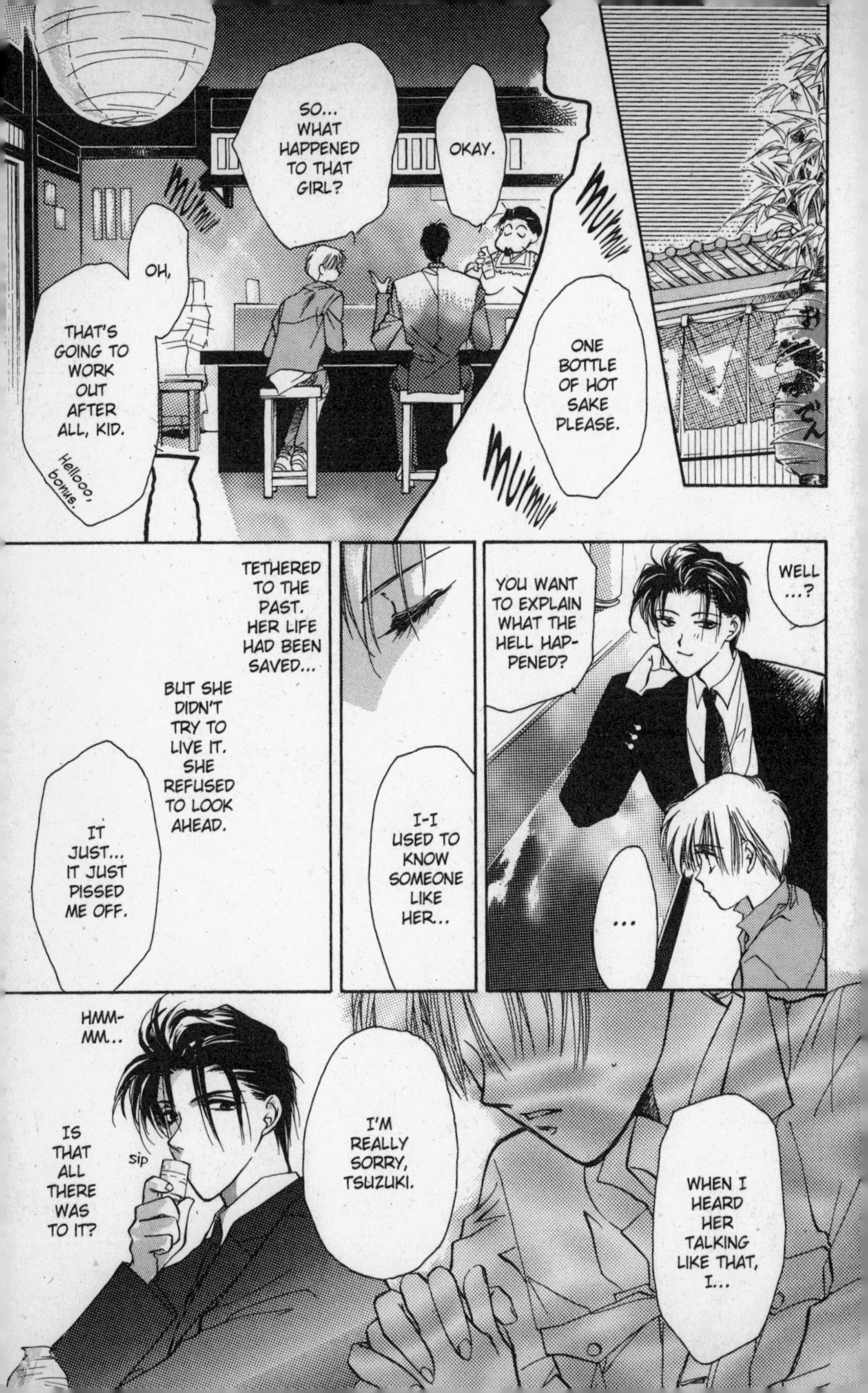
MUMU
ONE BOTTLE OF HOT SAKE PLEASE.
MUMU
OKAY.
SO... WHAT HAPPENED TO THAT GIRL?
MUMU
OH,
THAT'S GOING TO WORK OUT AFTER ALL, KID.
Hellooo, bonus.
WELL ...?
YOU WANT TO EXPLAIN WHAT THE HELL HAPPENED?
...
I-I USED TO KNOW SOMEONE LIKE HER...
TETHERED TO THE PAST. HER LIFE HAD BEEN SAVED...
BUT SHE DIDN'T TRY TO LIVE IT. SHE REFUSED TO LOOK AHEAD.
IT JUST... IT JUST PISSED ME OFF.
WHEN I HEARD HER TALKING LIKE THAT, I...
I'M REALLY SORRY, TSUZUKI.
HMM-MM...
sip
IS THAT ALL THERE WAS TO IT?

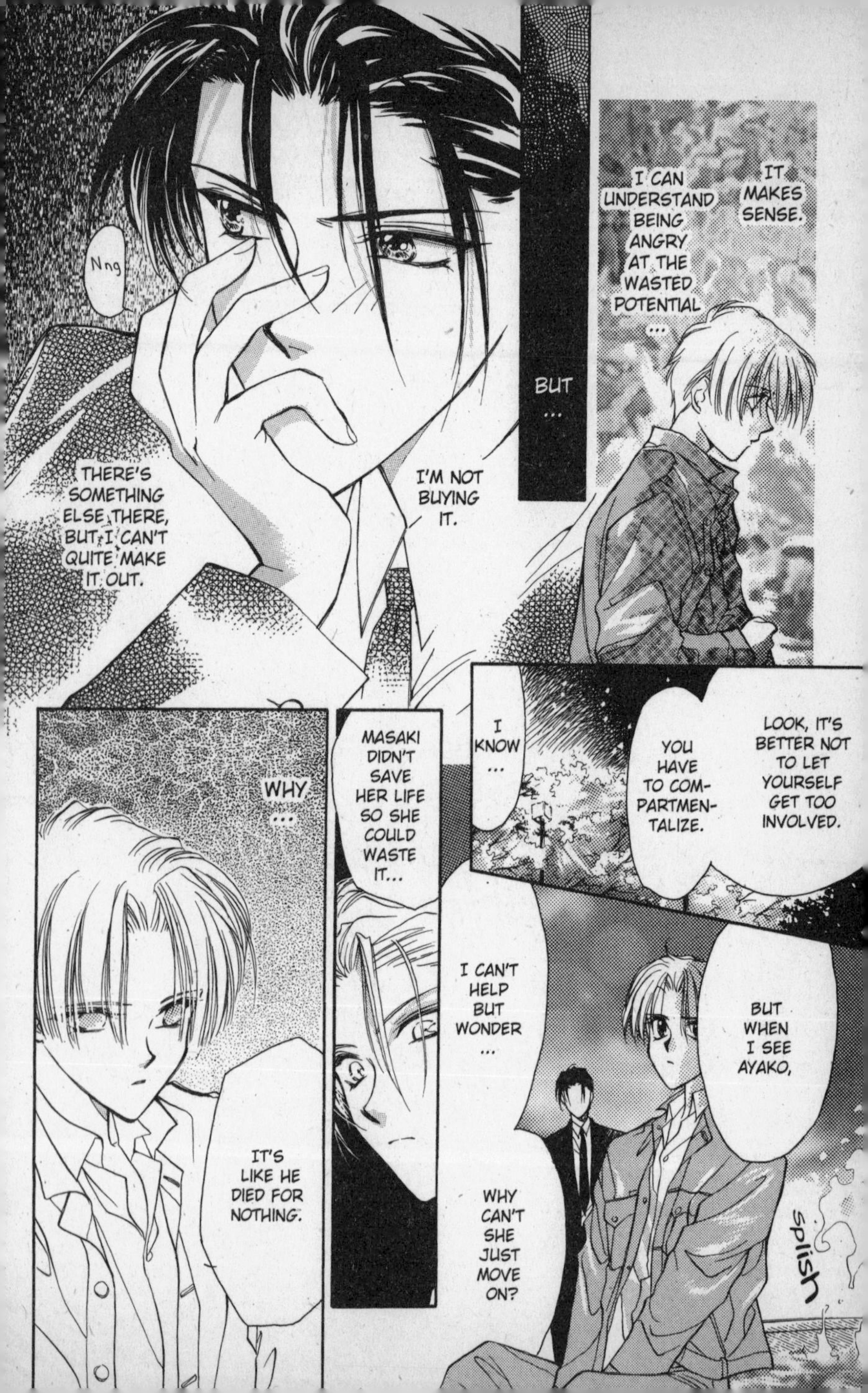
IT MAKES SENSE.
I CAN UNDERSTAND BEING ANGRY AT THE WASTED POTENTIAL ...
BUT ...
I'M NOT BUYING IT.
THERE'S SOMETHING ELSE THERE, BUT I CAN'T QUITE MAKE IT OUT.
Nng
LOOK, IT'S BETTER NOT TO LET YOURSELF GET TOO INVOLVED.
YOU HAVE TO COM-PARTMEN-TALIZE.
I KNOW ...
BUT WHEN I SEE AYAKO,
I CAN'T HELP BUT WONDER ...
WHY CAN'T SHE JUST MOVE ON?
splish
MASAKI DIDN'T SAVE HER LIFE SO SHE COULD WASTE IT...
WHY ...
IT'S LIKE HE DIED FOR NOTHING.

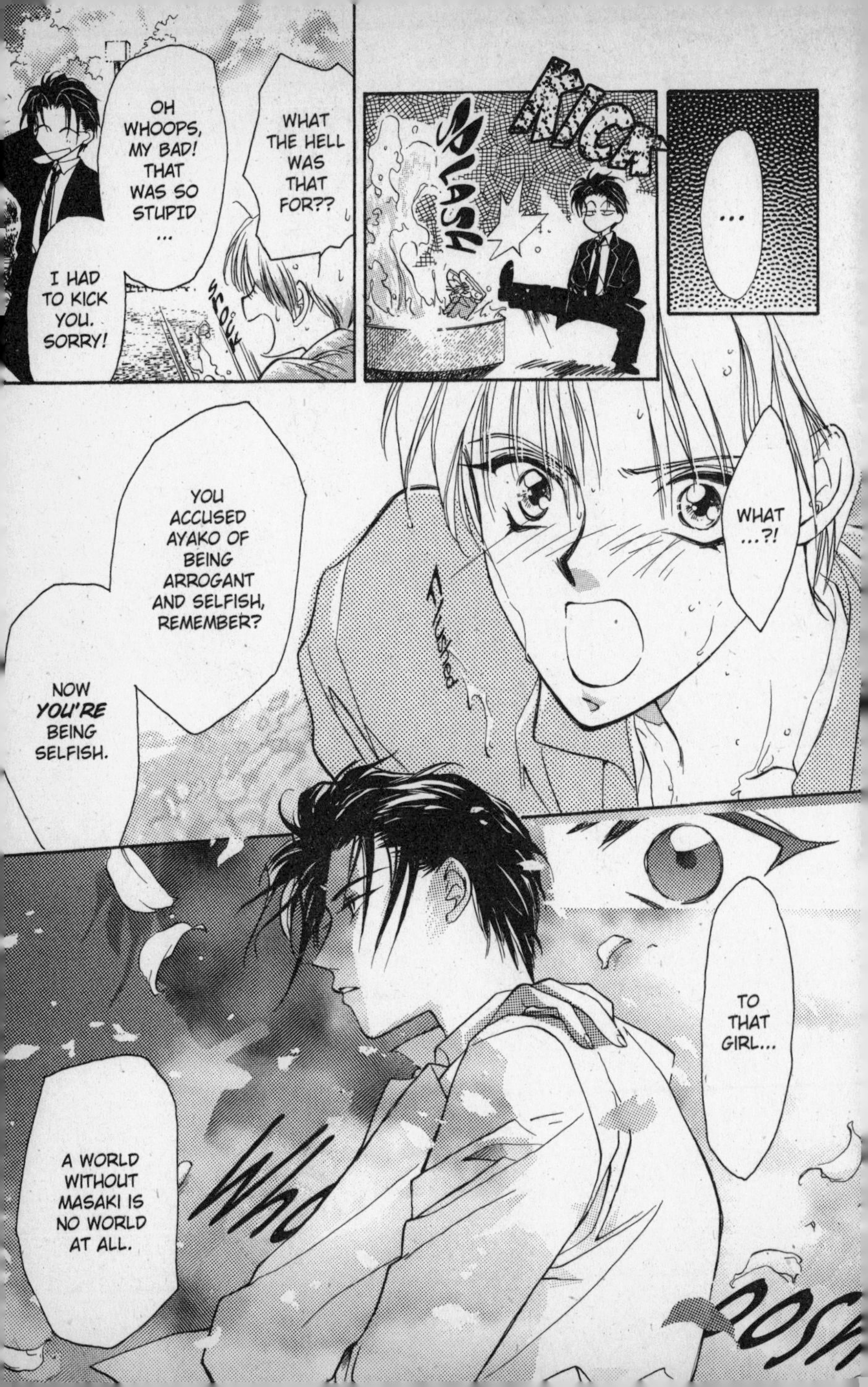
...
KICK
SPLASH
WHAT THE HELL WAS THAT FOR??
OH WHOOPS, MY BAD! THAT WAS SO STUPID ...
I HAD TO KICK YOU. SORRY!
WHAT ...?!
Flushed
YOU ACCUSED AYAKO OF BEING ARROGANT AND SELFISH, REMEMBER?
NOW *YOU'RE* BEING SELFISH.
TO THAT GIRL...
A WORLD WITHOUT MASAKI IS NO WORLD AT ALL.

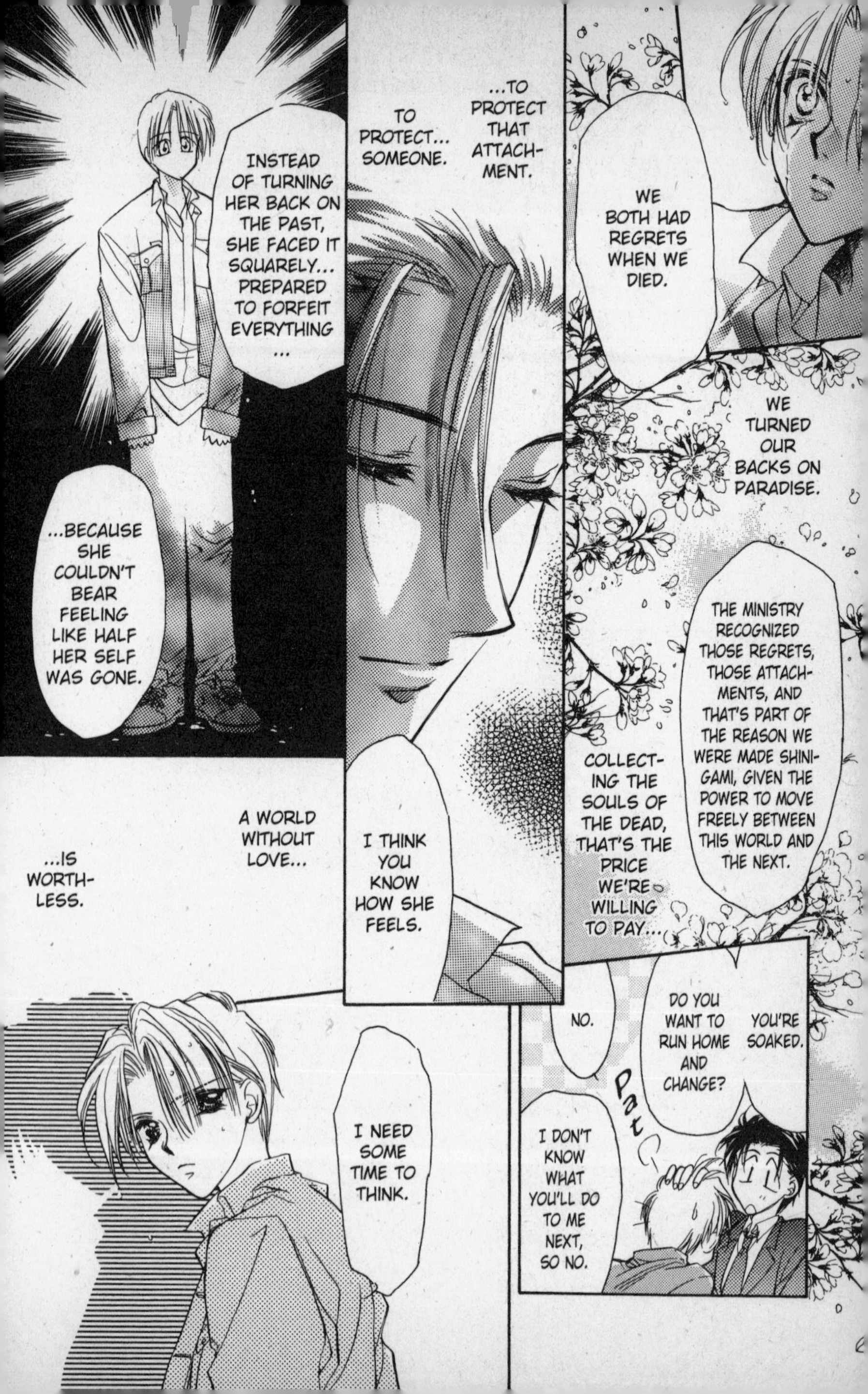

WE BOTH HAD REGRETS WHEN WE DIED.
WE TURNED OUR BACKS ON PARADISE.
THE MINISTRY RECOGNIZED THOSE REGRETS, THOSE ATTACH-MENTS, AND THAT'S PART OF THE REASON WE WERE MADE SHINI-GAMI, GIVEN THE POWER TO MOVE FREELY BETWEEN THIS WORLD AND THE NEXT.
COLLECT-ING THE SOULS OF THE DEAD, THAT'S THE PRICE WE'RE WILLING TO PAY...
...TO PROTECT THAT ATTACH-MENT.
TO PROTECT... SOMEONE.
INSTEAD OF TURNING HER BACK ON THE PAST, SHE FACED IT SQUARELY... PREPARED TO FORFEIT EVERYTHING ...
...BECAUSE SHE COULDN'T BEAR FEELING LIKE HALF HER SELF WAS GONE.
I THINK YOU KNOW HOW SHE FEELS.
A WORLD WITHOUT LOVE...
...IS WORTH-LESS.
I NEED SOME TIME TO THINK.
YOU'RE SOAKED.
DO YOU WANT TO RUN HOME AND CHANGE?
NO.
Pat
I DON'T KNOW WHAT YOU'LL DO TO ME NEXT, SO NO.

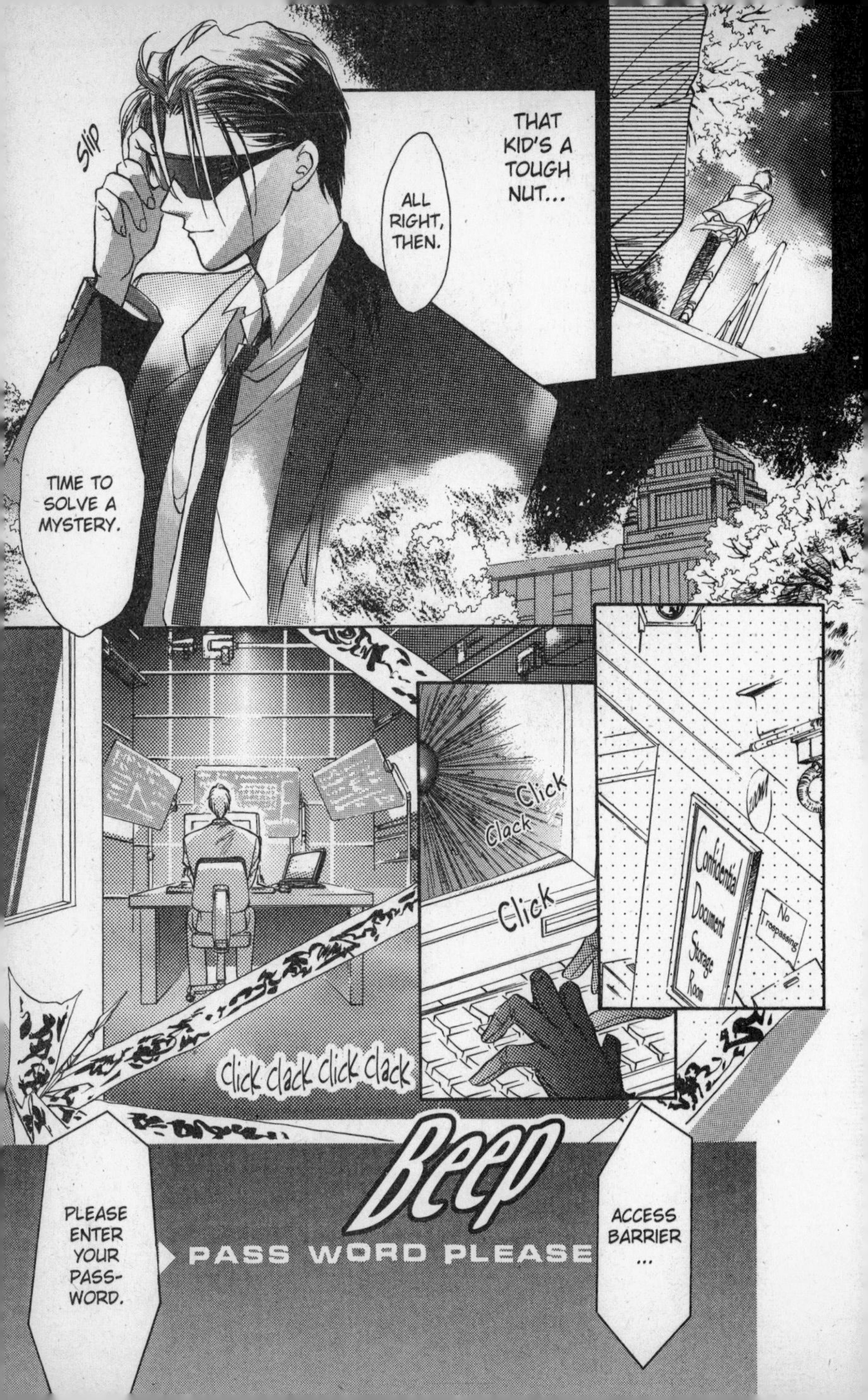
THAT KID'S A TOUGH NUT...
ALL RIGHT, THEN.
Slip
TIME TO SOLVE A MYSTERY.
Confidential Document Storage Room
No Trespassing
Click
Clack
Click
Click clack click clack
ACCESS BARRIER ...
Beep
PASS WORD PLEASE
PLEASE ENTER YOUR PASS-WORD.

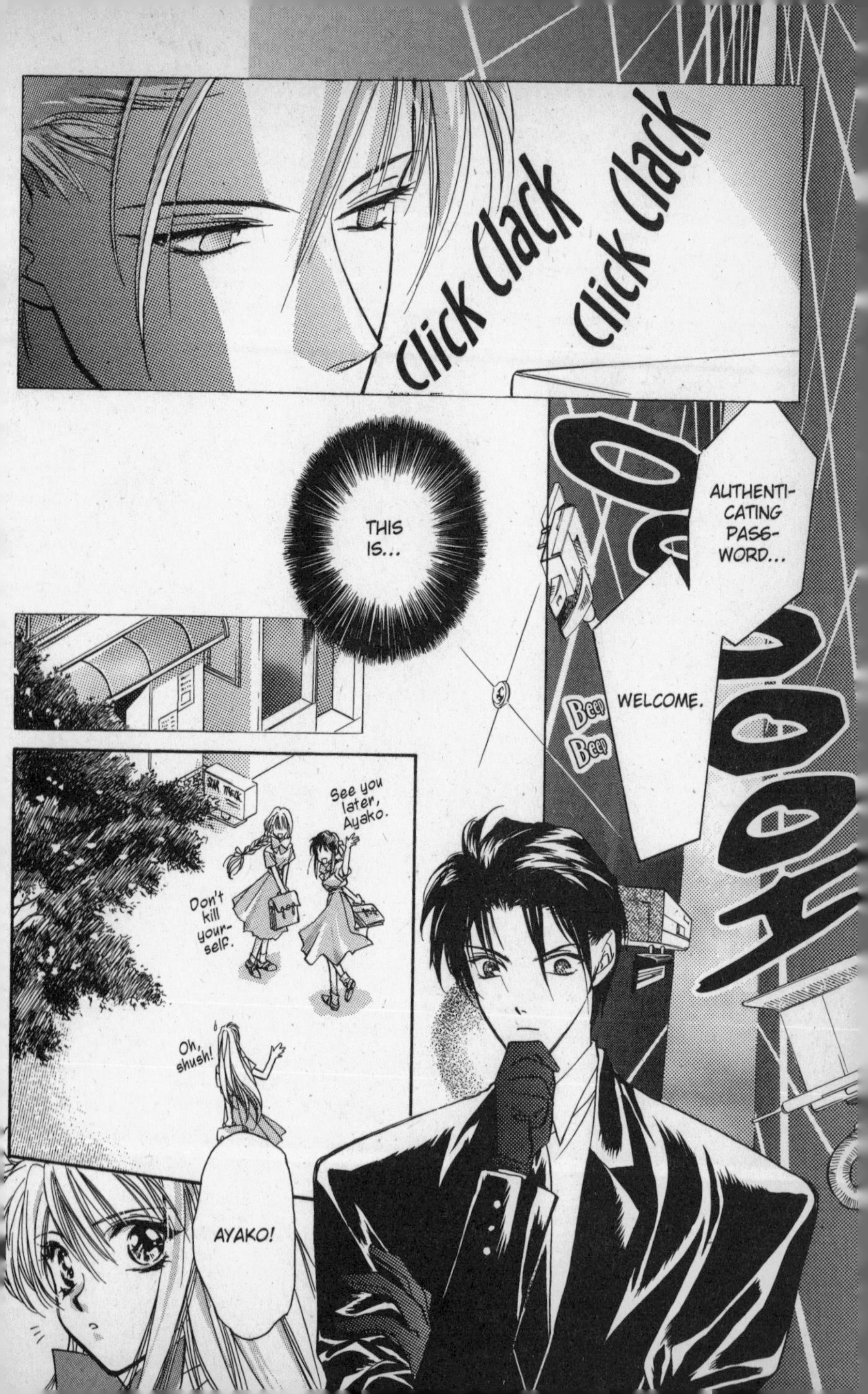
Click Clack
Click Clack
AUTHENTI-CATING PASS-WORD...
Beep Beep
WELCOME.
THIS IS...
See you later, Ayako.
Don't kill your-self.
Oh, shush!
AYAKO!

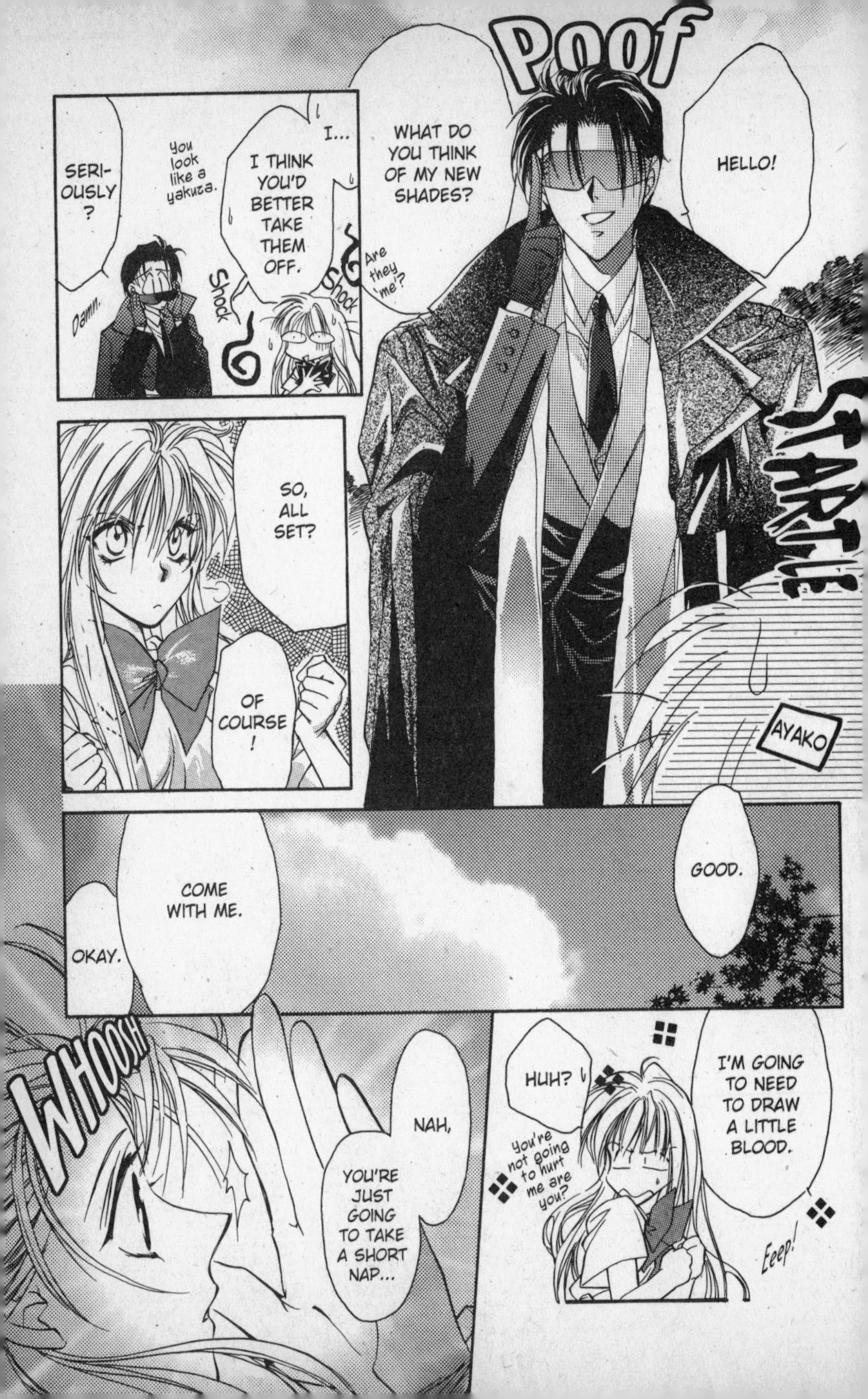
Poof
HELLO!
WHAT DO YOU THINK OF MY NEW SHADES?
STARTLE
AYAKO
Are they 'me'?
I...
I THINK YOU'D BETTER TAKE THEM OFF.
Shock
Shock
SERI-OUSLY?
You look like a yakuza.
Damn.
SO, ALL SET?
OF COURSE!
GOOD.
COME WITH ME.
OKAY.
I'M GOING TO NEED TO DRAW A LITTLE BLOOD.
HUH?
You're not going to hurt me are you?
Eeep!
NAH,
YOU'RE JUST GOING TO TAKE A SHORT NAP...
WHOOSH

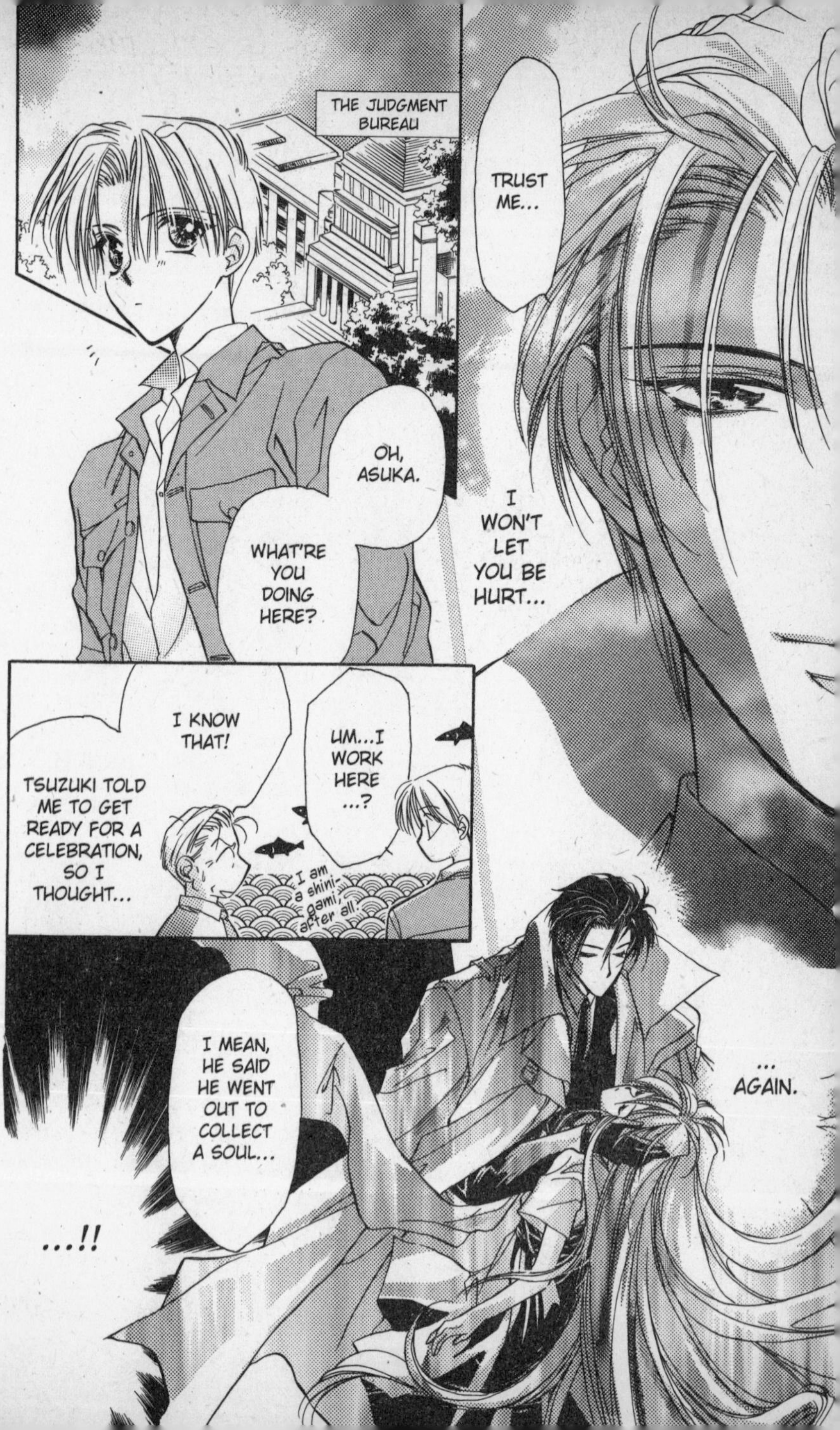

TRUST ME...
I WON'T LET YOU BE HURT...
... AGAIN.
THE JUDGMENT BUREAU
OH, ASUKA.
WHAT'RE YOU DOING HERE?
UM...I WORK HERE ...?
I am a shini-gami, after all.
I KNOW THAT!
TSUZUKI TOLD ME TO GET READY FOR A CELEBRATION, SO I THOUGHT...
I MEAN, HE SAID HE WENT OUT TO COLLECT A SOUL...
...!!

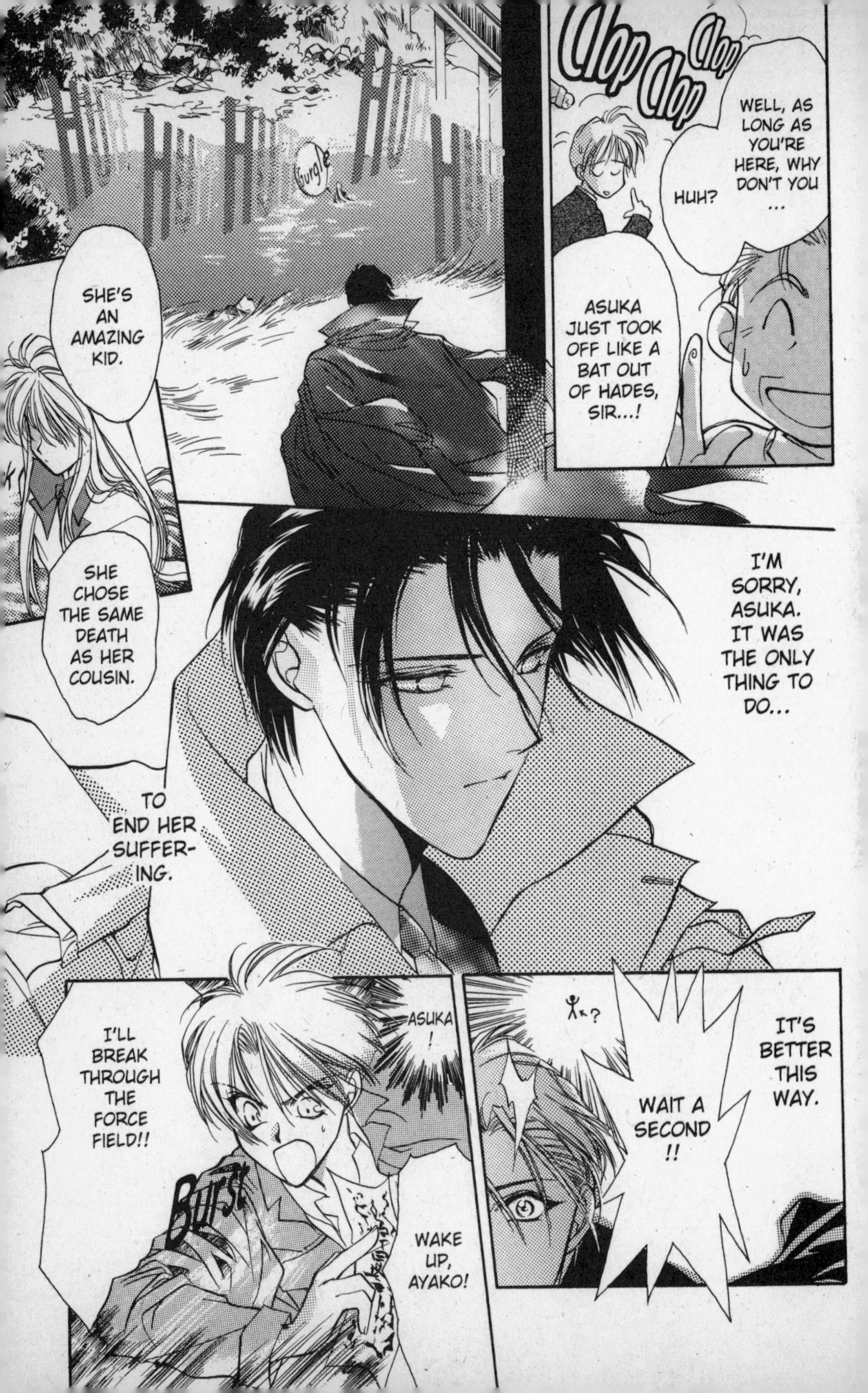
Clop Clop Clop
WELL, AS LONG AS YOU'RE HERE, WHY DON'T YOU ...
HUH?
ASUKA JUST TOOK OFF LIKE A BAT OUT OF HADES, SIR...!
Gurgle
SHE'S AN AMAZING KID.
SHE CHOSE THE SAME DEATH AS HER COUSIN.
I'M SORRY, ASUKA. IT WAS THE ONLY THING TO DO...
TO END HER SUFFER-ING.
IT'S BETTER THIS WAY.
?
WAIT A SECOND !!
ASUKA !
I'LL BREAK THROUGH THE FORCE FIELD!!
Burst
WAKE UP, AYAKO!

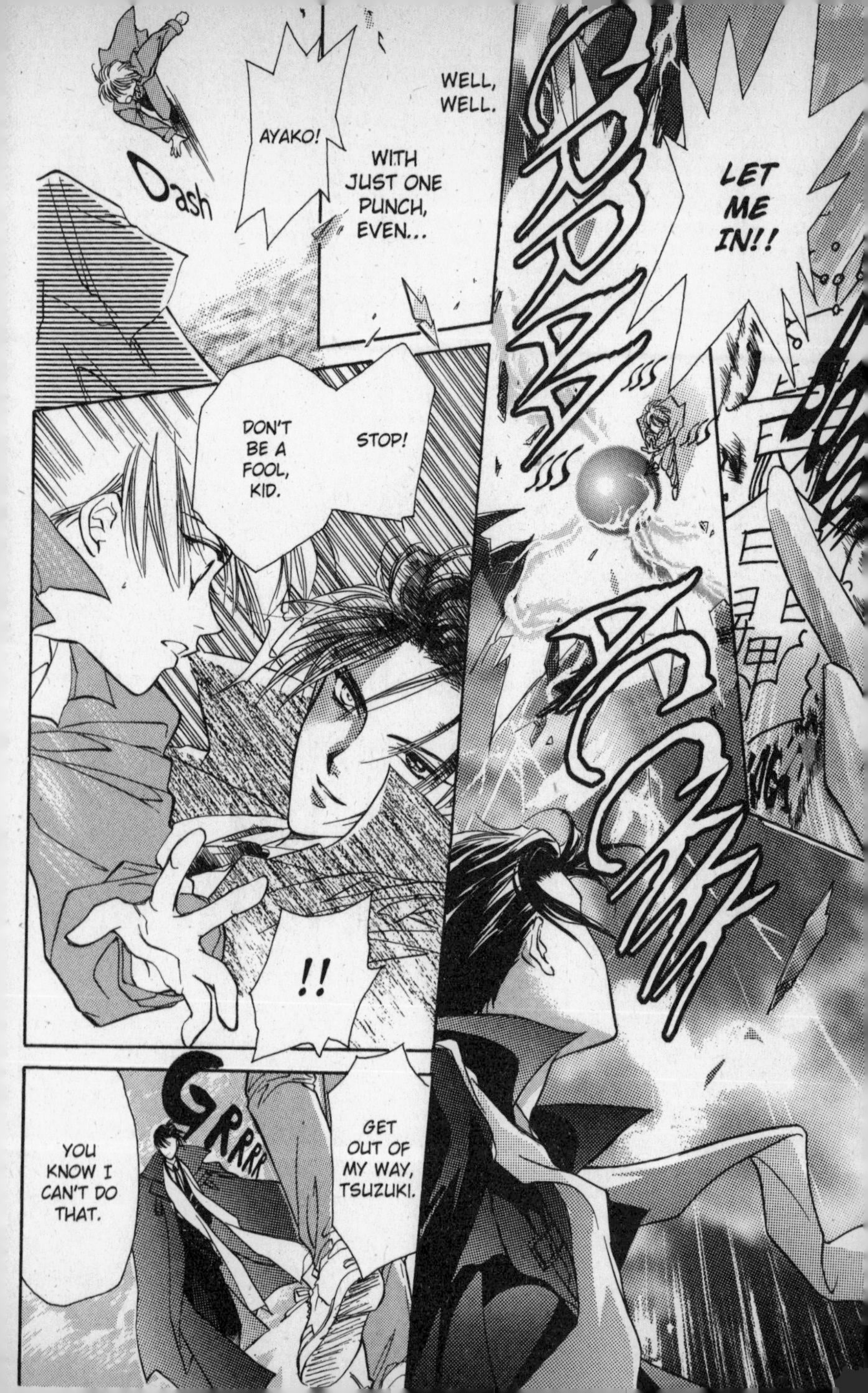
LET ME IN!!
WELL, WELL.
WITH JUST ONE PUNCH, EVEN...
AYAKO!
Dash
STOP!
DON'T BE A FOOL, KID.
!!
GET OUT OF MY WAY, TSUZUKI.
GRRRR
YOU KNOW I CAN'T DO THAT.

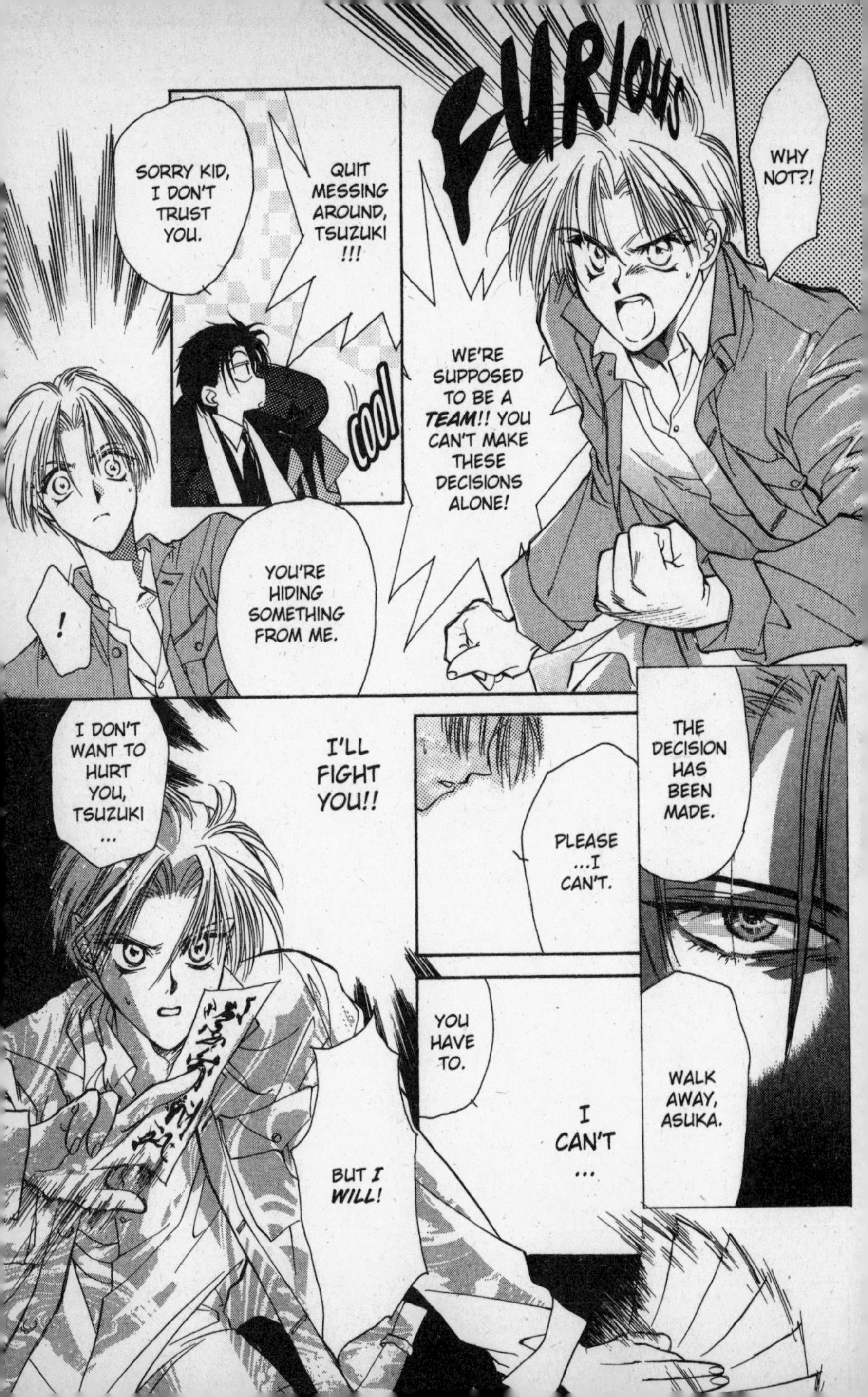
WHY NOT?!
FURIOUS
WE'RE SUPPOSED TO BE A TEAM!! YOU CAN'T MAKE THESE DECISIONS ALONE!
QUIT MESSING AROUND, TSUZUKI!!!
SORRY KID, I DON'T TRUST YOU.
COOL
YOU'RE HIDING SOMETHING FROM ME.
!
THE DECISION HAS BEEN MADE.
WALK AWAY, ASUKA.
PLEASE ...I CAN'T.
YOU HAVE TO.
I CAN'T ...
I'LL FIGHT YOU!!
I DON'T WANT TO HURT YOU, TSUZUKI ...
BUT I WILL!

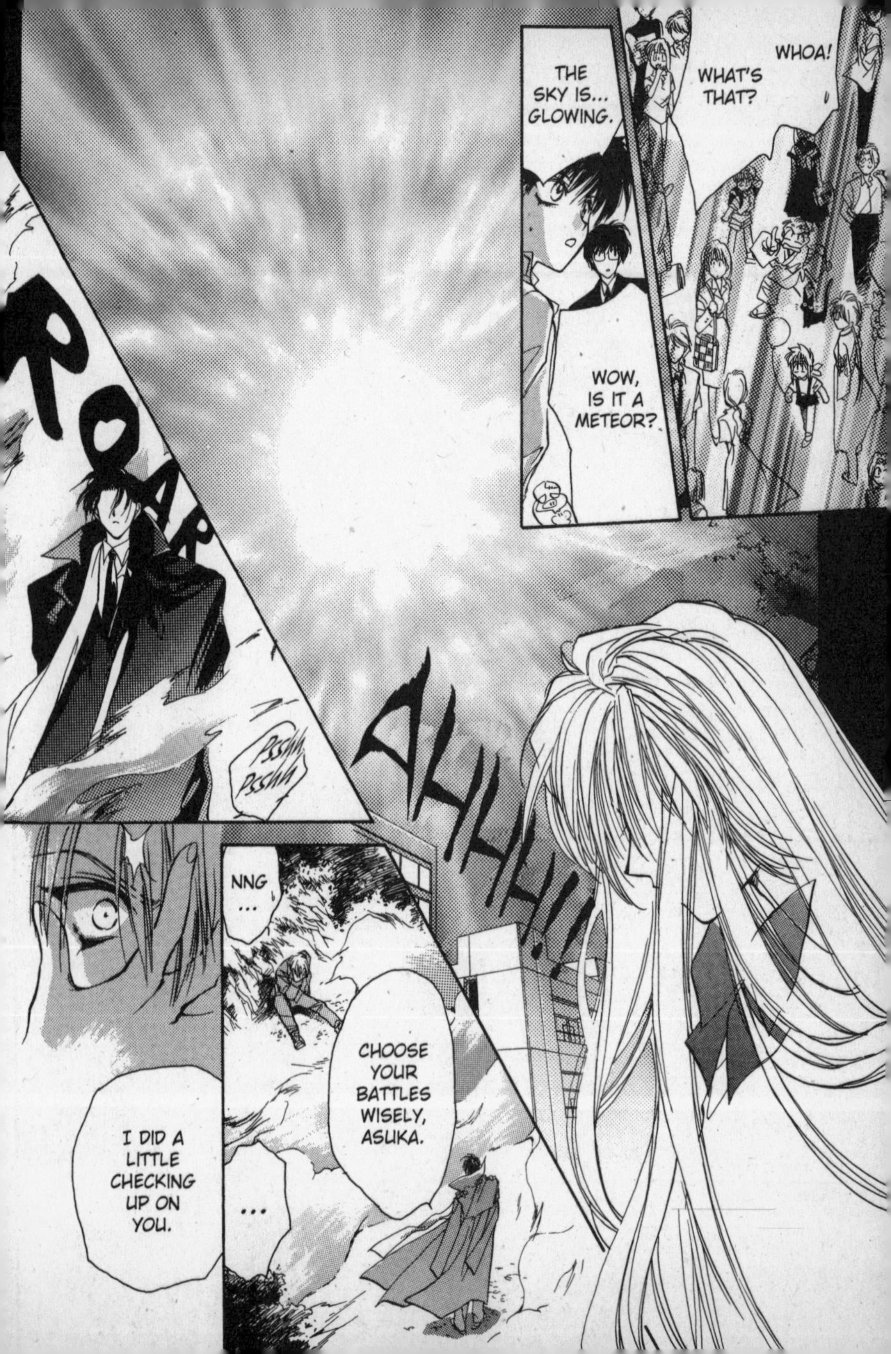
WHOA!
WHAT'S THAT?
THE SKY IS... GLOWING.
WOW, IS IT A METEOR?
ROAR
Psshh Psshh
AHHH!!!
NNG ...
CHOOSE YOUR BATTLES WISELY, ASUKA.
...
I DID A LITTLE CHECKING UP ON YOU.

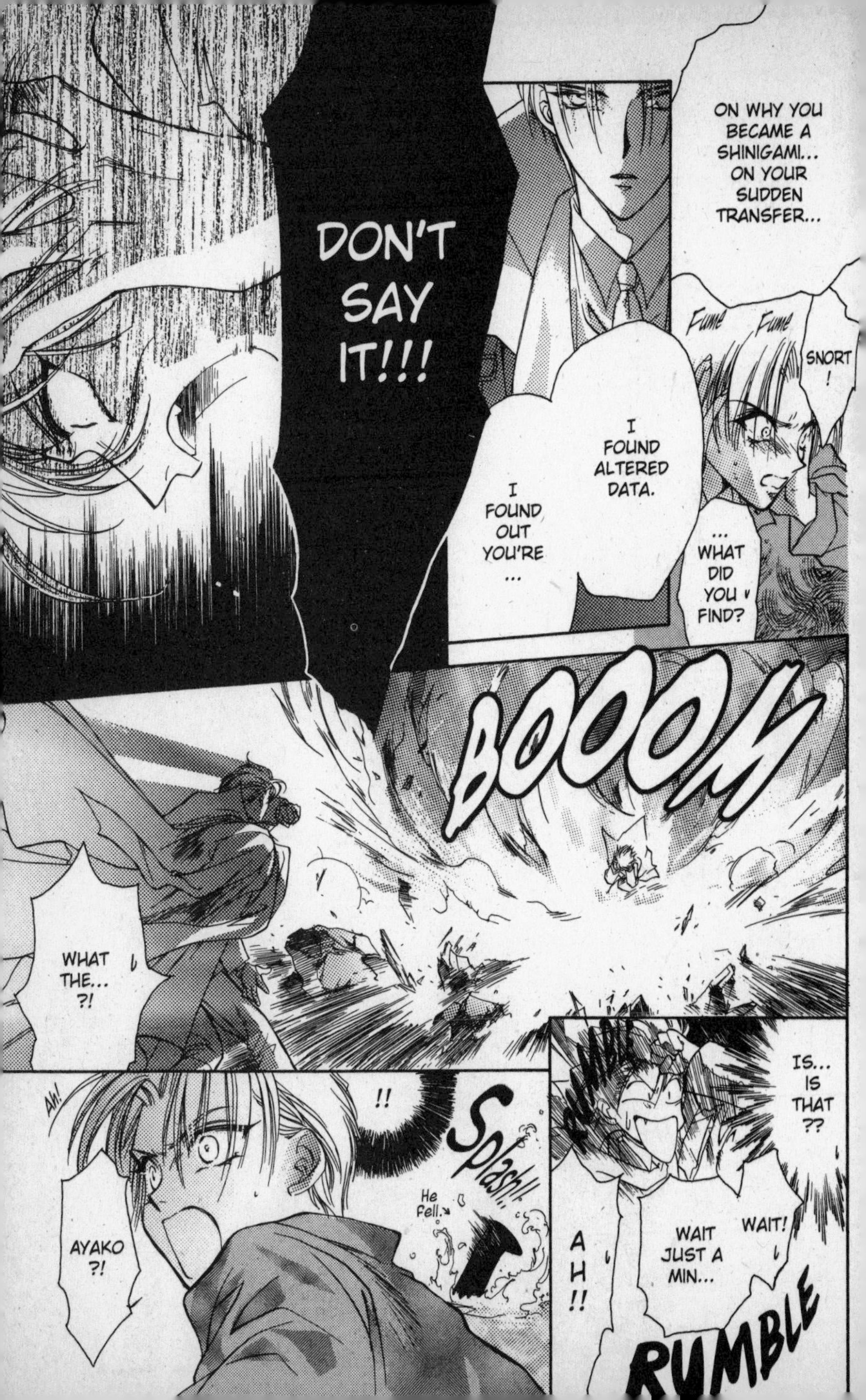
Fume Fume
SNORT!
I FOUND ALTERED DATA.
... WHAT DID YOU FIND?
ON WHY YOU BECAME A SHINIGAMI... ON YOUR SUDDEN TRANSFER...
I FOUND OUT YOU'RE ...
DON'T SAY IT!!!
BOOOM
WHAT THE... ?!
IS... IS THAT??
WAIT!
WAIT JUST A MIN...
AH!!
RUMBLE
!!
Splash!!
He fell.
Ah!
AYAKO ?!

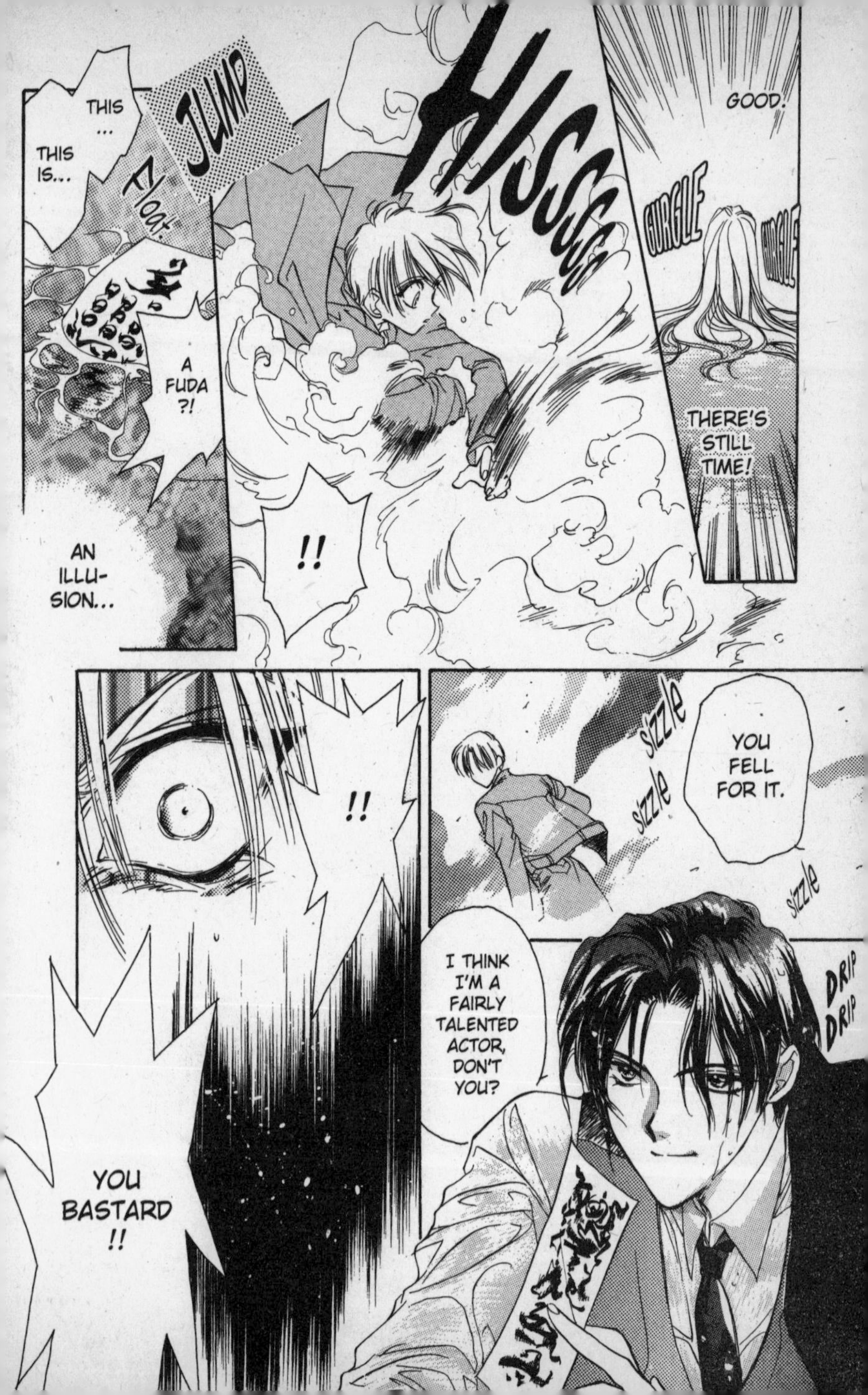
GOOD!
GURGLE
GURGLE
THERE'S STILL TIME!
HISSSSS
!!
THIS... THIS IS...
JUMP
Float
A FUDA?!
AN ILLUSION...
sizzle
sizzle
YOU FELL FOR IT.
sizzle
!!
I THINK I'M A FAIRLY TALENTED ACTOR, DON'T YOU?
DRIP DRIP
YOU BASTARD!!

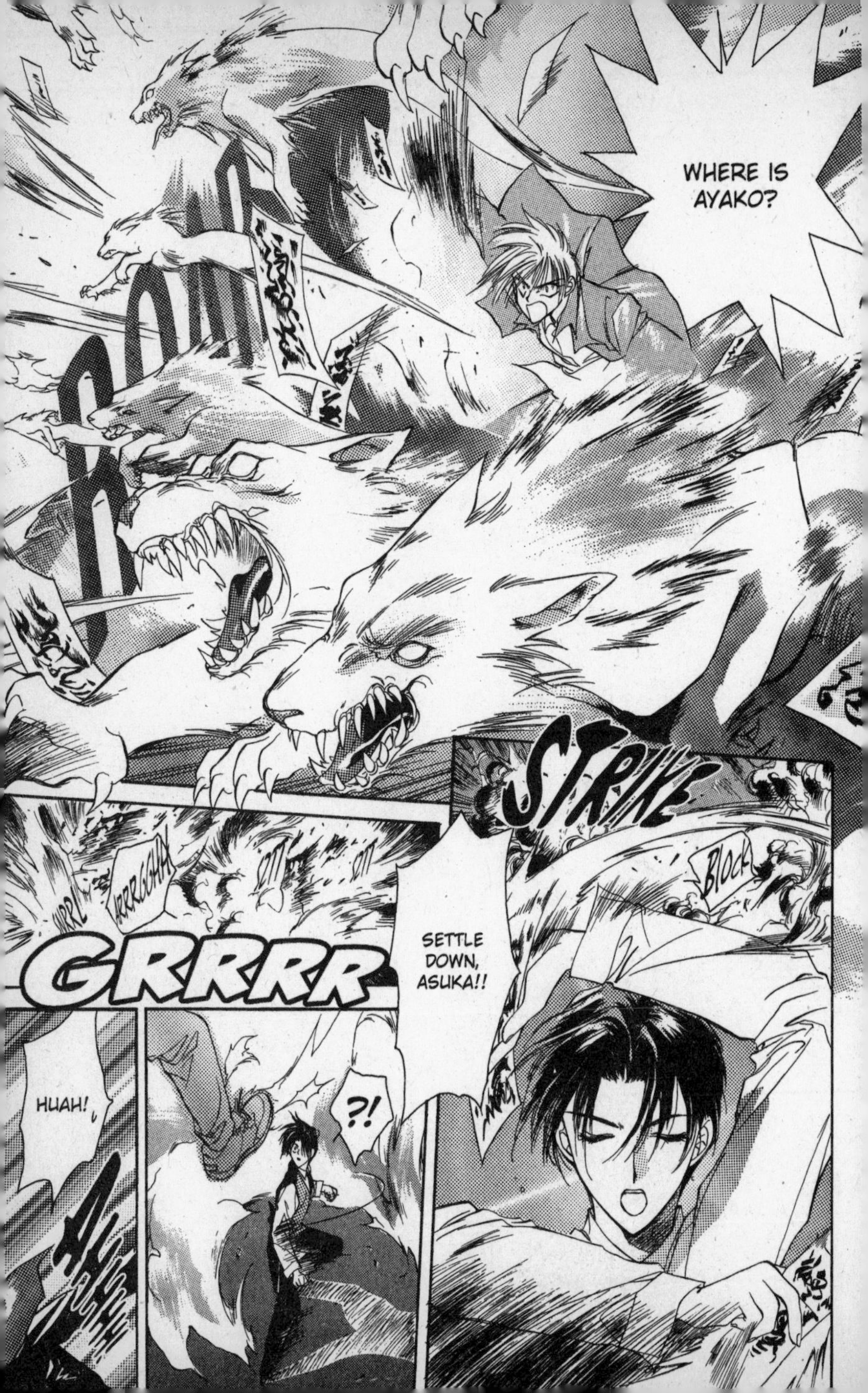
WHERE IS AYAKO?
STRIKE
BLOCK
ARRRGGHH
GRRRR
SETTLE DOWN, ASUKA!!
?!
HUAH!

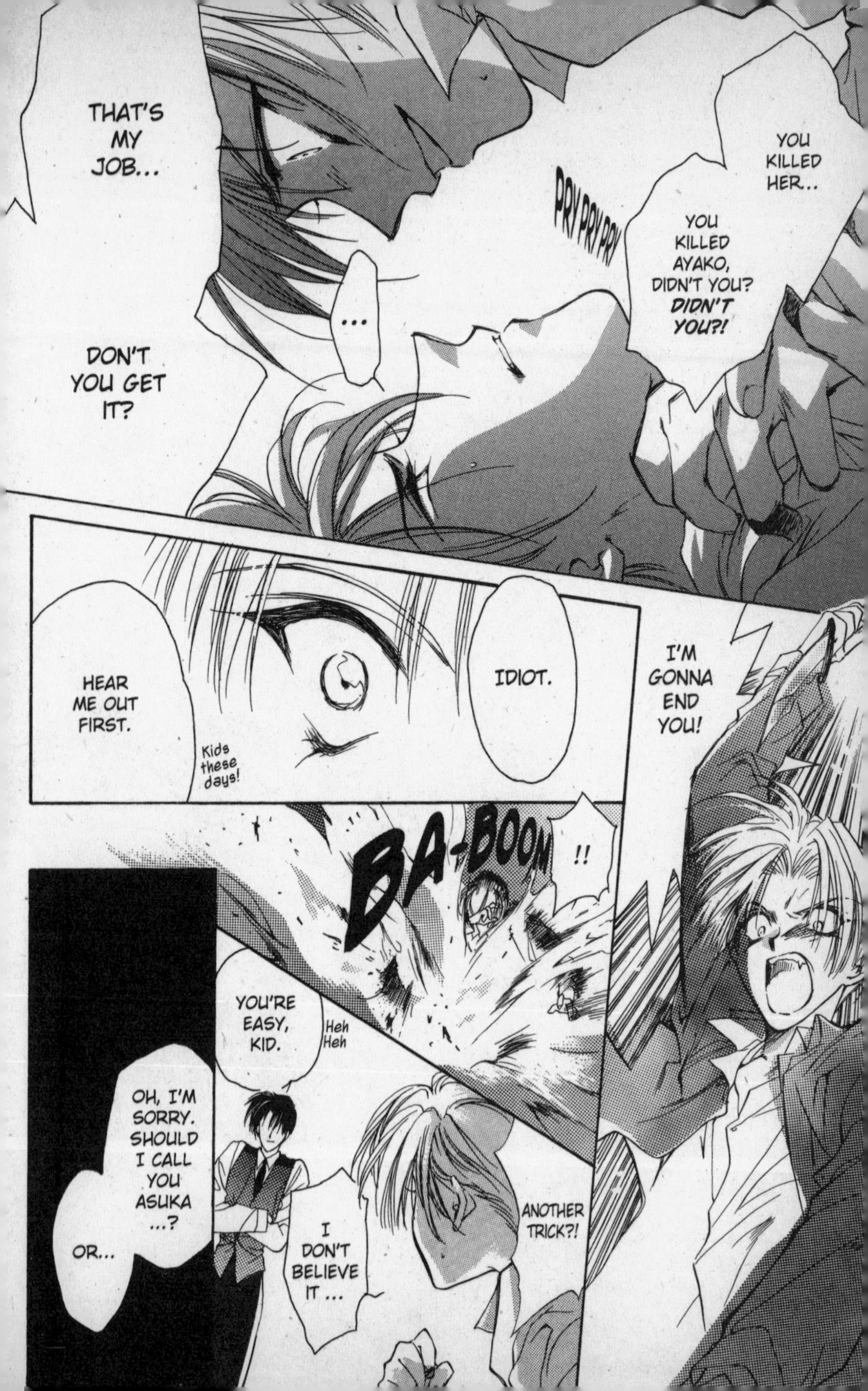
YOU KILLED HER...
YOU KILLED AYAKO, DIDN'T YOU? *DIDN'T YOU?!*
PRY PRY PRY
...
THAT'S MY JOB...
DON'T YOU GET IT?
I'M GONNA END YOU!
IDIOT.
HEAR ME OUT FIRST.
Kids these days!
BA-BOOM !!
YOU'RE EASY, KID.
Heh Heh
ANOTHER TRICK?!
I DON'T BELIEVE IT ...
OH, I'M SORRY. SHOULD I CALL YOU ASUKA ...?
OR...

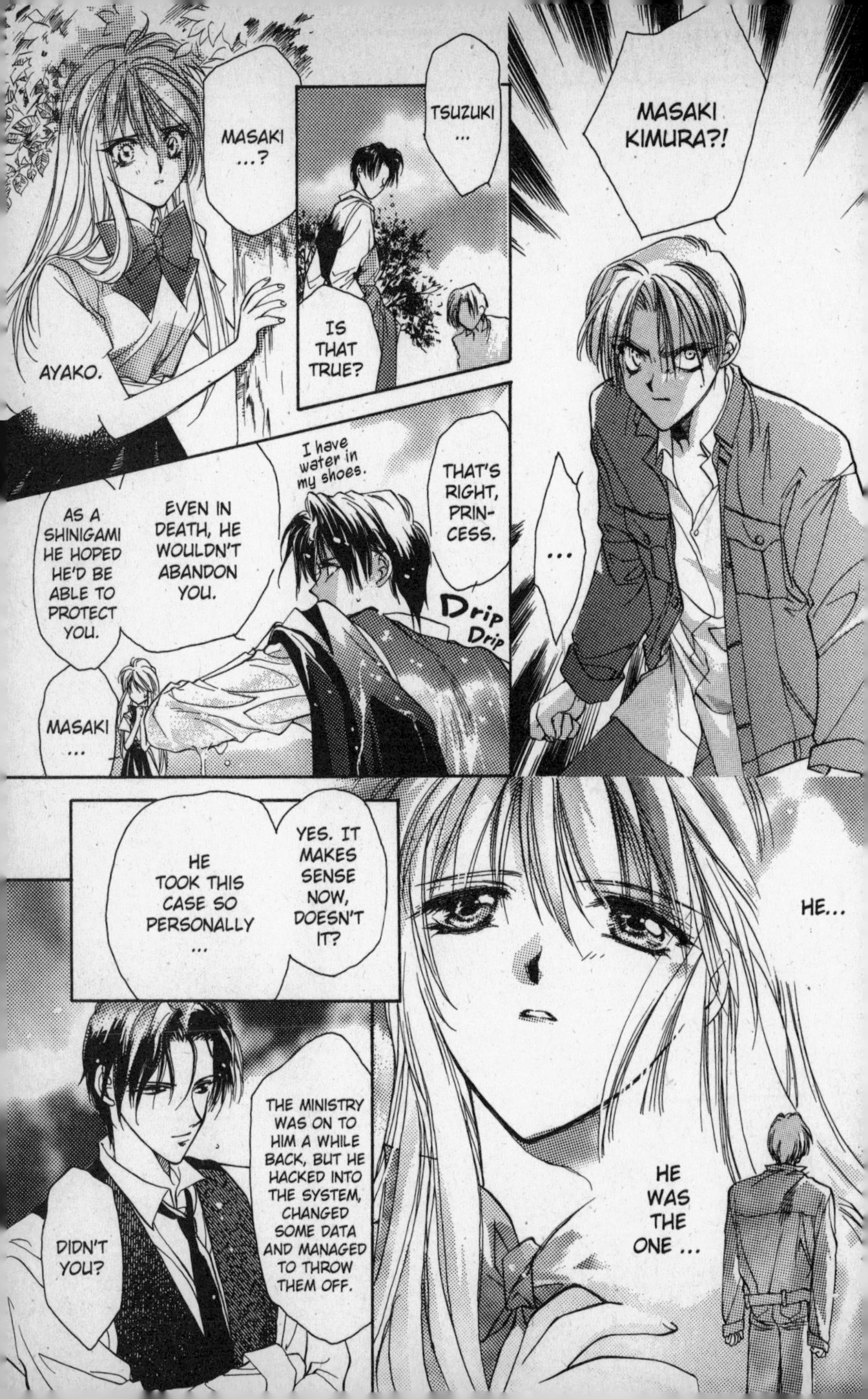
MASAKI KIMURA?!
...
TSUZUKI ...
IS THAT TRUE?
MASAKI ...?
AYAKO.
THAT'S RIGHT, PRINCESS.
I have water in my shoes.
EVEN IN DEATH, HE WOULDN'T ABANDON YOU.
AS A SHINIGAMI HE HOPED HE'D BE ABLE TO PROTECT YOU.
Drip Drip
MASAKI ...
HE...
HE WAS THE ONE ...
YES. IT MAKES SENSE NOW, DOESN'T IT?
HE TOOK THIS CASE SO PERSONALLY ...
THE MINISTRY WAS ON TO HIM A WHILE BACK, BUT HE HACKED INTO THE SYSTEM, CHANGED SOME DATA AND MANAGED TO THROW THEM OFF.
DIDN'T YOU?

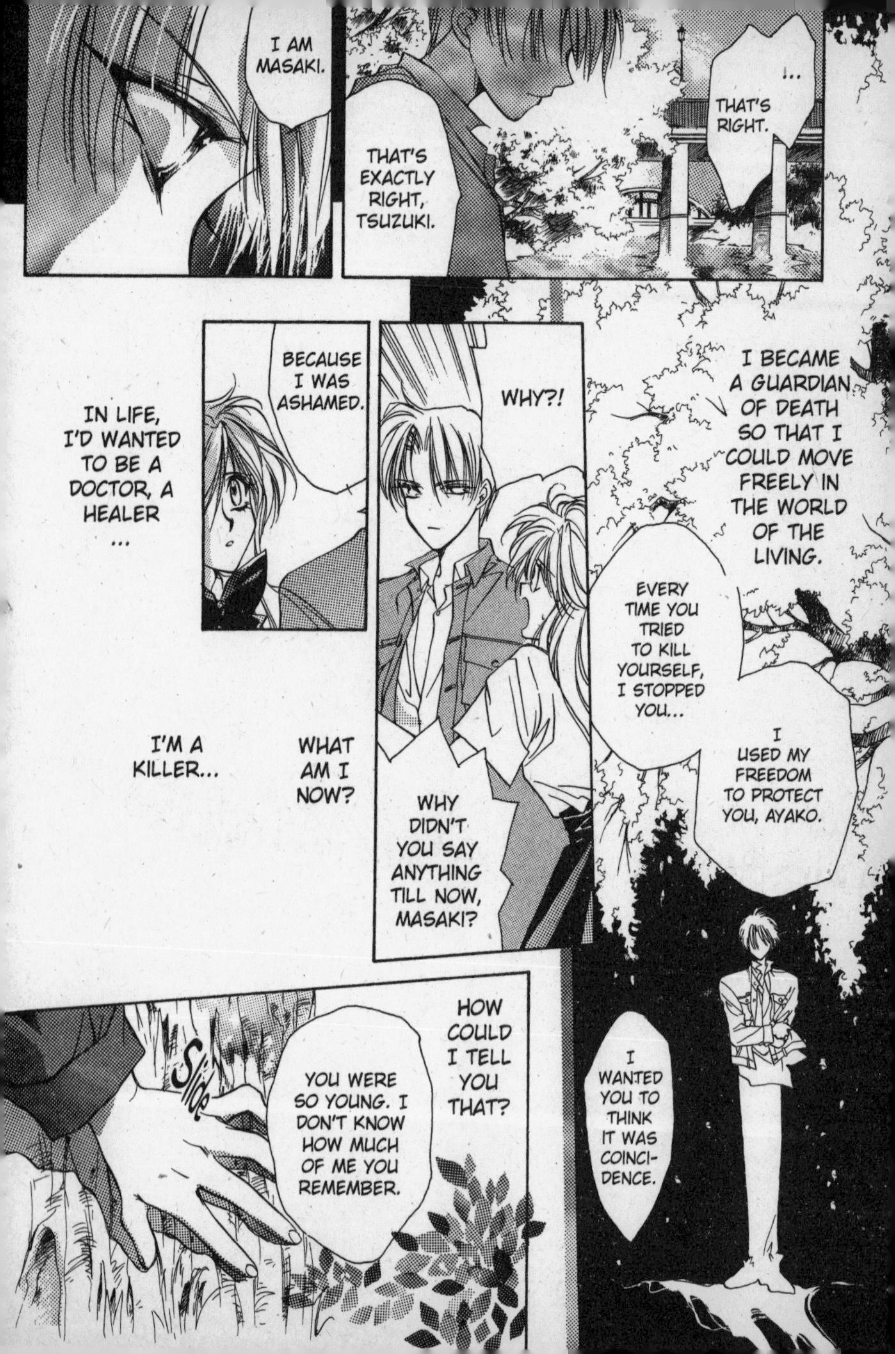
...
THAT'S RIGHT.
THAT'S EXACTLY RIGHT, TSUZUKI.
I AM MASAKI.
I BECAME A GUARDIAN OF DEATH SO THAT I COULD MOVE FREELY IN THE WORLD OF THE LIVING.
EVERY TIME YOU TRIED TO KILL YOURSELF, I STOPPED YOU...
I USED MY FREEDOM TO PROTECT YOU, AYAKO.
I WANTED YOU TO THINK IT WAS COINCIDENCE.
WHY?!
WHY DIDN'T YOU SAY ANYTHING TILL NOW, MASAKI?
BECAUSE I WAS ASHAMED.
IN LIFE, I'D WANTED TO BE A DOCTOR, A HEALER ...
WHAT AM I NOW?
I'M A KILLER...
HOW COULD I TELL YOU THAT?
YOU WERE SO YOUNG. I DON'T KNOW HOW MUCH OF ME YOU REMEMBER.
Slide

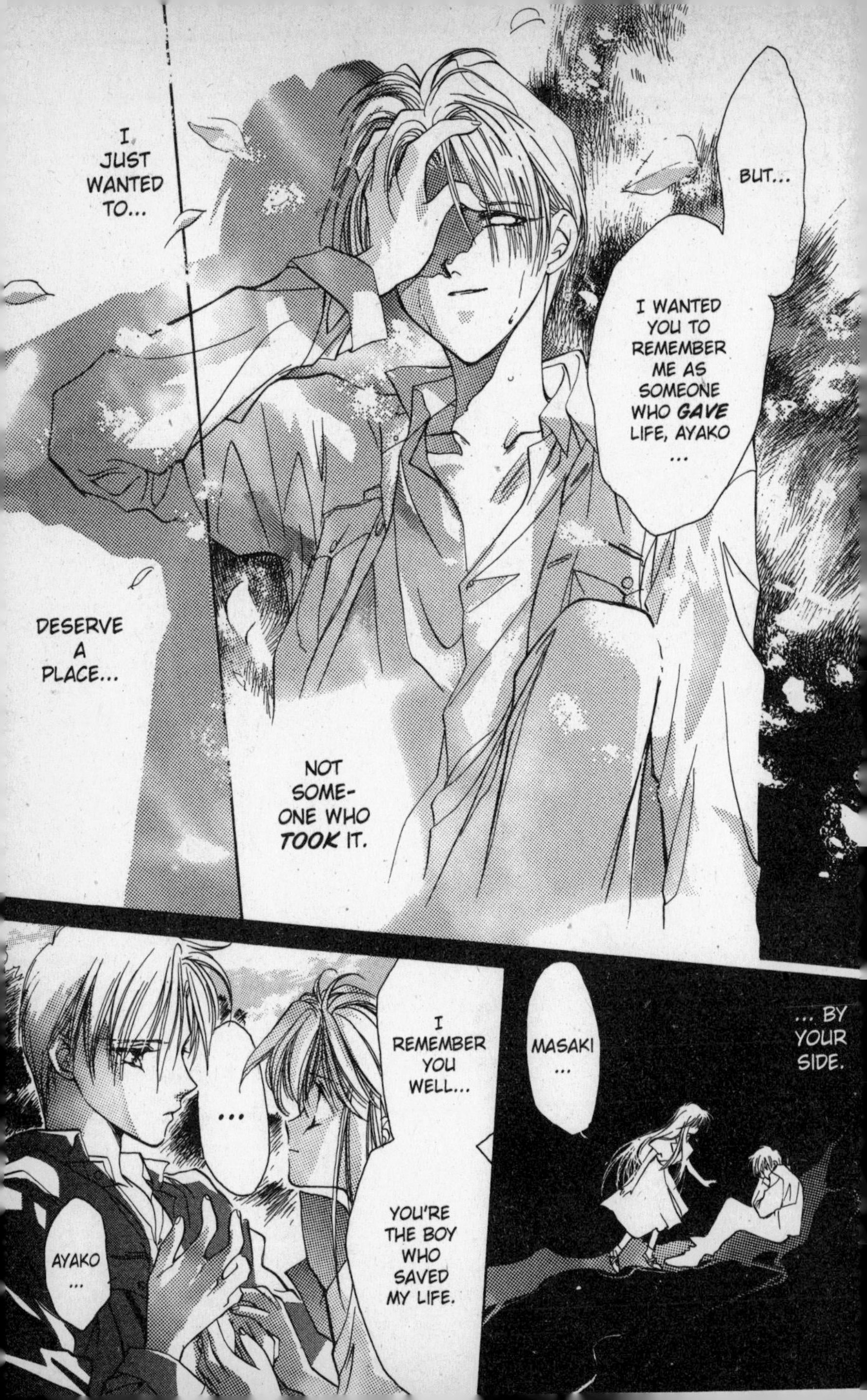
BUT...
I WANTED YOU TO REMEMBER ME AS SOMEONE WHO **GAVE** LIFE, AYAKO ...
NOT SOME-ONE WHO **TOOK** IT.
I JUST WANTED TO...
DESERVE A PLACE...
... BY YOUR SIDE.
MASAKI ...
I REMEMBER YOU WELL...
YOU'RE THE BOY WHO SAVED MY LIFE.
...
AYAKO ...

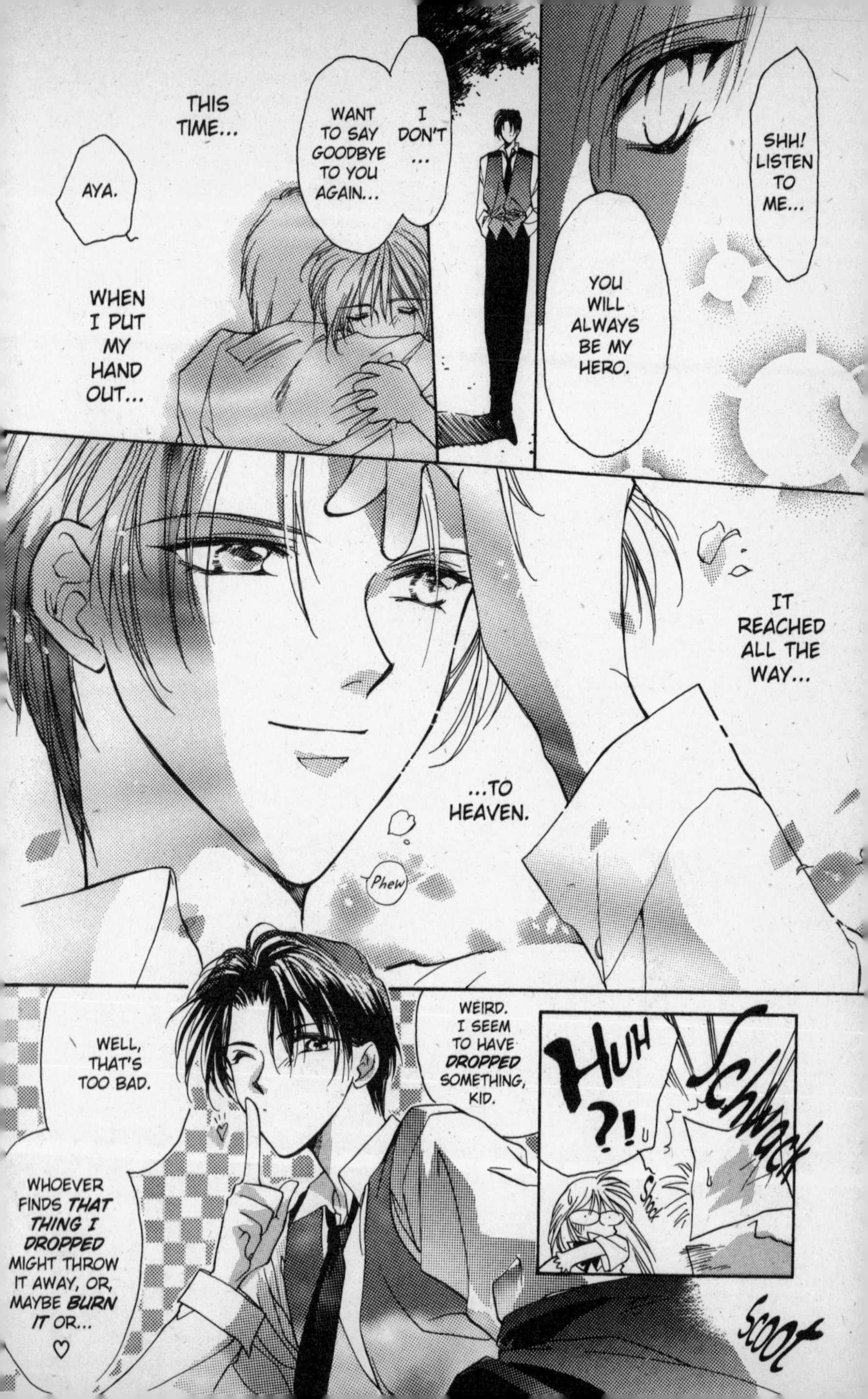
SHH! LISTEN TO ME...
YOU WILL ALWAYS BE MY HERO.
I DON'T ...
WANT TO SAY GOODBYE TO YOU AGAIN...
THIS TIME...
AYA.
WHEN I PUT MY HAND OUT...
IT REACHED ALL THE WAY...
...TO HEAVEN.
Phew
Schwack
HUH ?!
Shock
scoot
WEIRD. I SEEM TO HAVE *DROPPED* SOMETHING, KID.
WELL, THAT'S TOO BAD.
WHOEVER FINDS ***THAT THING I DROPPED*** MIGHT THROW IT AWAY, OR, MAYBE ***BURN IT*** OR... ♡

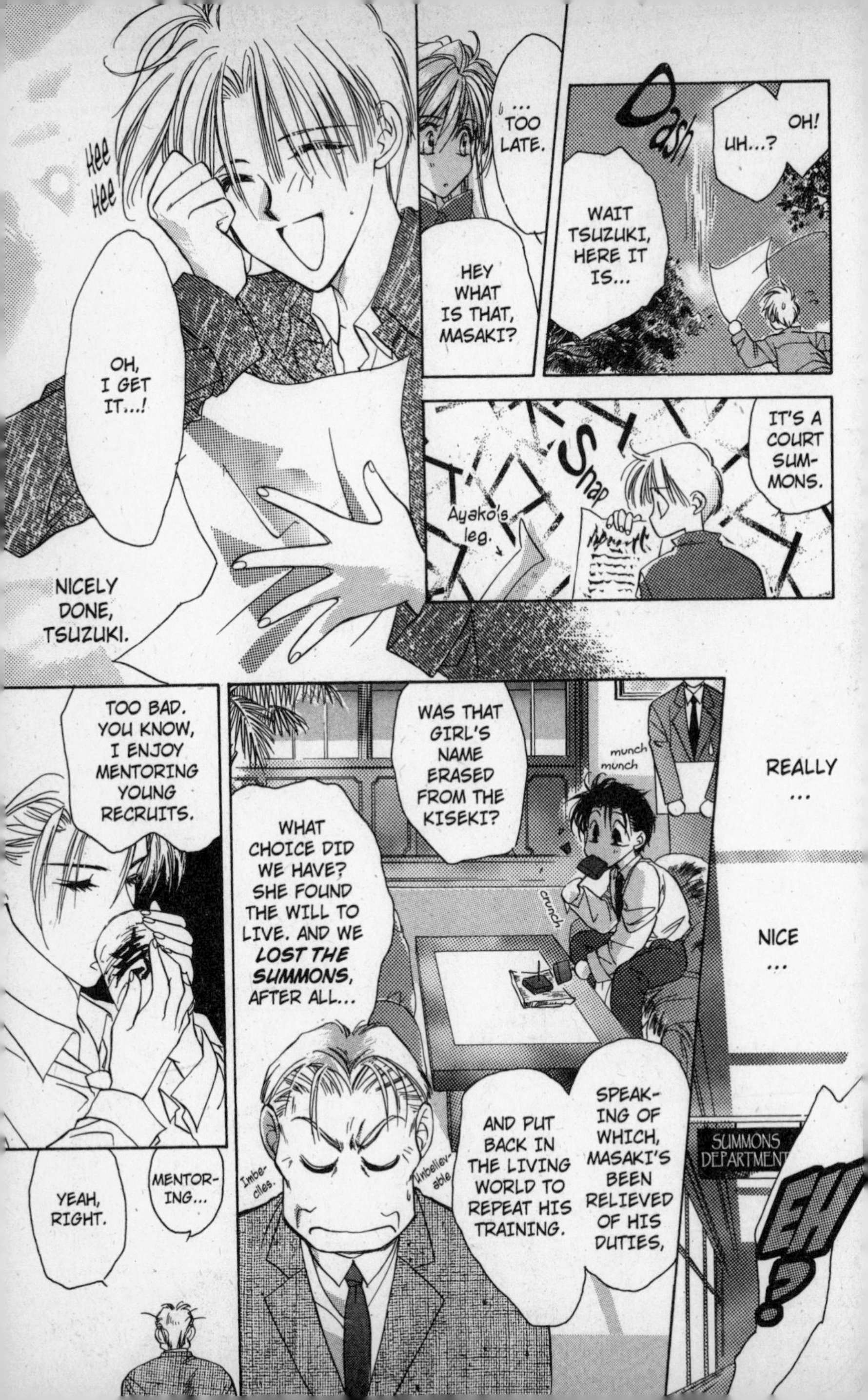
OH!
UH...?
Dash
WAIT TSUZUKI, HERE IT IS...
... TOO LATE.
HEY WHAT IS THAT, MASAKI?
IT'S A COURT SUMMONS.
Snap
Ayako's leg.
Hee Hee
OH, I GET IT...!
NICELY DONE, TSUZUKI.
REALLY ...
NICE ...
EH!?
SUMMONS DEPARTMENT
WAS THAT GIRL'S NAME ERASED FROM THE KISEKI?
munch munch
WHAT CHOICE DID WE HAVE? SHE FOUND THE WILL TO LIVE. AND WE *LOST THE SUMMONS*, AFTER ALL...
crunch
SPEAK-ING OF WHICH, MASAKI'S BEEN RELIEVED OF HIS DUTIES,
AND PUT BACK IN THE LIVING WORLD TO REPEAT HIS TRAINING.
Unbelievable
Imbeciles.
TOO BAD. YOU KNOW, I ENJOY MENTORING YOUNG RECRUITS.
MENTOR-ING...
YEAH, RIGHT.

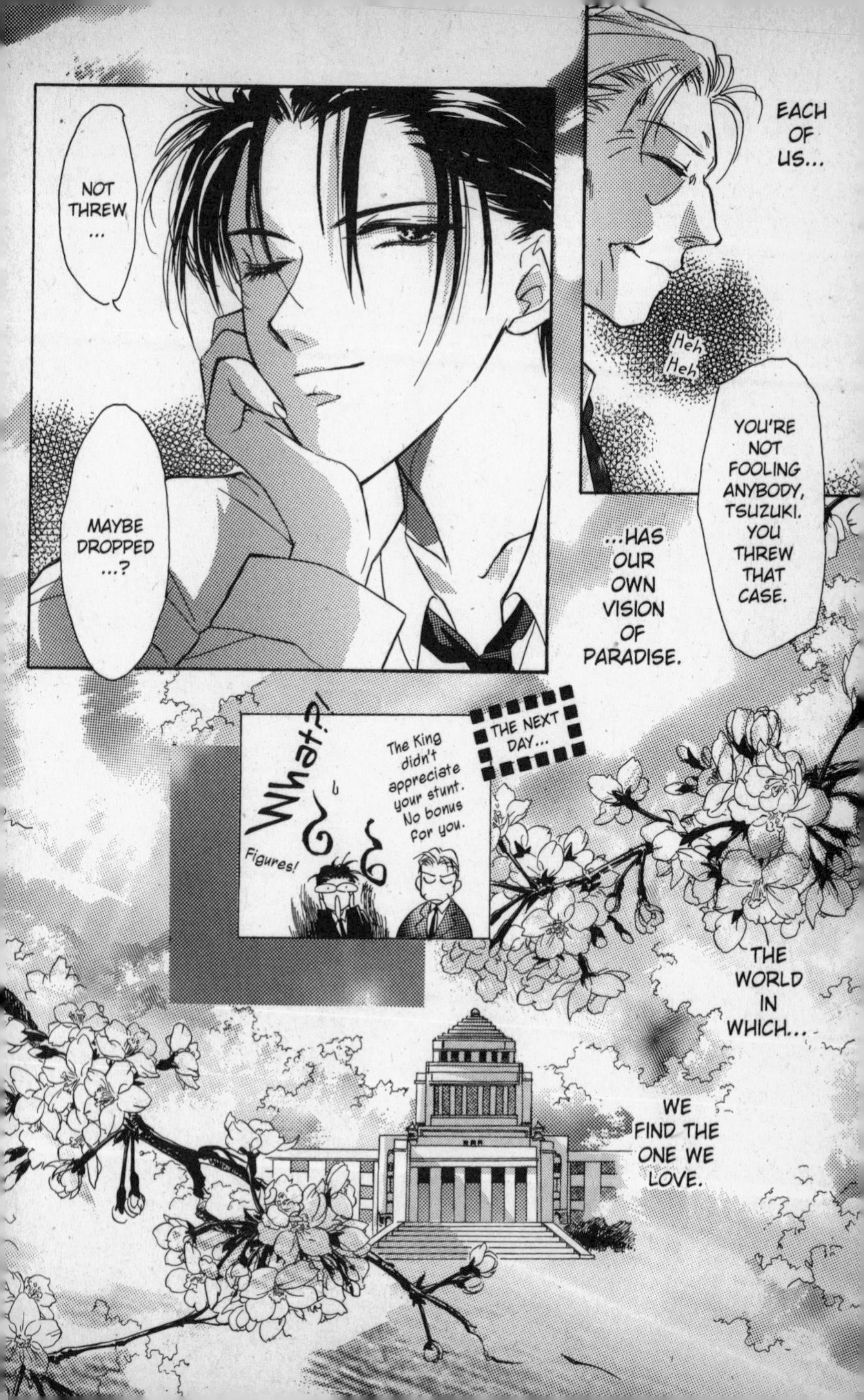
EACH OF US...
Heh Heh
YOU'RE NOT FOOLING ANYBODY, TSUZUKI. YOU THREW THAT CASE.
NOT THREW ...
MAYBE DROPPED ...?
...HAS OUR OWN VISION OF PARADISE.
THE NEXT DAY...
The King didn't appreciate your stunt. No bonus for you.
What?!
Figures!
THE WORLD IN WHICH...
WE FIND THE ONE WE LOVE.

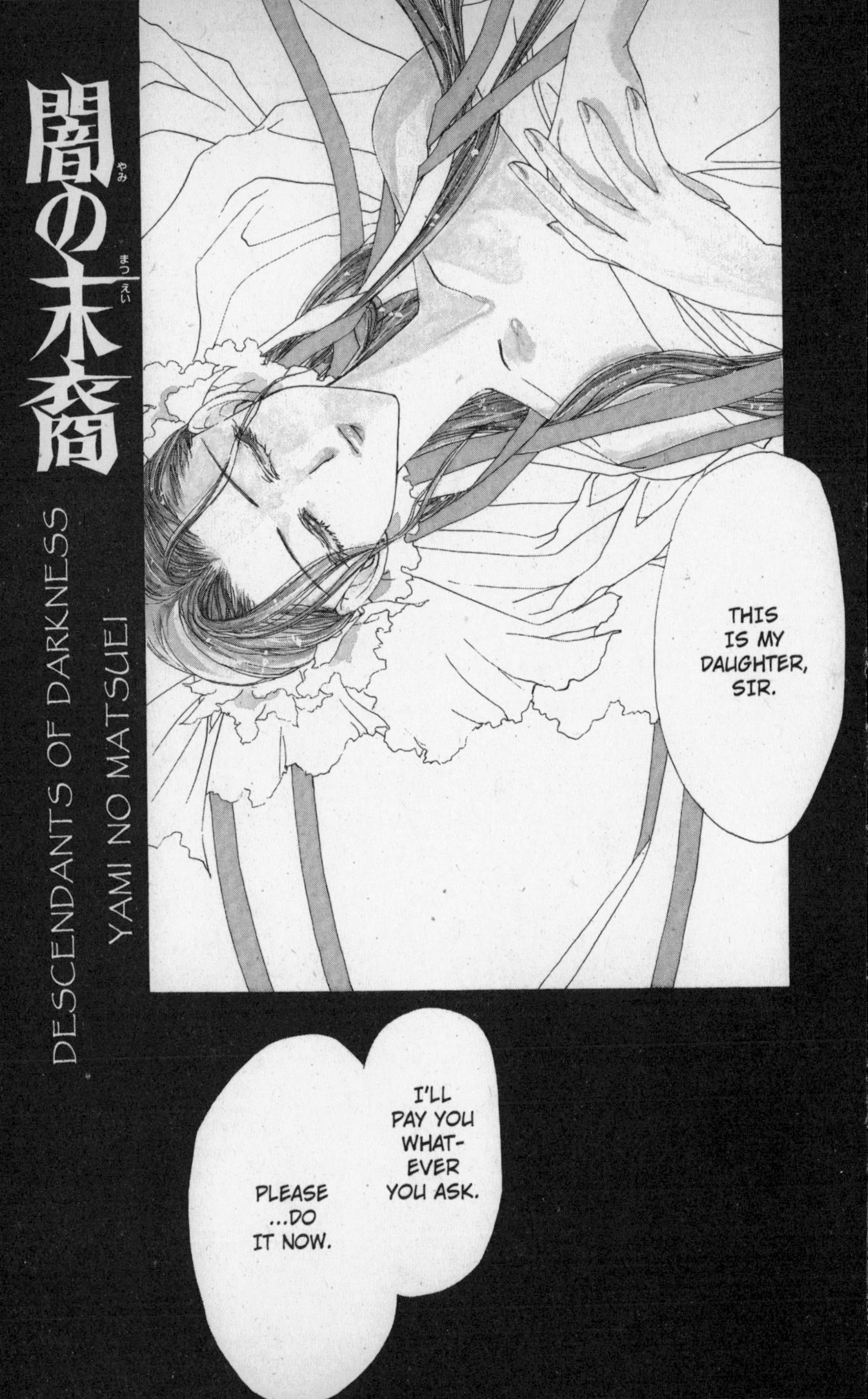
THIS IS MY DAUGHTER, SIR.
I'LL PAY YOU WHAT-EVER YOU ASK.
PLEASE ...DO IT NOW.
闇(やみ)の末裔(まつえい)
DESCENDANTS OF DARKNESS
YAMI NO MATSUEI

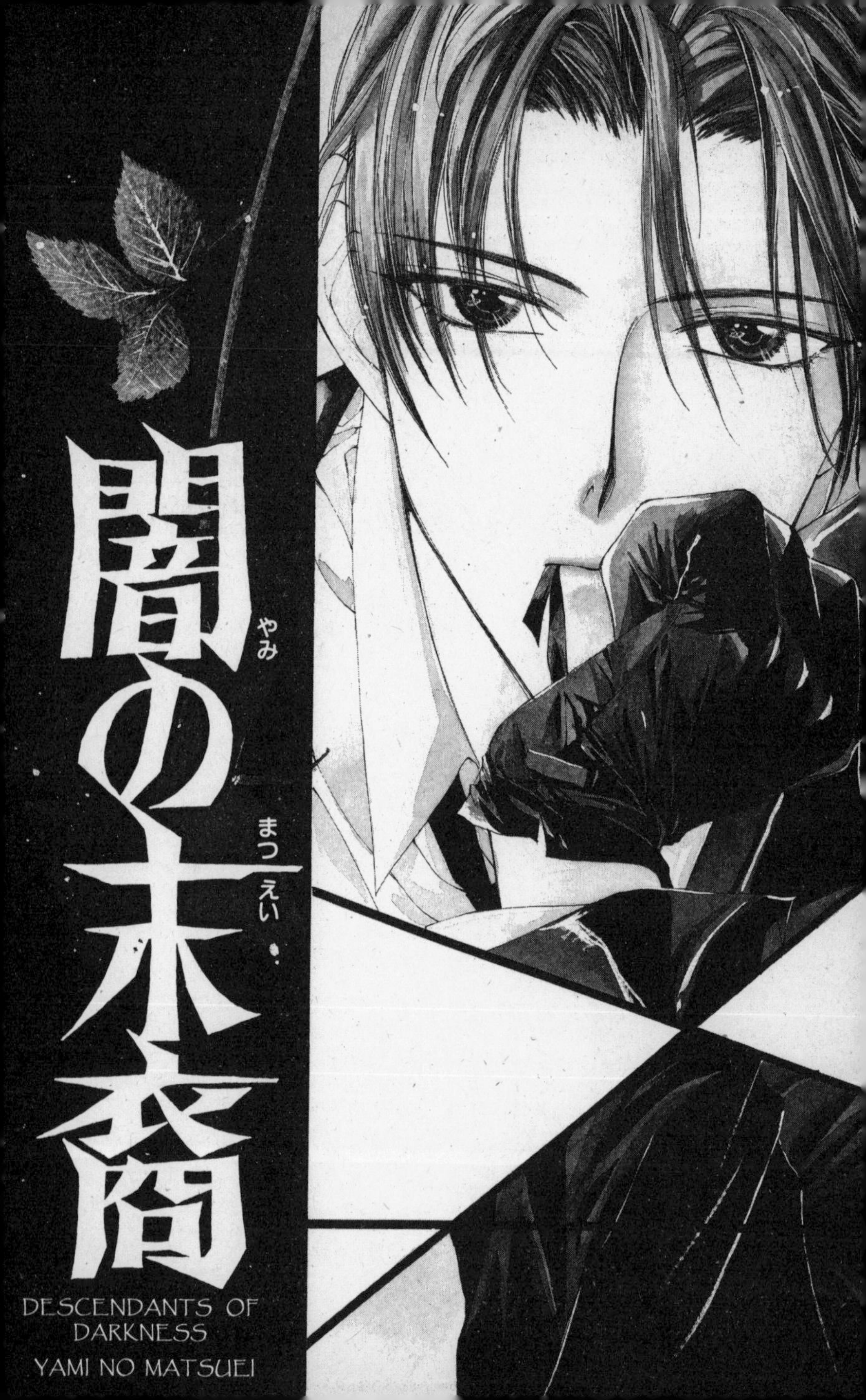
闇の末裔
DESCENDANTS OF DARKNESS
YAMI NO MATSUEI

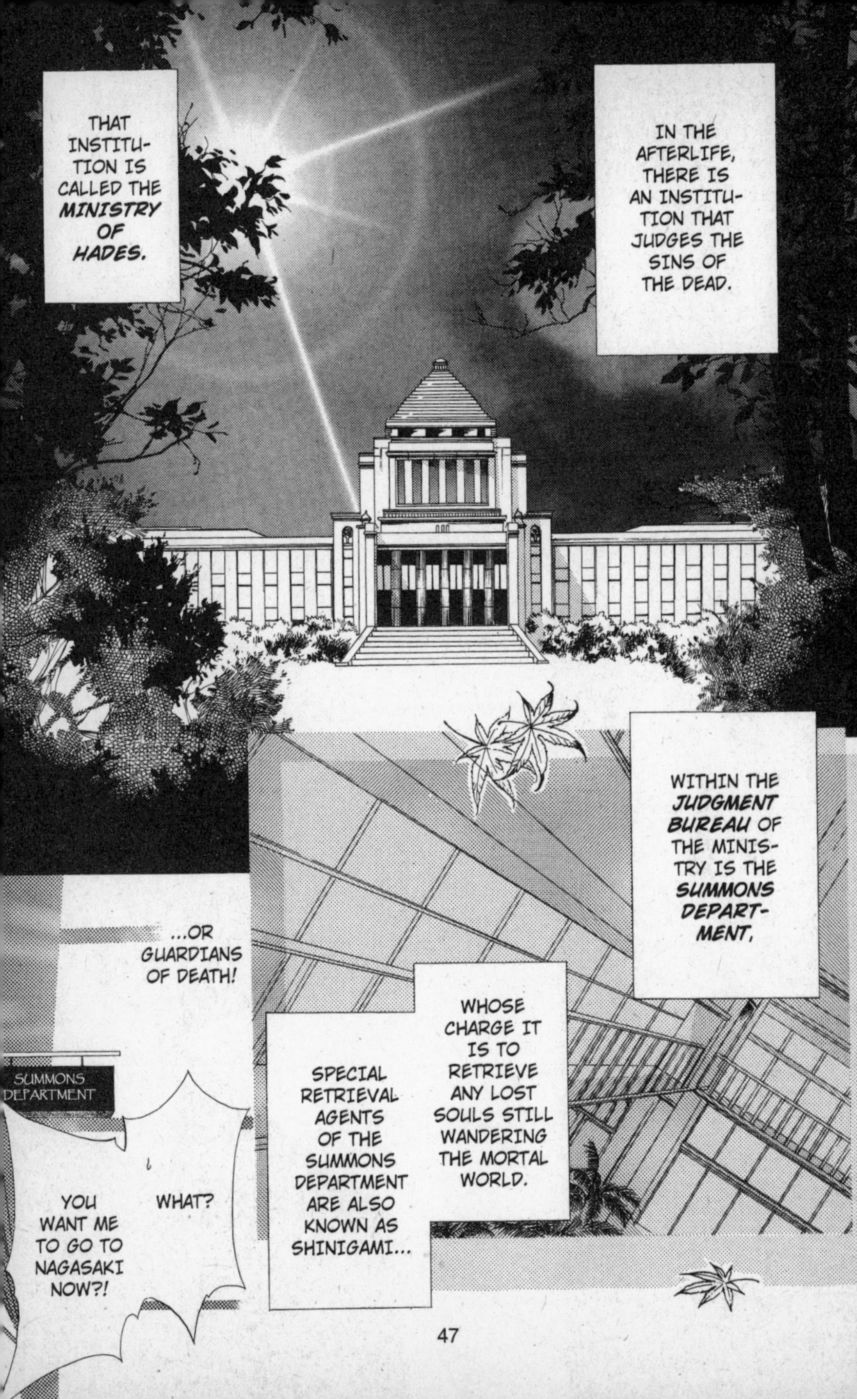
IN THE AFTERLIFE, THERE IS AN INSTITUTION THAT JUDGES THE SINS OF THE DEAD.
THAT INSTITUTION IS CALLED THE MINISTRY OF HADES.
WITHIN THE JUDGMENT BUREAU OF THE MINISTRY IS THE SUMMONS DEPARTMENT,
WHOSE CHARGE IT IS TO RETRIEVE ANY LOST SOULS STILL WANDERING THE MORTAL WORLD.
SPECIAL RETRIEVAL AGENTS OF THE SUMMONS DEPARTMENT ARE ALSO KNOWN AS SHINIGAMI...
...OR GUARDIANS OF DEATH!
SUMMONS DEPARTMENT
WHAT?
YOU WANT ME TO GO TO NAGASAKI NOW?!

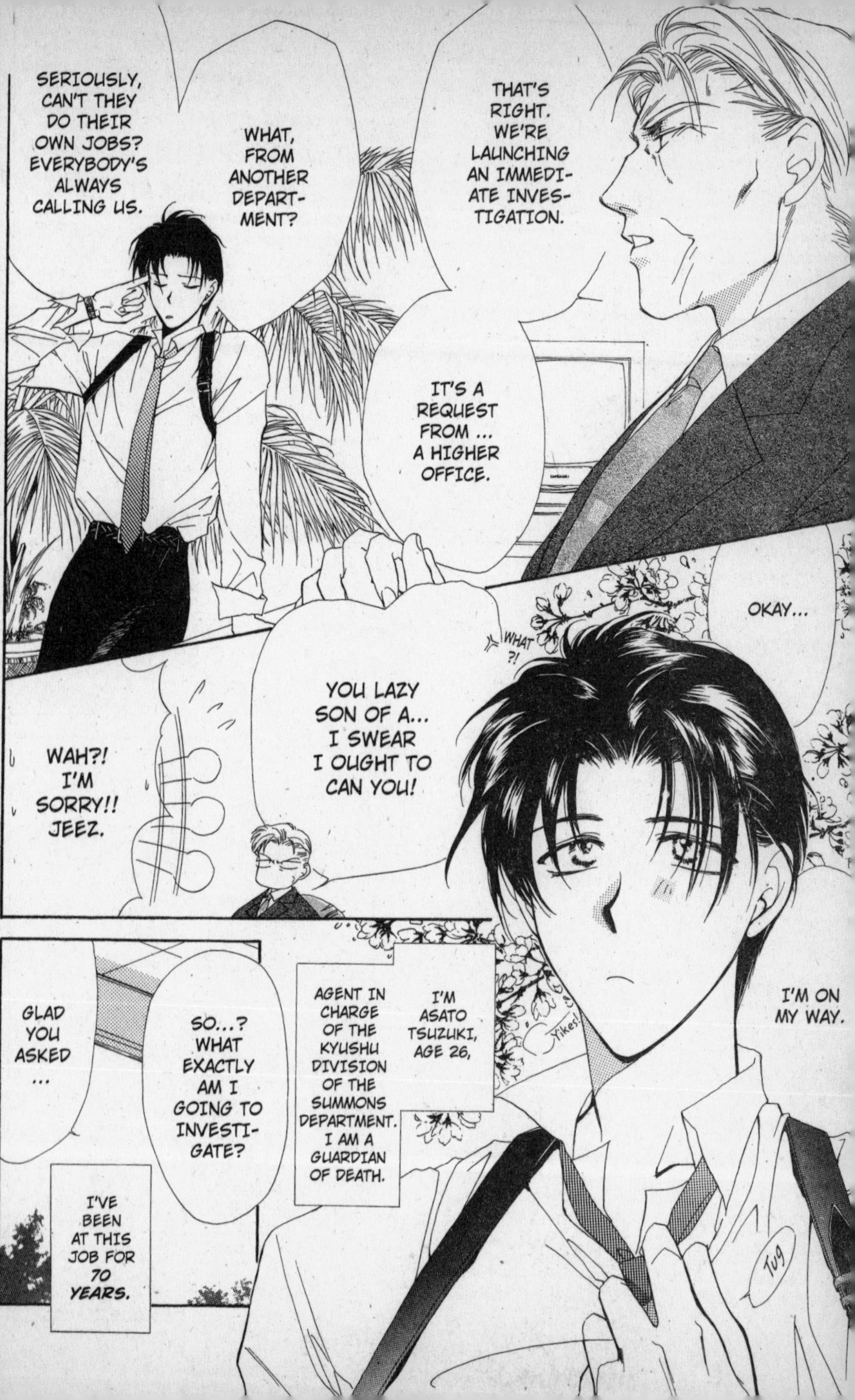
THAT'S RIGHT. WE'RE LAUNCHING AN IMMEDIATE INVESTIGATION.
WHAT, FROM ANOTHER DEPARTMENT?
IT'S A REQUEST FROM ... A HIGHER OFFICE.
SERIOUSLY, CAN'T THEY DO THEIR OWN JOBS? EVERYBODY'S ALWAYS CALLING US.
OKAY...
WHAT ?!
I'M ON MY WAY.
Yikes!
I'M ASATO TSUZUKI, AGE 26,
AGENT IN CHARGE OF THE KYUSHU DIVISION OF THE SUMMONS DEPARTMENT. I AM A GUARDIAN OF DEATH.
Tug
YOU LAZY SON OF A... I SWEAR I OUGHT TO CAN YOU!
WAH?! I'M SORRY!! JEEZ.
SO...? WHAT EXACTLY AM I GOING TO INVESTIGATE?
GLAD YOU ASKED ...
I'VE BEEN AT THIS JOB FOR 70 YEARS.

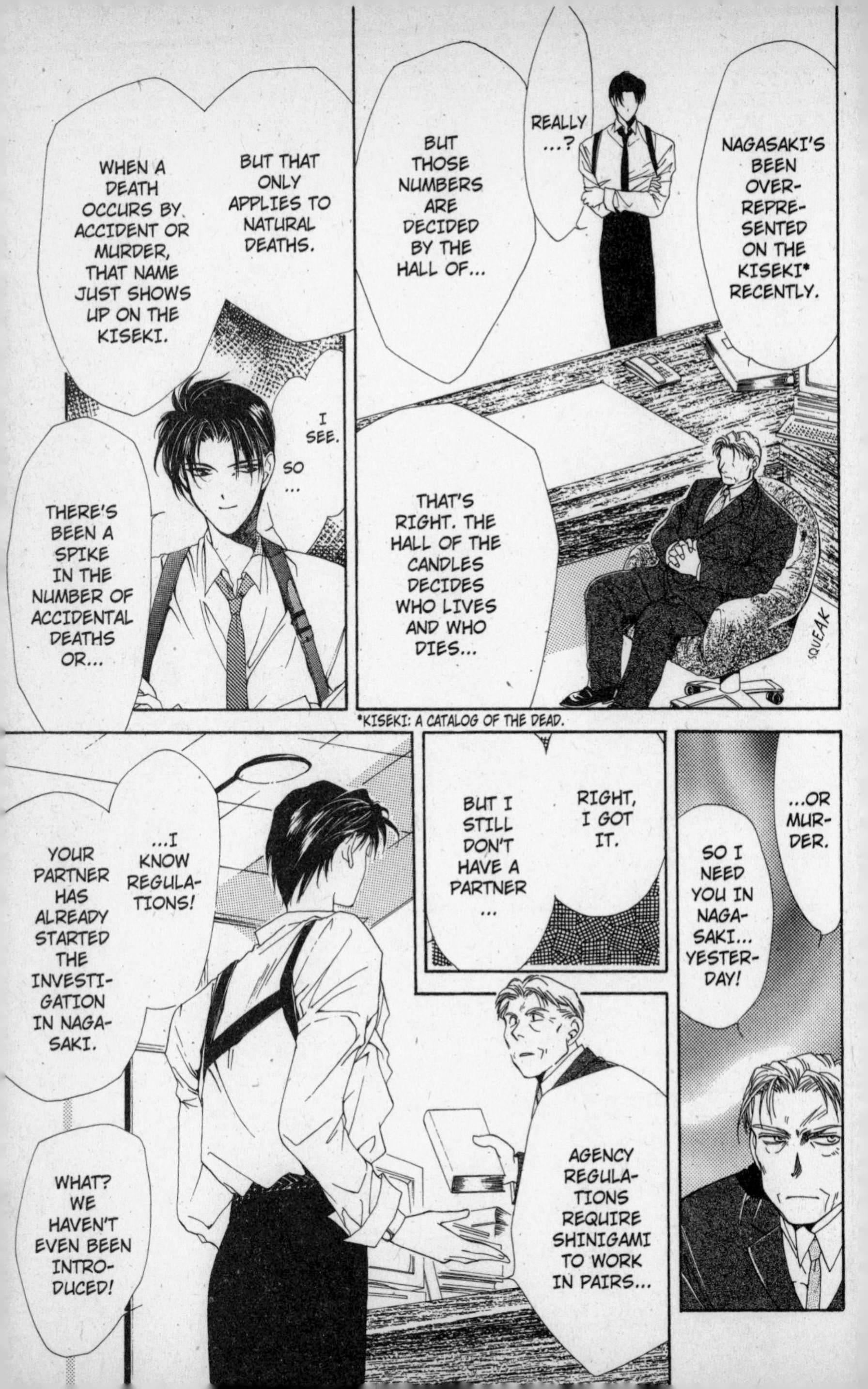
NAGASAKI'S BEEN OVER-REPRESENTED ON THE KISEKI* RECENTLY.
REALLY ...?
BUT THOSE NUMBERS ARE DECIDED BY THE HALL OF...
THAT'S RIGHT. THE HALL OF THE CANDLES DECIDES WHO LIVES AND WHO DIES...
SQUEAK
I SEE.
SO ...
BUT THAT ONLY APPLIES TO NATURAL DEATHS.
WHEN A DEATH OCCURS BY ACCIDENT OR MURDER, THAT NAME JUST SHOWS UP ON THE KISEKI.
THERE'S BEEN A SPIKE IN THE NUMBER OF ACCIDENTAL DEATHS OR...
*KISEKI: A CATALOG OF THE DEAD.
...OR MURDER.
SO I NEED YOU IN NAGASAKI... YESTERDAY!
RIGHT, I GOT IT.
BUT I STILL DON'T HAVE A PARTNER ...
AGENCY REGULATIONS REQUIRE SHINIGAMI TO WORK IN PAIRS...
...I KNOW REGULATIONS!
YOUR PARTNER HAS ALREADY STARTED THE INVESTIGATION IN NAGASAKI.
WHAT? WE HAVEN'T EVEN BEEN INTRODUCED!

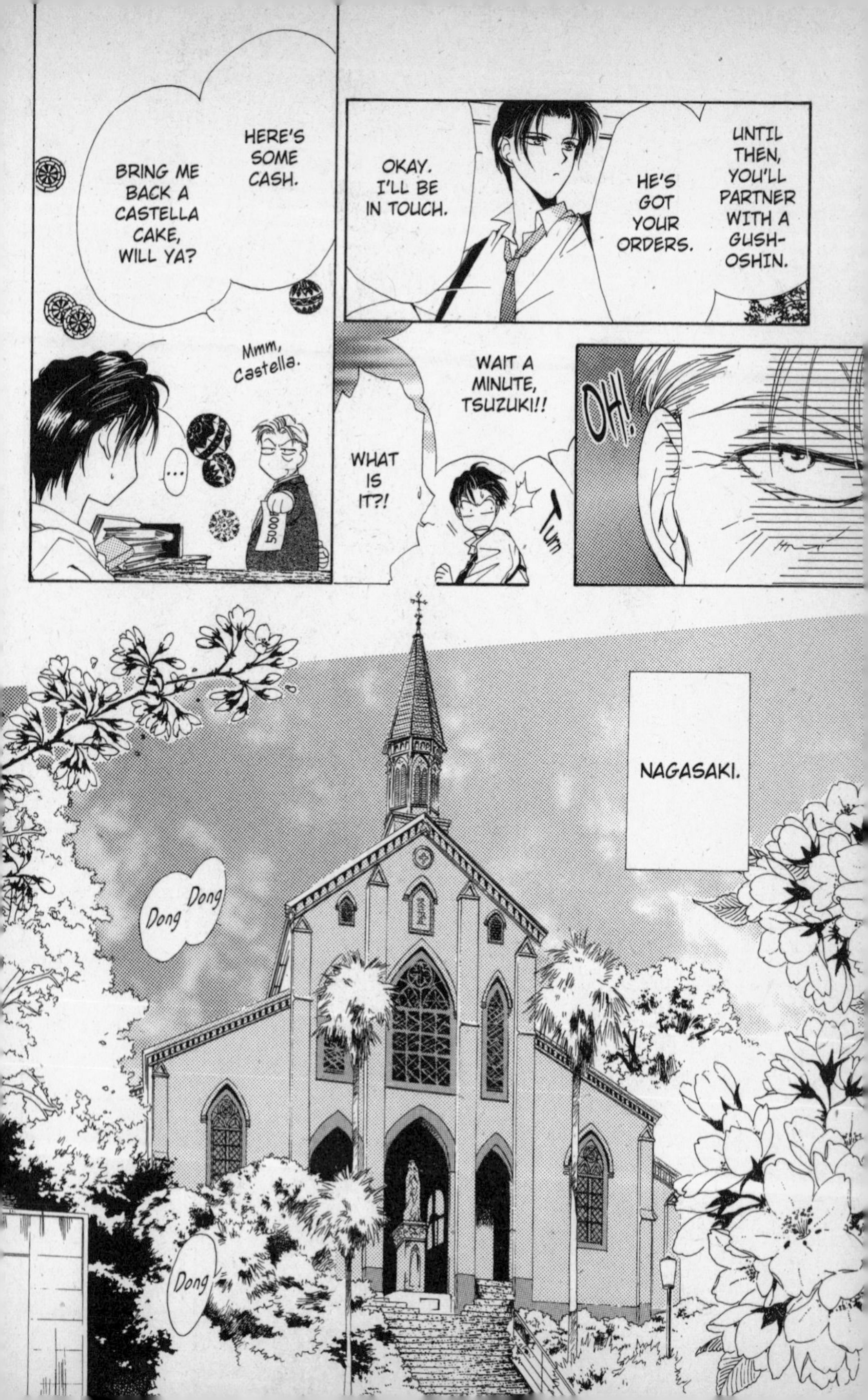
UNTIL THEN, YOU'LL PARTNER WITH A GUSH-OSHIN.
HE'S GOT YOUR ORDERS.
OKAY. I'LL BE IN TOUCH.
OH!
WAIT A MINUTE, TSUZUKI!!
Turn
WHAT IS IT?!
HERE'S SOME CASH.
BRING ME BACK A CASTELLA CAKE, WILL YA?
Mmm, Castella.
...
NAGASAKI.
Dong Dong
Dong

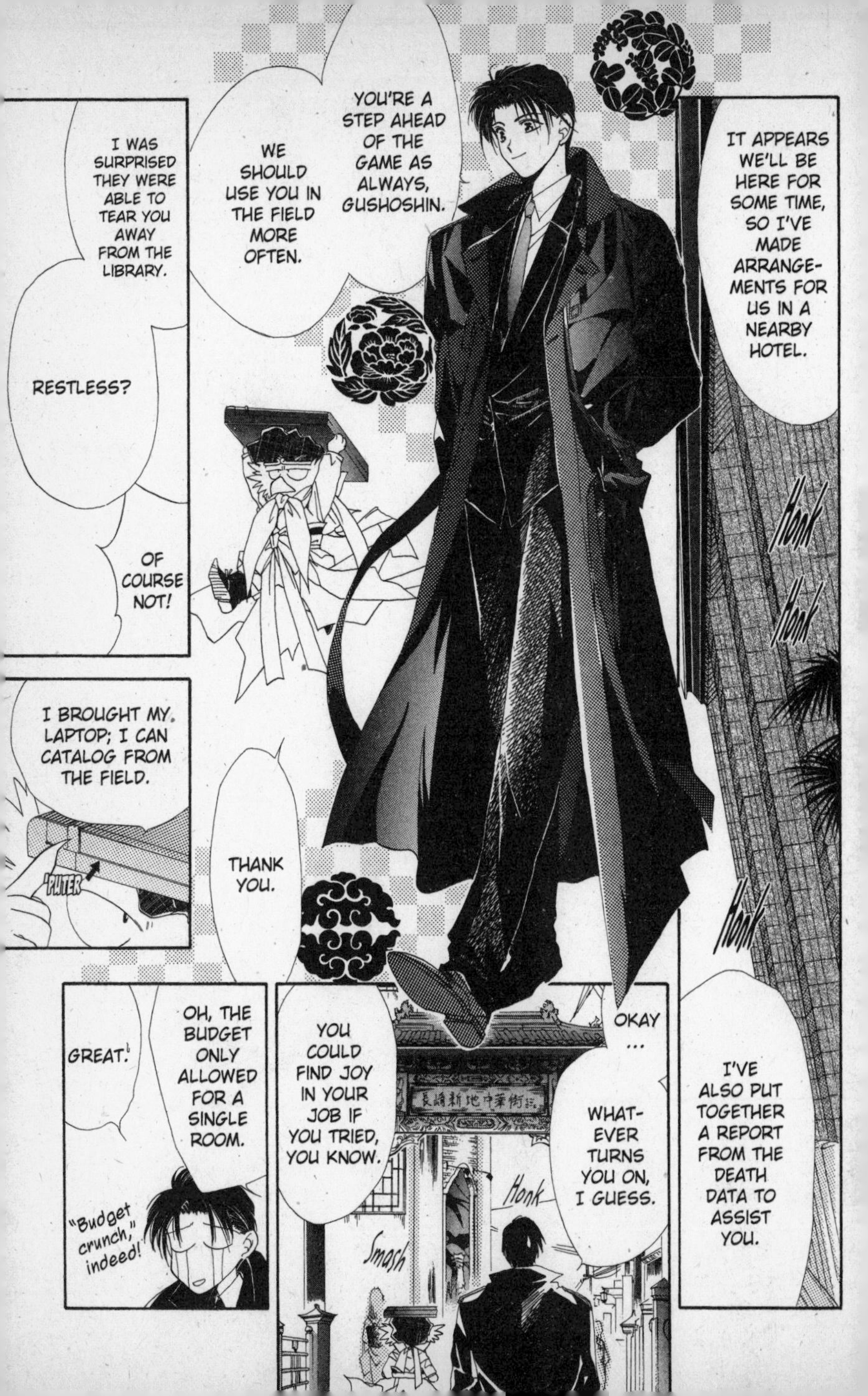
IT APPEARS WE'LL BE HERE FOR SOME TIME, SO I'VE MADE ARRANGEMENTS FOR US IN A NEARBY HOTEL.
Honk
Honk
Honk
YOU'RE A STEP AHEAD OF THE GAME AS ALWAYS, GUSHOSHIN.
WE SHOULD USE YOU IN THE FIELD MORE OFTEN.
I WAS SURPRISED THEY WERE ABLE TO TEAR YOU AWAY FROM THE LIBRARY.
RESTLESS?
OF COURSE NOT!
I BROUGHT MY LAPTOP; I CAN CATALOG FROM THE FIELD.
'PUTER
THANK YOU.
I'VE ALSO PUT TOGETHER A REPORT FROM THE DEATH DATA TO ASSIST YOU.
OKAY ...
WHATEVER TURNS YOU ON, I GUESS.
Honk
Smash
YOU COULD FIND JOY IN YOUR JOB IF YOU TRIED, YOU KNOW.
OH, THE BUDGET ONLY ALLOWED FOR A SINGLE ROOM.
GREAT.
"Budget crunch," indeed!

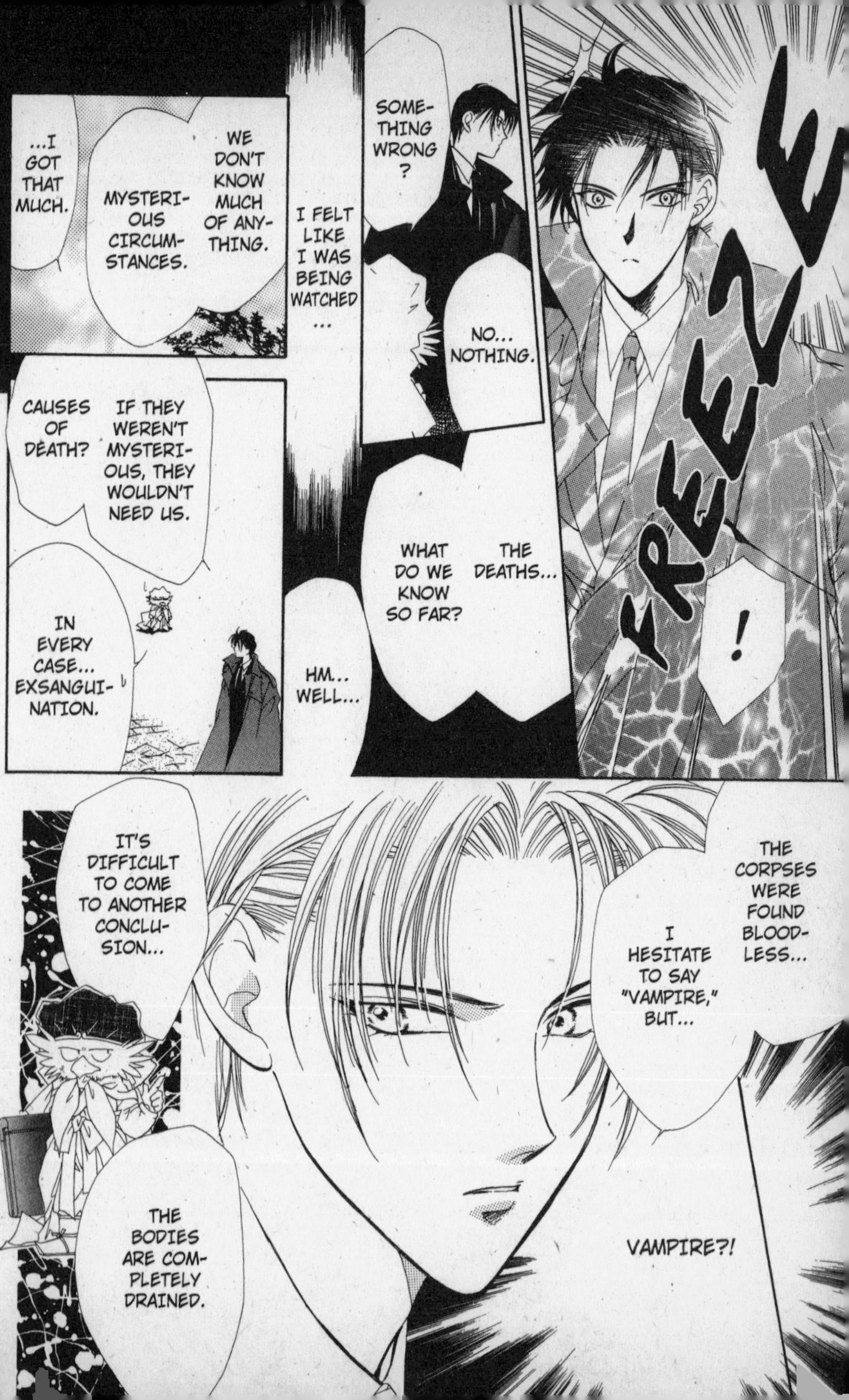
FREEZE
!
SOMETHING WRONG?
I FELT LIKE I WAS BEING WATCHED...
NO... NOTHING.
THE DEATHS...
WHAT DO WE KNOW SO FAR?
HM... WELL...
WE DON'T KNOW MUCH OF ANYTHING.
MYSTERIOUS CIRCUMSTANCES.
...I GOT THAT MUCH.
IF THEY WEREN'T MYSTERIOUS, THEY WOULDN'T NEED US.
CAUSES OF DEATH?
IN EVERY CASE... EXSANGUINATION.
THE CORPSES WERE FOUND BLOODLESS...
I HESITATE TO SAY "VAMPIRE," BUT...
IT'S DIFFICULT TO COME TO ANOTHER CONCLUSION...
VAMPIRE?!
THE BODIES ARE COMPLETELY DRAINED.

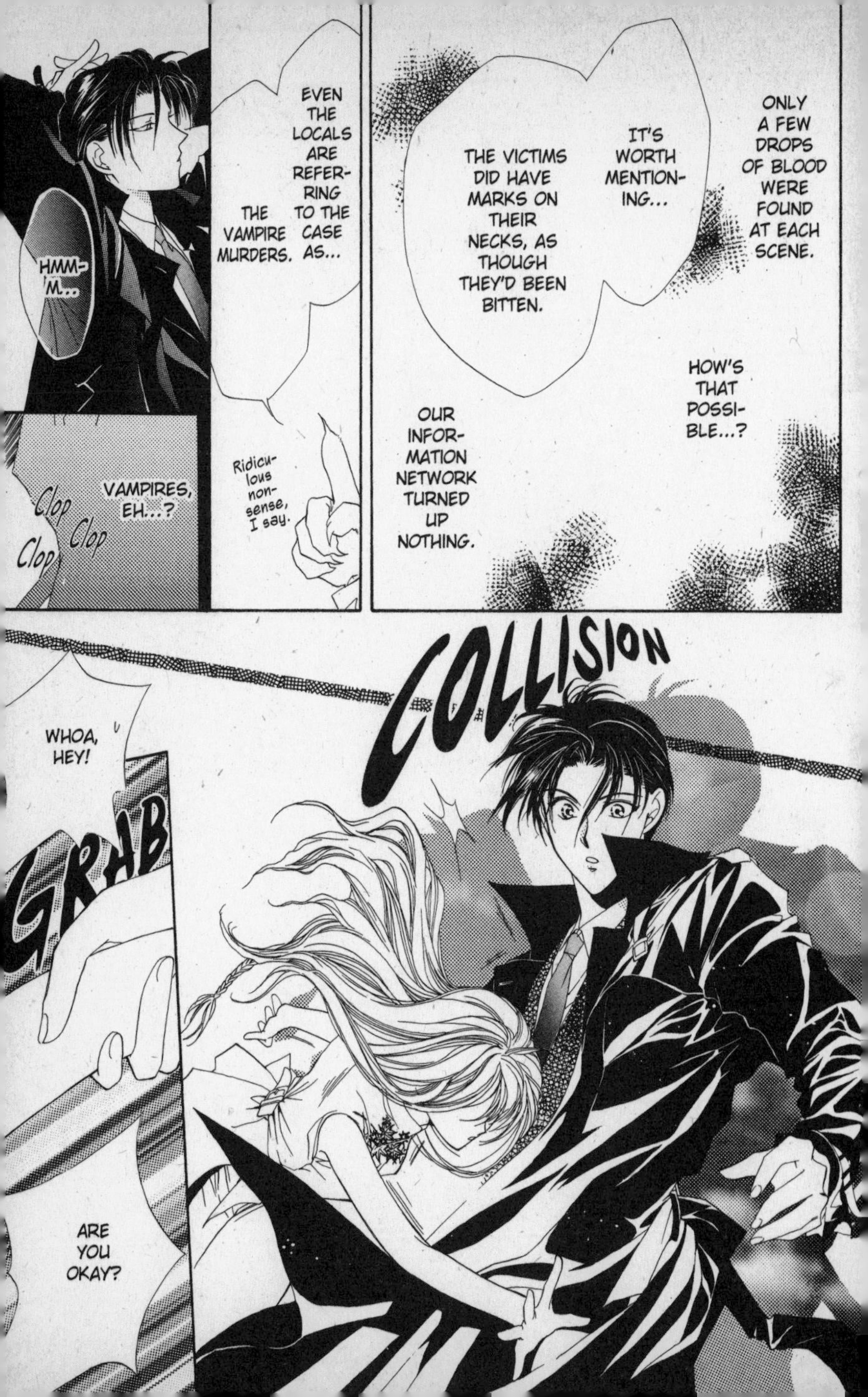
ONLY A FEW DROPS OF BLOOD WERE FOUND AT EACH SCENE.
IT'S WORTH MENTIONING...
THE VICTIMS DID HAVE MARKS ON THEIR NECKS, AS THOUGH THEY'D BEEN BITTEN.
HOW'S THAT POSSIBLE...?
OUR INFORMATION NETWORK TURNED UP NOTHING.
EVEN THE LOCALS ARE REFERRING TO THE CASE AS...
THE VAMPIRE MURDERS.
Ridiculous nonsense, I say.
HMM-M...
VAMPIRES, EH...?
Clop Clop Clop
COLLISION
WHOA, HEY!
GRAB
ARE YOU OKAY?

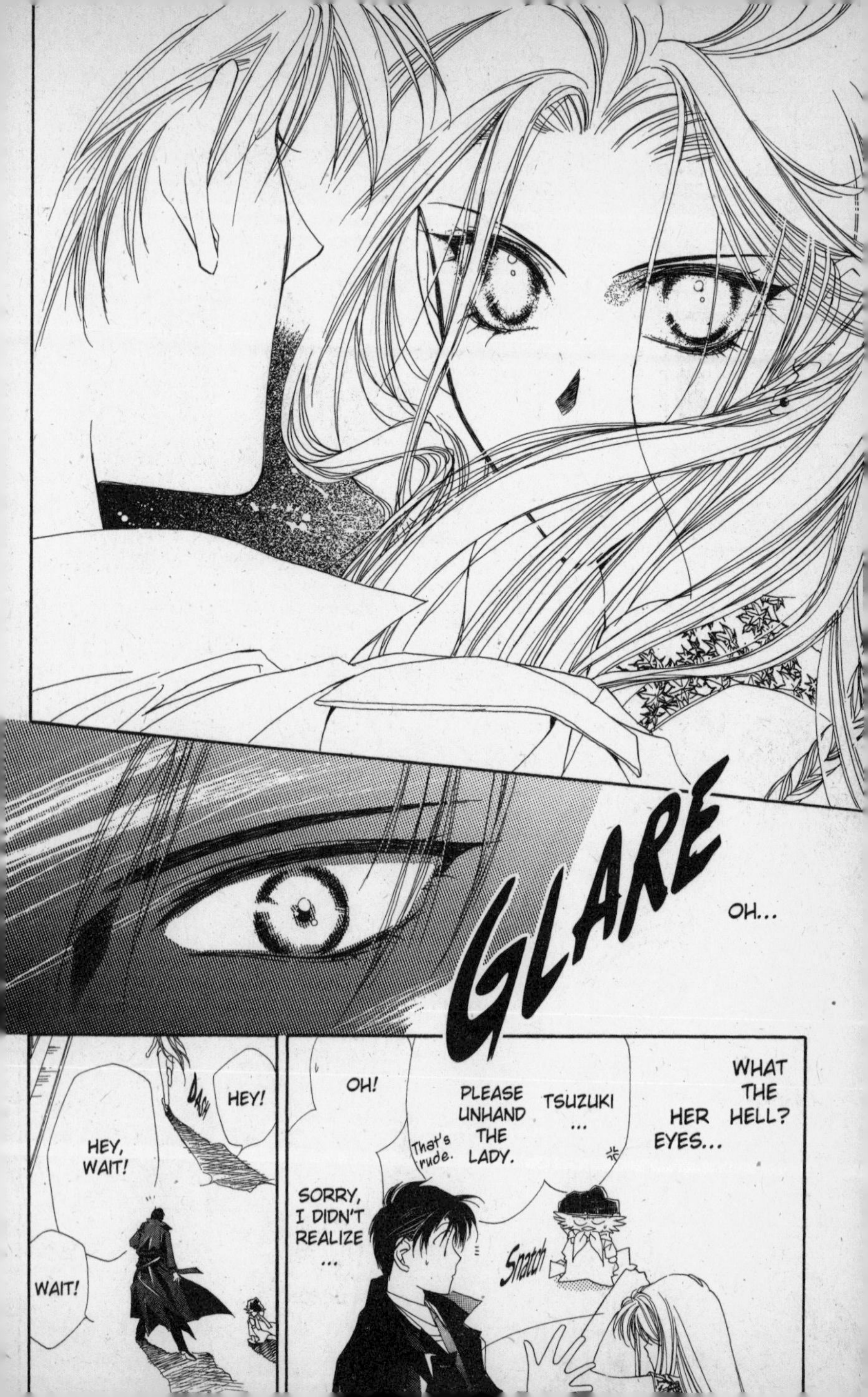
GLARE
OH...
WHAT THE HELL?
HER EYES...
TSUZUKI ...
PLEASE UNHAND THE LADY.
That's rude.
OH!
SORRY, I DIDN'T REALIZE ...
Snatch
HEY!
DASH
HEY, WAIT!
WAIT!

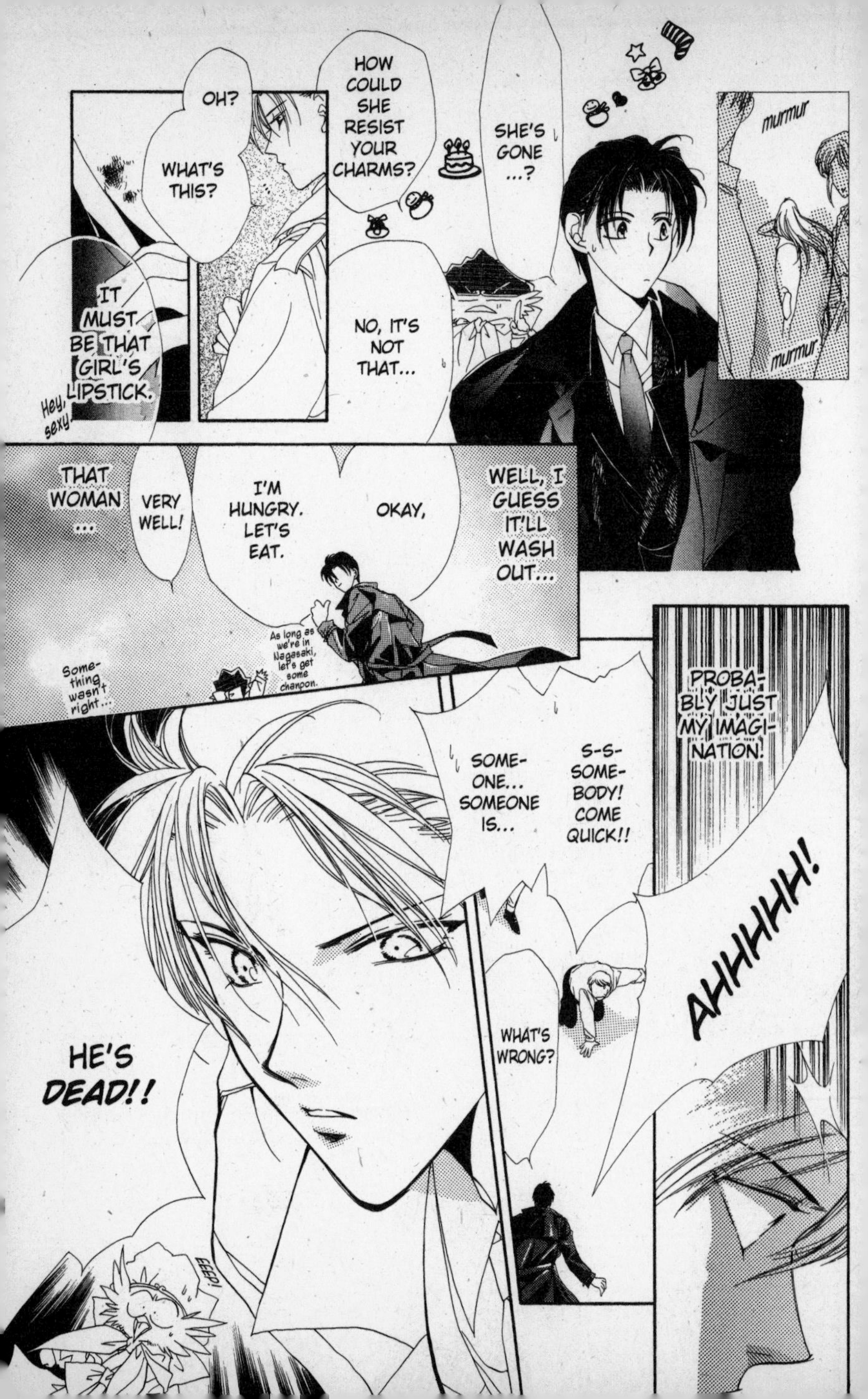
murmur
murmur
SHE'S GONE ...?
HOW COULD SHE RESIST YOUR CHARMS?
NO, IT'S NOT THAT...
OH?
WHAT'S THIS?
IT MUST BE THAT GIRL'S LIPSTICK.
Hey, sexy.
WELL, I GUESS IT'LL WASH OUT...
OKAY,
I'M HUNGRY. LET'S EAT.
As long as we're in Nagasaki, let's get some chanpon.
VERY WELL!
THAT WOMAN ...
Some-thing wasn't right...
PROBA-BLY JUST MY IMAGI-NATION!
AHHHH!
S-S-SOME-BODY! COME QUICK!!
SOME-ONE... SOMEONE IS...
WHAT'S WRONG?
HE'S DEAD!!
EEEP!

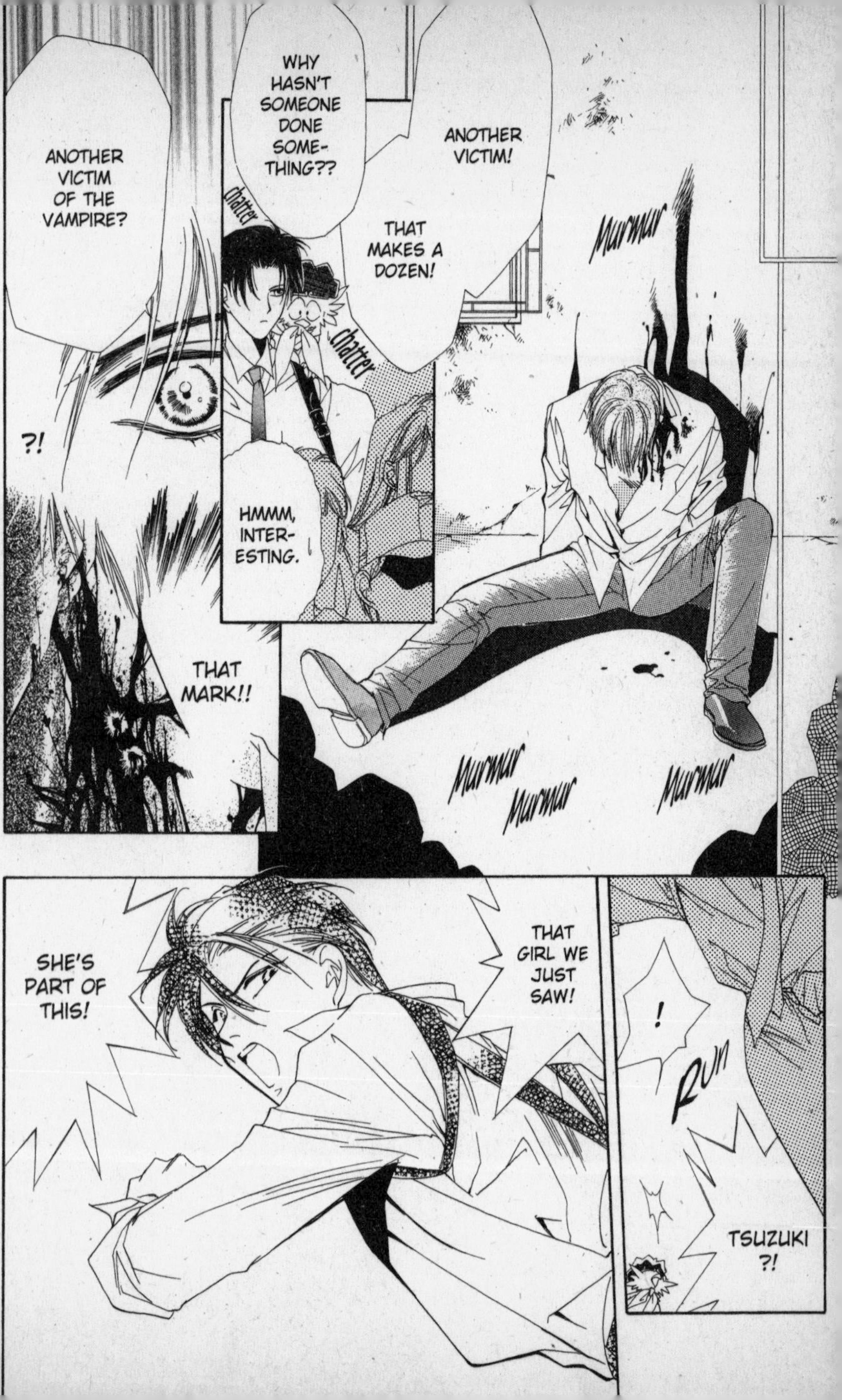
ANOTHER VICTIM!
WHY HASN'T SOMEONE DONE SOME-THING??
THAT MAKES A DOZEN!
Murmur
Murmur
Murmur
Murmur
chatter
chatter
HMMM, INTER-ESTING.
ANOTHER VICTIM OF THE VAMPIRE?
?!
THAT MARK!!
!
Run
TSUZUKI ?!
THAT GIRL WE JUST SAW!
SHE'S PART OF THIS!

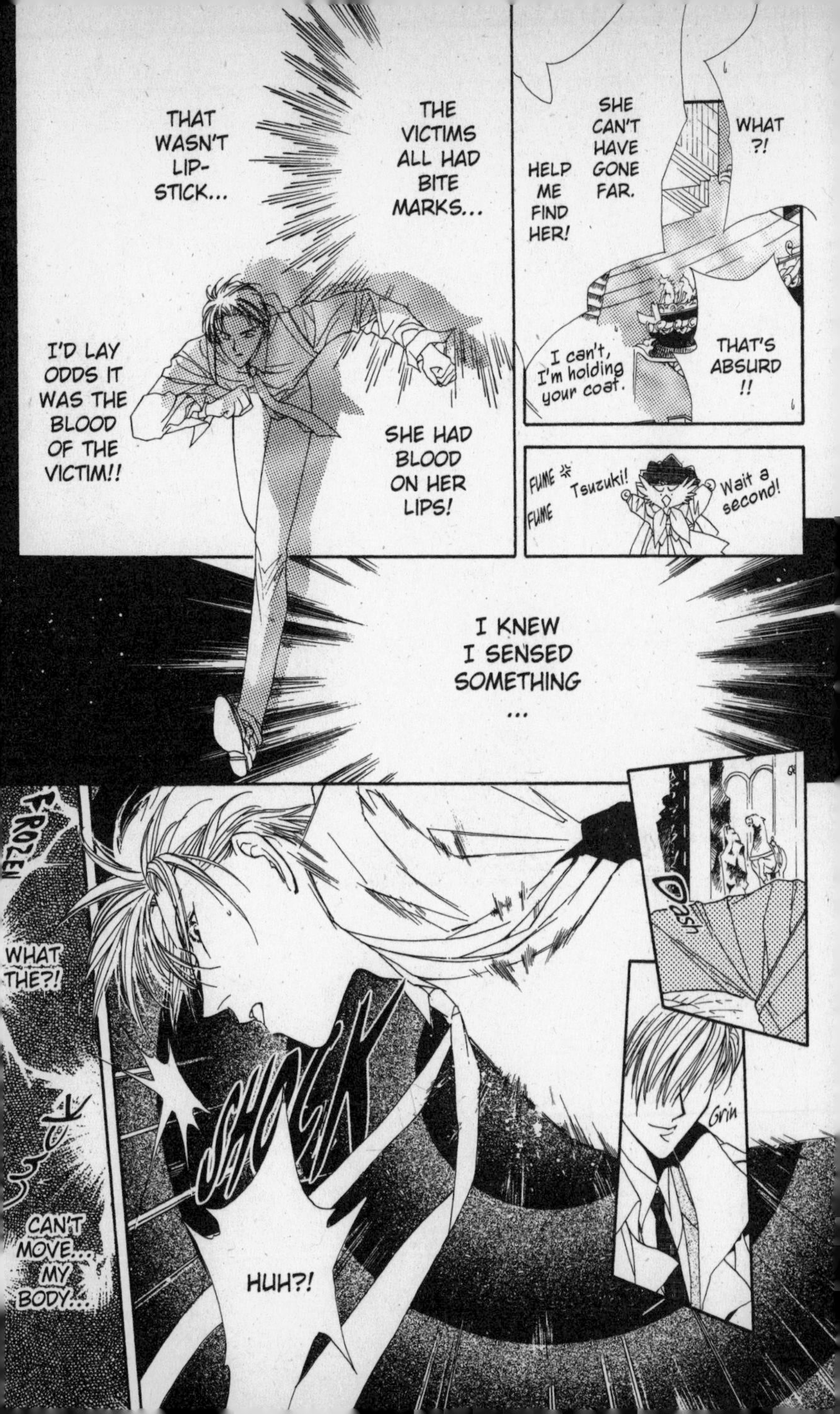
WHAT ?!
SHE CAN'T HAVE GONE FAR.
HELP ME FIND HER!
THAT'S ABSURD !!
I can't, I'm holding your coat.
FUME FUME
Tsuzuki!
Wait a second!
THE VICTIMS ALL HAD BITE MARKS...
THAT WASN'T LIP-STICK...
SHE HAD BLOOD ON HER LIPS!
I'D LAY ODDS IT WAS THE BLOOD OF THE VICTIM!!
I KNEW I SENSED SOMETHING ...
Dash
Grin
FROZEN
WHAT THE?!
HUH?!
CAN'T MOVE... MY BODY...

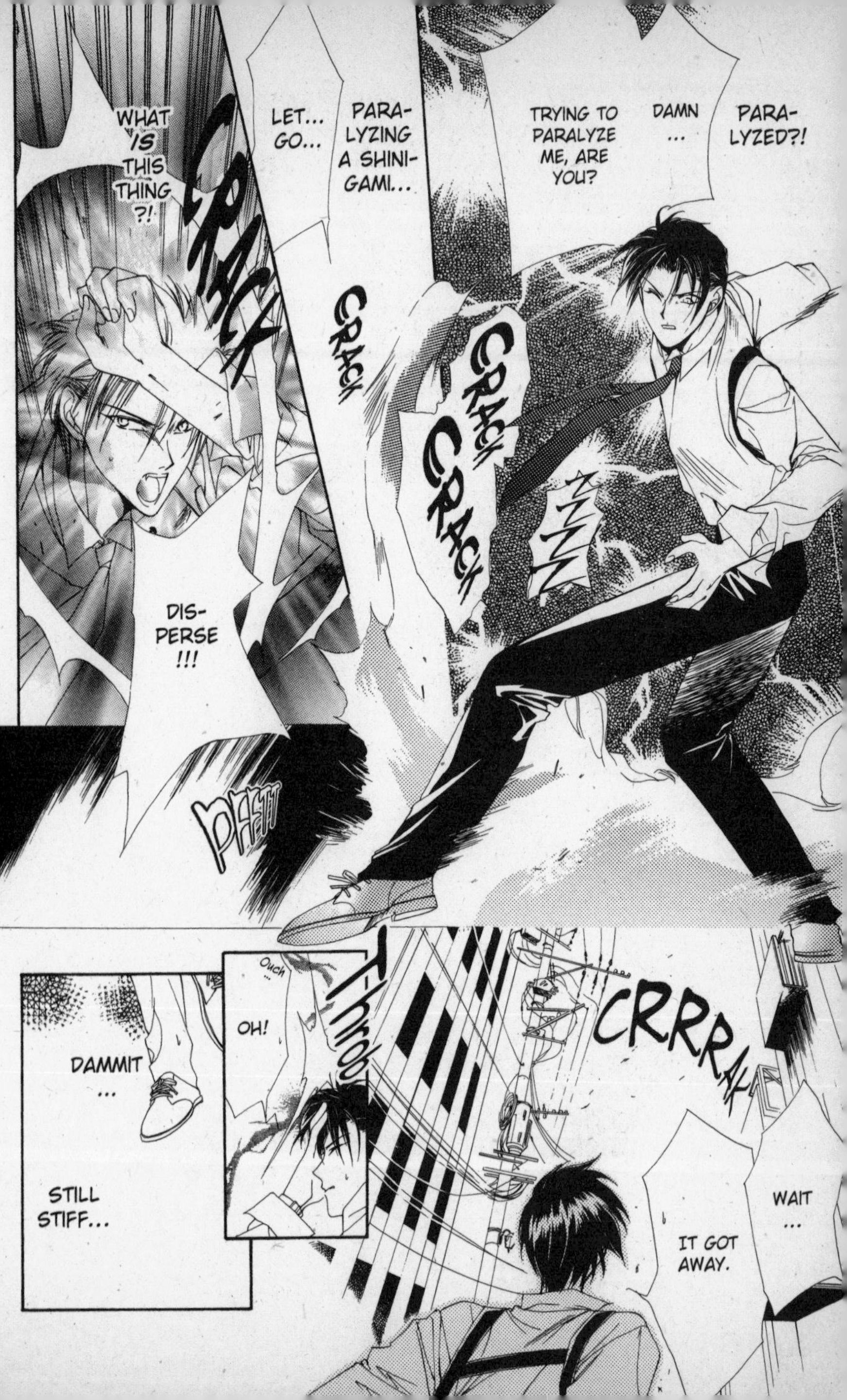
PARA-LYZED?!
DAMN ...
TRYING TO PARALYZE ME, ARE YOU?
CRACK
CRACK
CRACK
PARA-LYZING A SHINI-GAMI...
LET... GO...
CRACK
WHAT IS THIS THING?!
CRACK
DIS-PERSE!!!
CRRRAK
WAIT ...
IT GOT AWAY.
T-throb
Ouch ...
OH!
DAMMIT ...
STILL STIFF...

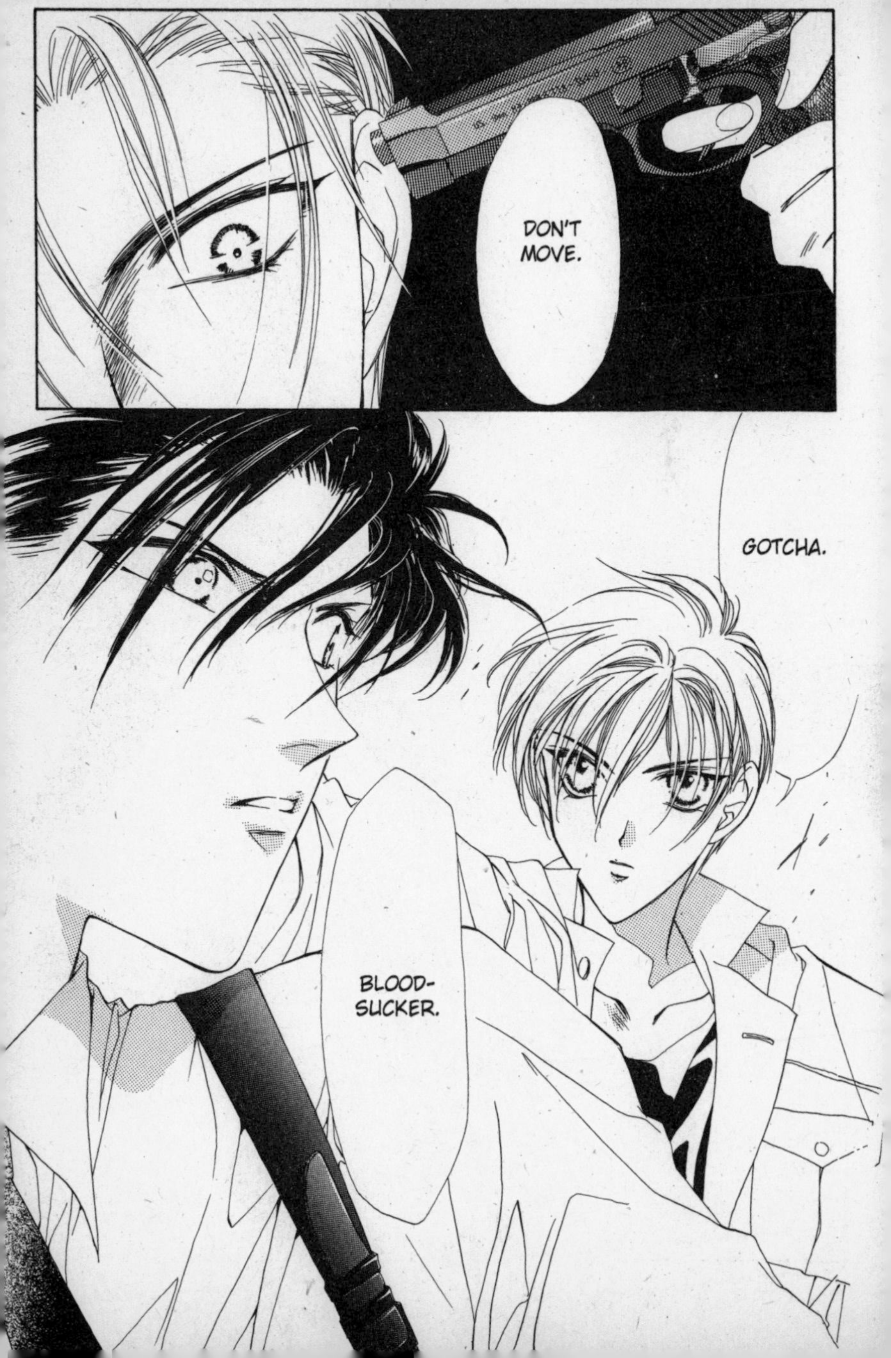
DON'T MOVE.
GOTCHA.
BLOOD-SUCKER.

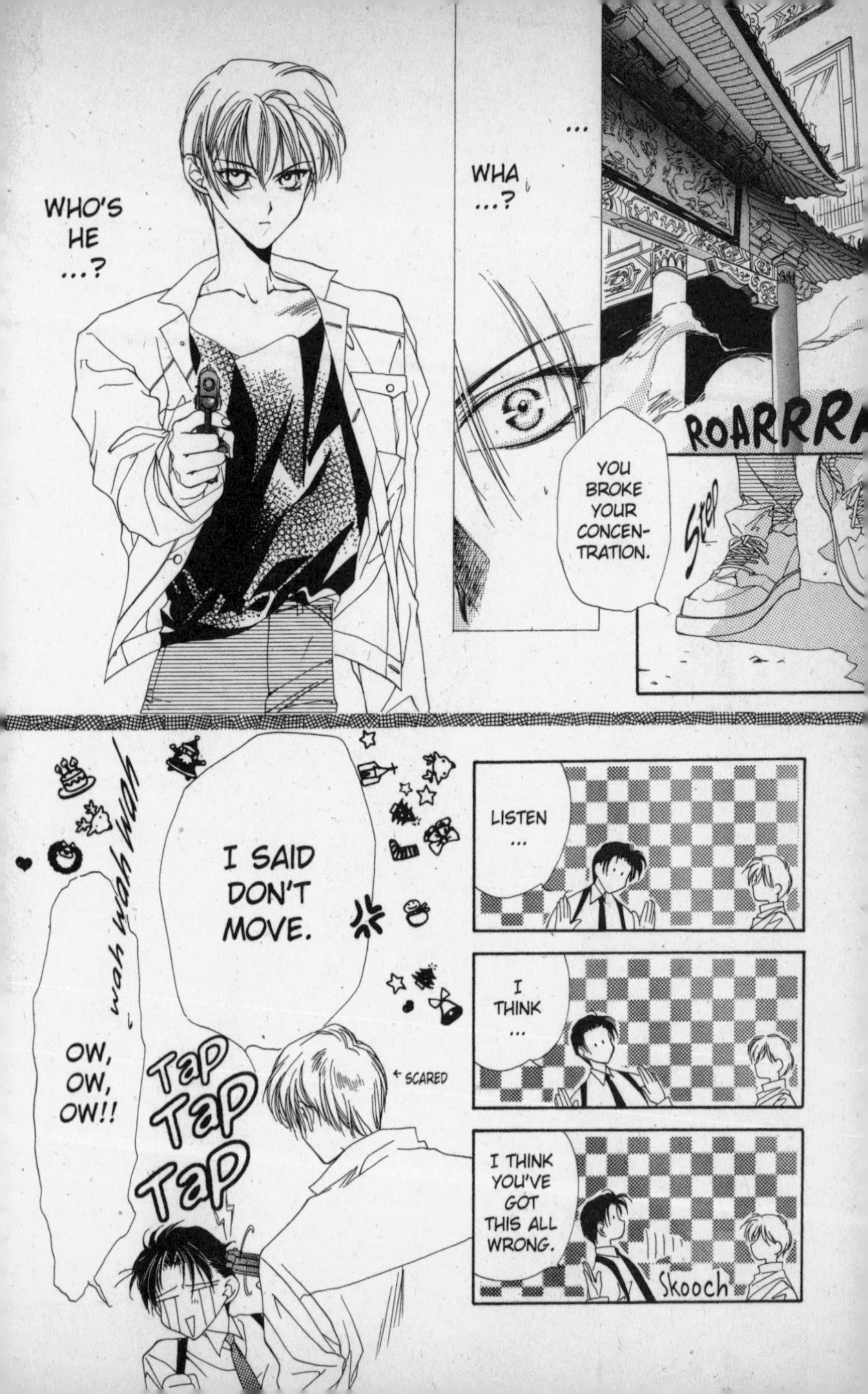
ROARRR
Step
...
WHA ...?
YOU BROKE YOUR CONCEN-TRATION.
WHO'S HE ...?
LISTEN ...
I THINK ...
I THINK YOU'VE GOT THIS ALL WRONG.
Skooch
I SAID DON'T MOVE.
Tap Tap Tap
SCARED
OW, OW, OW!!

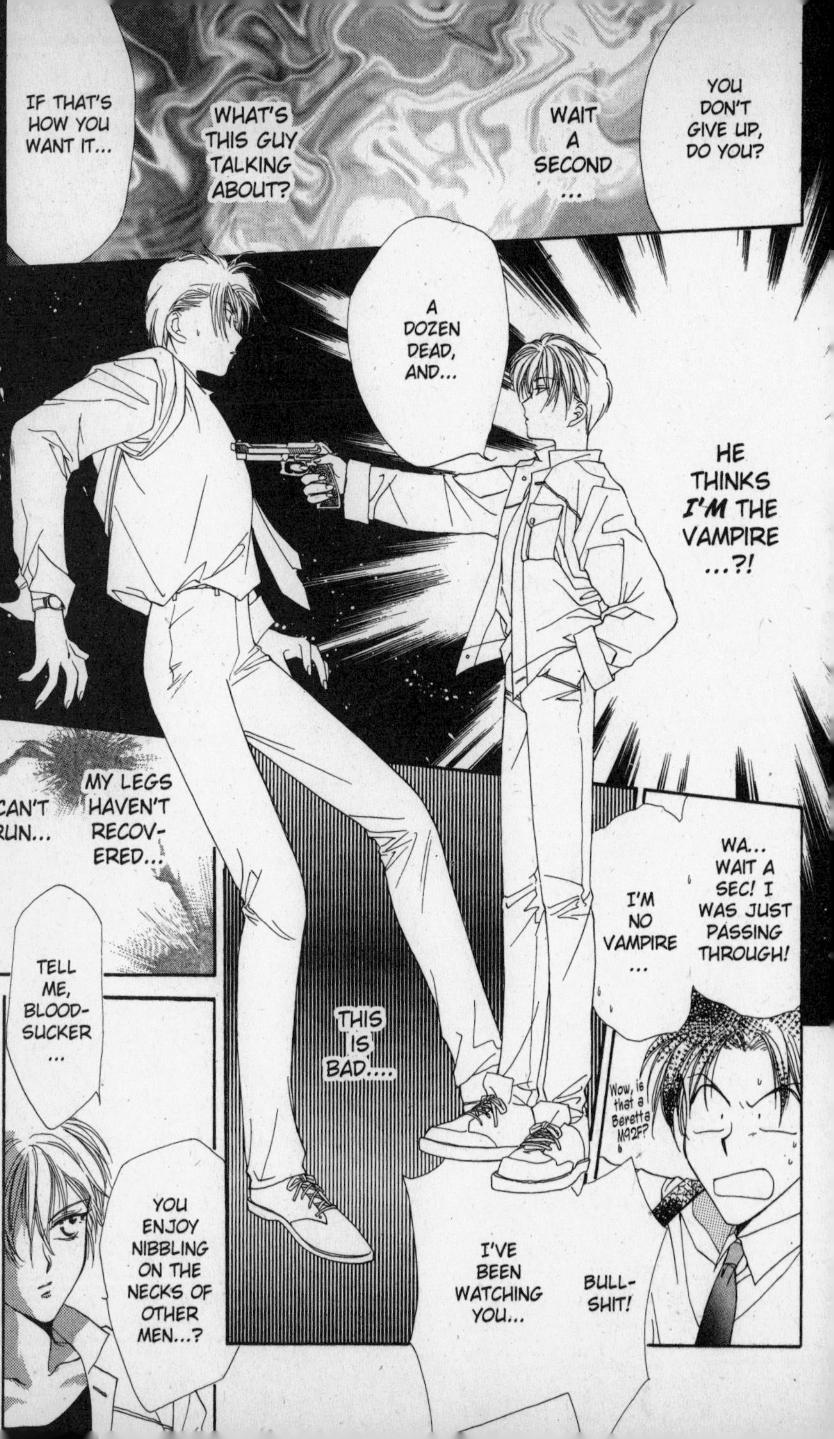
YOU DON'T GIVE UP, DO YOU?
WAIT A SECOND...
WHAT'S THIS GUY TALKING ABOUT?
IF THAT'S HOW YOU WANT IT...
A DOZEN DEAD, AND...
HE THINKS *I'M* THE VAMPIRE...?!
MY LEGS HAVEN'T RECOVERED...
CAN'T RUN...
WA... WAIT A SEC! I WAS JUST PASSING THROUGH!
I'M NO VAMPIRE...
Wow, is that a Beretta M92F?
BULL-SHIT!
I'VE BEEN WATCHING YOU...
THIS IS BAD....
TELL ME, BLOOD-SUCKER...
YOU ENJOY NIBBLING ON THE NECKS OF OTHER MEN...?

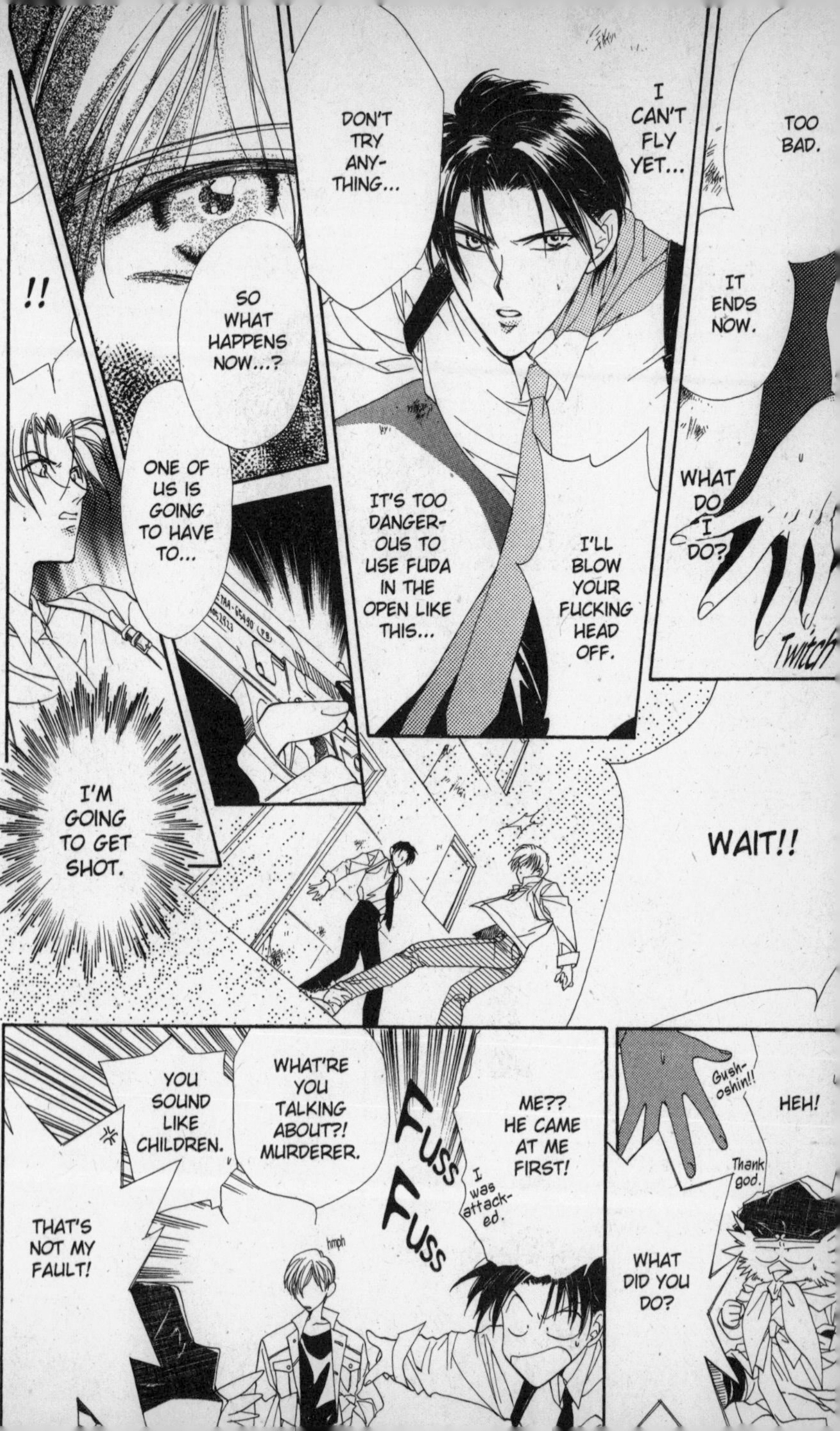
TOO BAD.
IT ENDS NOW.
WHAT DO I DO?
Twitch
I CAN'T FLY YET...
DON'T TRY ANYTHING...
I'LL BLOW YOUR FUCKING HEAD OFF.
IT'S TOO DANGEROUS TO USE FUDA IN THE OPEN LIKE THIS...
SO WHAT HAPPENS NOW...?
ONE OF US IS GOING TO HAVE TO...
!!
I'M GOING TO GET SHOT.
WAIT!!
Gush-oshin!!
HEH!
Thank god.
WHAT DID YOU DO?
ME?? HE CAME AT ME FIRST!
I was attacked.
FUSS FUSS
WHAT'RE YOU TALKING ABOUT?! MURDERER.
hmph
YOU SOUND LIKE CHILDREN.
THAT'S NOT MY FAULT!

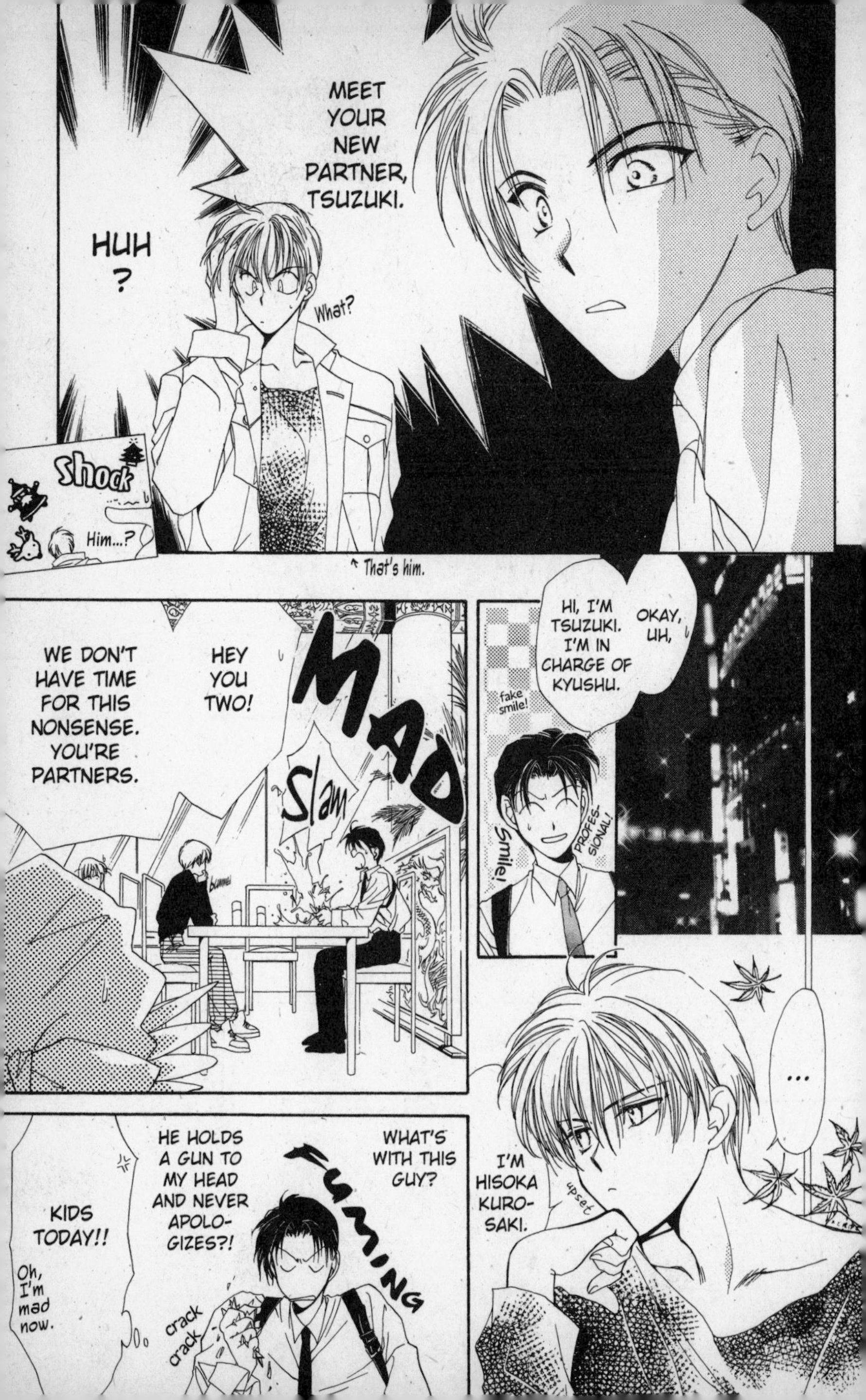
MEET YOUR NEW PARTNER, TSUZUKI.
HUH?
What?
Shock
Him...?
That's him.
OKAY, UH,
HI, I'M TSUZUKI. I'M IN CHARGE OF KYUSHU.
fake smile!
PROFES-SIONAL!
Smile!
...
I'M HISOKA KURO-SAKI.
upset
MAD
HEY YOU TWO!
WE DON'T HAVE TIME FOR THIS NONSENSE. YOU'RE PARTNERS.
Slam
WHAT'S WITH THIS GUY?
FUMING
HE HOLDS A GUN TO MY HEAD AND NEVER APOLO-GIZES?!
KIDS TODAY!!
Oh, I'm mad now.
crack crack

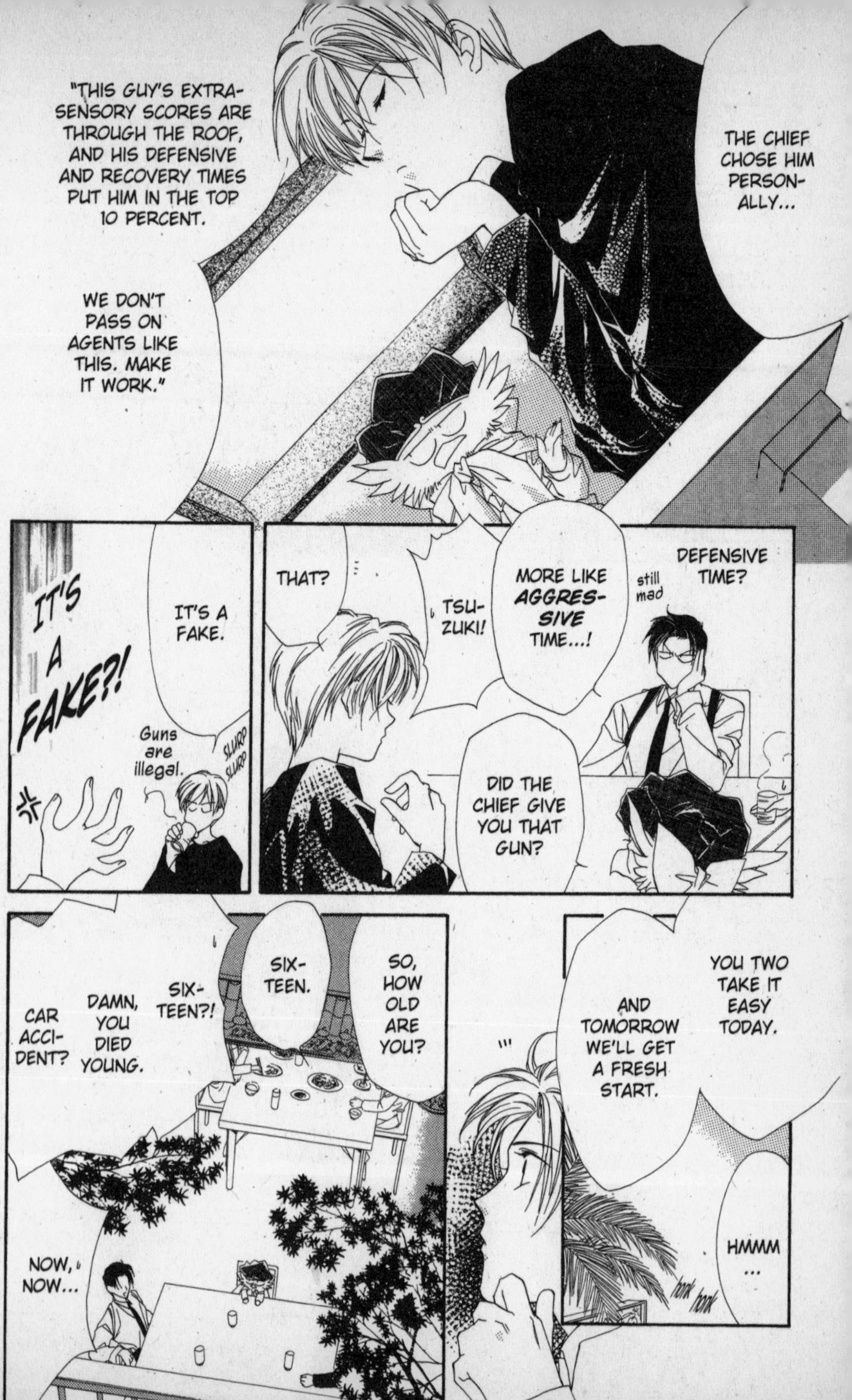
THE CHIEF CHOSE HIM PERSONALLY...
"THIS GUY'S EXTRA-SENSORY SCORES ARE THROUGH THE ROOF, AND HIS DEFENSIVE AND RECOVERY TIMES PUT HIM IN THE TOP 10 PERCENT.
WE DON'T PASS ON AGENTS LIKE THIS. MAKE IT WORK."
DEFENSIVE TIME?
still mad
MORE LIKE AGGRESSIVE TIME...!
TSUZUKI!
THAT?
DID THE CHIEF GIVE YOU THAT GUN?
IT'S A FAKE.
IT'S A FAKE?!
SLURP SLURP
Guns are illegal.
YOU TWO TAKE IT EASY TODAY.
AND TOMORROW WE'LL GET A FRESH START.
HMMM...
hook hook
SO, HOW OLD ARE YOU?
SIXTEEN.
SIXTEEN?!
DAMN, YOU DIED YOUNG.
CAR ACCIDENT?
NOW, NOW...

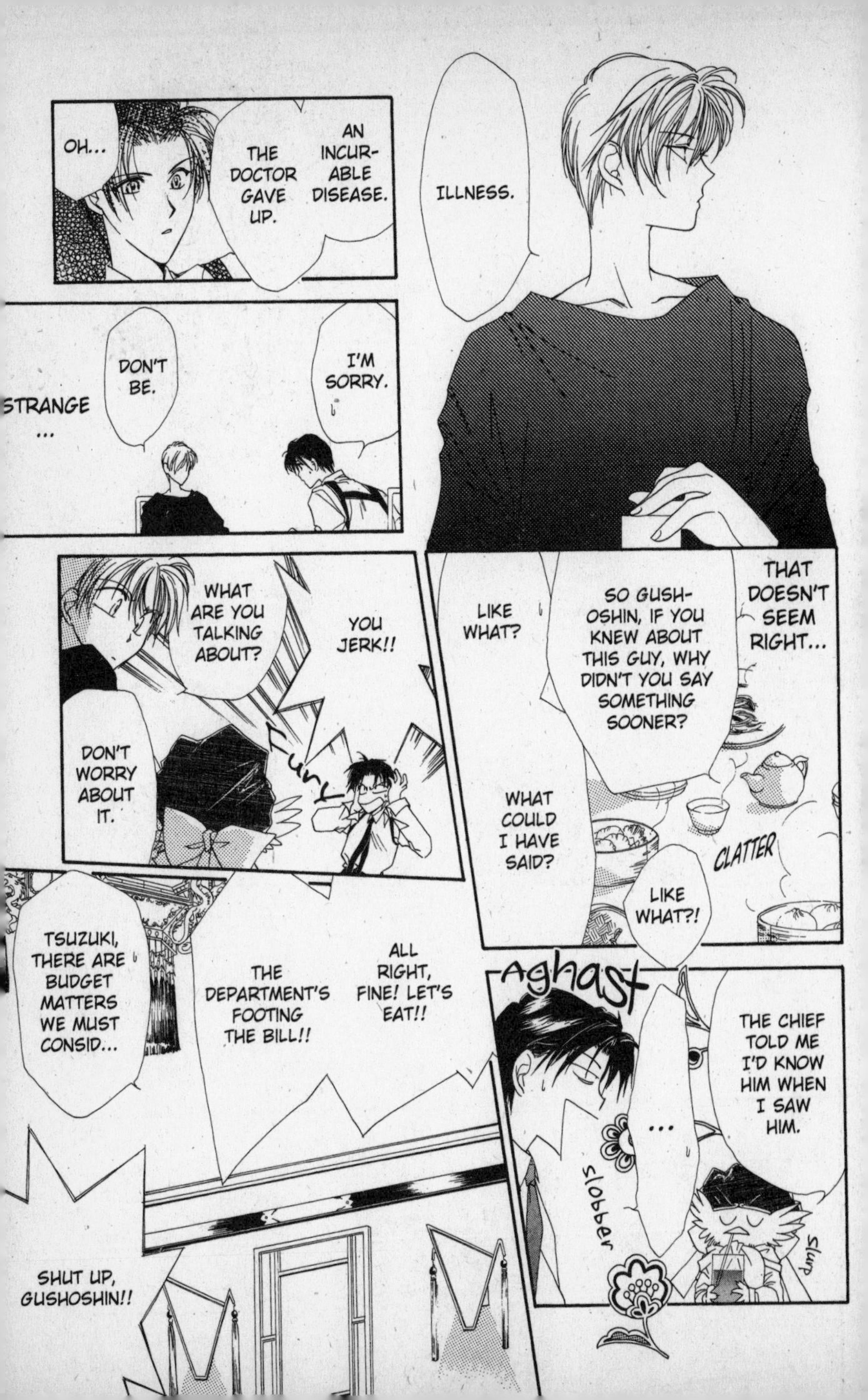
ILLNESS.
AN INCURABLE DISEASE.
THE DOCTOR GAVE UP.
OH...
I'M SORRY.
DON'T BE.
STRANGE...
THAT DOESN'T SEEM RIGHT...
SO GUSHOSHIN, IF YOU KNEW ABOUT THIS GUY, WHY DIDN'T YOU SAY SOMETHING SOONER?
LIKE WHAT?
WHAT COULD I HAVE SAID?
CLATTER
LIKE WHAT?!
YOU JERK!!
WHAT ARE YOU TALKING ABOUT?
DON'T WORRY ABOUT IT.
THE CHIEF TOLD ME I'D KNOW HIM WHEN I SAW HIM.
Aghast
...
slobber
slurp
ALL RIGHT, FINE! LET'S EAT!!
THE DEPARTMENT'S FOOTING THE BILL!!
TSUZUKI, THERE ARE BUDGET MATTERS WE MUST CONSID...
SHUT UP, GUSHOSHIN!!

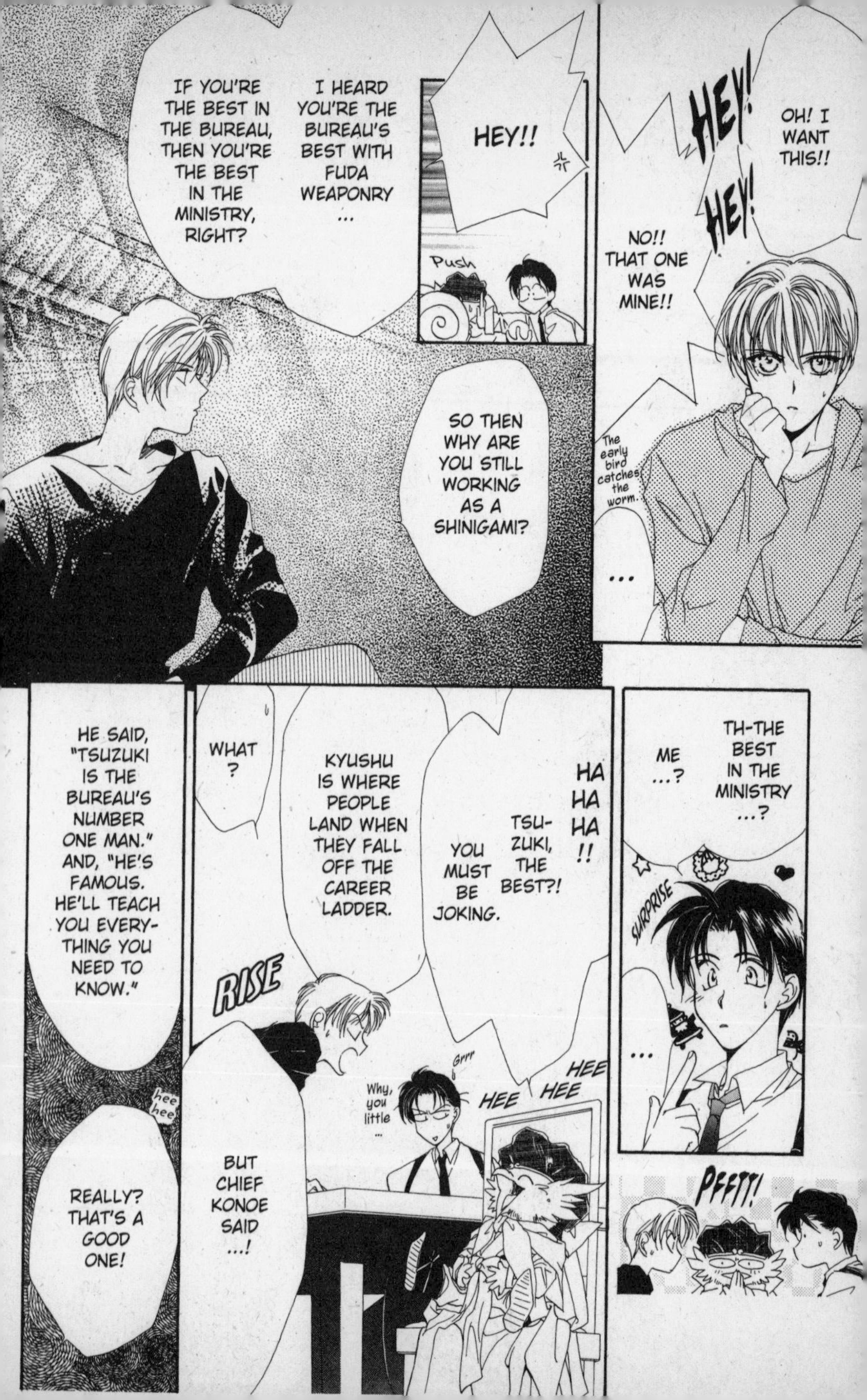
OH! I WANT THIS!!
HEY!
HEY!
NO!! THAT ONE WAS MINE!!
The early bird catches the worm.
...
HEY!!
Push
I HEARD YOU'RE THE BUREAU'S BEST WITH FUDA WEAPONRY ...
IF YOU'RE THE BEST IN THE BUREAU, THEN YOU'RE THE BEST IN THE MINISTRY, RIGHT?
SO THEN WHY ARE YOU STILL WORKING AS A SHINIGAMI?
TH-THE BEST IN THE MINISTRY ...?
ME ...?
SURPRISE
...
PFFTT!
HA HA HA !!
TSU-ZUKI, THE BEST?!
YOU MUST BE JOKING.
KYUSHU IS WHERE PEOPLE LAND WHEN THEY FALL OFF THE CAREER LADDER.
WHAT?
RISE
HEE HEE
HEE HEE
Grrr
Why, you little ...
BUT CHIEF KONOE SAID ...!
HE SAID, "TSUZUKI IS THE BUREAU'S NUMBER ONE MAN." AND, "HE'S FAMOUS. HE'LL TEACH YOU EVERY-THING YOU NEED TO KNOW."
hee hee
REALLY? THAT'S A GOOD ONE!

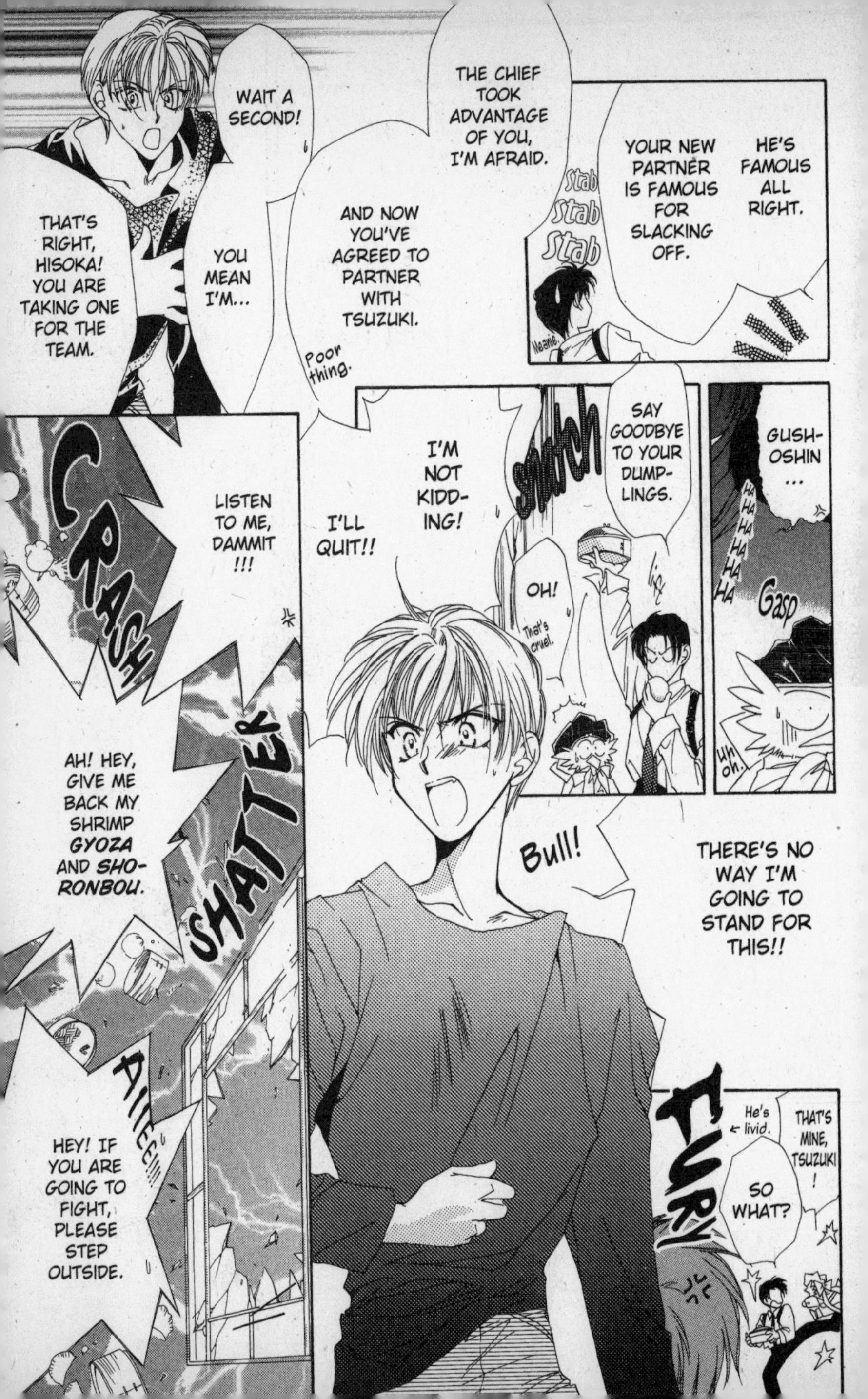
HE'S FAMOUS ALL RIGHT.
YOUR NEW PARTNER IS FAMOUS FOR SLACKING OFF.
Stab Stab Stab
Meanie.
THE CHIEF TOOK ADVANTAGE OF YOU, I'M AFRAID.
AND NOW YOU'VE AGREED TO PARTNER WITH TSUZUKI.
Poor thing.
WAIT A SECOND!
YOU MEAN I'M...
THAT'S RIGHT, HISOKA! YOU ARE TAKING ONE FOR THE TEAM.
GUSH-OSHIN...
HA HA HA HA HA HA
Gasp
Uh oh.
SAY GOODBYE TO YOUR DUMPLINGS.
snatch
OH!
That's cruel.
I'M NOT KIDDING!
I'LL QUIT!!
LISTEN TO ME, DAMMIT!!!
Bull!
THERE'S NO WAY I'M GOING TO STAND FOR THIS!!
FURY
THAT'S MINE, TSUZUKI!
He's livid.
SO WHAT?
CRASH
AH! HEY, GIVE ME BACK MY SHRIMP *GYOZA* AND *SHO-RONBOU*.
SHATTER
AIIIEE!!!
HEY! IF YOU ARE GOING TO FIGHT, PLEASE STEP OUTSIDE.

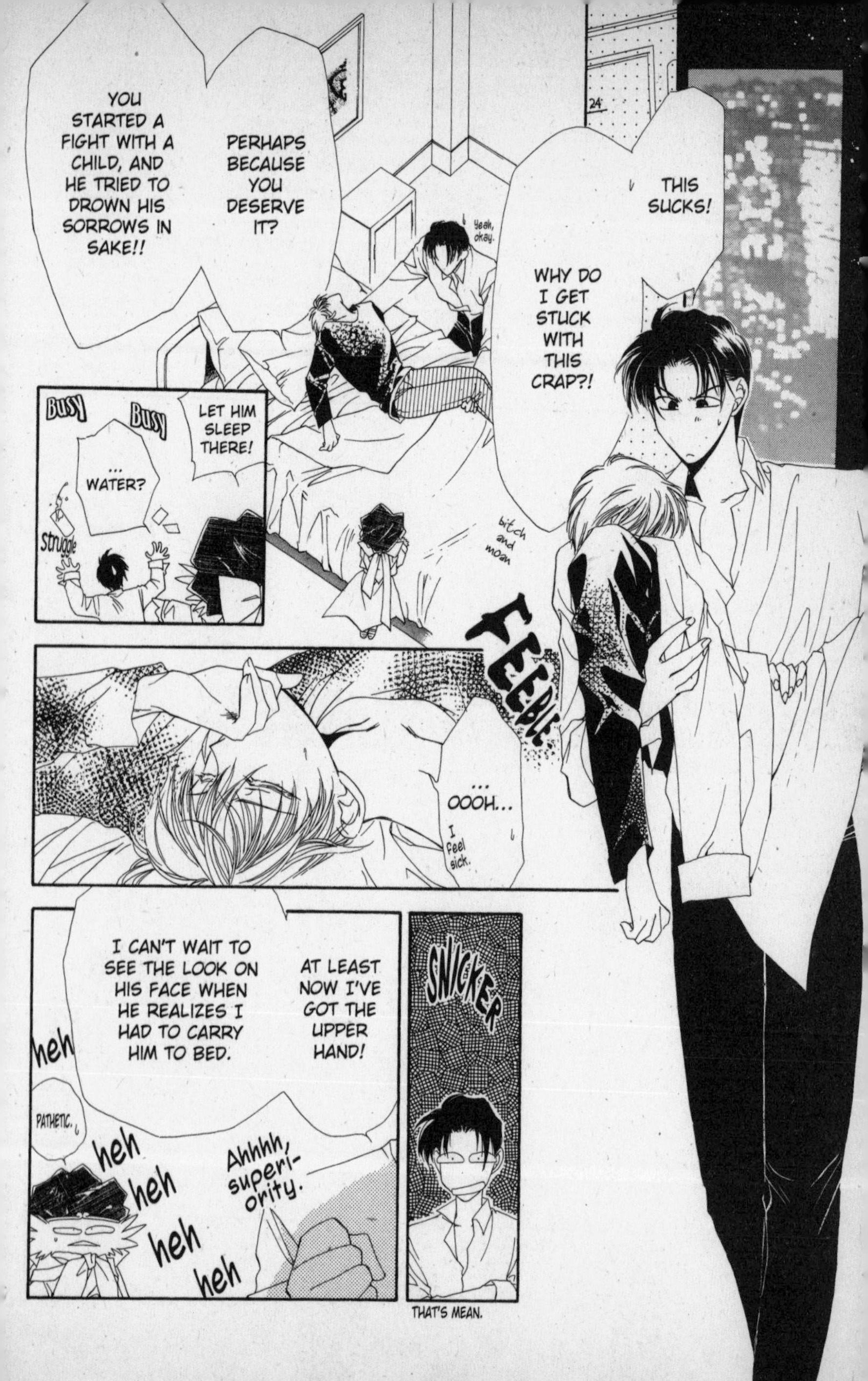
THIS SUCKS!
WHY DO I GET STUCK WITH THIS CRAP?!
bitch and moan
FEEBLE
PERHAPS BECAUSE YOU DESERVE IT?
YOU STARTED A FIGHT WITH A CHILD, AND HE TRIED TO DROWN HIS SORROWS IN SAKE!!
Yeah, okay.
LET HIM SLEEP THERE!
... WATER?
Busy
Busy
struggle
... OOOH...
I feel sick.
SNICKER
AT LEAST NOW I'VE GOT THE UPPER HAND!
I CAN'T WAIT TO SEE THE LOOK ON HIS FACE WHEN HE REALIZES I HAD TO CARRY HIM TO BED.
heh
heh
heh
heh
heh
Ahhhh, superi-ority.
PATHETIC.
THAT'S MEAN.

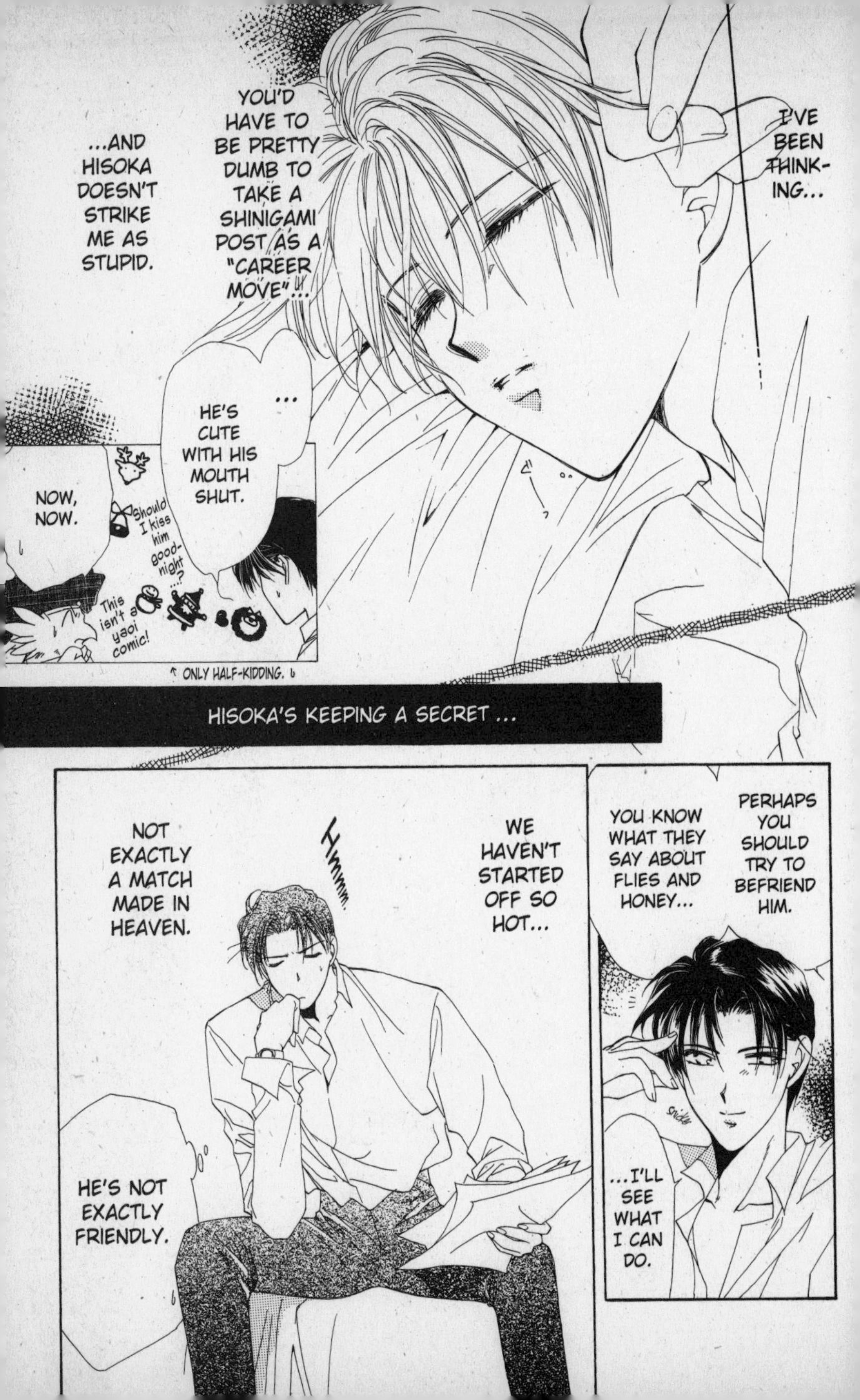
I'VE BEEN THINKING...
YOU'D HAVE TO BE PRETTY DUMB TO TAKE A SHINIGAMI POST AS A "CAREER MOVE"...
...AND HISOKA DOESN'T STRIKE ME AS STUPID.
...
HE'S CUTE WITH HIS MOUTH SHUT.
Should I kiss him good-night...?
NOW, NOW.
This isn't a yaoi comic!
↑ ONLY HALF-KIDDING.
HISOKA'S KEEPING A SECRET...
PERHAPS YOU SHOULD TRY TO BEFRIEND HIM.
YOU KNOW WHAT THEY SAY ABOUT FLIES AND HONEY...
...I'LL SEE WHAT I CAN DO.
WE HAVEN'T STARTED OFF SO HOT...
Hmmm.
NOT EXACTLY A MATCH MADE IN HEAVEN.
HE'S NOT EXACTLY FRIENDLY.

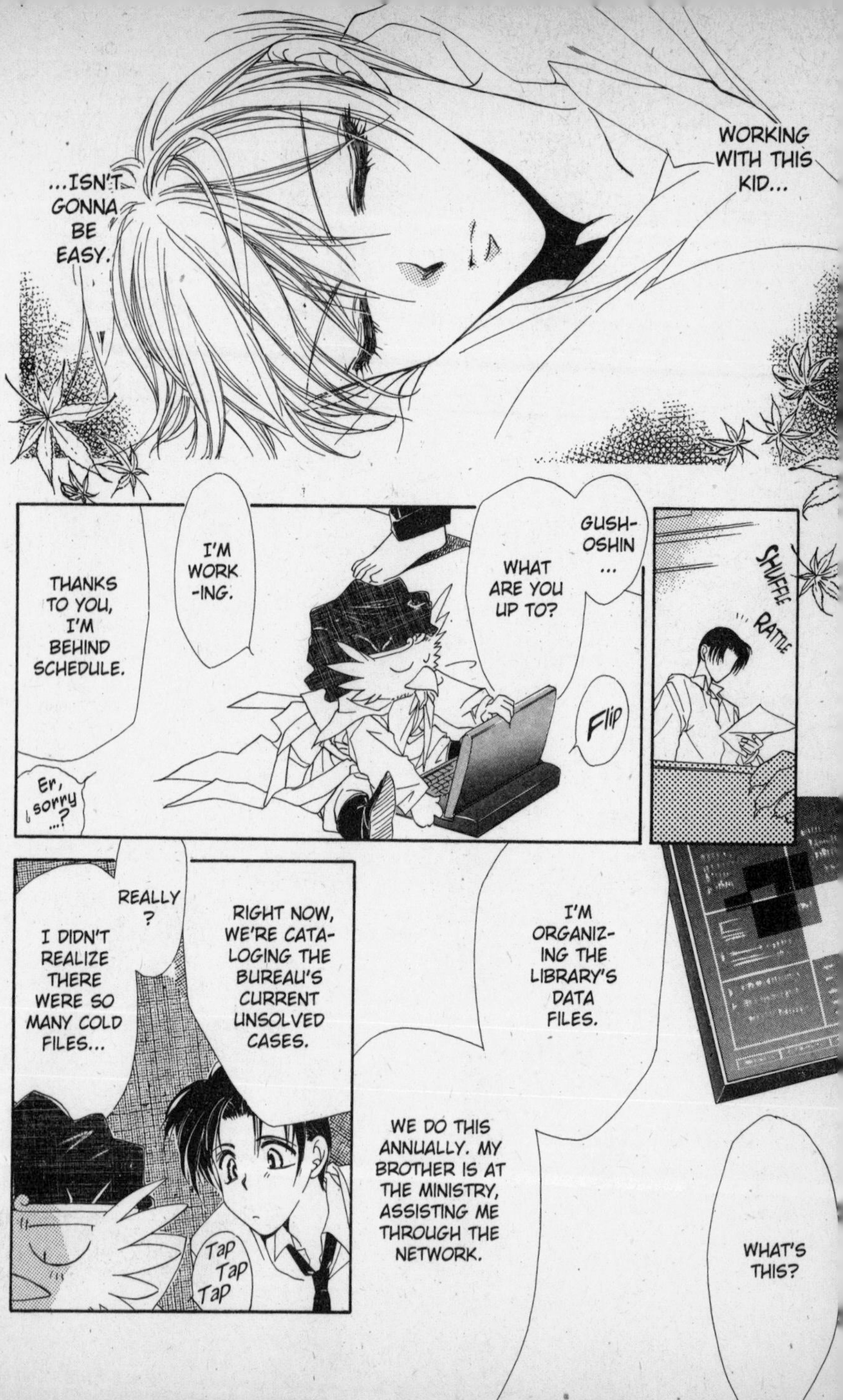
WORKING WITH THIS KID...
...ISN'T GONNA BE EASY.
SHUFFLE
RATTLE
GUSH-OSHIN ...
WHAT ARE YOU UP TO?
Flip
I'M WORK-ING.
THANKS TO YOU, I'M BEHIND SCHEDULE.
Er, sorry ...?
WHAT'S THIS?
I'M ORGANIZ-ING THE LIBRARY'S DATA FILES.
WE DO THIS ANNUALLY. MY BROTHER IS AT THE MINISTRY, ASSISTING ME THROUGH THE NETWORK.
RIGHT NOW, WE'RE CATA-LOGING THE BUREAU'S CURRENT UNSOLVED CASES.
REALLY?
I DIDN'T REALIZE THERE WERE SO MANY COLD FILES...
Tap Tap Tap

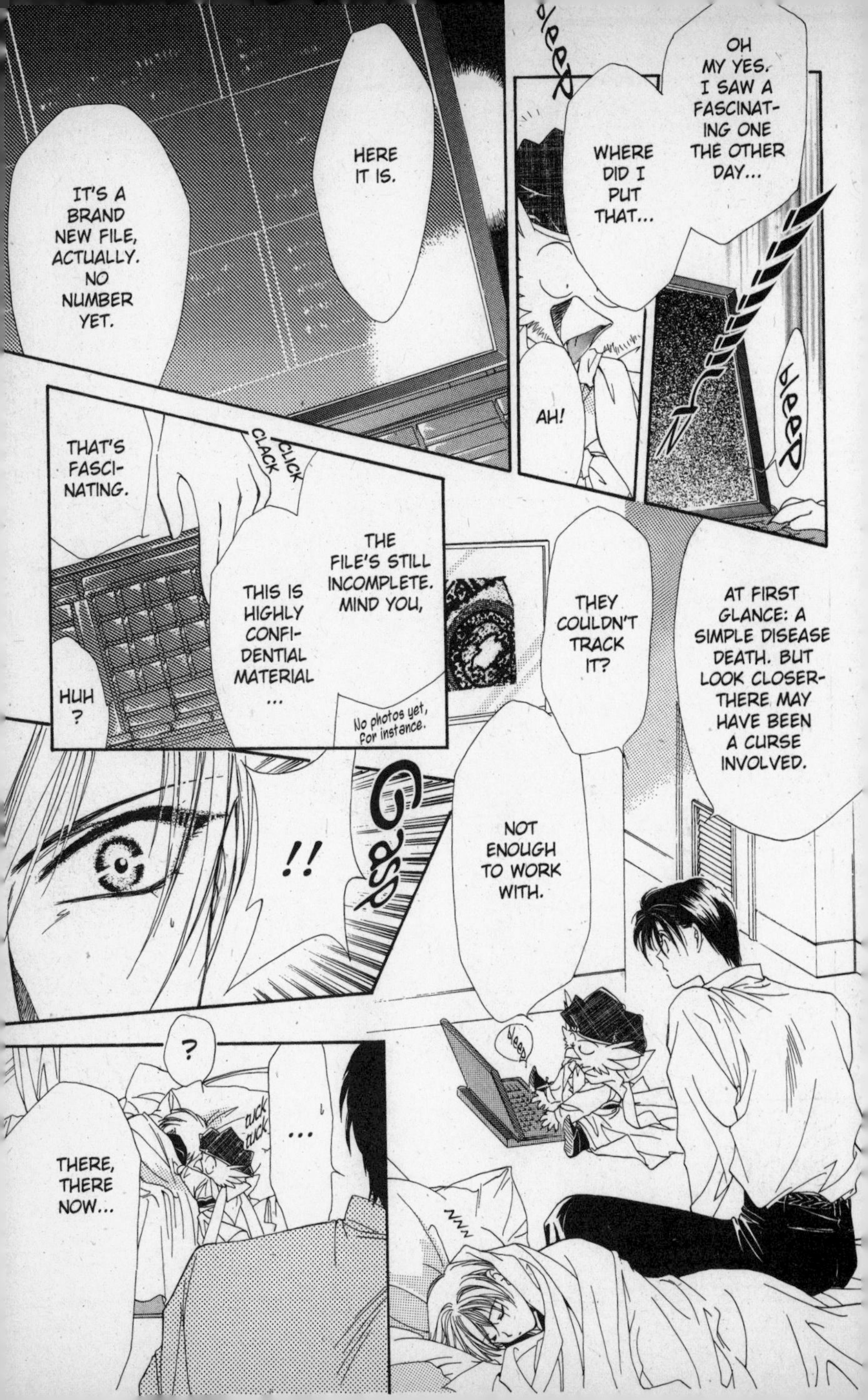
bleep
OH MY YES. I SAW A FASCINATING ONE THE OTHER DAY...
WHERE DID I PUT THAT...
bleep
AH!
HERE IT IS.
IT'S A BRAND NEW FILE, ACTUALLY. NO NUMBER YET.
AT FIRST GLANCE: A SIMPLE DISEASE DEATH. BUT LOOK CLOSER-THERE MAY HAVE BEEN A CURSE INVOLVED.
THEY COULDN'T TRACK IT?
NOT ENOUGH TO WORK WITH.
bleep
NNN
THE FILE'S STILL INCOMPLETE. MIND YOU,
No photos yet, for instance.
THIS IS HIGHLY CONFIDENTIAL MATERIAL...
CLICK CLACK
THAT'S FASCINATING.
HUH?
Gasp
!!
?
...
click click
THERE, THERE NOW...

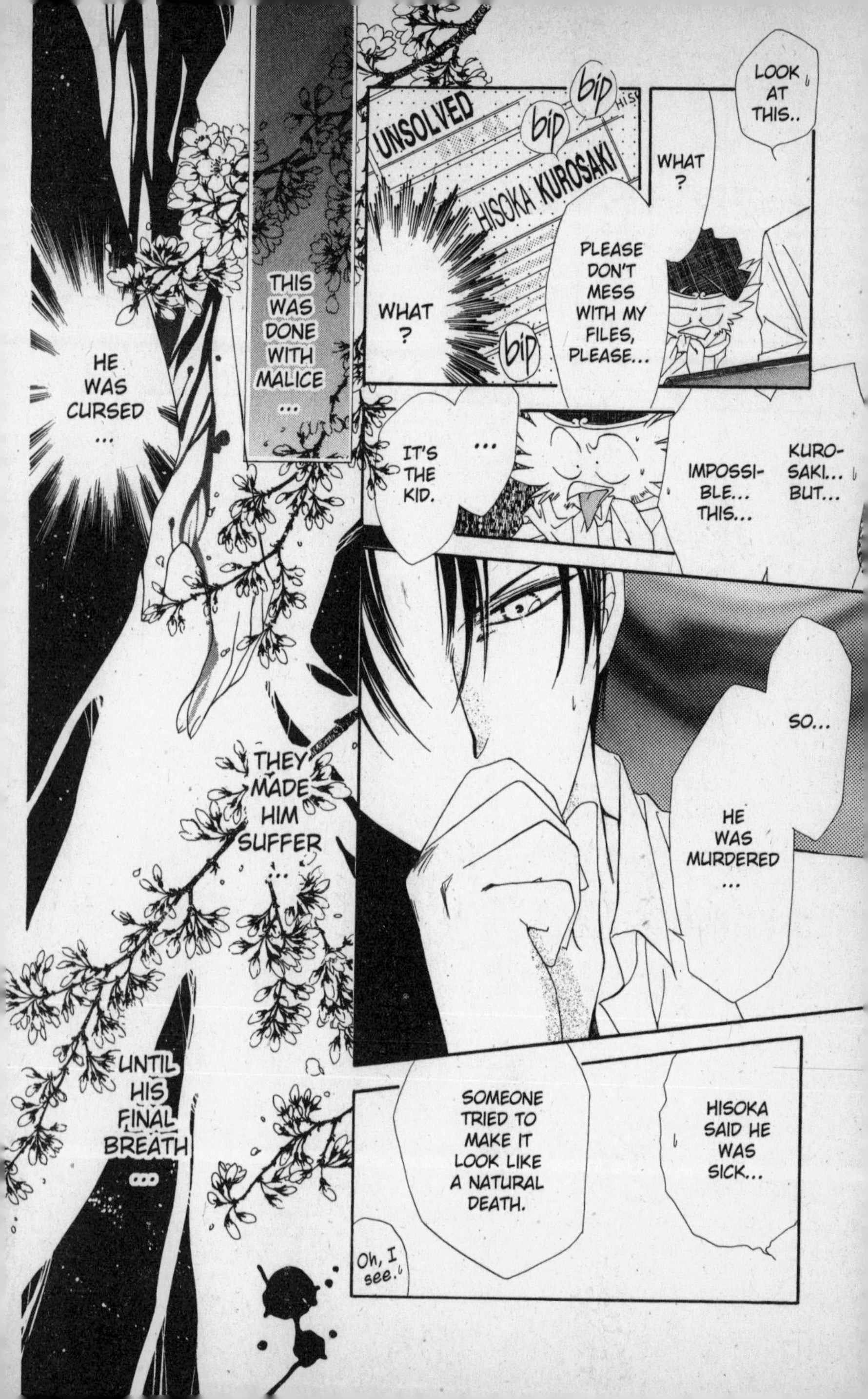

LOOK AT THIS..
WHAT?
bip
HISOKA KUROSAKI
UNSOLVED
bip
PLEASE DON'T MESS WITH MY FILES, PLEASE...
bip
WHAT?
KURO-SAKI... BUT...
IMPOSSI-BLE... THIS...
...
IT'S THE KID.
SO...
HE WAS MURDERED...
HISOKA SAID HE WAS SICK...
SOMEONE TRIED TO MAKE IT LOOK LIKE A NATURAL DEATH.
Oh, I see.
THIS WAS DONE WITH MALICE...
HE WAS CURSED...
THEY MADE HIM SUFFER...
UNTIL HIS FINAL BREATH...

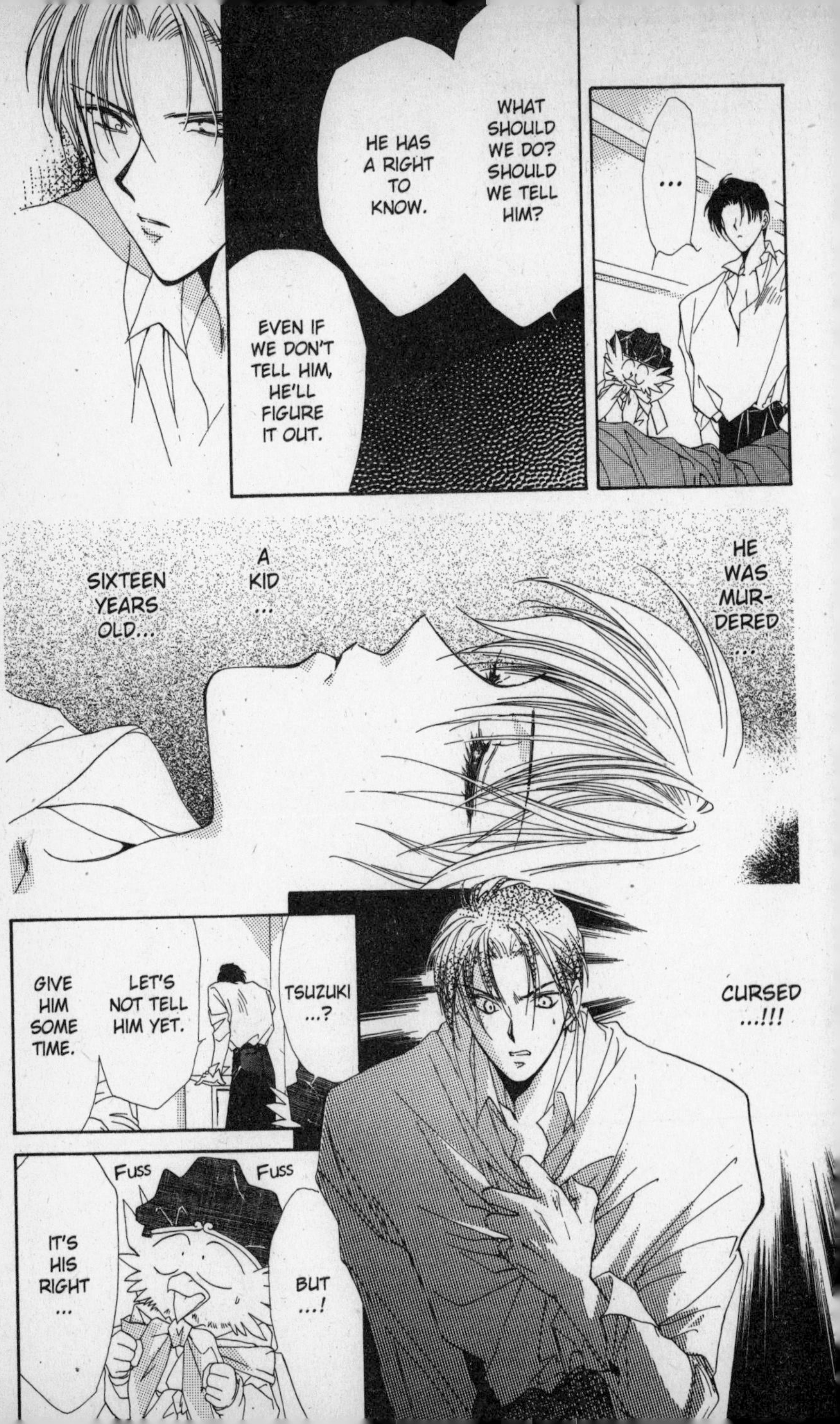
...
WHAT SHOULD WE DO? SHOULD WE TELL HIM?
HE HAS A RIGHT TO KNOW.
EVEN IF WE DON'T TELL HIM, HE'LL FIGURE IT OUT.
HE WAS MUR-DERED...
A KID...
SIXTEEN YEARS OLD...
CURSED...!!!
TSUZUKI...?
LET'S NOT TELL HIM YET.
GIVE HIM SOME TIME.
FUSS
FUSS
BUT...!
IT'S HIS RIGHT...

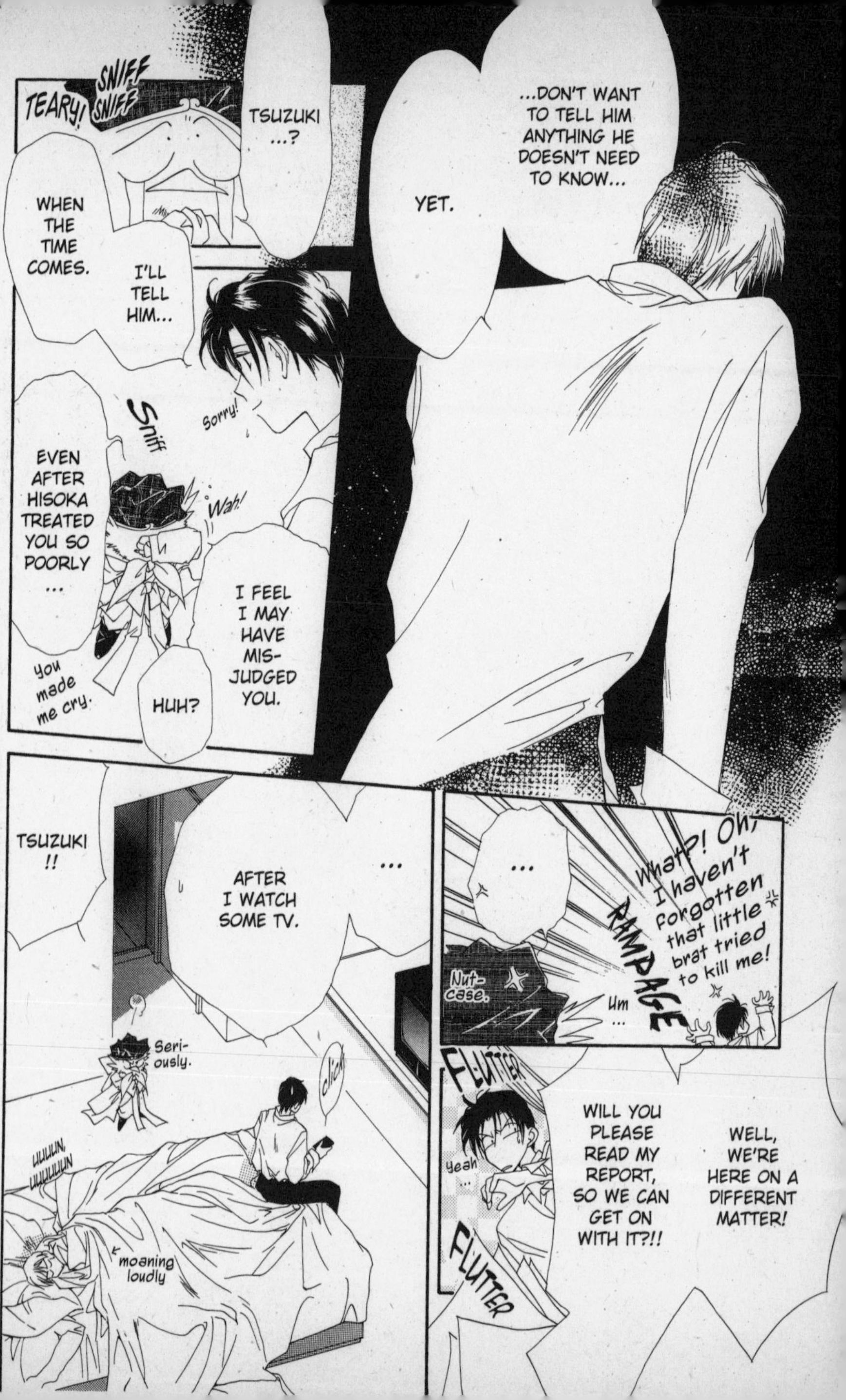
...DON'T WANT TO TELL HIM ANYTHING HE DOESN'T NEED TO KNOW...
YET.
TEARY!
SNIFF SNIFF
TSUZUKI ...?
I'LL TELL HIM...
WHEN THE TIME COMES.
Sorry!
I FEEL I MAY HAVE MIS-JUDGED YOU.
Wah!
Sniff
EVEN AFTER HISOKA TREATED YOU SO POORLY ...
HUH?
You made me cry.
WHAT?! Oh, I haven't forgotten that little brat tried to kill me!
RAMPAGE
...
Um ...
Nut-case.
WELL, WE'RE HERE ON A DIFFERENT MATTER!
WILL YOU PLEASE READ MY REPORT, SO WE CAN GET ON WITH IT?!!
FLUTTER
Yeah ...
FLUTTER
...
AFTER I WATCH SOME TV.
TSUZUKI !!
click
Seri-ously.
uuuun, uuuuuun
moaning loudly

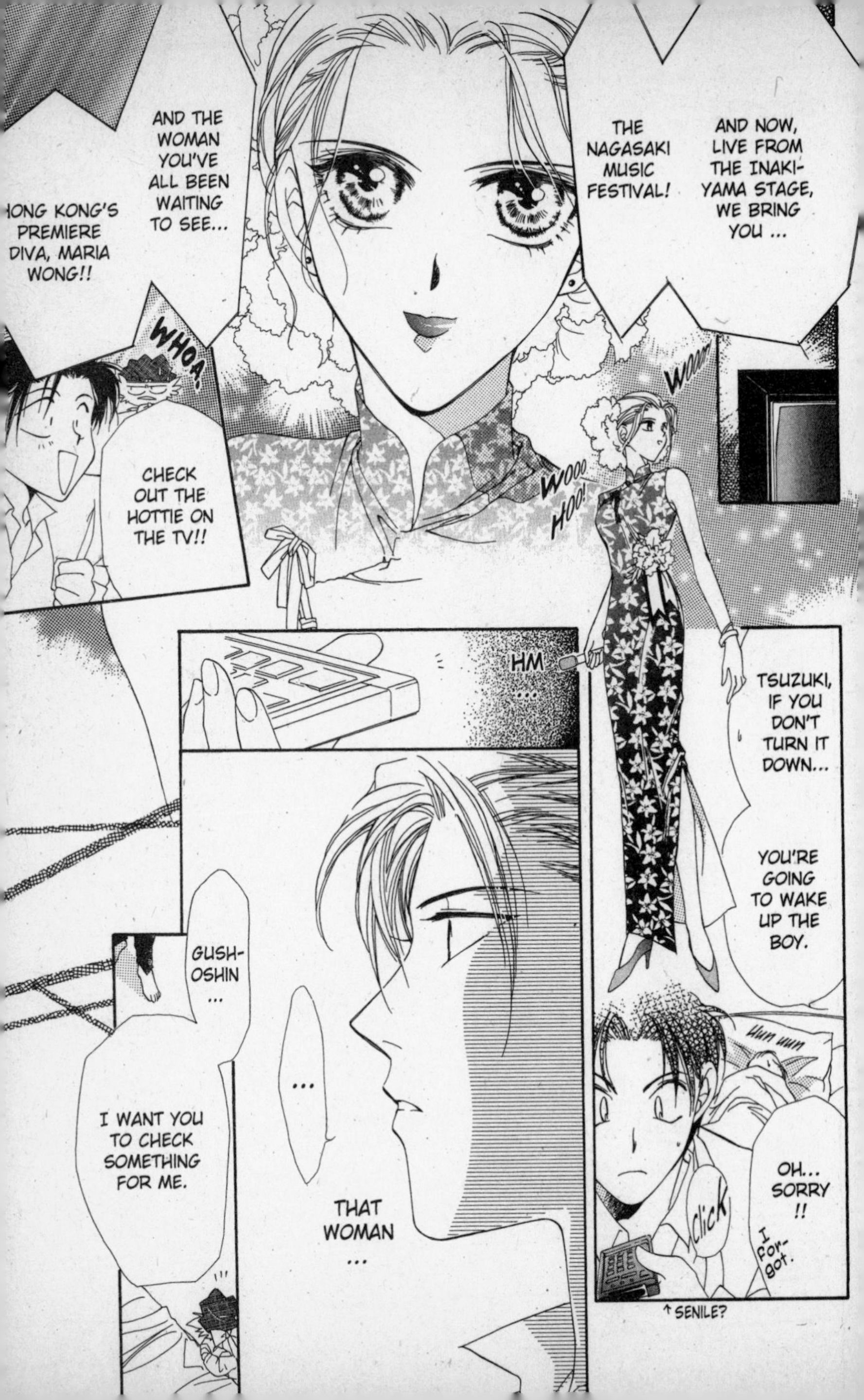
AND NOW, LIVE FROM THE INAKI-YAMA STAGE, WE BRING YOU ...
THE NAGASAKI MUSIC FESTIVAL!
AND THE WOMAN YOU'VE ALL BEEN WAITING TO SEE...
HONG KONG'S PREMIERE DIVA, MARIA WONG!!
WHOA
CHECK OUT THE HOTTIE ON THE TV!!
WOOO
WOOO HOO!
HM ...
TSUZUKI, IF YOU DON'T TURN IT DOWN...
YOU'RE GOING TO WAKE UP THE BOY.
Uun uun
OH... SORRY!!
click
I forgot.
↑SENILE?
...
THAT WOMAN ...
GUSH-OSHIN ...
I WANT YOU TO CHECK SOMETHING FOR ME.
!!!

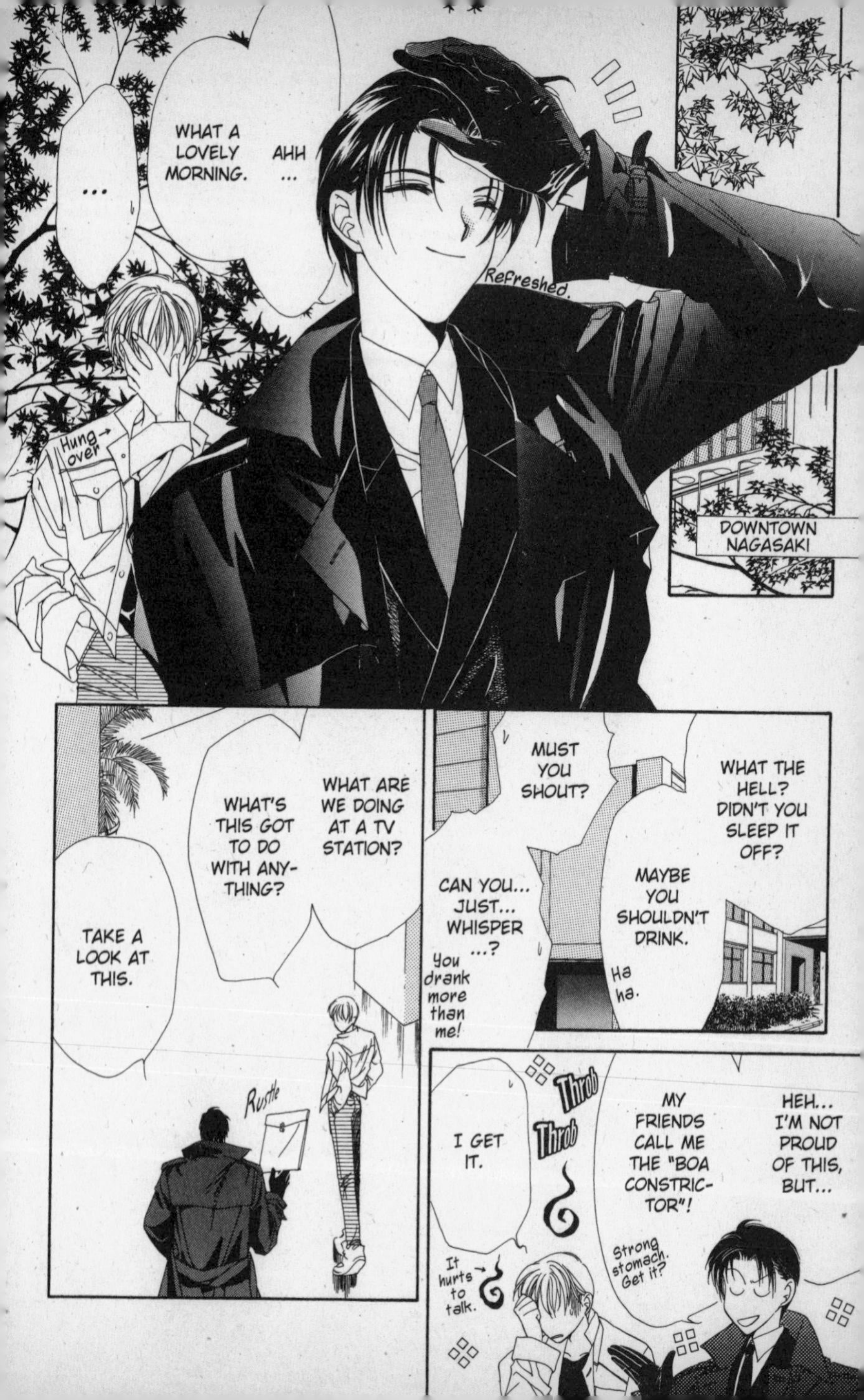
AHH ...
WHAT A LOVELY MORNING.
...
Refreshed.
Hung-over
DOWNTOWN NAGASAKI
WHAT THE HELL? DIDN'T YOU SLEEP IT OFF?
MUST YOU SHOUT?
MAYBE YOU SHOULDN'T DRINK.
Ha ha.
CAN YOU... JUST... WHISPER ...?
You drank more than me!
HEH... I'M NOT PROUD OF THIS, BUT...
MY FRIENDS CALL ME THE "BOA CONSTRICTOR"!
Strong stomach. Get it?
Throb
Throb
I GET IT.
It hurts to talk.
WHAT ARE WE DOING AT A TV STATION?
WHAT'S THIS GOT TO DO WITH ANY-THING?
TAKE A LOOK AT THIS.
Rustle

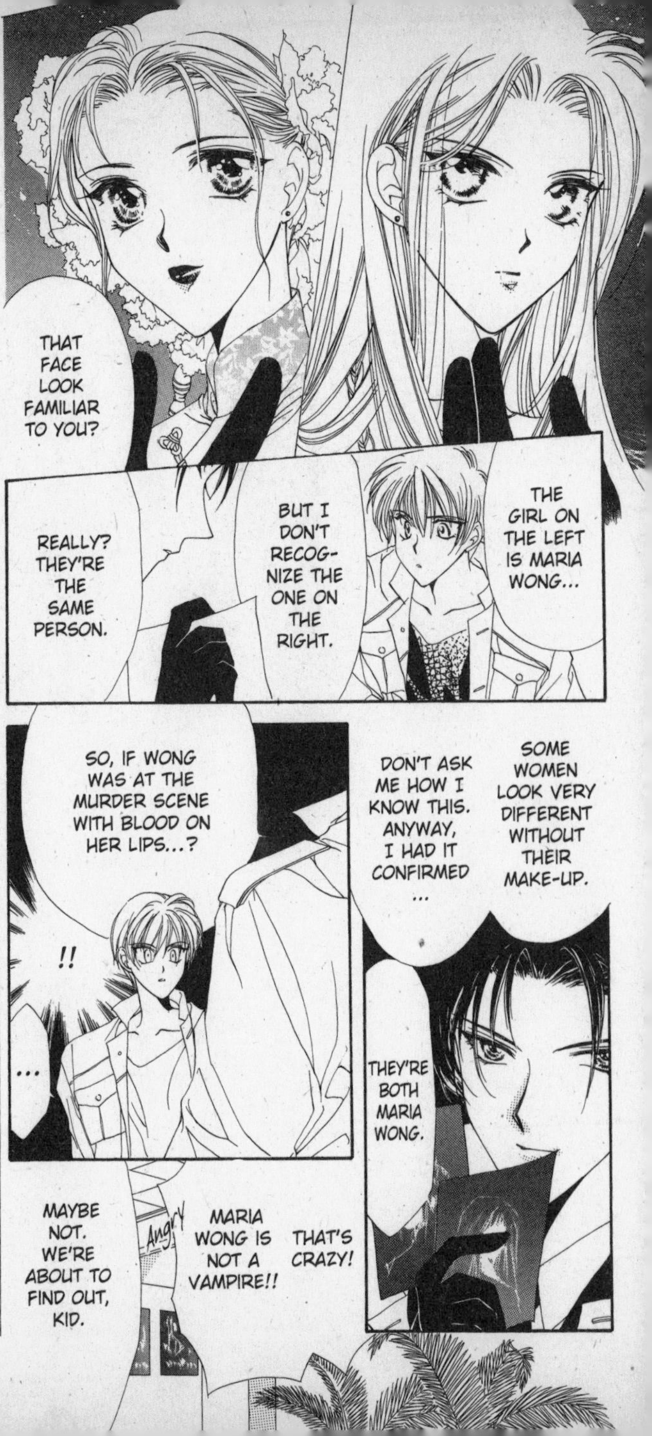
THAT FACE LOOK FAMILIAR TO YOU?
THE GIRL ON THE LEFT IS MARIA WONG...
BUT I DON'T RECOGNIZE THE ONE ON THE RIGHT.
REALLY? THEY'RE THE SAME PERSON.
SOME WOMEN LOOK VERY DIFFERENT WITHOUT THEIR MAKE-UP.
DON'T ASK ME HOW I KNOW THIS. ANYWAY, I HAD IT CONFIRMED ...
THEY'RE BOTH MARIA WONG.
SO, IF WONG WAS AT THE MURDER SCENE WITH BLOOD ON HER LIPS...?
!!
...
THAT'S CRAZY!
MARIA WONG IS NOT A VAMPIRE!!
Angry
MAYBE NOT. WE'RE ABOUT TO FIND OUT, KID.

Descendants of Darkness is now a series! This is the third story and Tsuzuki has a new partner. I considered giving him a female partner, but then I dreamed up Hisoka! Before I settled on this Hisoka, I considered giving him a couple of different personalities:

1. "Prototype Hisoka" very similar to Masaki; your average good student; and

2. "Strange Hisoka" a bad guy who sabotages Tsuzuki.

After much trial and error, I settled on "Grumpy and Exhausted Hisoka."

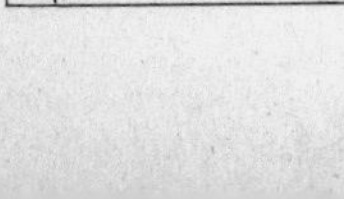
EXHAUSTED.
Whose fault is that?

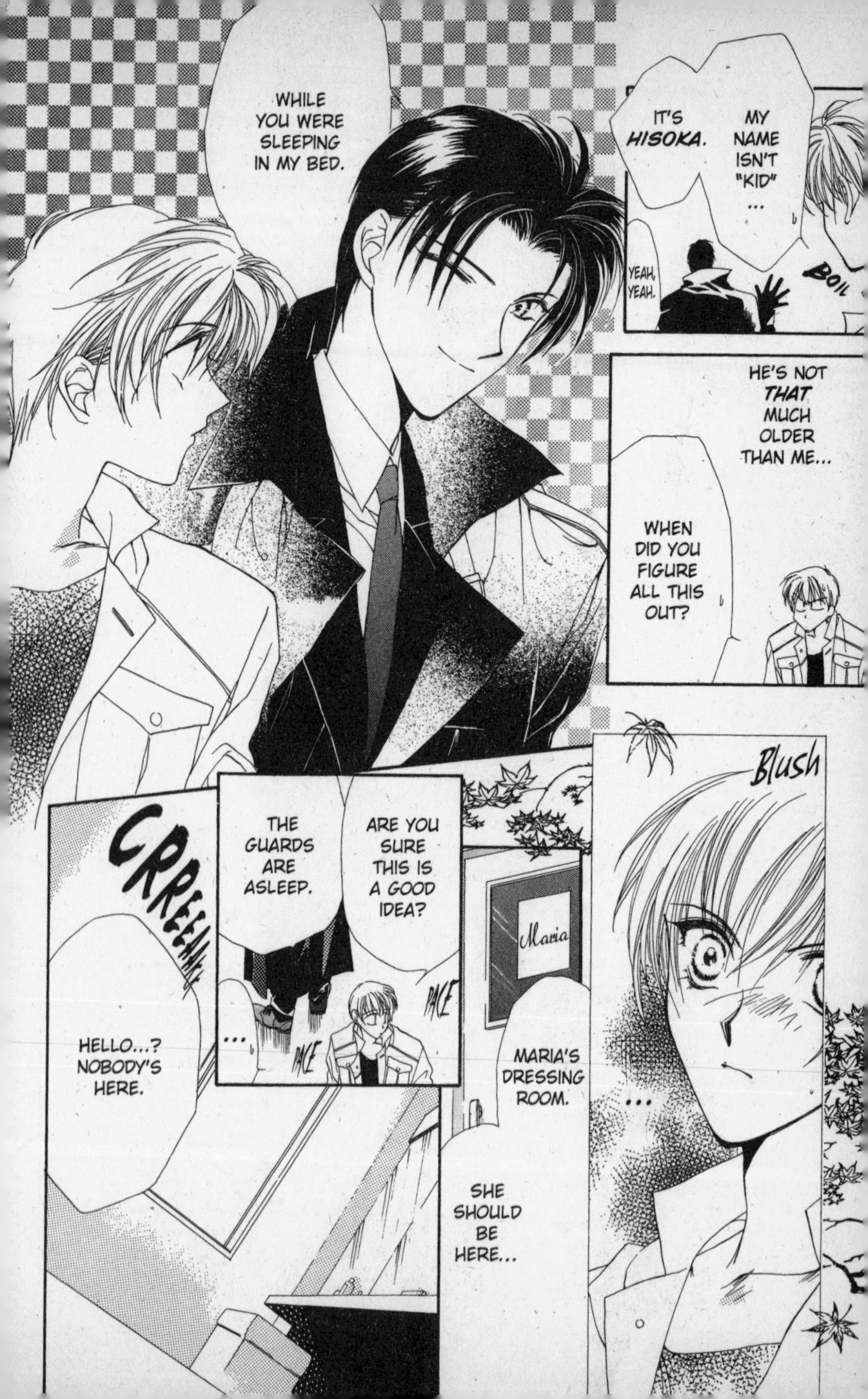
MY NAME ISN'T "KID" ...
IT'S HISOKA.
YEAH, YEAH.
BOIL
HE'S NOT THAT MUCH OLDER THAN ME...
WHEN DID YOU FIGURE ALL THIS OUT?
WHILE YOU WERE SLEEPING IN MY BED.
Blush
...
ARE YOU SURE THIS IS A GOOD IDEA?
THE GUARDS ARE ASLEEP.
PACE
PACE
...
Maria
MARIA'S DRESSING ROOM.
SHE SHOULD BE HERE...
CRREEAK
HELLO...? NOBODY'S HERE.

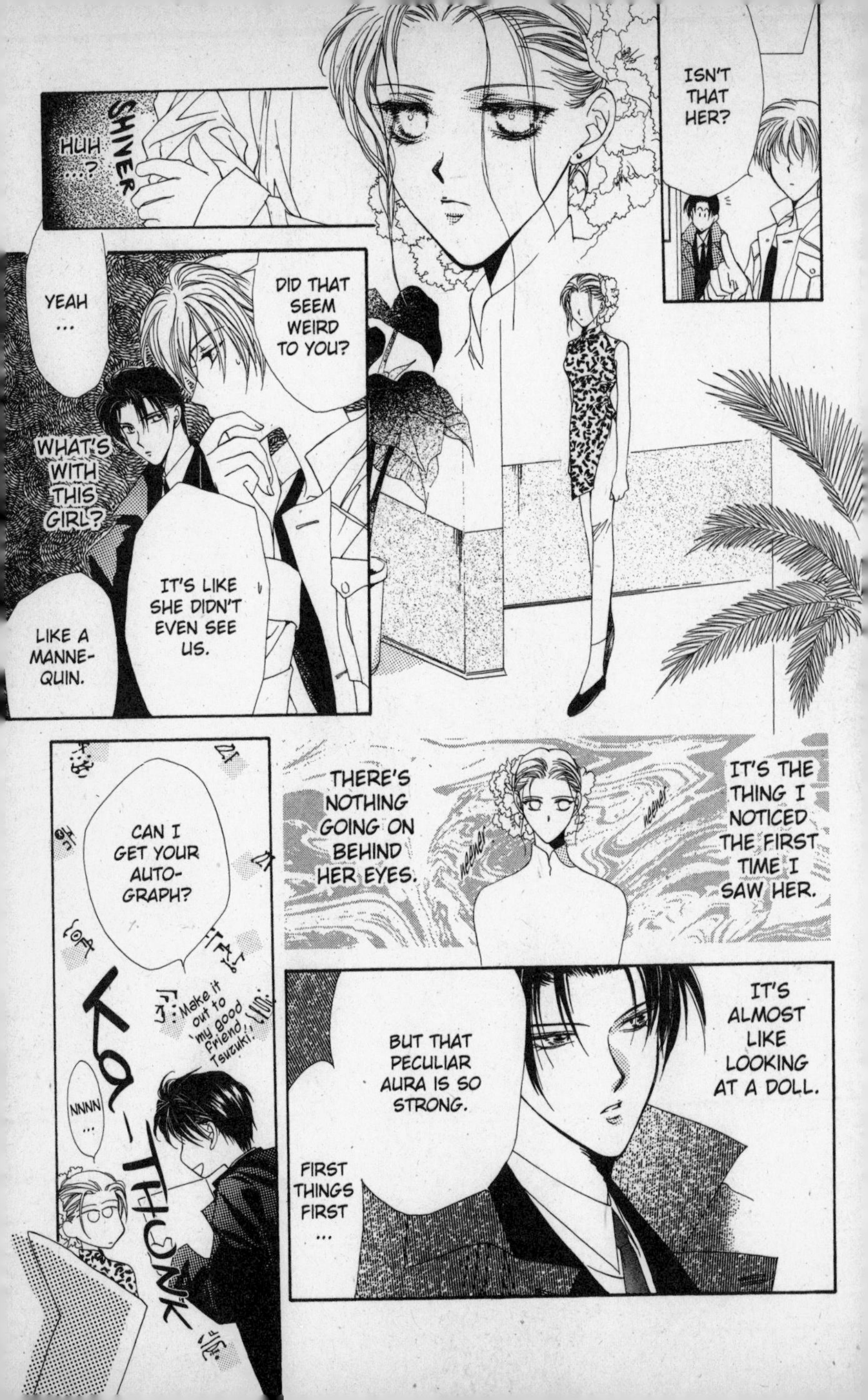
ISN'T THAT HER?
SHIVER
HUH ...?
DID THAT SEEM WEIRD TO YOU?
YEAH ...
WHAT'S WITH THIS GIRL?
IT'S LIKE SHE DIDN'T EVEN SEE US.
LIKE A MANNE-QUIN.
IT'S THE THING I NOTICED THE FIRST TIME I SAW HER.
neener
neener
THERE'S NOTHING GOING ON BEHIND HER EYES.
IT'S ALMOST LIKE LOOKING AT A DOLL.
BUT THAT PECULIAR AURA IS SO STRONG.
FIRST THINGS FIRST ...
CAN I GET YOUR AUTO-GRAPH?
Make it out to my good friend Tsuzuki.
NNNN ...
KA-THUNK

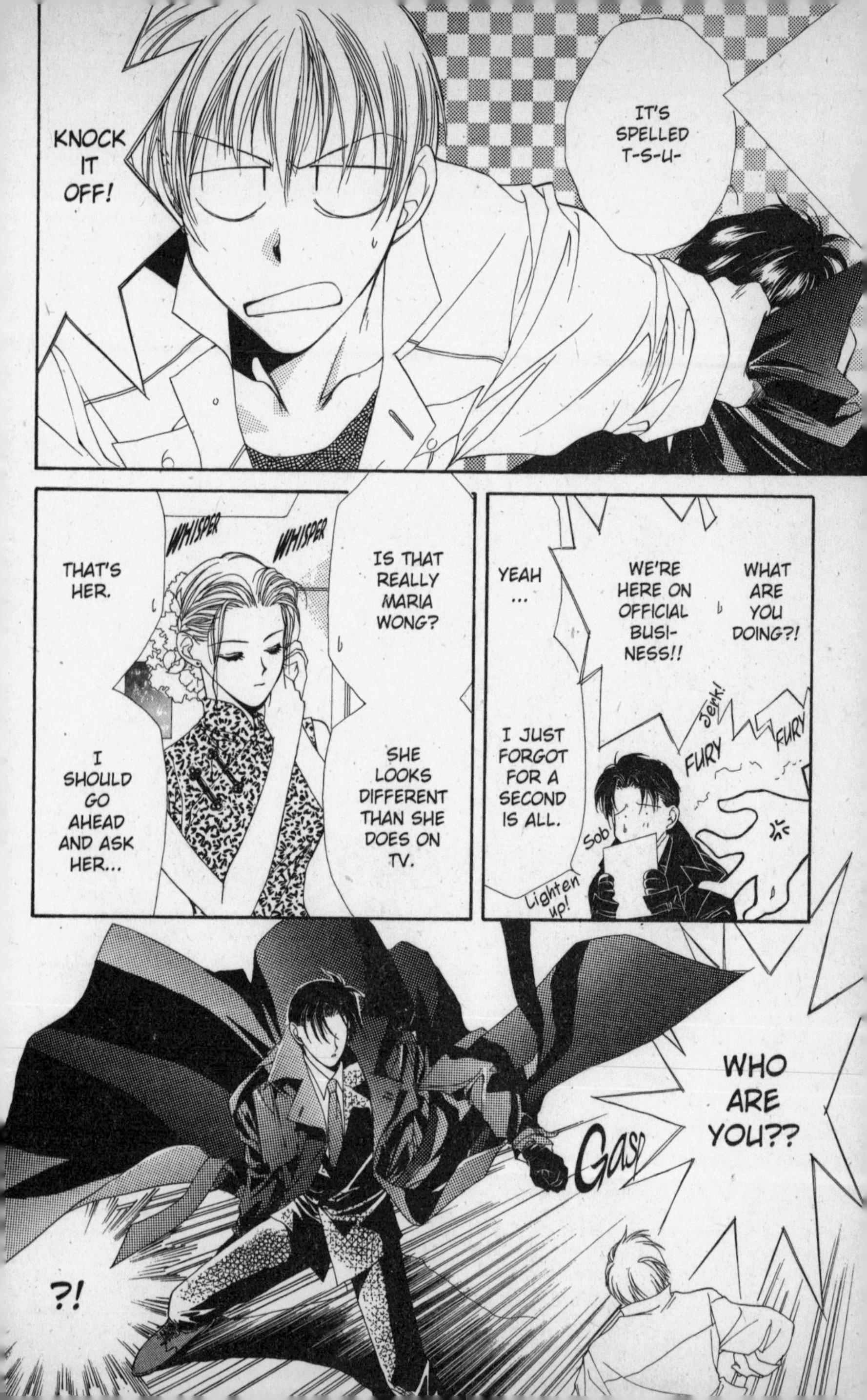
IT'S SPELLED T-S-U-
KNOCK IT OFF!
WHAT ARE YOU DOING?!
WE'RE HERE ON OFFICIAL BUSI-NESS!!
YEAH ...
Jerk!
FURY
FURY
I JUST FORGOT FOR A SECOND IS ALL.
Sob
Lighten up!
WHISPER
WHISPER
IS THAT REALLY MARIA WONG?
THAT'S HER.
SHE LOOKS DIFFERENT THAN SHE DOES ON TV.
I SHOULD GO AHEAD AND ASK HER...
WHO ARE YOU??
Gasp
?!

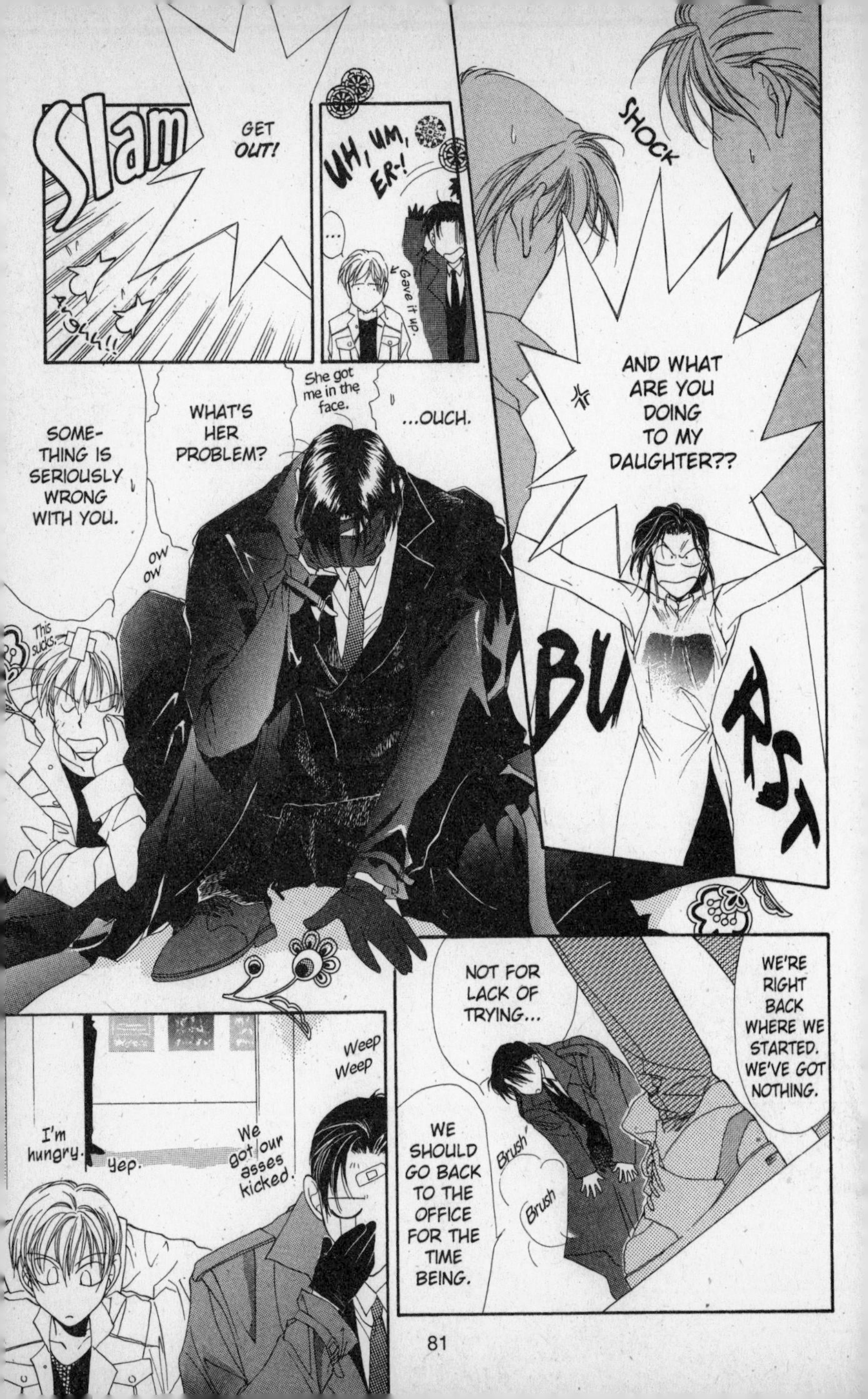
SHOCK
AND WHAT ARE YOU DOING TO MY DAUGHTER??
BURST
UH, UM, ER-!
...
Gave it up.
Slam
GET OUT!
...OUCH.
She got me in the face.
WHAT'S HER PROBLEM?
SOMETHING IS SERIOUSLY WRONG WITH YOU.
OW OW
This sucks.
WE'RE RIGHT BACK WHERE WE STARTED. WE'VE GOT NOTHING.
NOT FOR LACK OF TRYING...
Brush
Brush
WE SHOULD GO BACK TO THE OFFICE FOR THE TIME BEING.
Weep Weep
We got our asses kicked.
Yep.
I'm hungry.

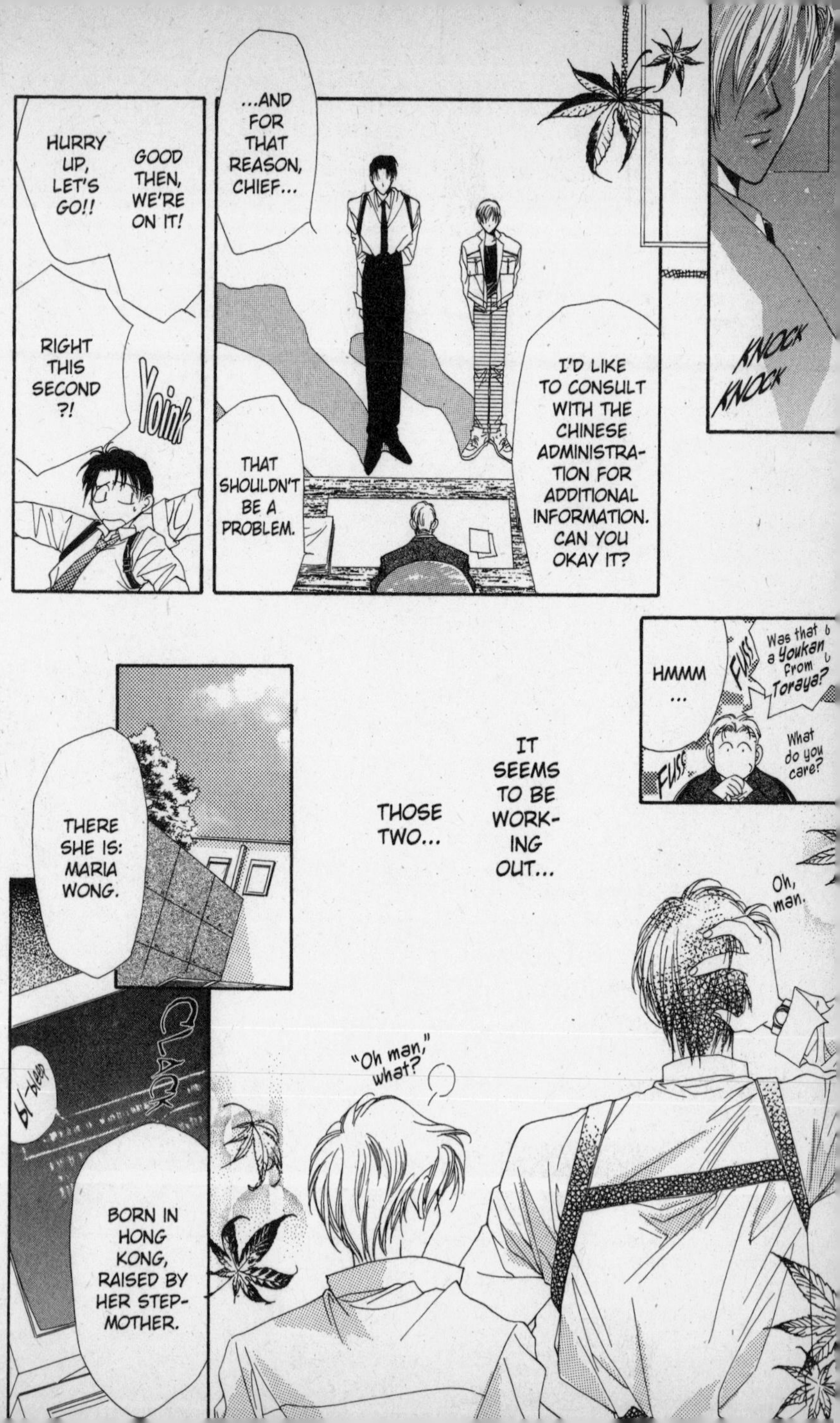
KNOCK KNOCK
...AND FOR THAT REASON, CHIEF...
I'D LIKE TO CONSULT WITH THE CHINESE ADMINISTRATION FOR ADDITIONAL INFORMATION. CAN YOU OKAY IT?
THAT SHOULDN'T BE A PROBLEM.
GOOD THEN, WE'RE ON IT!
HURRY UP, LET'S GO!!
Yoink
RIGHT THIS SECOND ?!
HMMM ...
FUSS
Was that a Youkan from Toraya?
What do you care?
FUSS
IT SEEMS TO BE WORKING OUT...
THOSE TWO...
Oh, man.
"Oh man," what?
THERE SHE IS: MARIA WONG.
CLACK
bl-bleep
BORN IN HONG KONG, RAISED BY HER STEP-MOTHER.

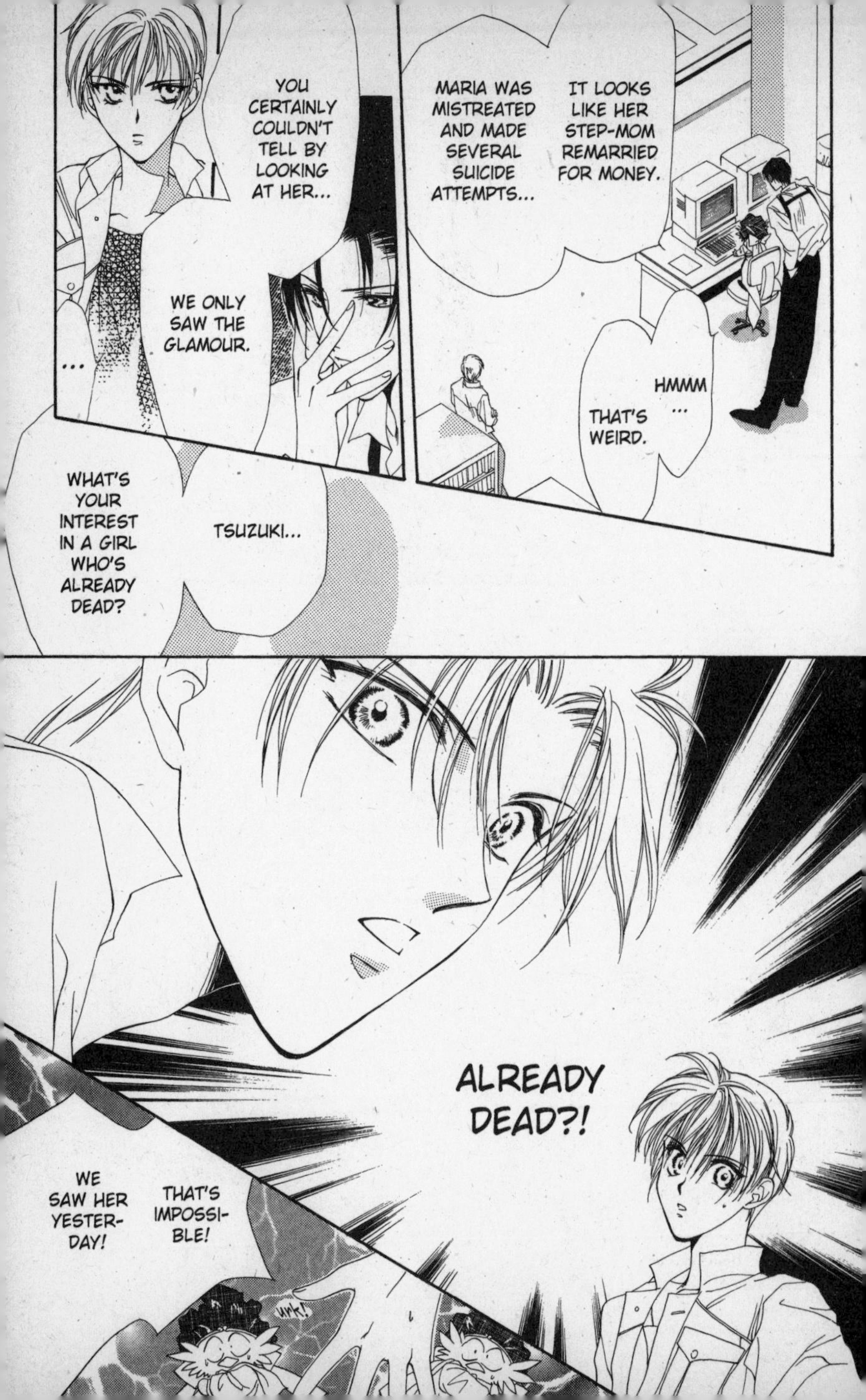
IT LOOKS LIKE HER STEP-MOM REMARRIED FOR MONEY.
MARIA WAS MISTREATED AND MADE SEVERAL SUICIDE ATTEMPTS...
HMMM...
THAT'S WEIRD.
YOU CERTAINLY COULDN'T TELL BY LOOKING AT HER...
WE ONLY SAW THE GLAMOUR.
...
TSUZUKI...
WHAT'S YOUR INTEREST IN A GIRL WHO'S ALREADY DEAD?
ALREADY DEAD?!
THAT'S IMPOSSIBLE!
WE SAW HER YESTERDAY!
UNK!

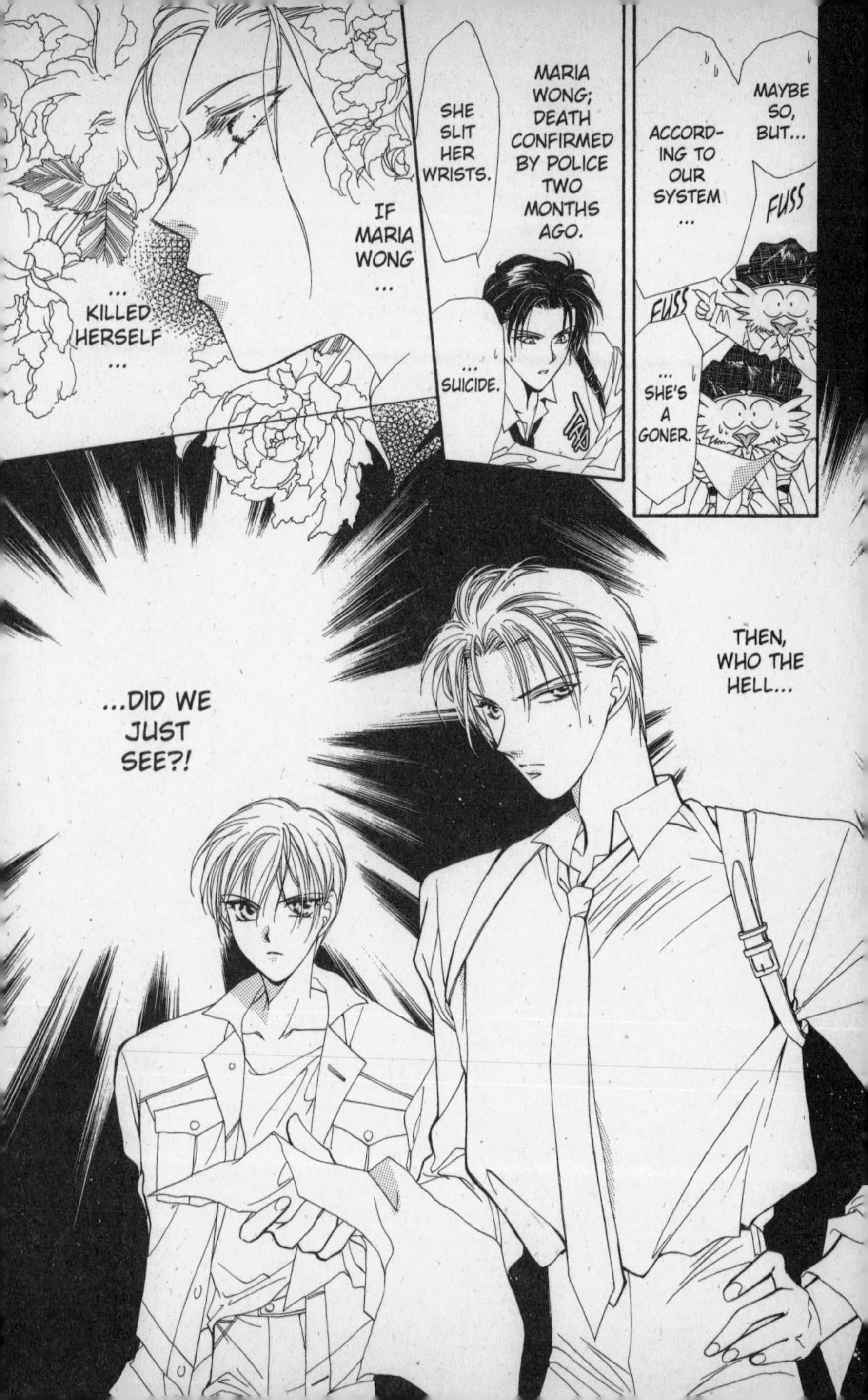
MAYBE SO, BUT...
ACCORD-ING TO OUR SYSTEM ...
FUSS
FUSS
... SHE'S A GONER.
MARIA WONG; DEATH CONFIRMED BY POLICE TWO MONTHS AGO.
SHE SLIT HER WRISTS.
... SUICIDE.
IF MARIA WONG ...
... KILLED HERSELF ...
THEN, WHO THE HELL...
...DID WE JUST SEE?!

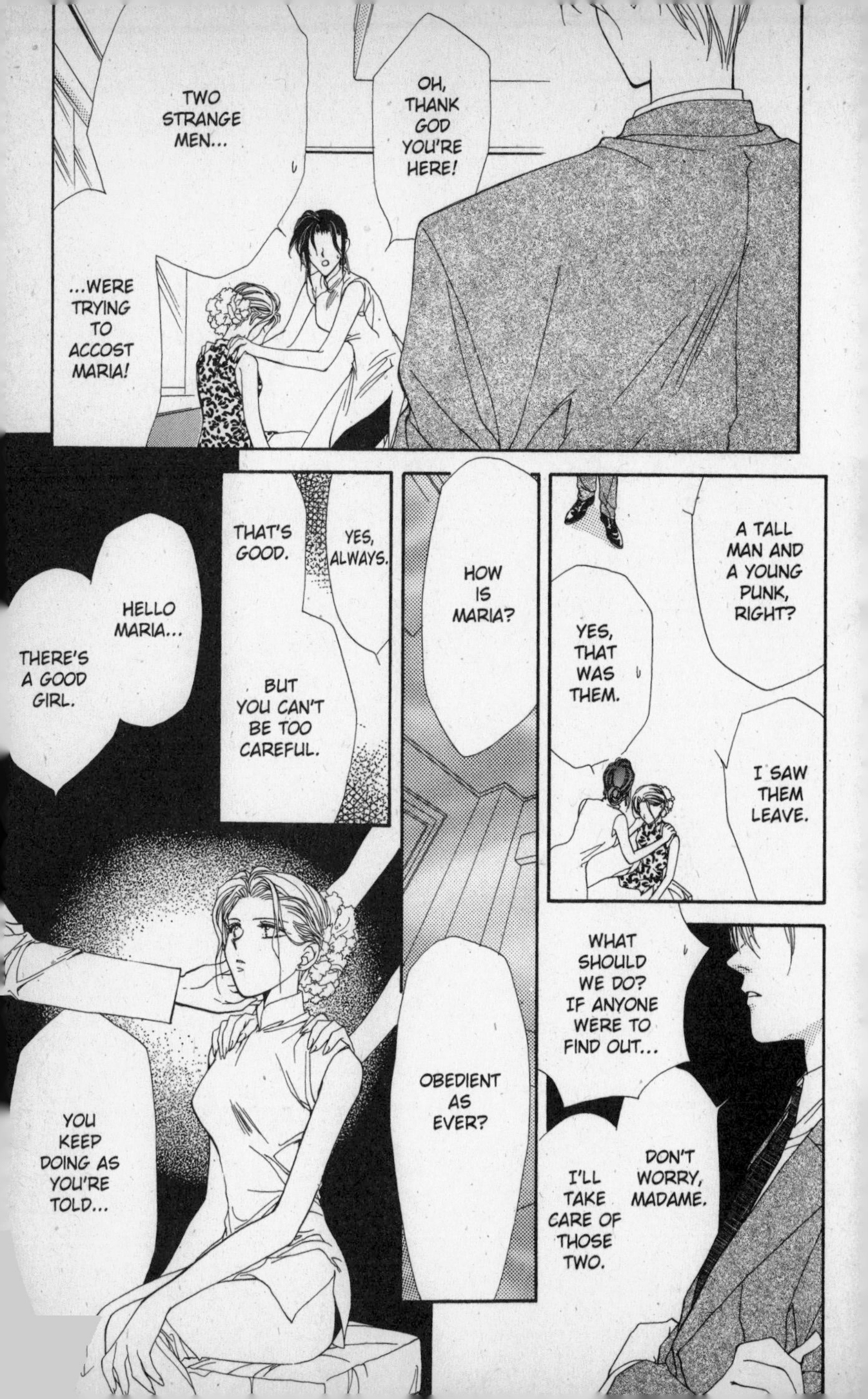
OH, THANK GOD YOU'RE HERE!
TWO STRANGE MEN...
...WERE TRYING TO ACCOST MARIA!
A TALL MAN AND A YOUNG PUNK, RIGHT?
YES, THAT WAS THEM.
I SAW THEM LEAVE.
HOW IS MARIA?
YES, ALWAYS.
THAT'S GOOD.
BUT YOU CAN'T BE TOO CAREFUL.
WHAT SHOULD WE DO? IF ANYONE WERE TO FIND OUT...
DON'T WORRY, MADAME.
I'LL TAKE CARE OF THOSE TWO.
OBEDIENT AS EVER?
HELLO MARIA...
THERE'S A GOOD GIRL.
YOU KEEP DOING AS YOU'RE TOLD...

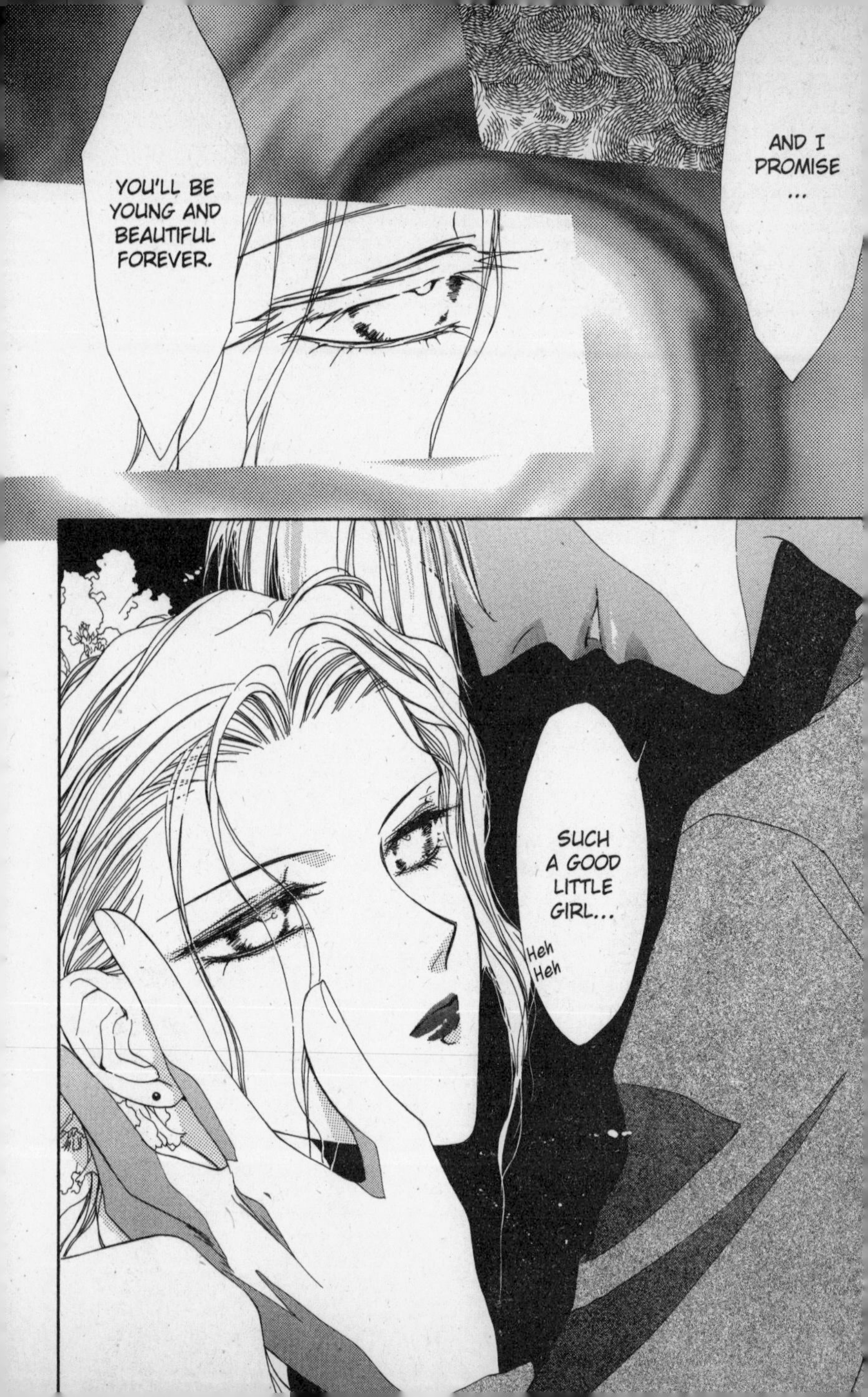
AND I PROMISE ...
YOU'LL BE YOUNG AND BEAUTIFUL FOREVER.
SUCH A GOOD LITTLE GIRL...
Heh Heh

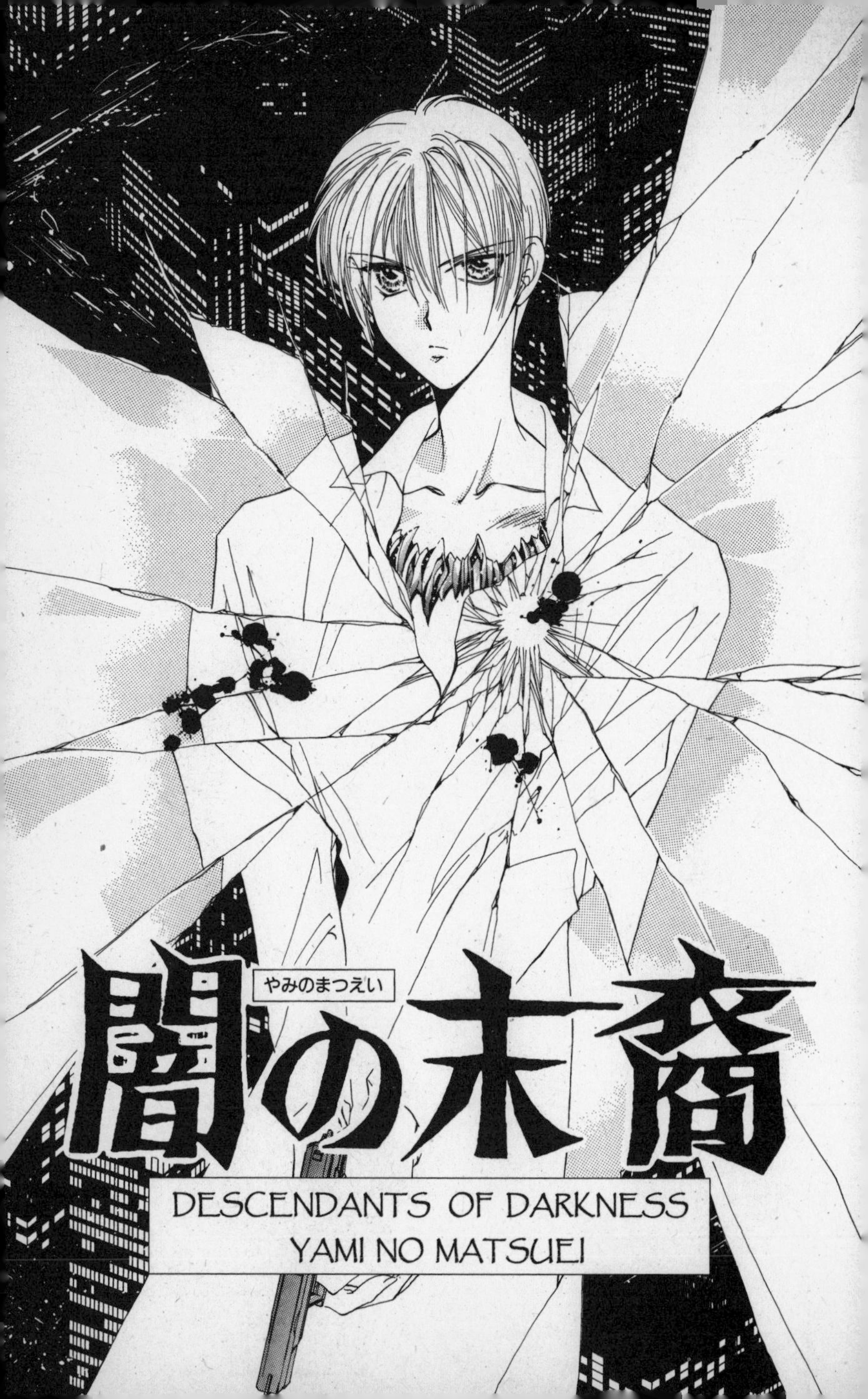

やみのまつえい
闇の末裔
DESCENDANTS OF DARKNESS
YAMI NO MATSUEI

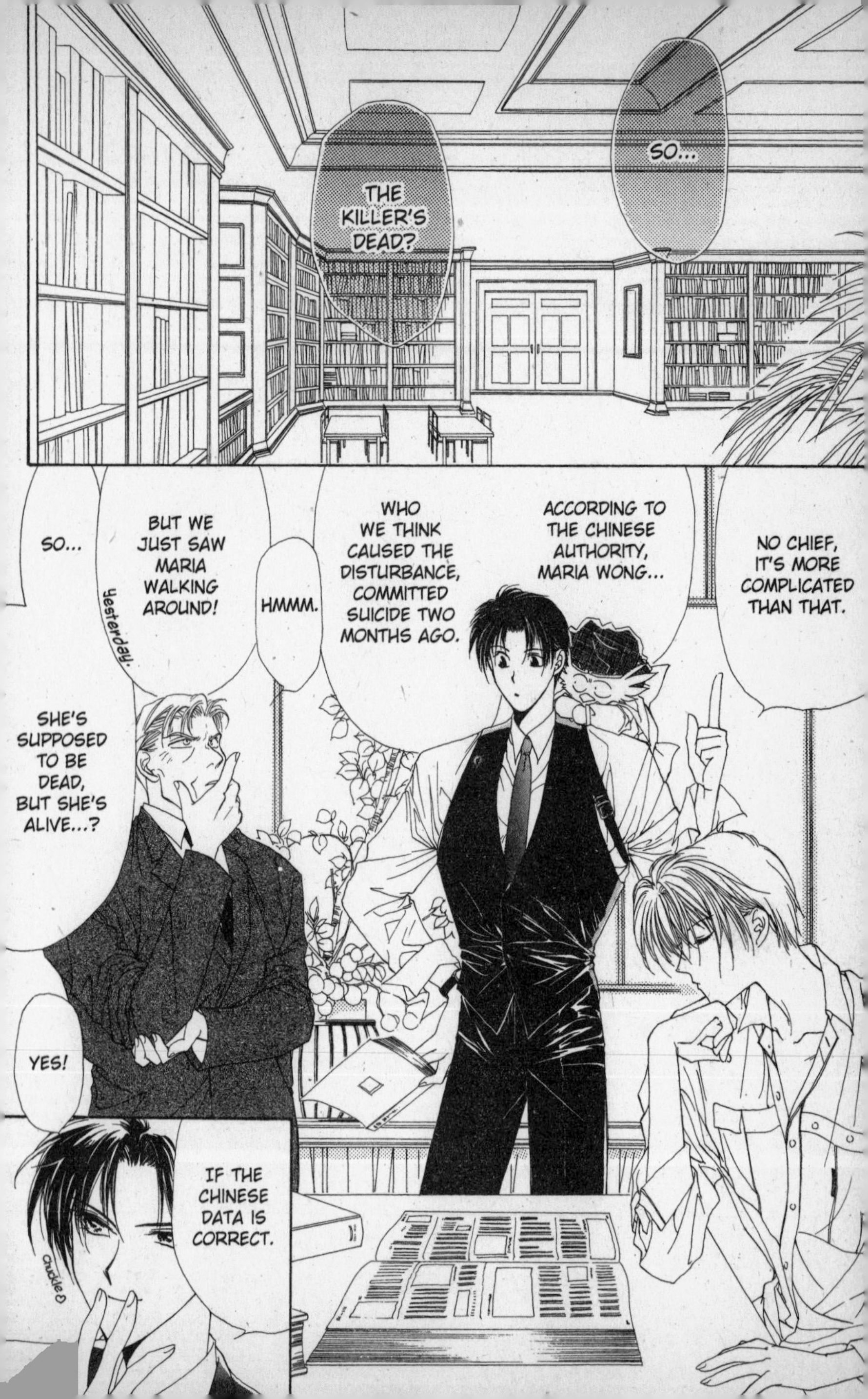
SO...
THE KILLER'S DEAD?
NO CHIEF, IT'S MORE COMPLICATED THAN THAT.
ACCORDING TO THE CHINESE AUTHORITY, MARIA WONG...
WHO WE THINK CAUSED THE DISTURBANCE, COMMITTED SUICIDE TWO MONTHS AGO.
HMMM.
BUT WE JUST SAW MARIA WALKING AROUND!
Yesterday.
SO...
SHE'S SUPPOSED TO BE DEAD, BUT SHE'S ALIVE...?
YES!
IF THE CHINESE DATA IS CORRECT.
chuckle♡

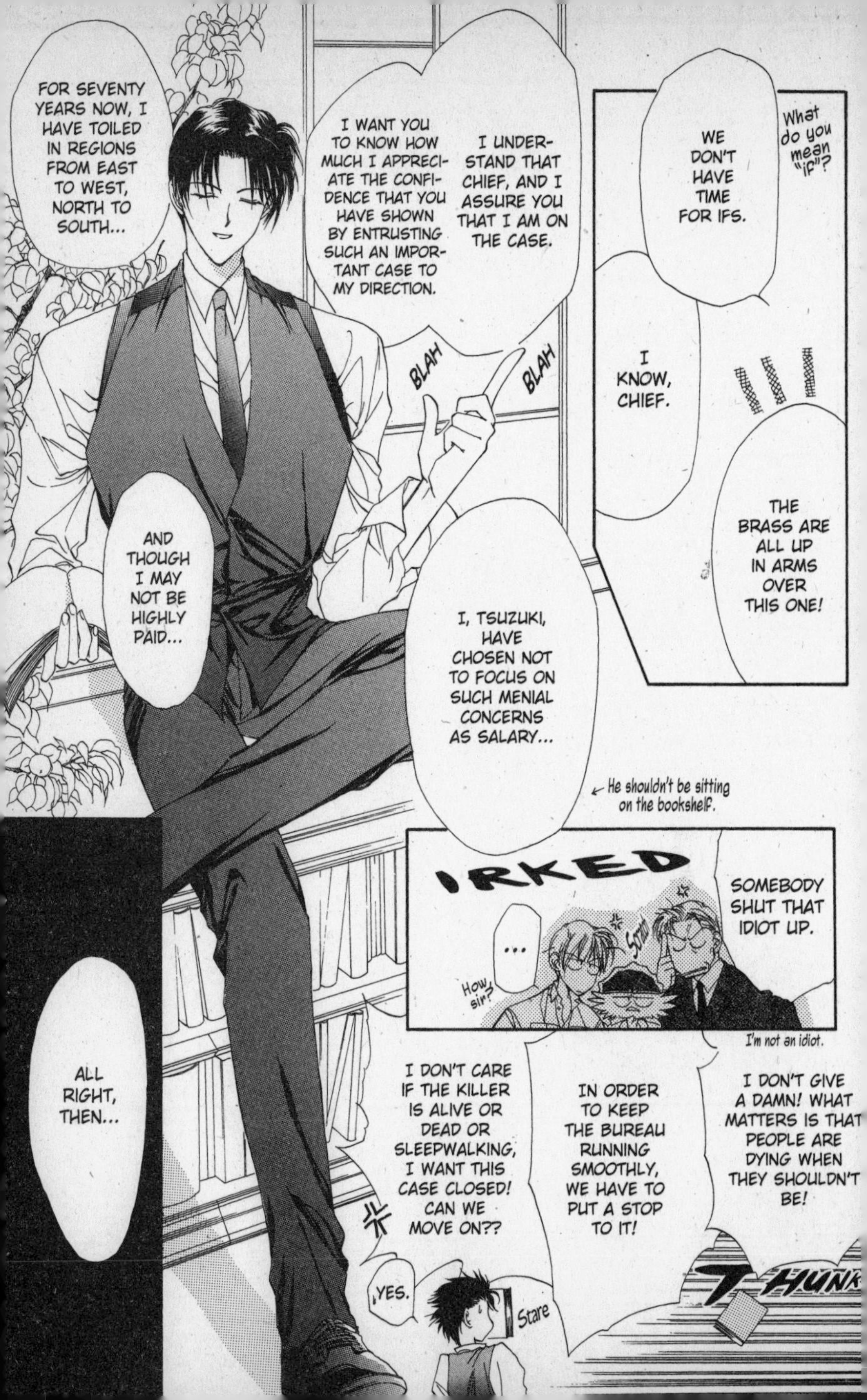
WE DON'T HAVE TIME FOR IFS.
What do you mean "if"?
I KNOW, CHIEF.
THE BRASS ARE ALL UP IN ARMS OVER THIS ONE!
I UNDER-STAND THAT CHIEF, AND I ASSURE YOU THAT I AM ON THE CASE.
I WANT YOU TO KNOW HOW MUCH I APPRECI-ATE THE CONFI-DENCE THAT YOU HAVE SHOWN BY ENTRUSTING SUCH AN IMPOR-TANT CASE TO MY DIRECTION.
BLAH
BLAH
FOR SEVENTY YEARS NOW, I HAVE TOILED IN REGIONS FROM EAST TO WEST, NORTH TO SOUTH...
AND THOUGH I MAY NOT BE HIGHLY PAID...
I, TSUZUKI, HAVE CHOSEN NOT TO FOCUS ON SUCH MENIAL CONCERNS AS SALARY...
← He shouldn't be sitting on the bookshelf.
IRKED
SOMEBODY SHUT THAT IDIOT UP.
...
How, sir?
I'm not an idiot.
T-HUNK
I DON'T GIVE A DAMN! WHAT MATTERS IS THAT PEOPLE ARE DYING WHEN THEY SHOULDN'T BE!
IN ORDER TO KEEP THE BUREAU RUNNING SMOOTHLY, WE HAVE TO PUT A STOP TO IT!
I DON'T CARE IF THE KILLER IS ALIVE OR DEAD OR SLEEPWALKING, I WANT THIS CASE CLOSED! CAN WE MOVE ON??
Stare
YES.
ALL RIGHT, THEN...

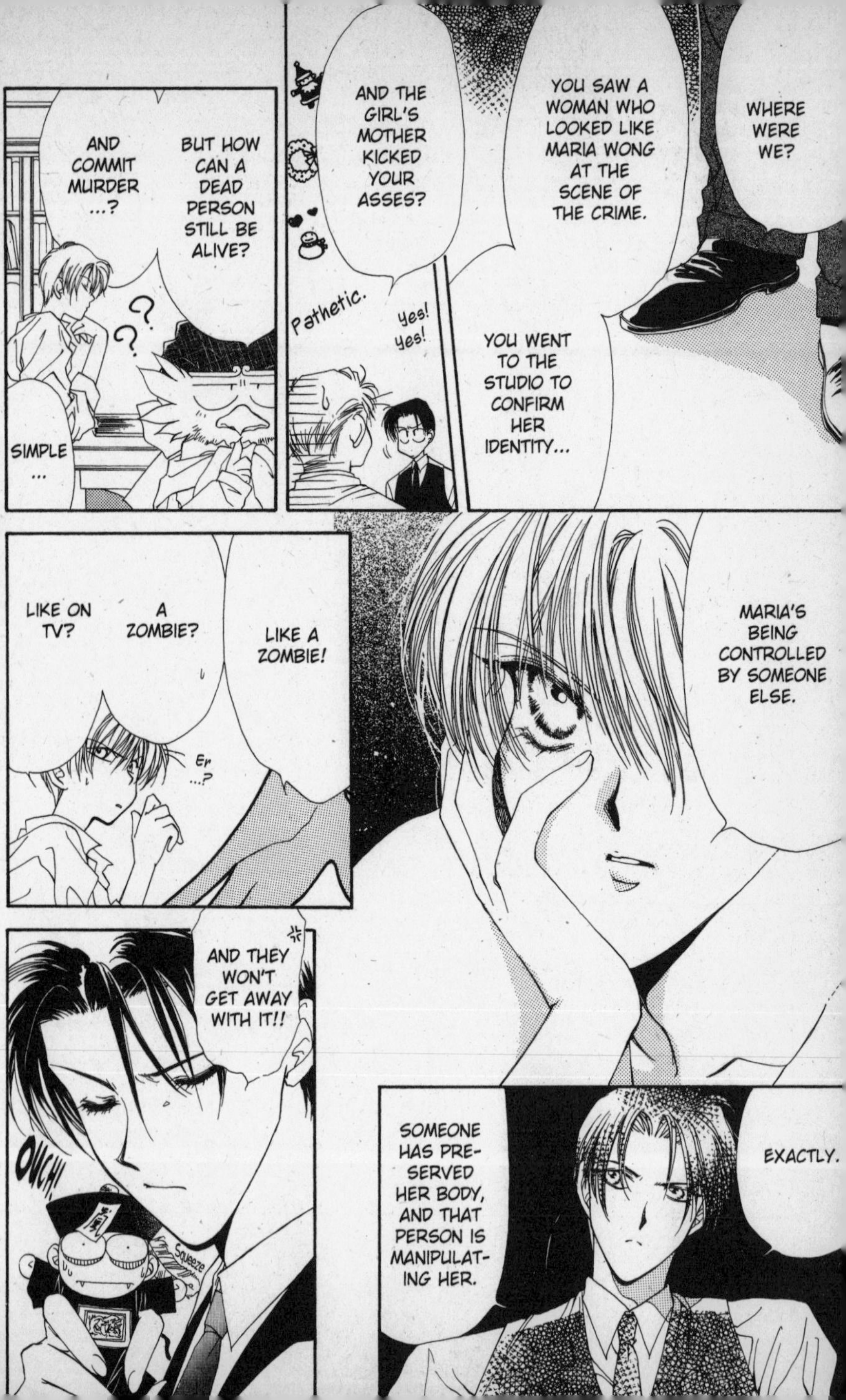
WHERE WERE WE?
YOU SAW A WOMAN WHO LOOKED LIKE MARIA WONG AT THE SCENE OF THE CRIME.
YOU WENT TO THE STUDIO TO CONFIRM HER IDENTITY...
AND THE GIRL'S MOTHER KICKED YOUR ASSES?
Yes! Yes!
Pathetic.
BUT HOW CAN A DEAD PERSON STILL BE ALIVE?
AND COMMIT MURDER ...?
SIMPLE ...
MARIA'S BEING CONTROLLED BY SOMEONE ELSE.
LIKE A ZOMBIE!
A ZOMBIE?
LIKE ON TV?
Er ...?
EXACTLY.
SOMEONE HAS PRE-SERVED HER BODY, AND THAT PERSON IS MANIPULAT-ING HER.
AND THEY WON'T GET AWAY WITH IT!!
OUCH!
Squeeze

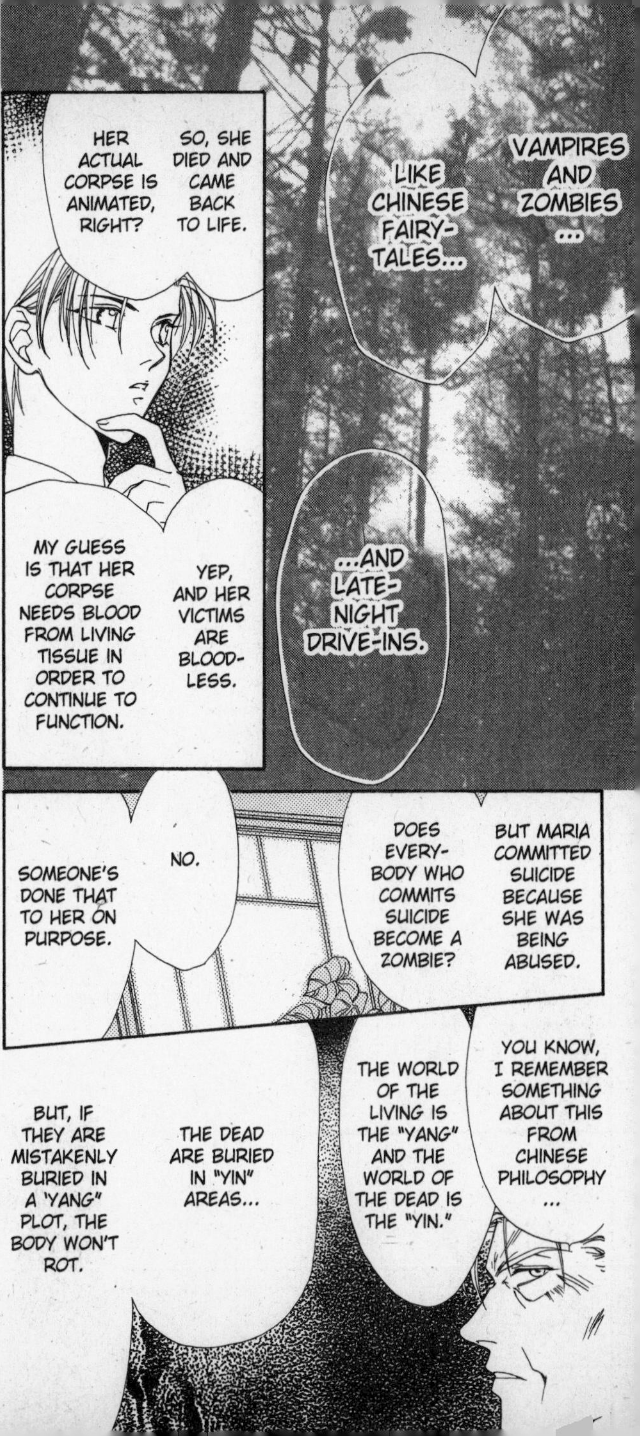
VAMPIRES AND ZOMBIES ...
LIKE CHINESE FAIRY-TALES...
...AND LATE-NIGHT DRIVE-INS.
SO, SHE DIED AND CAME BACK TO LIFE.
HER ACTUAL CORPSE IS ANIMATED, RIGHT?
YEP, AND HER VICTIMS ARE BLOOD-LESS.
MY GUESS IS THAT HER CORPSE NEEDS BLOOD FROM LIVING TISSUE IN ORDER TO CONTINUE TO FUNCTION.
BUT MARIA COMMITTED SUICIDE BECAUSE SHE WAS BEING ABUSED.
DOES EVERY-BODY WHO COMMITS SUICIDE BECOME A ZOMBIE?
NO.
SOMEONE'S DONE THAT TO HER ON PURPOSE.
YOU KNOW, I REMEMBER SOMETHING ABOUT THIS FROM CHINESE PHILOSOPHY ...
THE WORLD OF THE LIVING IS THE "YANG" AND THE WORLD OF THE DEAD IS THE "YIN."
THE DEAD ARE BURIED IN "YIN" AREAS...
BUT, IF THEY ARE MISTAKENLY BURIED IN A 'YANG" PLOT, THE BODY WON'T ROT.

Tsuzuki's story mainly takes place in Kyushu. The Judgment Bureau is in Tokyo, but I decided to make Kyushu the center of the story... I guess rebellion is in my blood. (I'm type AB!)

Just for fun, I've included a chart at the back of the books, telling you in which part of Japan each department of Ministry is located.

This chapter takes place in Nagasaki. I love the exotic atmosphere. And I can't think of Nagasaki without thinking of Castella Cake—the kind Chief Konoe, wanted to eat!! I've never actually tasted Fukusaya's Castella, but I like the places that sell 7 or 10 pieces for ¥1,000, which is really cheap. (Yay, bargain!)

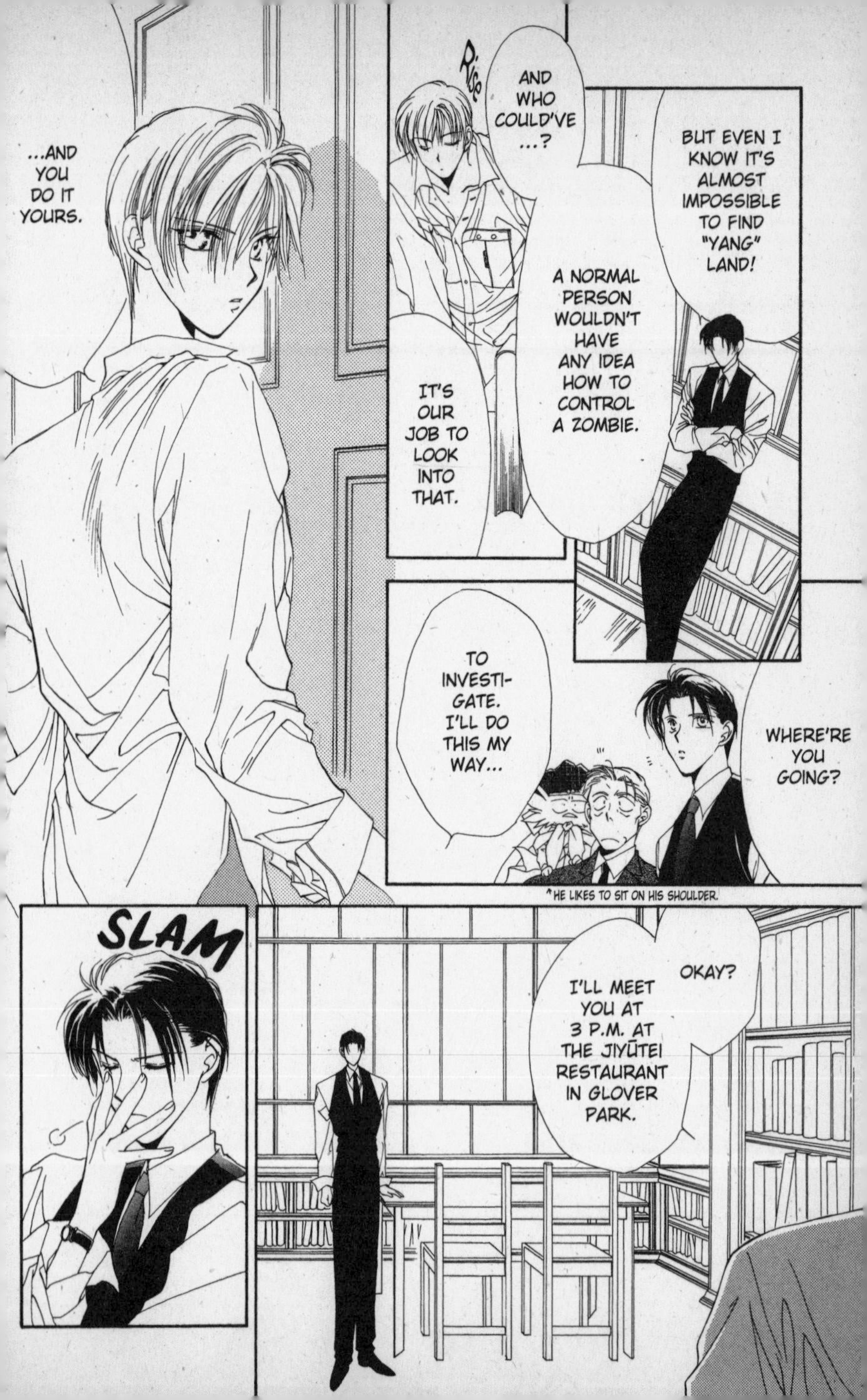
BUT EVEN I KNOW IT'S ALMOST IMPOSSIBLE TO FIND "YANG" LAND!
A NORMAL PERSON WOULDN'T HAVE ANY IDEA HOW TO CONTROL A ZOMBIE.
Rise
AND WHO COULD'VE ...?
IT'S OUR JOB TO LOOK INTO THAT.
WHERE'RE YOU GOING?
TO INVESTI-GATE. I'LL DO THIS MY WAY...
*HE LIKES TO SIT ON HIS SHOULDER.
...AND YOU DO IT YOURS.
OKAY?
I'LL MEET YOU AT 3 P.M. AT THE JIYŪTEI RESTAURANT IN GLOVER PARK.
SLAM

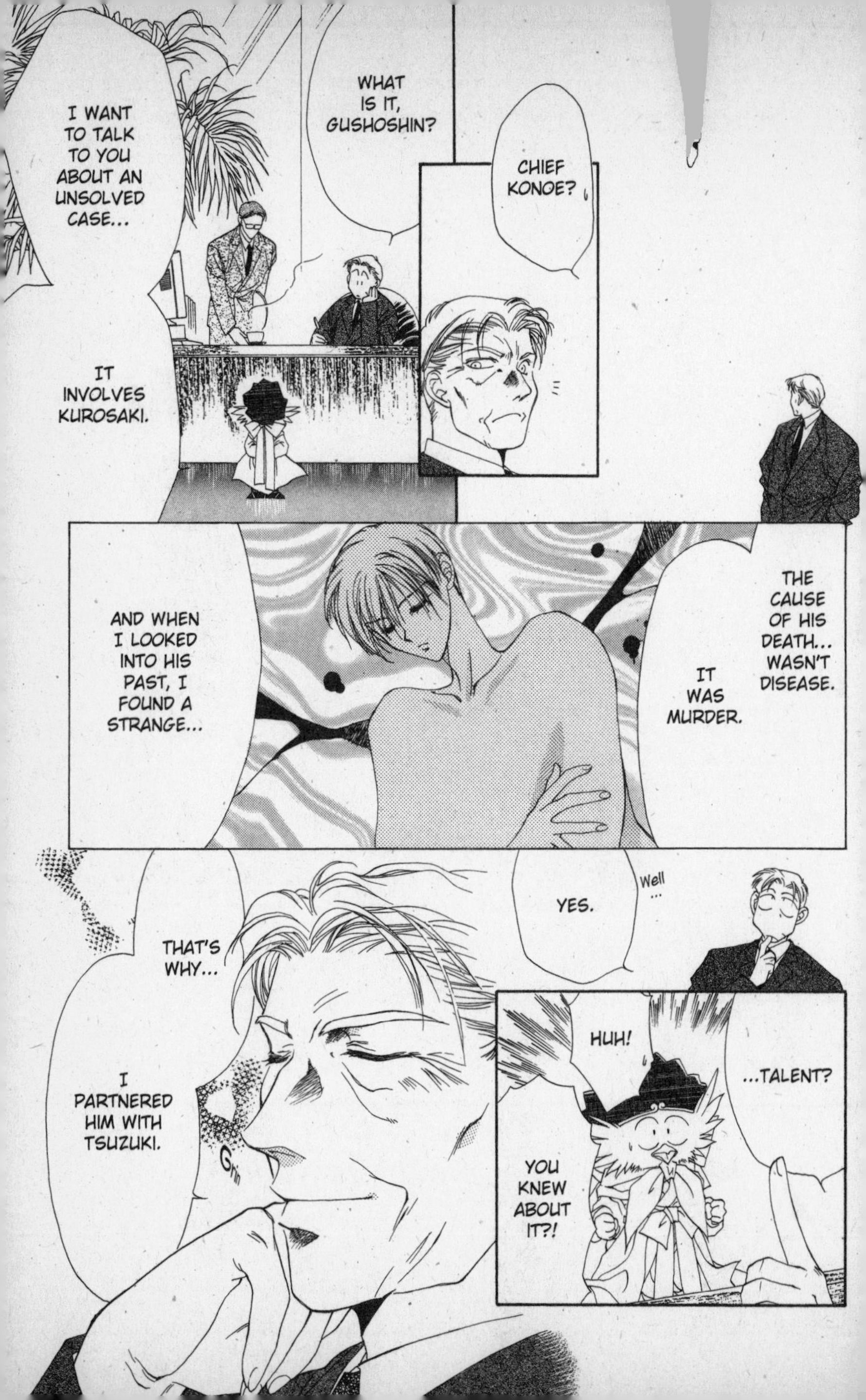
CHIEF KONOE?
WHAT IS IT, GUSHOSHIN?
I WANT TO TALK TO YOU ABOUT AN UNSOLVED CASE...
IT INVOLVES KUROSAKI.
THE CAUSE OF HIS DEATH... WASN'T DISEASE.
IT WAS MURDER.
AND WHEN I LOOKED INTO HIS PAST, I FOUND A STRANGE...
...TALENT?
Well ...
YES.
HUH!
YOU KNEW ABOUT IT?!
THAT'S WHY...
Grin
I PARTNERED HIM WITH TSUZUKI.

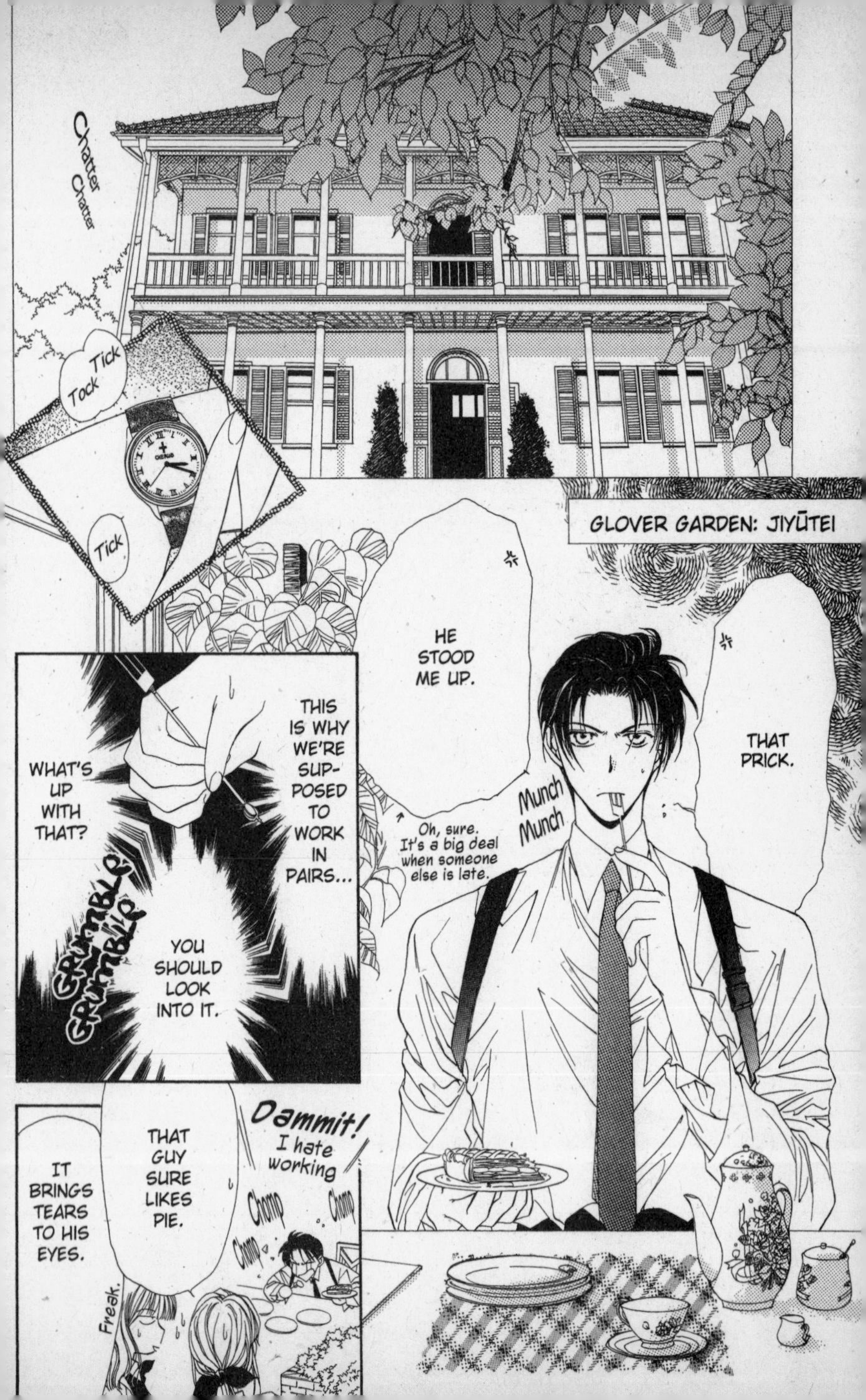
Tick Tock
Tick
Chatter Chatter
GLOVER GARDEN: JIYŪTEI
THAT PRICK.
HE STOOD ME UP.
Munch Munch
Oh, sure. It's a big deal when someone else is late.
THIS IS WHY WE'RE SUP-POSED TO WORK IN PAIRS...
WHAT'S UP WITH THAT?
GRUMBLE GRUMBLE
YOU SHOULD LOOK INTO IT.
Dammit! I hate working
Chomp Chomp Chomp
THAT GUY SURE LIKES PIE.
IT BRINGS TEARS TO HIS EYES.
Freak.

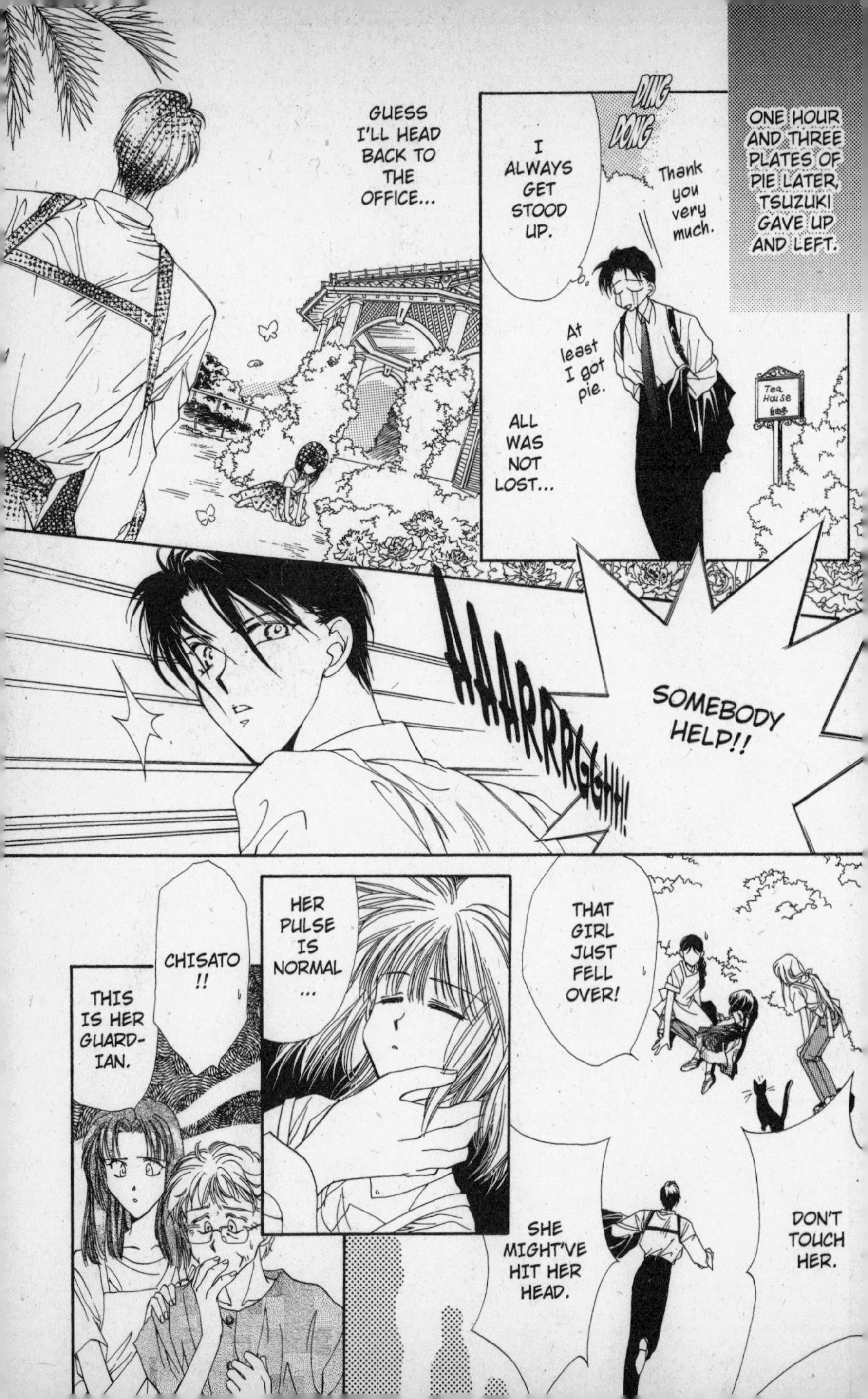
ONE HOUR AND THREE PLATES OF PIE LATER, TSUZUKI GAVE UP AND LEFT.
DING DONG
Thank you very much.
I ALWAYS GET STOOD UP.
Tea House
At least I got pie.
ALL WAS NOT LOST...
GUESS I'LL HEAD BACK TO THE OFFICE...
SOMEBODY HELP!!
AAARRRGGHH!!
THAT GIRL JUST FELL OVER!
SHE MIGHT'VE HIT HER HEAD.
DON'T TOUCH HER.
HER PULSE IS NORMAL ...
CHISATO!!
THIS IS HER GUARDIAN.

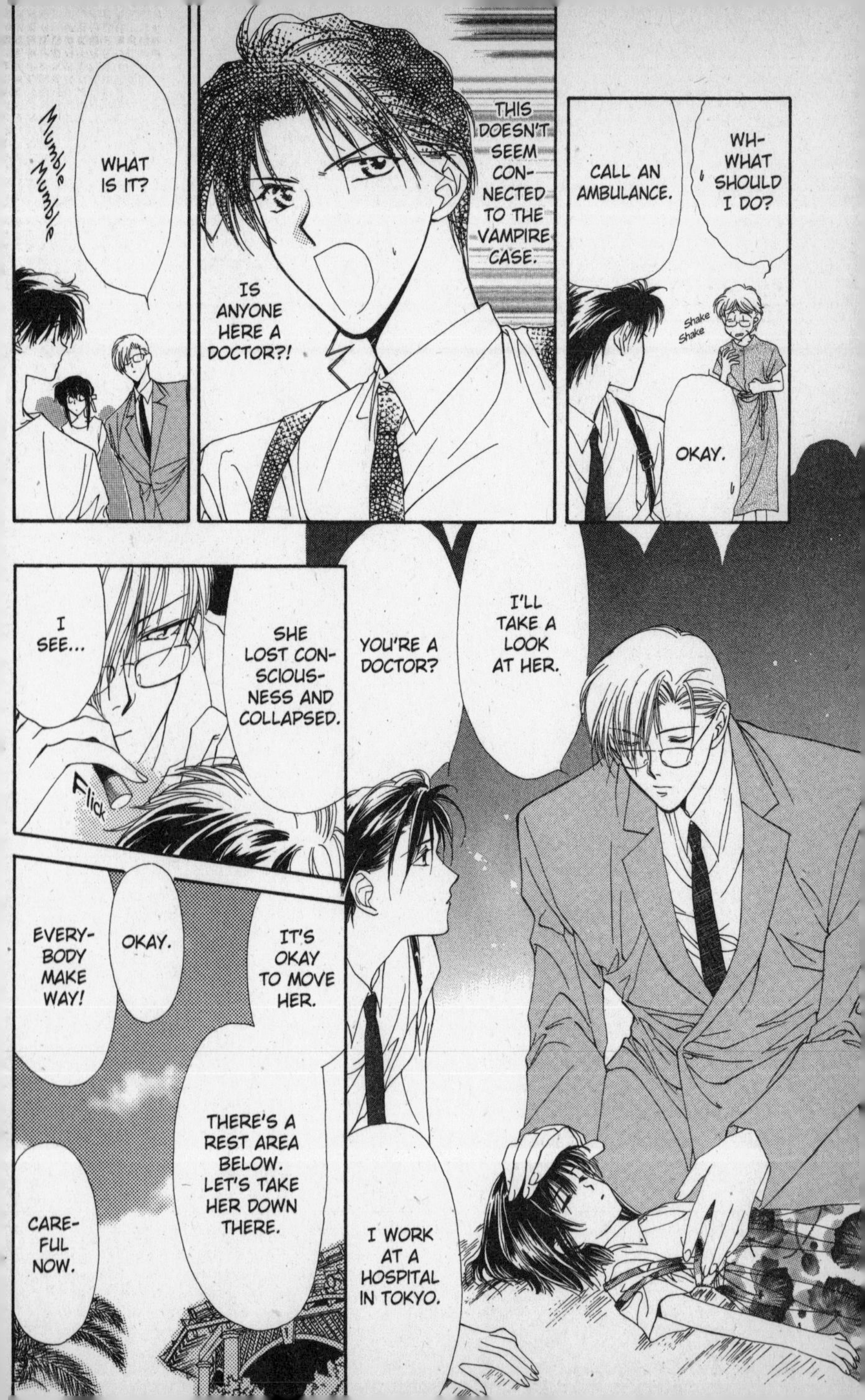
WH- WHAT SHOULD I DO?
CALL AN AMBULANCE.
Shake Shake
OKAY.
THIS DOESN'T SEEM CON-NECTED TO THE VAMPIRE CASE.
IS ANYONE HERE A DOCTOR?!
WHAT IS IT?
Mumble Mumble
I'LL TAKE A LOOK AT HER.
YOU'RE A DOCTOR?
I WORK AT A HOSPITAL IN TOKYO.
SHE LOST CON-SCIOUS-NESS AND COLLAPSED.
I SEE...
Flick
IT'S OKAY TO MOVE HER.
OKAY.
EVERY-BODY MAKE WAY!
THERE'S A REST AREA BELOW. LET'S TAKE HER DOWN THERE.
CARE-FUL NOW.

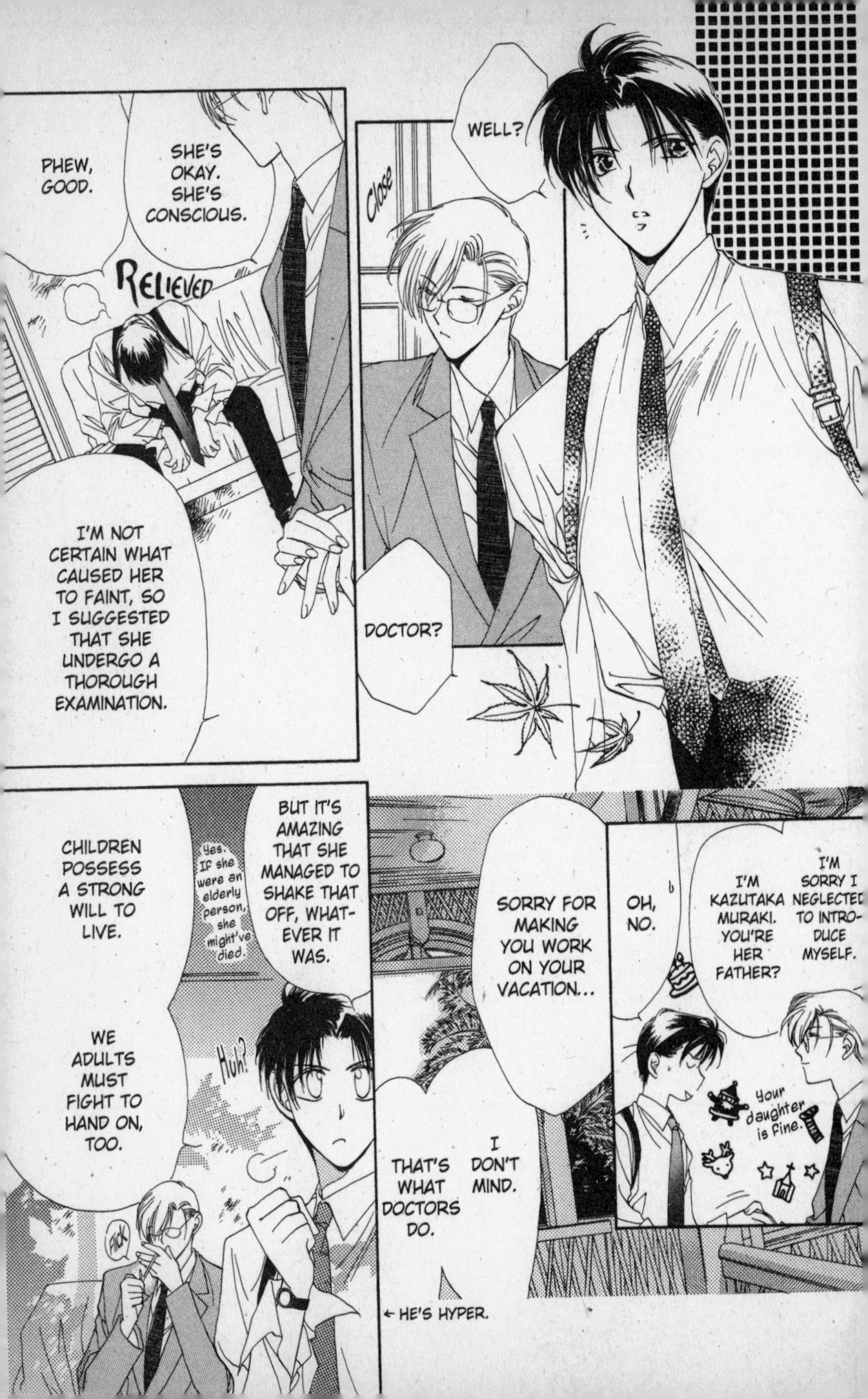
WELL?
Close
DOCTOR?
SHE'S OKAY. SHE'S CONSCIOUS.
PHEW, GOOD.
RELIEVED
I'M NOT CERTAIN WHAT CAUSED HER TO FAINT, SO I SUGGESTED THAT SHE UNDERGO A THOROUGH EXAMINATION.
I'M SORRY I NEGLECTED TO INTRODUCE MYSELF.
I'M KAZUTAKA MURAKI. YOU'RE HER FATHER?
Your daughter is fine.
OH, NO.
SORRY FOR MAKING YOU WORK ON YOUR VACATION...
I DON'T MIND.
THAT'S WHAT DOCTORS DO.
← HE'S HYPER.
BUT IT'S AMAZING THAT SHE MANAGED TO SHAKE THAT OFF, WHATEVER IT WAS.
Yes. If she were an elderly person, she might've died.
CHILDREN POSSESS A STRONG WILL TO LIVE.
Huh?
WE ADULTS MUST FIGHT TO HANG ON, TOO.
Flick

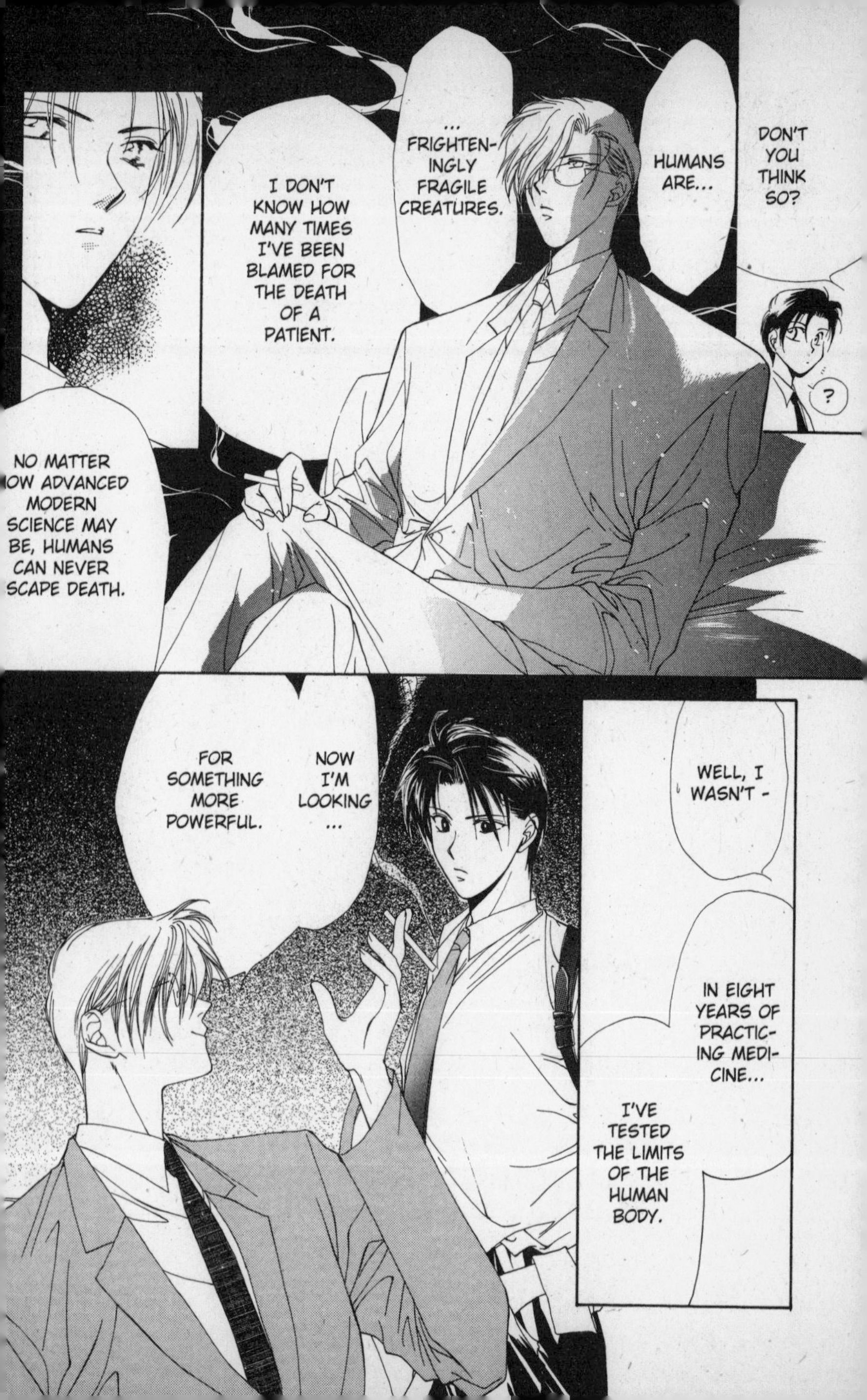
DON'T YOU THINK SO?
?
HUMANS ARE...
... FRIGHTEN-INGLY FRAGILE CREATURES.
I DON'T KNOW HOW MANY TIMES I'VE BEEN BLAMED FOR THE DEATH OF A PATIENT.
NO MATTER OW ADVANCED MODERN SCIENCE MAY BE, HUMANS CAN NEVER SCAPE DEATH.
WELL, I WASN'T -
IN EIGHT YEARS OF PRACTIC-ING MEDI-CINE...
I'VE TESTED THE LIMITS OF THE HUMAN BODY.
NOW I'M LOOKING ...
FOR SOMETHING MORE POWERFUL.

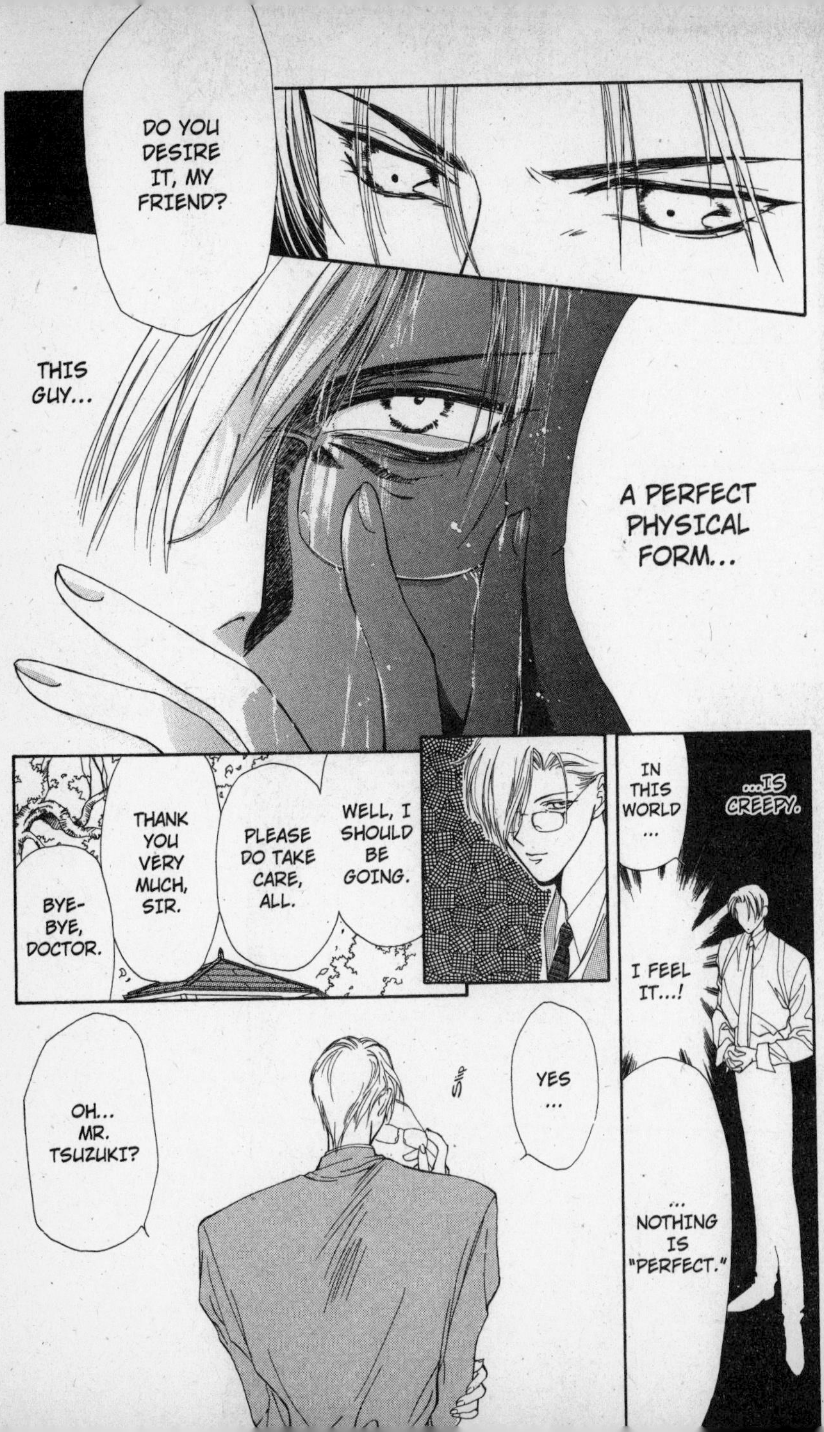

DO YOU DESIRE IT, MY FRIEND?
A PERFECT PHYSICAL FORM...
THIS GUY...
...IS CREEPY.
IN THIS WORLD ...
I FEEL IT...!
... NOTHING IS "PERFECT."
WELL, I SHOULD BE GOING.
PLEASE DO TAKE CARE, ALL.
THANK YOU VERY MUCH, SIR.
BYE-BYE, DOCTOR.
YES ...
Slip
OH... MR. TSUZUKI?

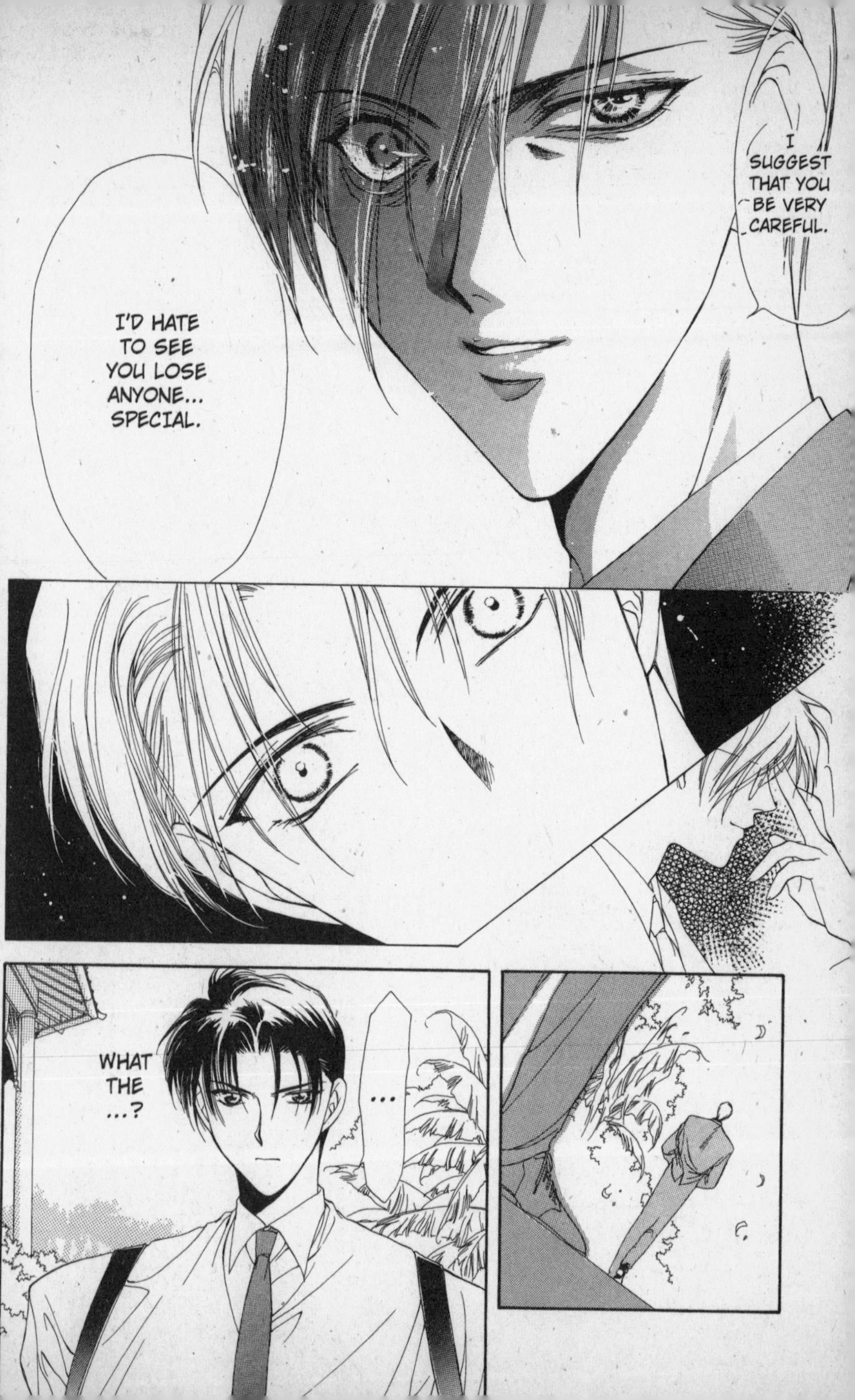
I SUGGEST THAT YOU BE VERY CAREFUL.
I'D HATE TO SEE YOU LOSE ANYONE... SPECIAL.
...
WHAT THE ...?

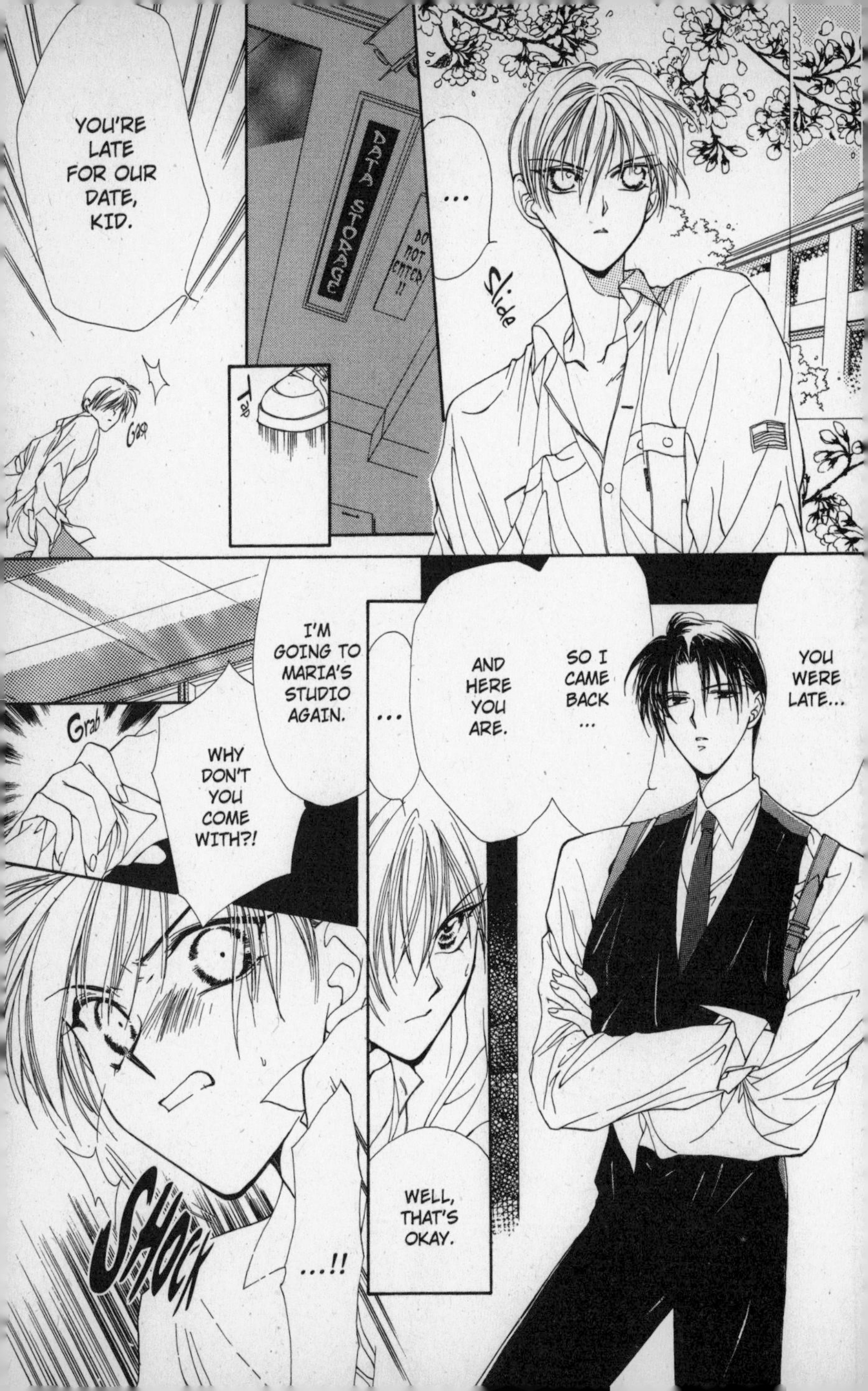
...
Slide
DATA STORAGE
DO NOT ENTER!!
Tap
YOU'RE LATE FOR OUR DATE, KID.
Gasp
YOU WERE LATE...
SO I CAME BACK...
AND HERE YOU ARE.
...
WELL, THAT'S OKAY.
I'M GOING TO MARIA'S STUDIO AGAIN.
Grab
WHY DON'T YOU COME WITH?!
...!!
SHOCK

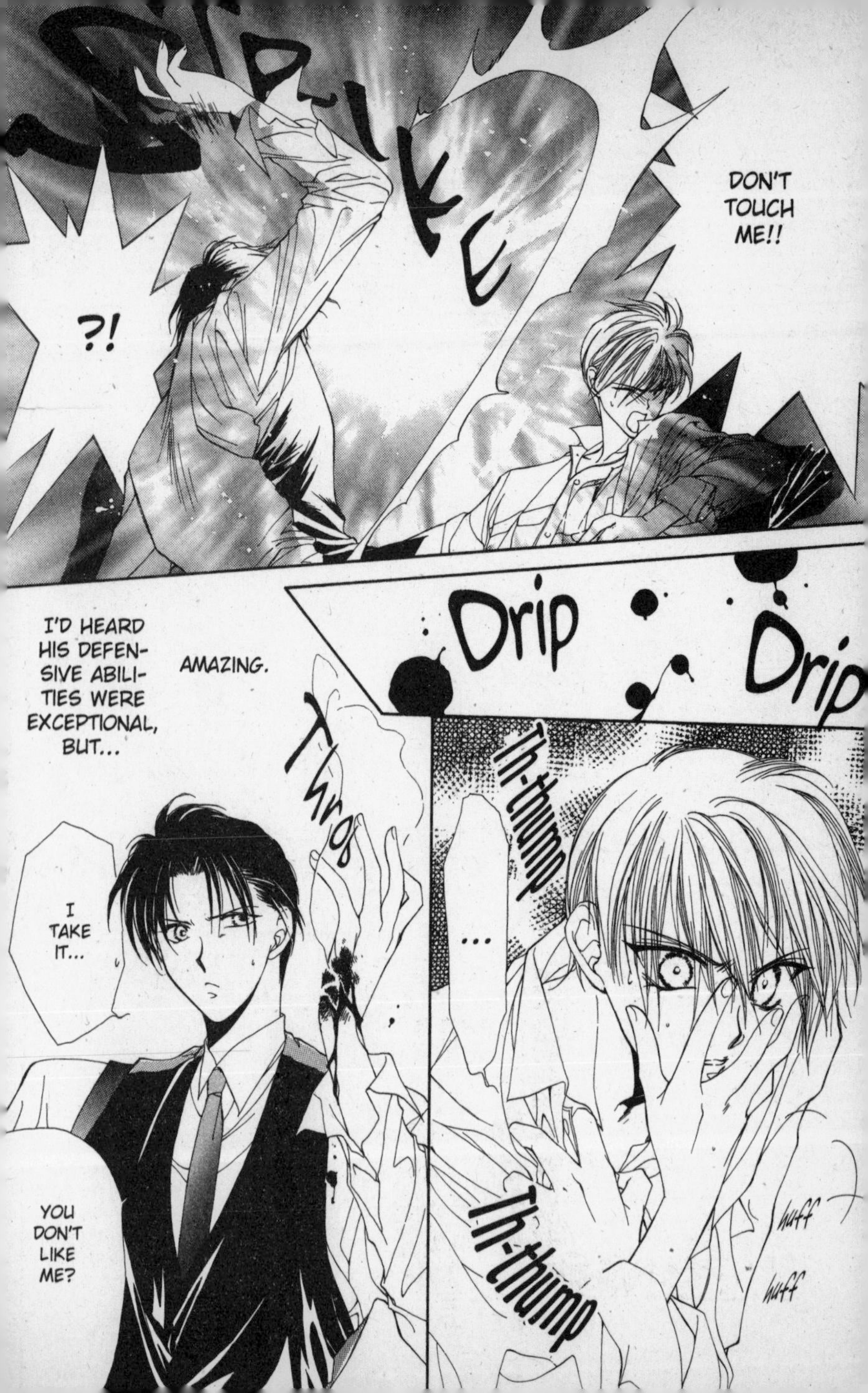
DON'T TOUCH ME!!
?!
Drip
Drip
Th-thump
...
Th-thump
huff
huff
AMAZING.
I'D HEARD HIS DEFEN-SIVE ABILI-TIES WERE EXCEPTIONAL, BUT...
Throb
I TAKE IT...
YOU DON'T LIKE ME?

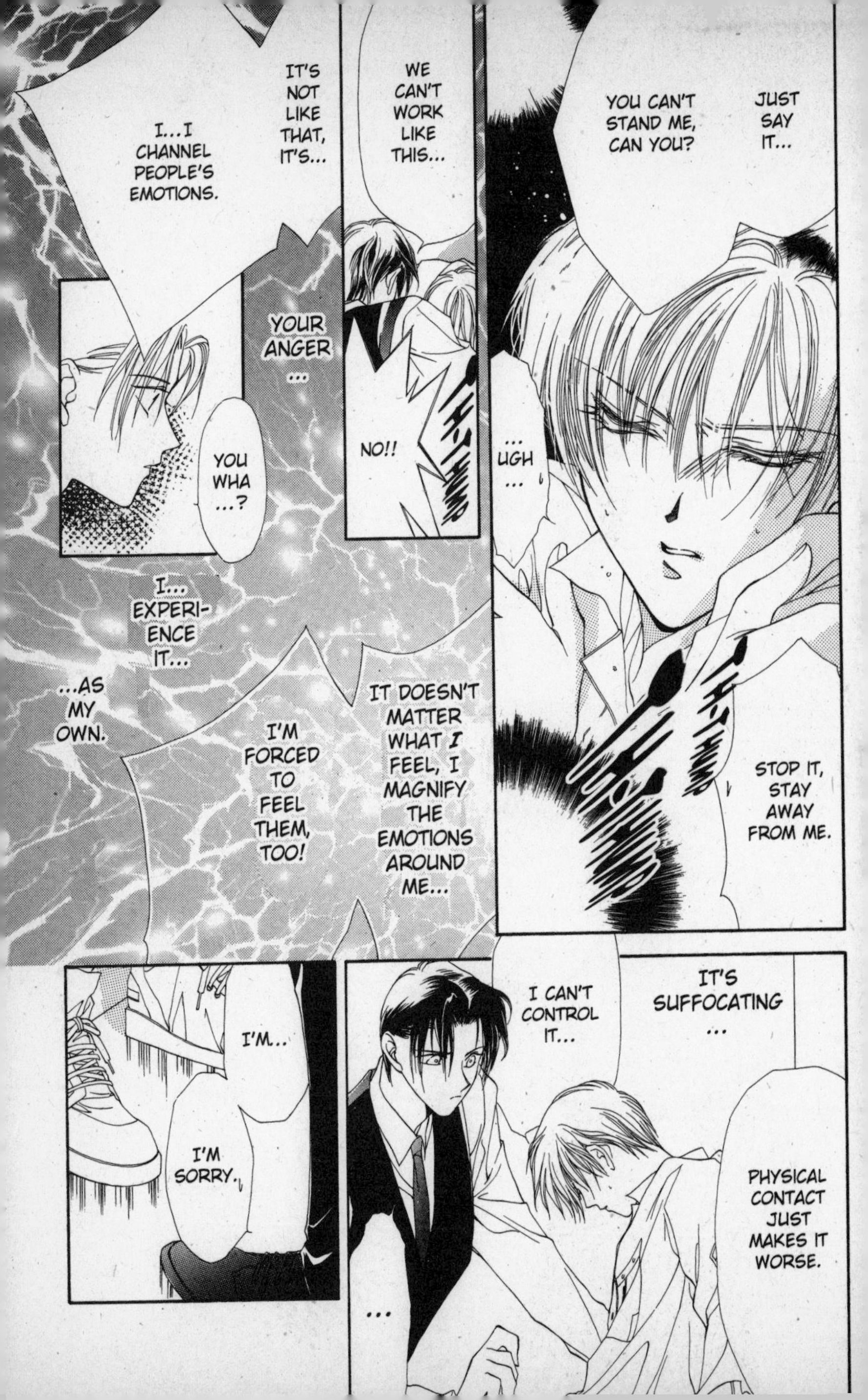
JUST SAY IT...
YOU CAN'T STAND ME, CAN YOU?
...UGH...
STOP IT, STAY AWAY FROM ME.
WE CAN'T WORK LIKE THIS...
NO!!
IT'S NOT LIKE THAT, IT'S...
I...I CHANNEL PEOPLE'S EMOTIONS.
YOUR ANGER...
YOU WHA...?
I... EXPERIENCE IT...
...AS MY OWN.
IT DOESN'T MATTER WHAT I FEEL, I MAGNIFY THE EMOTIONS AROUND ME...
I'M FORCED TO FEEL THEM, TOO!
IT'S SUFFOCATING...
I CAN'T CONTROL IT...
PHYSICAL CONTACT JUST MAKES IT WORSE.
...
I'M...
I'M SORRY.

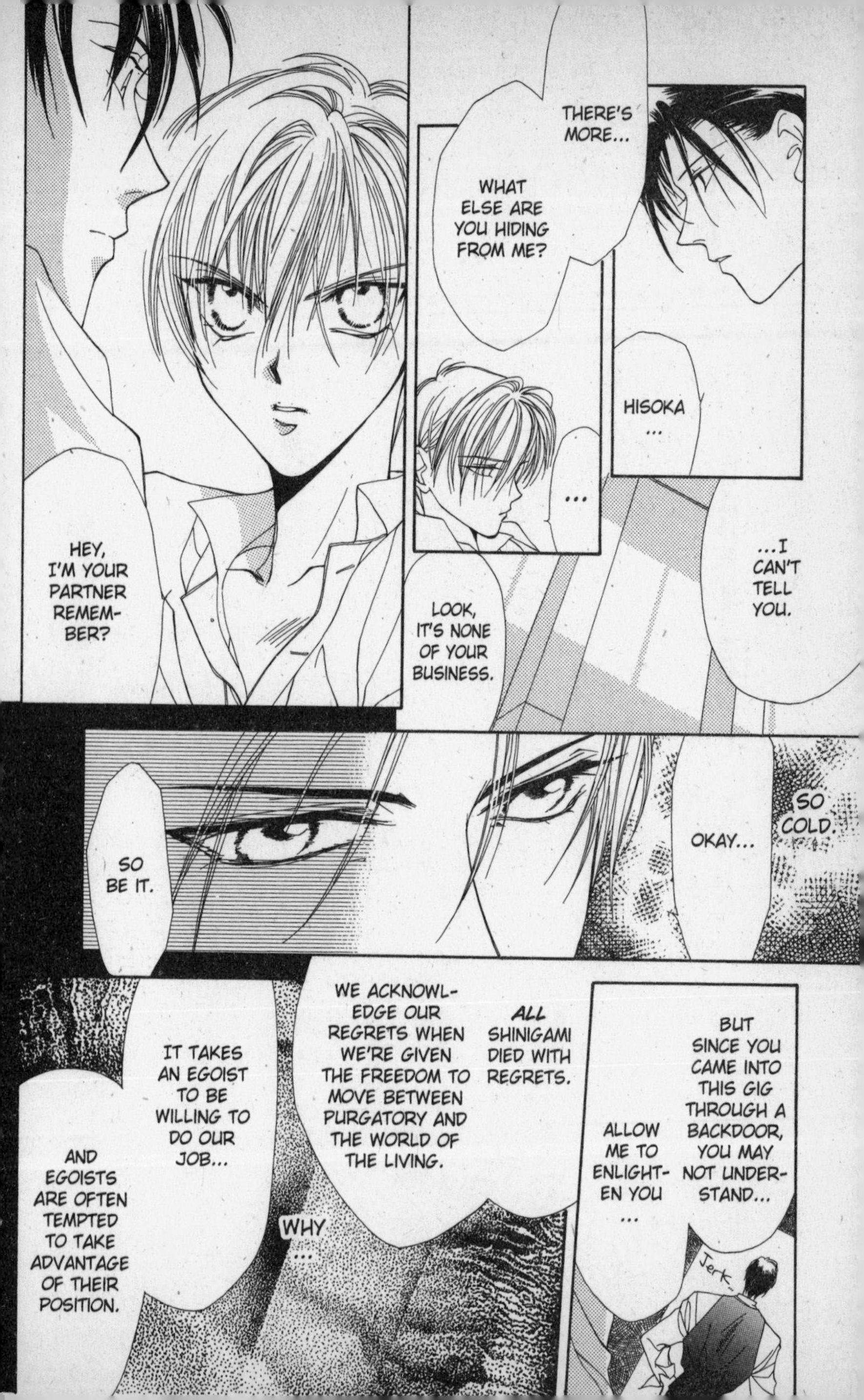
THERE'S MORE...
WHAT ELSE ARE YOU HIDING FROM ME?
HISOKA ...
...
...I CAN'T TELL YOU.
LOOK, IT'S NONE OF YOUR BUSINESS.
HEY, I'M YOUR PARTNER REMEMBER?
SO COLD.
OKAY...
SO BE IT.
BUT SINCE YOU CAME INTO THIS GIG THROUGH A BACKDOOR, YOU MAY NOT UNDERSTAND...
ALLOW ME TO ENLIGHTEN YOU ...
Jerk.
*ALL* SHINIGAMI DIED WITH REGRETS.
WE ACKNOWLEDGE OUR REGRETS WHEN WE'RE GIVEN THE FREEDOM TO MOVE BETWEEN PURGATORY AND THE WORLD OF THE LIVING.
IT TAKES AN EGOIST TO BE WILLING TO DO OUR JOB...
WHY ...
AND EGOISTS ARE OFTEN TEMPTED TO TAKE ADVANTAGE OF THEIR POSITION.

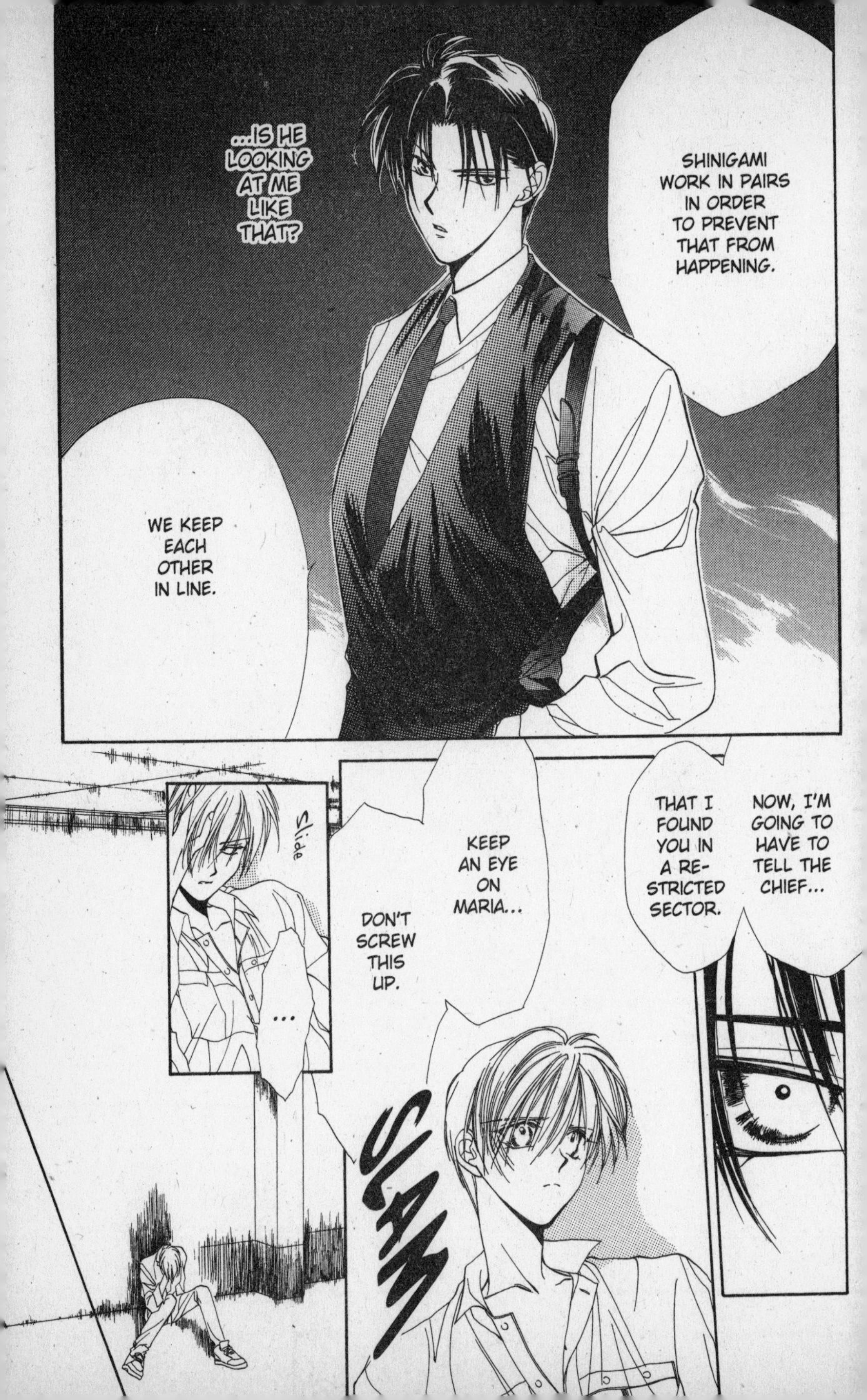
SHINIGAMI WORK IN PAIRS IN ORDER TO PREVENT THAT FROM HAPPENING.
...IS HE LOOKING AT ME LIKE THAT?
WE KEEP EACH OTHER IN LINE.
NOW, I'M GOING TO HAVE TO TELL THE CHIEF...
THAT I FOUND YOU IN A RE-STRICTED SECTOR.
KEEP AN EYE ON MARIA...
DON'T SCREW THIS UP.
SLAM
Slide
...

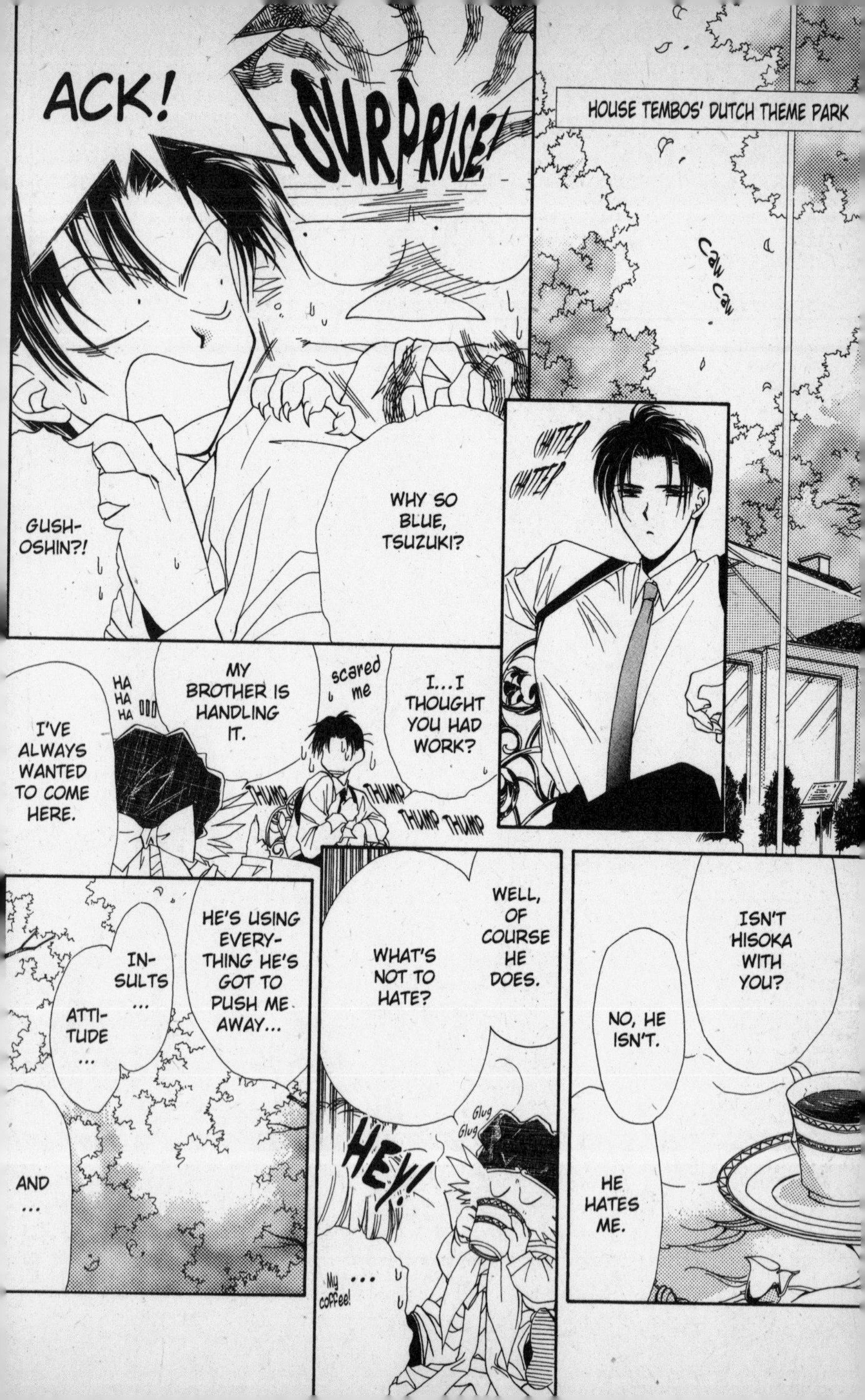
HOUSE TEMBOS' DUTCH THEME PARK
Caw caw
CHATTER CHATTER
SURPRISE!
ACK!
WHY SO BLUE, TSUZUKI?
GUSH-OSHIN?!
I...I THOUGHT YOU HAD WORK?
scared me
THUMP THUMP THUMP THUMP
MY BROTHER IS HANDLING IT.
HA HA HA
I'VE ALWAYS WANTED TO COME HERE.
ISN'T HISOKA WITH YOU?
NO, HE ISN'T.
HE HATES ME.
WELL, OF COURSE HE DOES.
WHAT'S NOT TO HATE?
HEY!
Glug Glug
My coffee!
...
HE'S USING EVERY-THING HE'S GOT TO PUSH ME AWAY...
IN-SULTS...
ATTI-TUDE...
AND...

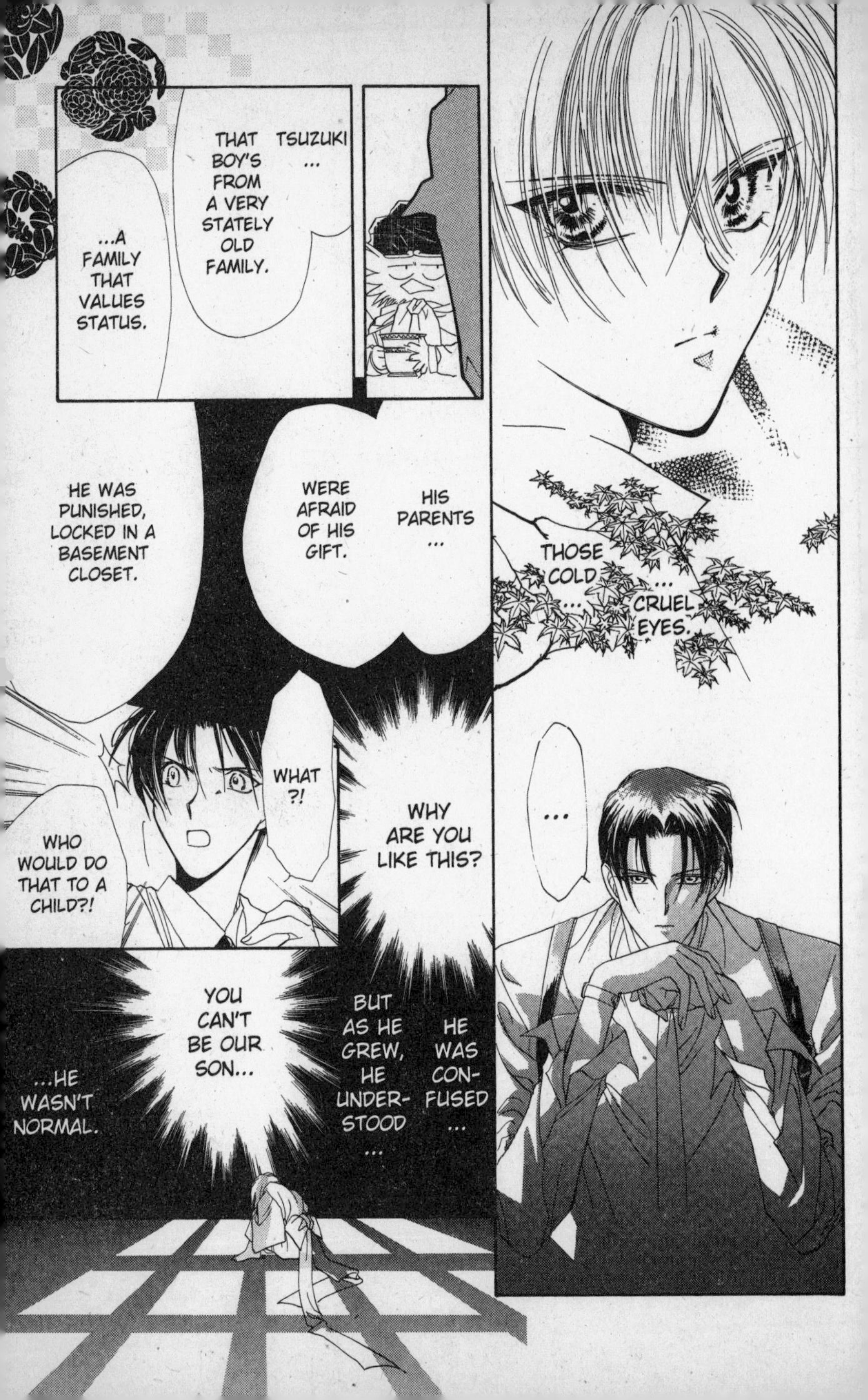
THOSE COLD ... ...CRUEL EYES.
...
TSUZUKI ...
THAT BOY'S FROM A VERY STATELY OLD FAMILY.
...A FAMILY THAT VALUES STATUS.
HIS PARENTS ...
WERE AFRAID OF HIS GIFT.
HE WAS PUNISHED, LOCKED IN A BASEMENT CLOSET.
WHY ARE YOU LIKE THIS?
WHAT?!
WHO WOULD DO THAT TO A CHILD?!
HE WAS CON-FUSED ...
BUT AS HE GREW, HE UNDER-STOOD ...
YOU CAN'T BE OUR SON...
...HE WASN'T NORMAL.

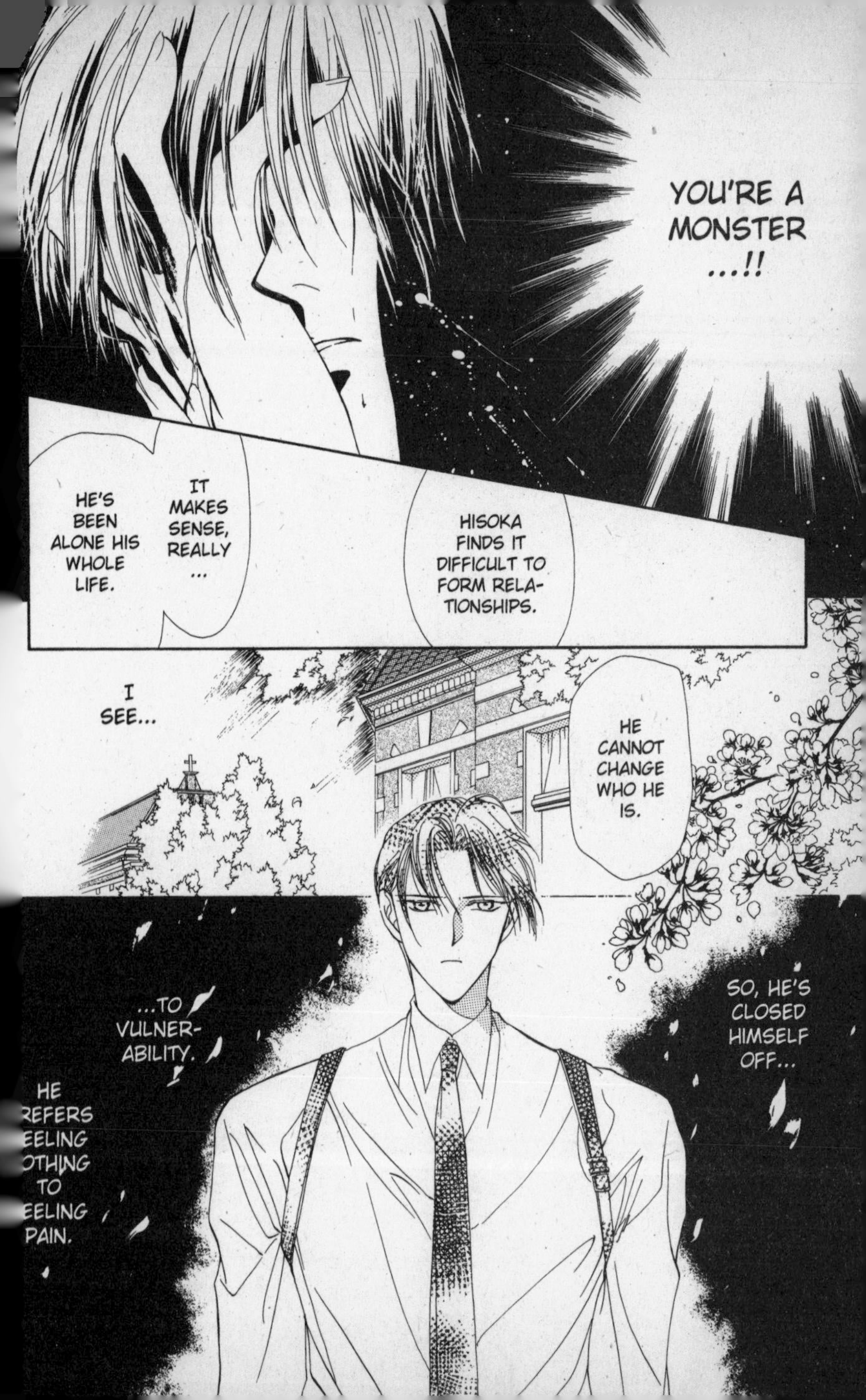
YOU'RE A MONSTER ...!!
HISOKA FINDS IT DIFFICULT TO FORM RELA-TIONSHIPS.
IT MAKES SENSE, REALLY ...
HE'S BEEN ALONE HIS WHOLE LIFE.
HE CANNOT CHANGE WHO HE IS.
I SEE...
SO, HE'S CLOSED HIMSELF OFF...
...TO VULNER-ABILITY.
HE REFERS EELING OTHING TO EELING PAIN.

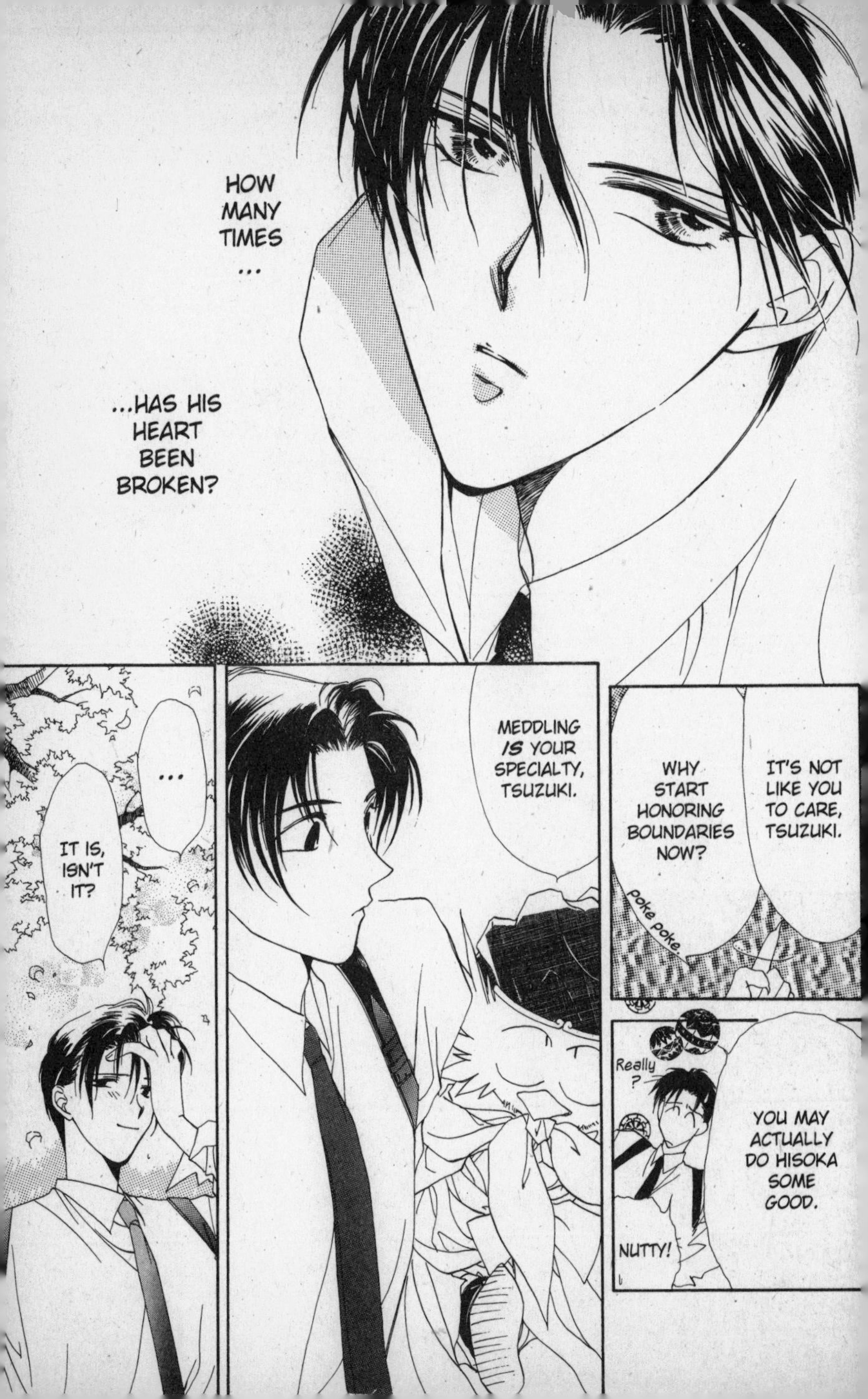
HOW MANY TIMES ...
...HAS HIS HEART BEEN BROKEN?
IT'S NOT LIKE YOU TO CARE, TSUZUKI.
WHY START HONORING BOUNDARIES NOW?
poke poke.
YOU MAY ACTUALLY DO HISOKA SOME GOOD.
Really?
NUTTY!
MEDDLING *IS* YOUR SPECIALTY, TSUZUKI.
...
IT IS, ISN'T IT?

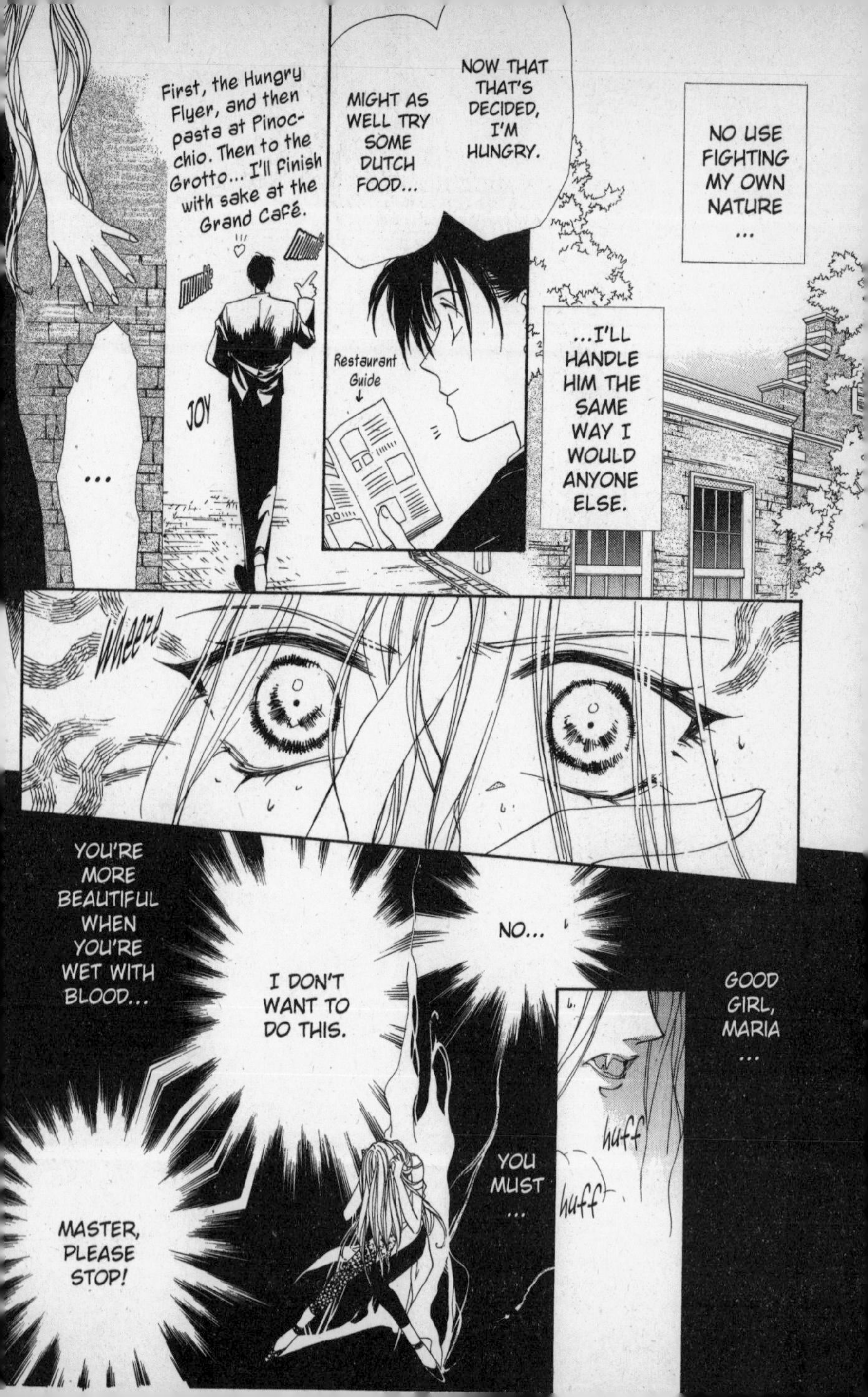
NO USE FIGHTING MY OWN NATURE...
...I'LL HANDLE HIM THE SAME WAY I WOULD ANYONE ELSE.
NOW THAT THAT'S DECIDED, I'M HUNGRY.
MIGHT AS WELL TRY SOME DUTCH FOOD...
Restaurant Guide
First, the Hungry Flyer, and then pasta at Pinocchio. Then to the Grotto... I'll finish with sake at the Grand Café.
mumble
mumble
JOY
...
wheeze
GOOD GIRL, MARIA...
NO...
YOU MUST...
huff
huff
I DON'T WANT TO DO THIS.
YOU'RE MORE BEAUTIFUL WHEN YOU'RE WET WITH BLOOD...
MASTER, PLEASE STOP!

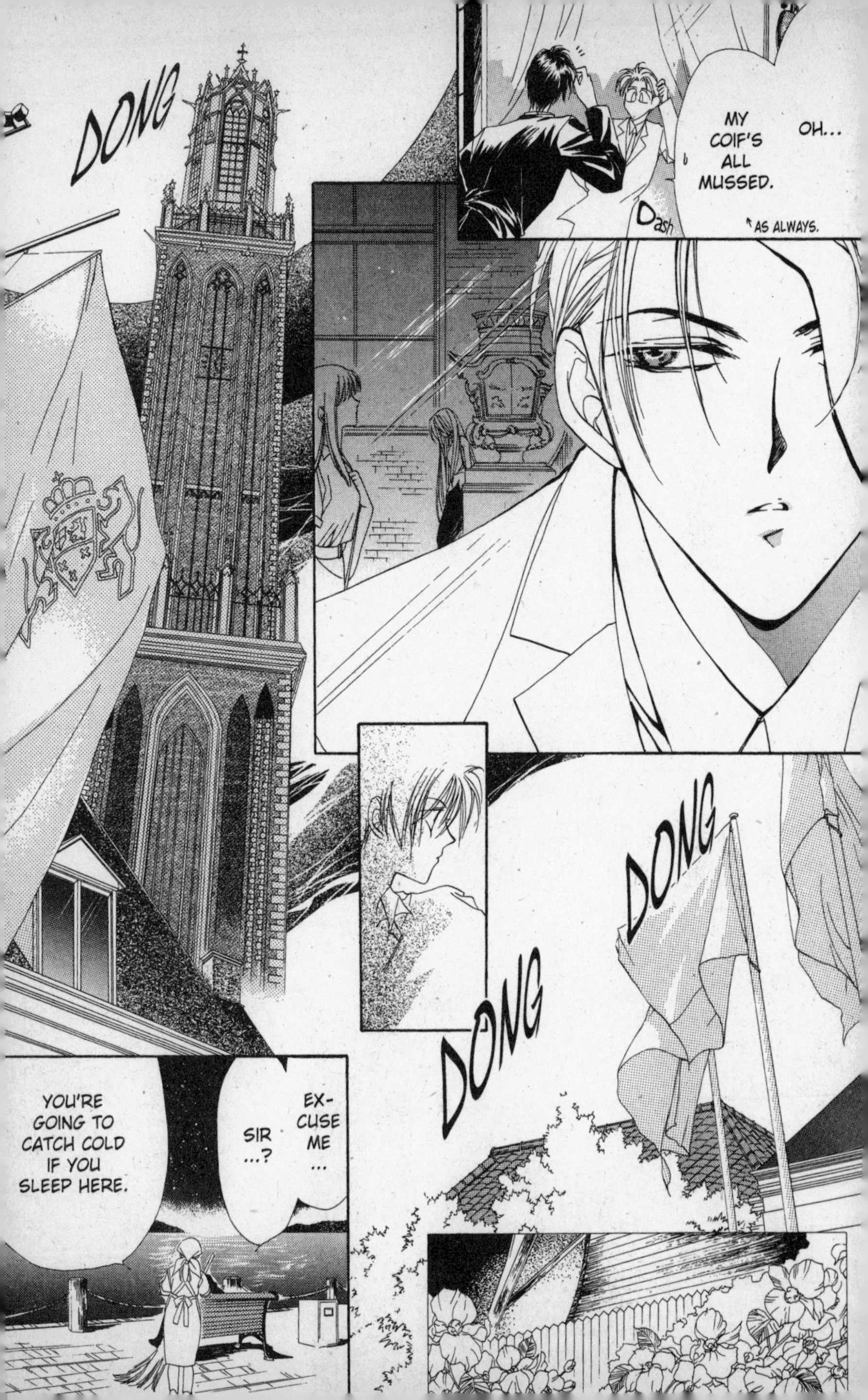

OH...
MY COIF'S ALL MUSSED.
Dash
AS ALWAYS.
DONG
DONG
DONG
EX-CUSE ME ...
SIR ...?
YOU'RE GOING TO CATCH COLD IF YOU SLEEP HERE.

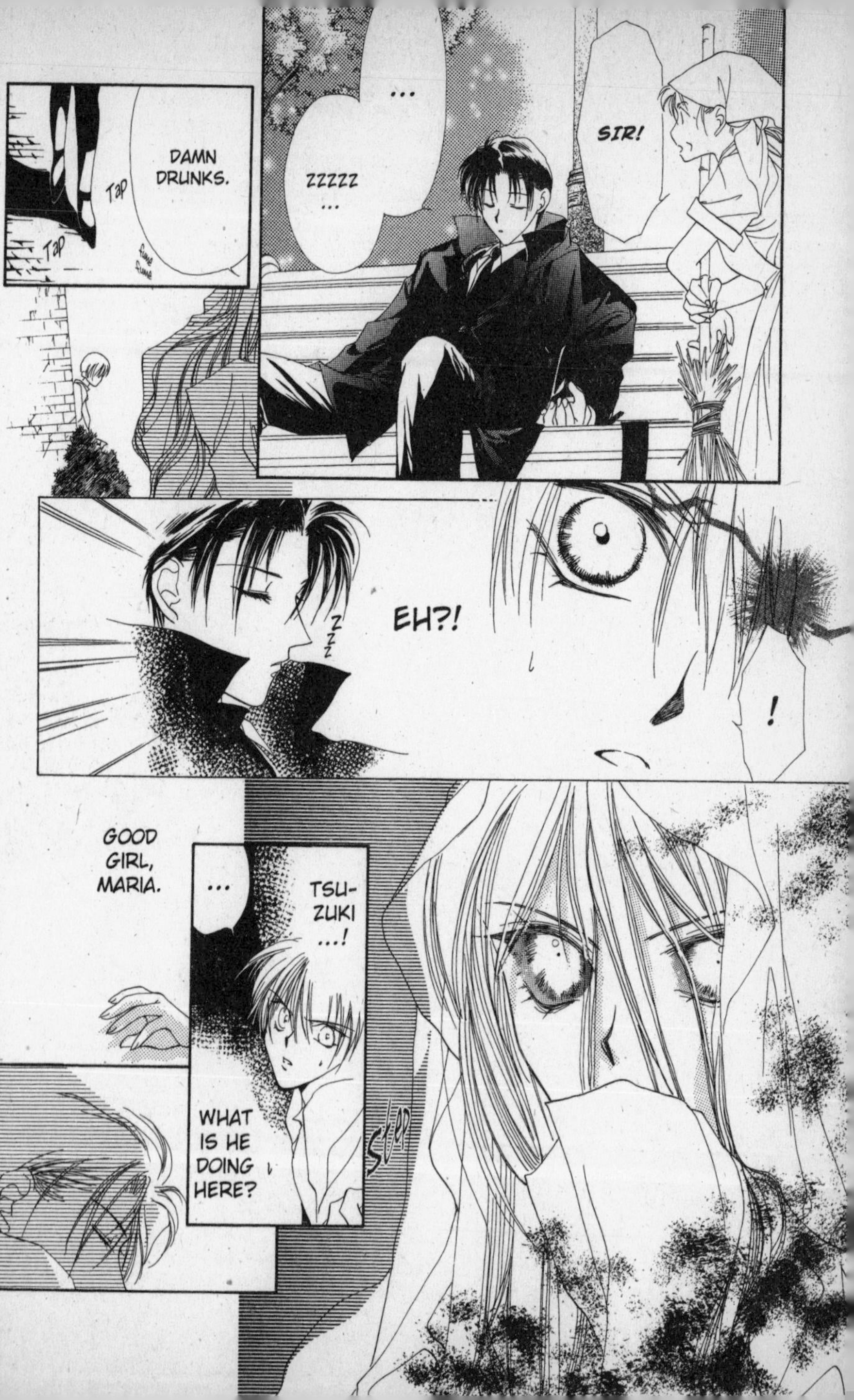
SIR!
...
ZZZZZ ...
DAMN DRUNKS.
Tap
Tap
fume fume
!
EH?!
ZZZ
TSU-ZUKI ...!
...
WHAT IS HE DOING HERE?
Step
GOOD GIRL, MARIA.

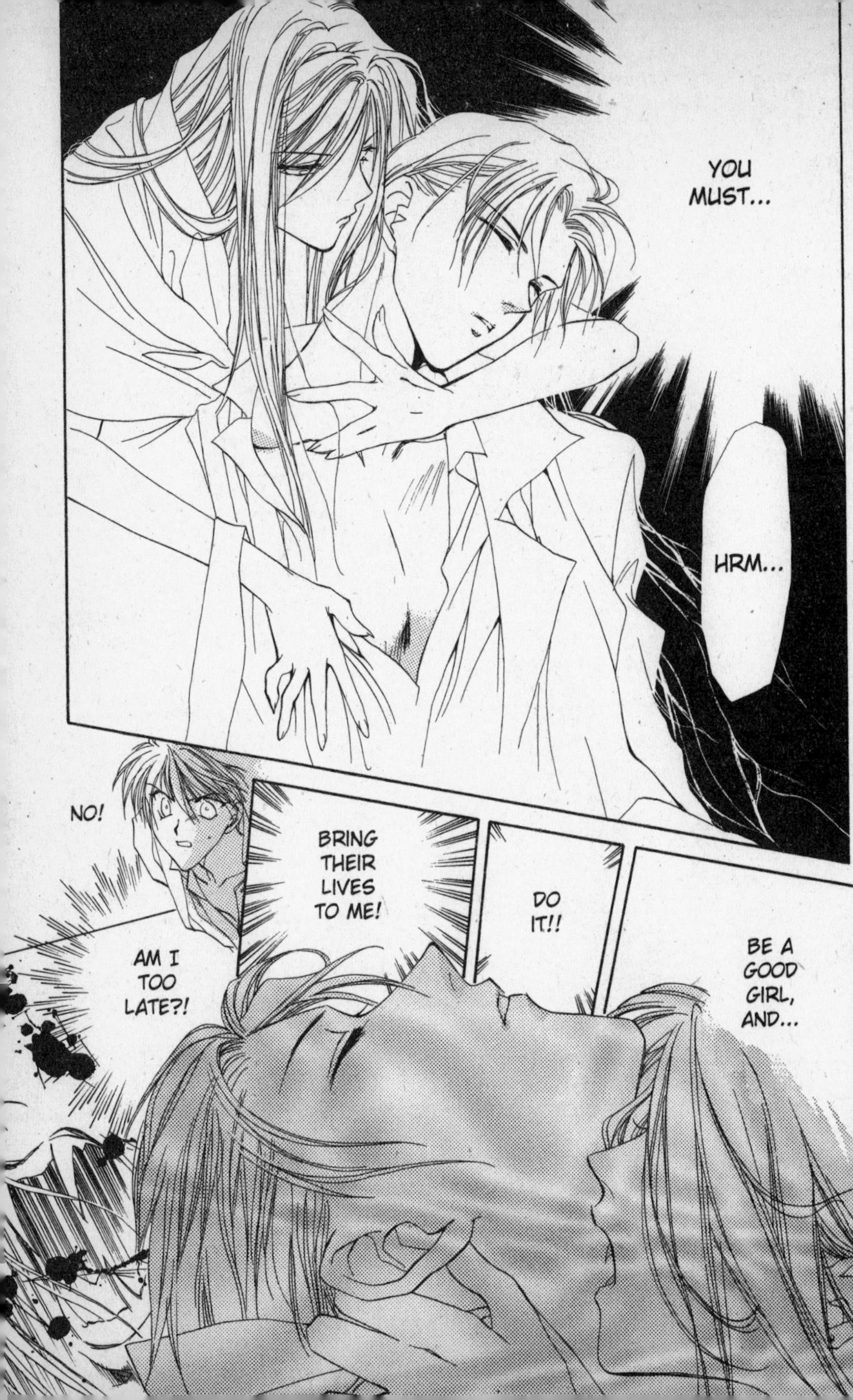
YOU MUST...
HRM...
BE A GOOD GIRL, AND...
DO IT!!
BRING THEIR LIVES TO ME!
NO!
AM I TOO LATE?!

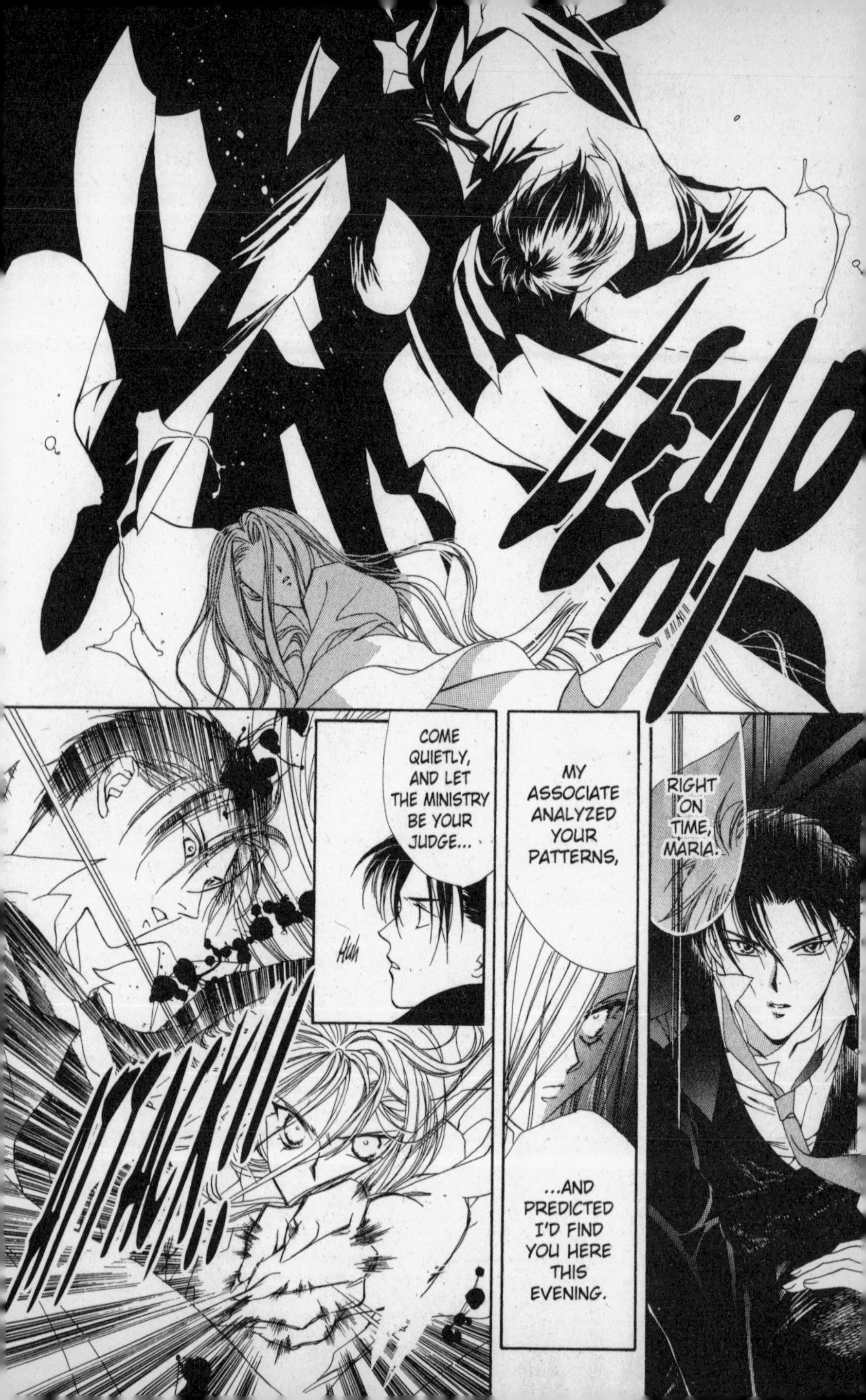
RIGHT ON TIME, MARIA.
MY ASSOCIATE ANALYZED YOUR PATTERNS,
...AND PREDICTED I'D FIND YOU HERE THIS EVENING.
COME QUIETLY, AND LET THE MINISTRY BE YOUR JUDGE...
Huh

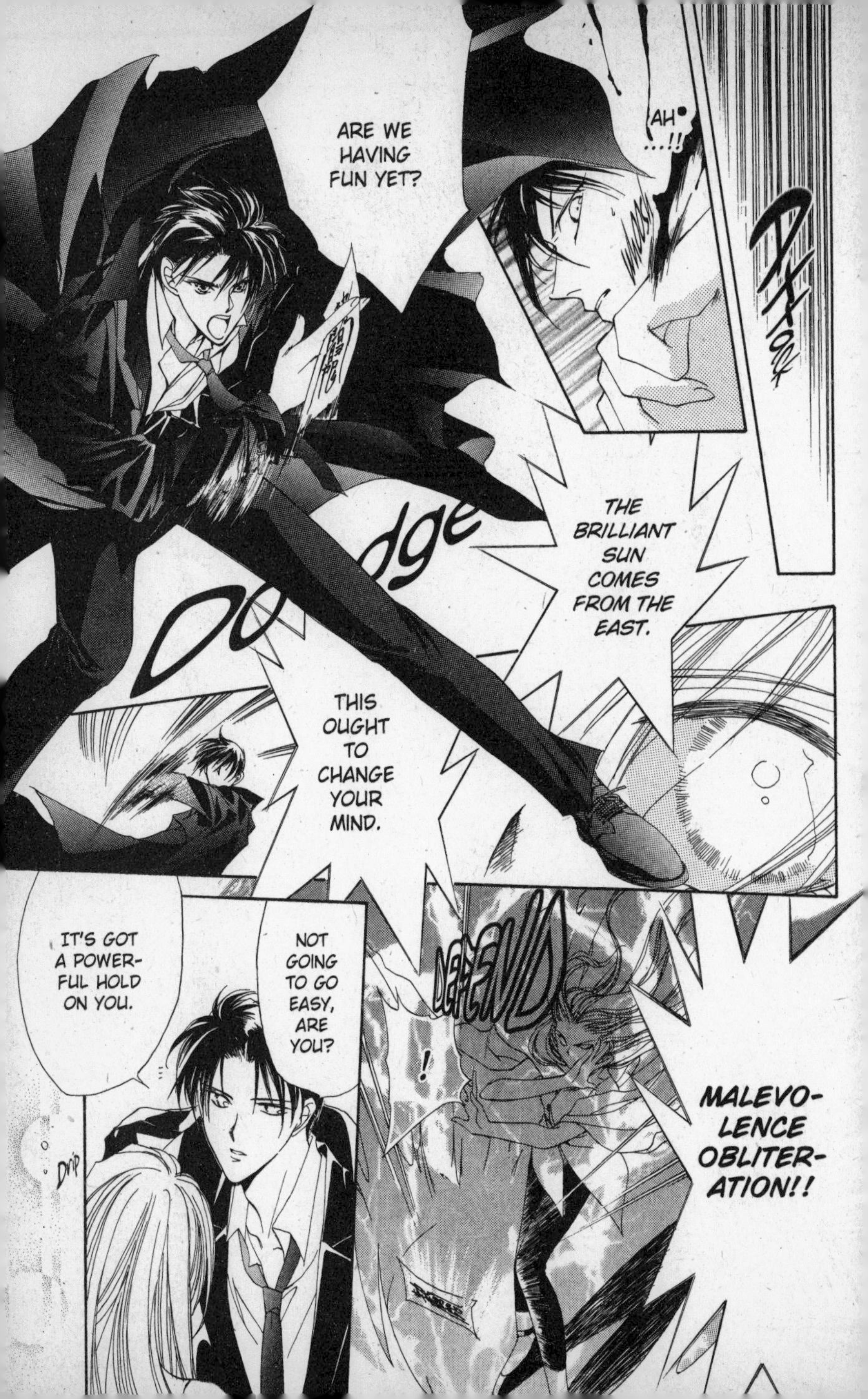
AH ...!!
ARE WE HAVING FUN YET?
THE BRILLIANT SUN COMES FROM THE EAST.
THIS OUGHT TO CHANGE YOUR MIND.
MALEVO-LENCE OBLITER-ATION!!
!
NOT GOING TO GO EASY, ARE YOU?
IT'S GOT A POWER-FUL HOLD ON YOU.
Drip

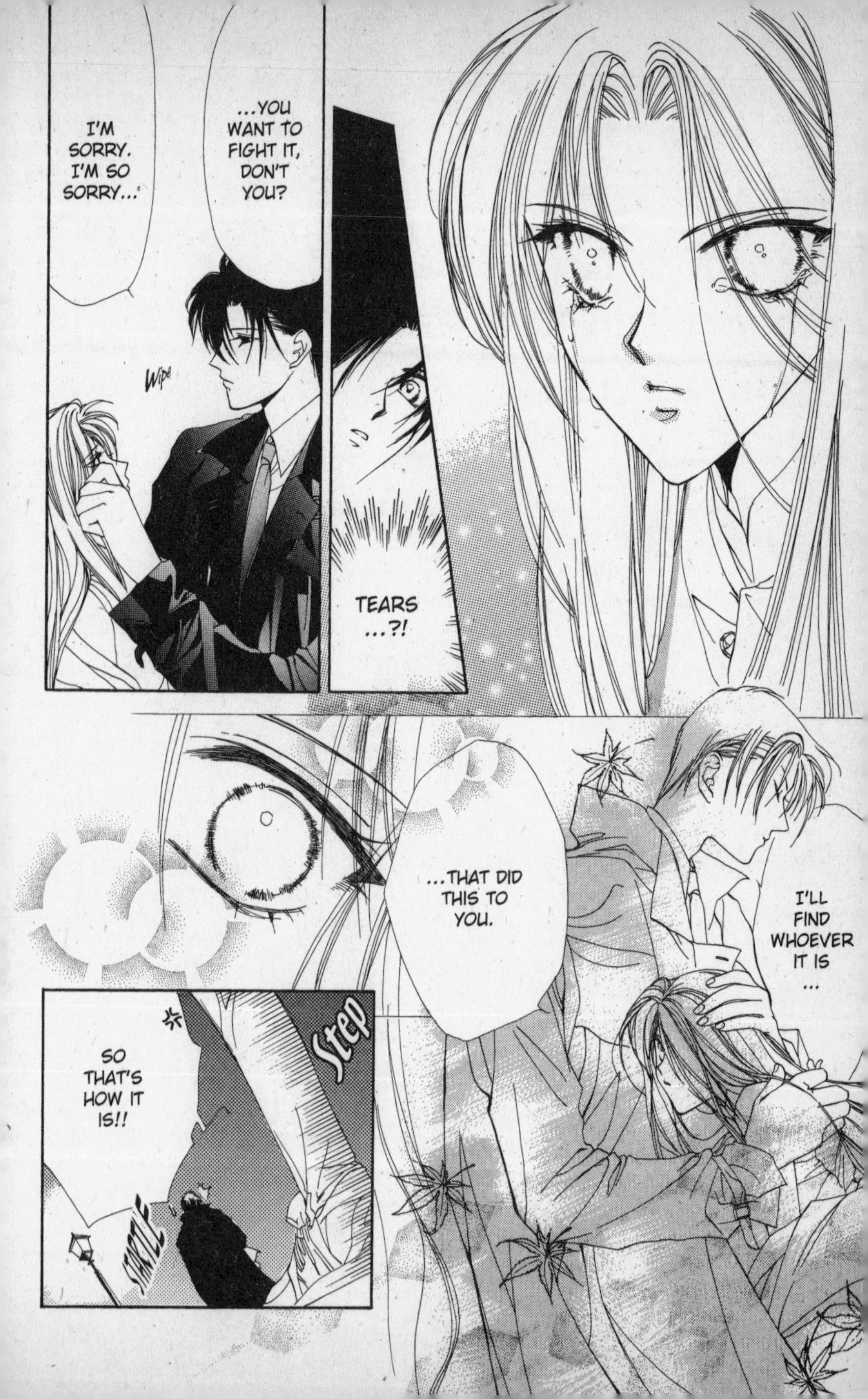
...YOU WANT TO FIGHT IT, DON'T YOU?
TEARS ...?!
I'M SORRY. I'M SO SORRY...
Wipe
I'LL FIND WHOEVER IT IS ...
...THAT DID THIS TO YOU.
Step
SO THAT'S HOW IT IS!!
STARTLE

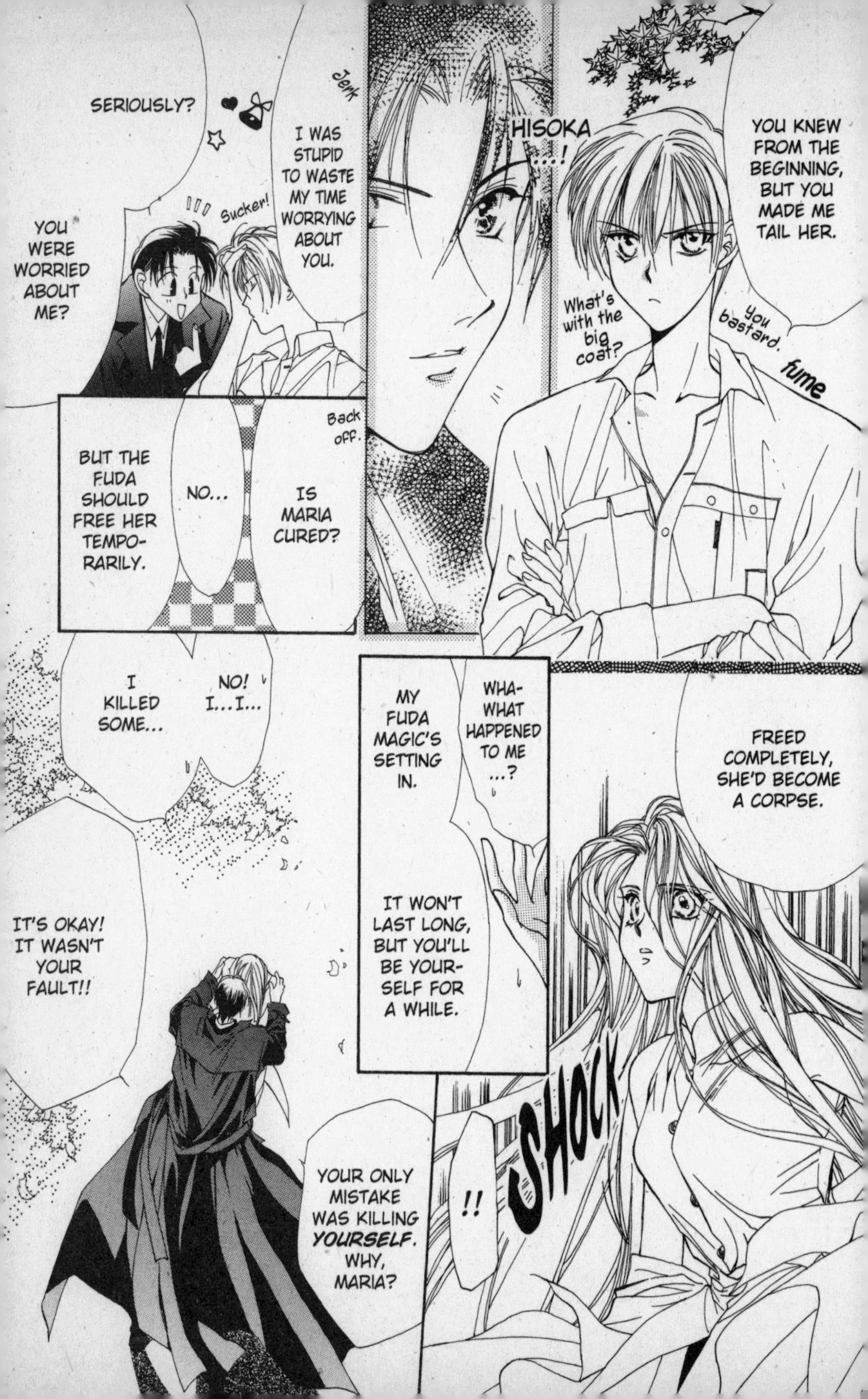
YOU KNEW FROM THE BEGINNING, BUT YOU MADE ME TAIL HER.
You bastard.
fume
What's with the big coat?
HISOKA ...!
Jerk
I WAS STUPID TO WASTE MY TIME WORRYING ABOUT YOU.
Sucker!
SERIOUSLY?
YOU WERE WORRIED ABOUT ME?
Back off.
IS MARIA CURED?
NO...
BUT THE FUDA SHOULD FREE HER TEMPORARILY.
FREED COMPLETELY, SHE'D BECOME A CORPSE.
SHOCK
!!
WHA-WHAT HAPPENED TO ME ...?
MY FUDA MAGIC'S SETTING IN.
IT WON'T LAST LONG, BUT YOU'LL BE YOURSELF FOR A WHILE.
NO! I...I...
I KILLED SOME...
IT'S OKAY! IT WASN'T YOUR FAULT!!
YOUR ONLY MISTAKE WAS KILLING *YOURSELF*. WHY, MARIA?

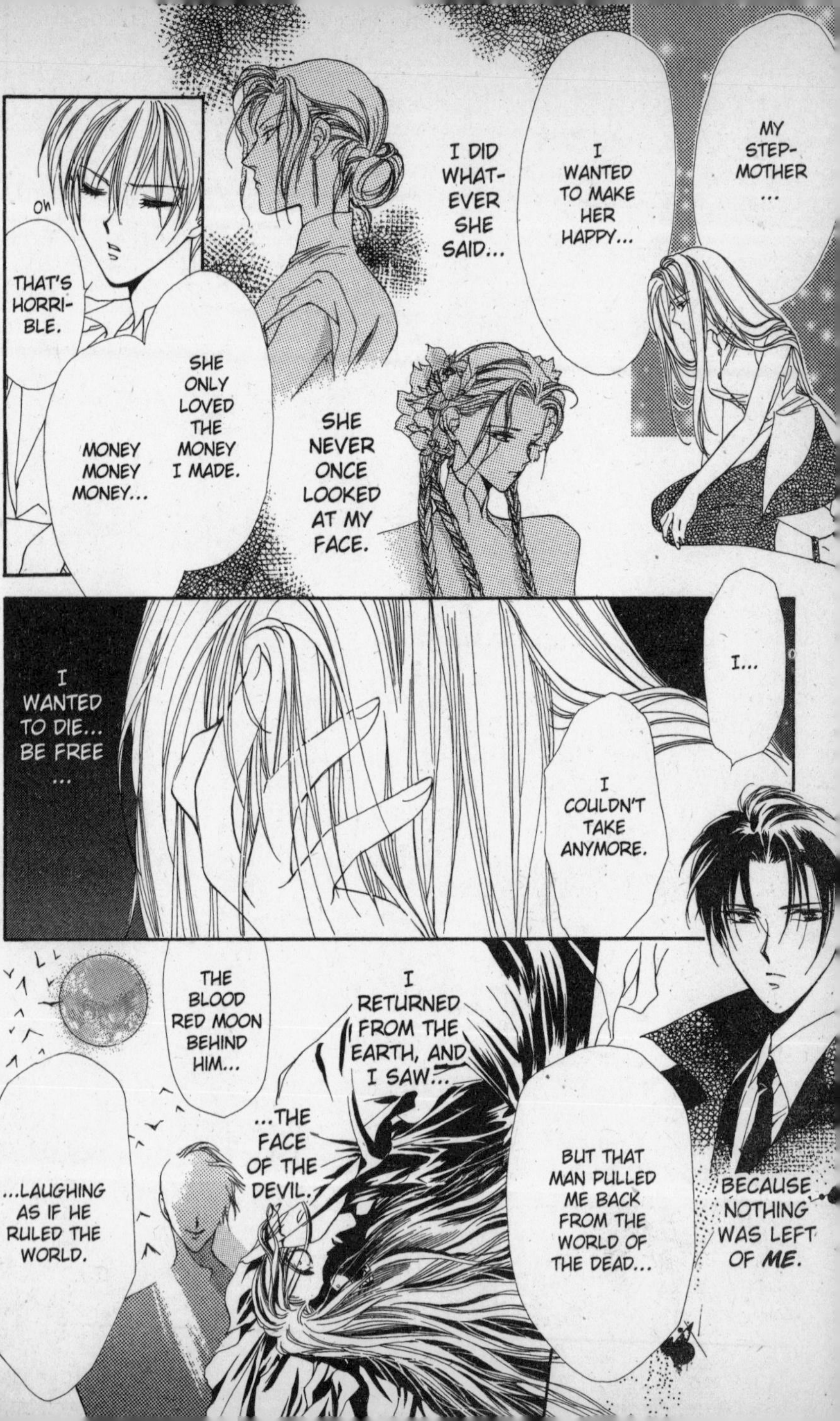
MY STEP-MOTHER...
I WANTED TO MAKE HER HAPPY...
I DID WHAT-EVER SHE SAID...
SHE NEVER ONCE LOOKED AT MY FACE.
SHE ONLY LOVED THE MONEY I MADE.
MONEY MONEY MONEY...
Oh
THAT'S HORRI-BLE.
I...
I COULDN'T TAKE ANYMORE.
I WANTED TO DIE... BE FREE...
BECAUSE NOTHING WAS LEFT OF *ME*.
BUT THAT MAN PULLED ME BACK FROM THE WORLD OF THE DEAD...
I RETURNED FROM THE EARTH, AND I SAW...
...THE FACE OF THE DEVIL.
THE BLOOD RED MOON BEHIND HIM...
...LAUGHING AS IF HE RULED THE WORLD.

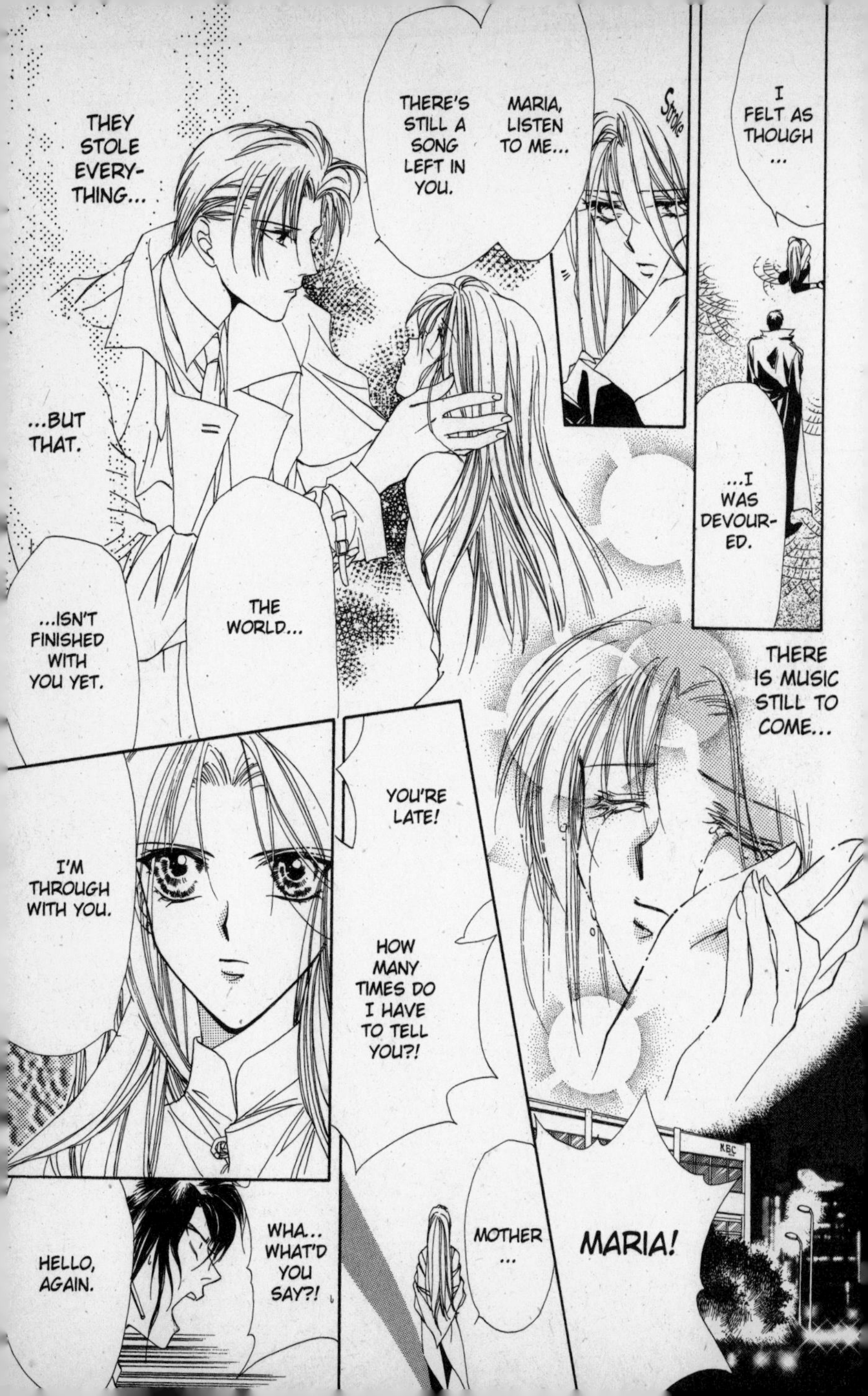
I FELT AS THOUGH ...
...I WAS DEVOUR-ED.
Stroke
MARIA, LISTEN TO ME...
THERE'S STILL A SONG LEFT IN YOU.
THEY STOLE EVERY-THING...
...BUT THAT.
THE WORLD...
...ISN'T FINISHED WITH YOU YET.
THERE IS MUSIC STILL TO COME...
MARIA!
MOTHER ...
KBC
YOU'RE LATE!
HOW MANY TIMES DO I HAVE TO TELL YOU?!
I'M THROUGH WITH YOU.
WHA... WHAT'D YOU SAY?!
HELLO, AGAIN.

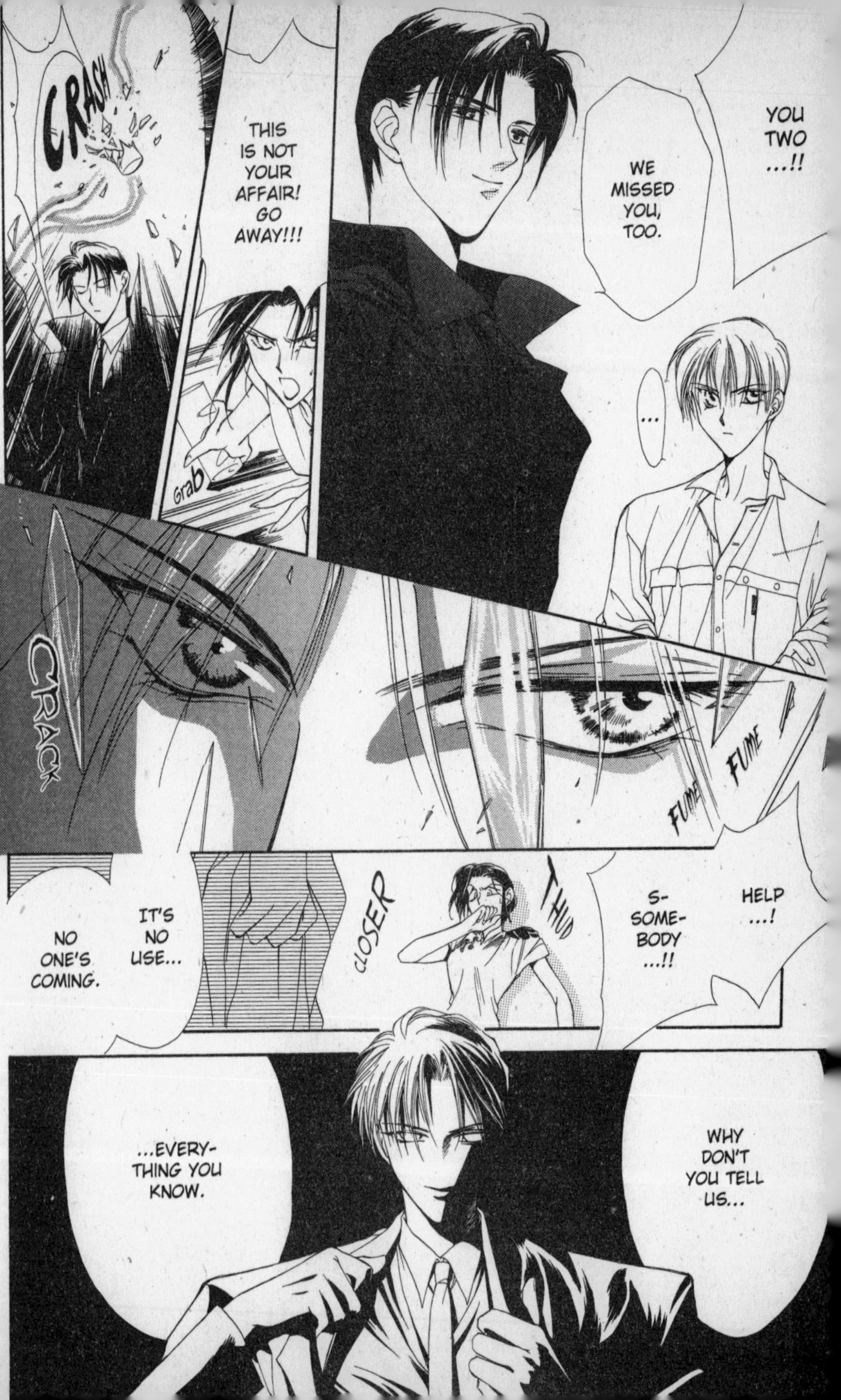

YOU TWO ...!!
WE MISSED YOU, TOO.
...
THIS IS NOT YOUR AFFAIR! GO AWAY!!!
Grab
CRASH
FUME
FUME
CRACK
HELP ...!
S-SOMEBODY ...!!
THUD
CLOSER
IT'S NO USE...
NO ONE'S COMING.
WHY DON'T YOU TELL US...
...EVERY-THING YOU KNOW.

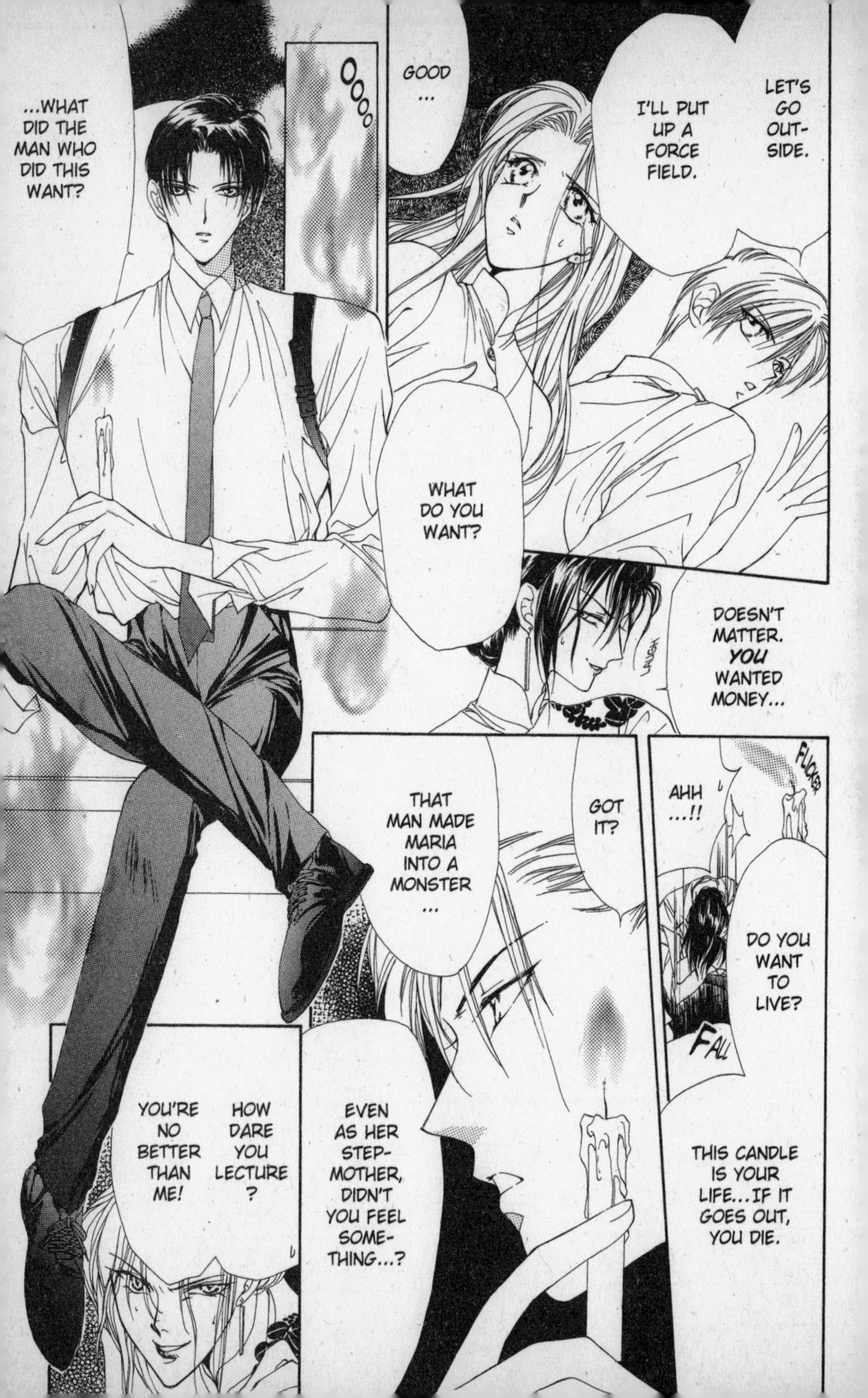
LET'S GO OUT-SIDE.
I'LL PUT UP A FORCE FIELD.
GOOD ...
OOOO
...WHAT DID THE MAN WHO DID THIS WANT?
WHAT DO YOU WANT?
DOESN'T MATTER. **YOU** WANTED MONEY...
LAUGH
FLICKER
AHH ...!!
DO YOU WANT TO LIVE?
FALL
GOT IT?
THAT MAN MADE MARIA INTO A MONSTER ...
THIS CANDLE IS YOUR LIFE...IF IT GOES OUT, YOU DIE.
EVEN AS HER STEP-MOTHER, DIDN'T YOU FEEL SOME-THING...?
HOW DARE YOU LECTURE ?
YOU'RE NO BETTER THAN ME!

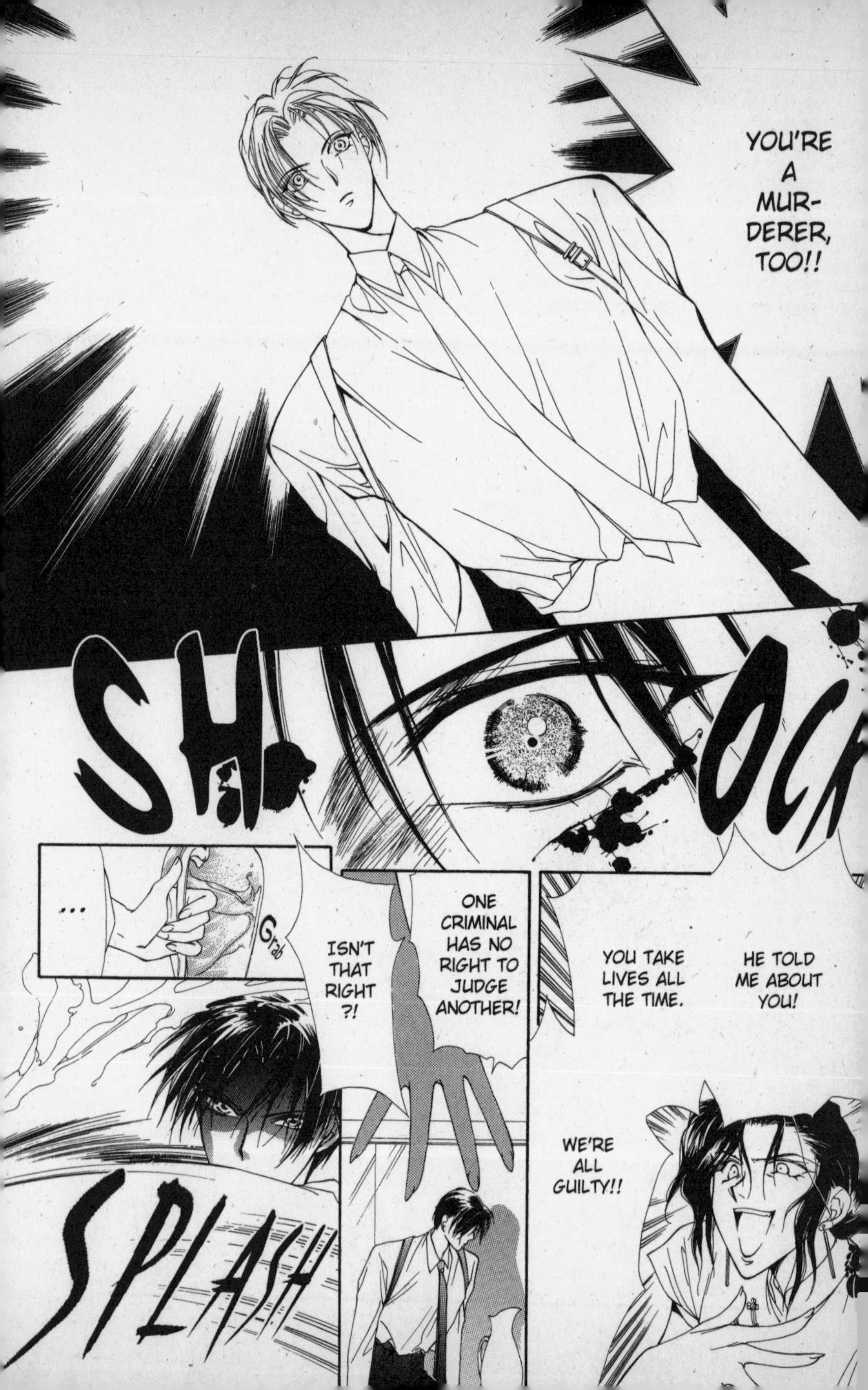
YOU'RE A MURDERER, TOO!!
SHOCK
HE TOLD ME ABOUT YOU!
YOU TAKE LIVES ALL THE TIME.
WE'RE ALL GUILTY!!
ONE CRIMINAL HAS NO RIGHT TO JUDGE ANOTHER!
ISN'T THAT RIGHT ?!
...
Grab
SPLASH

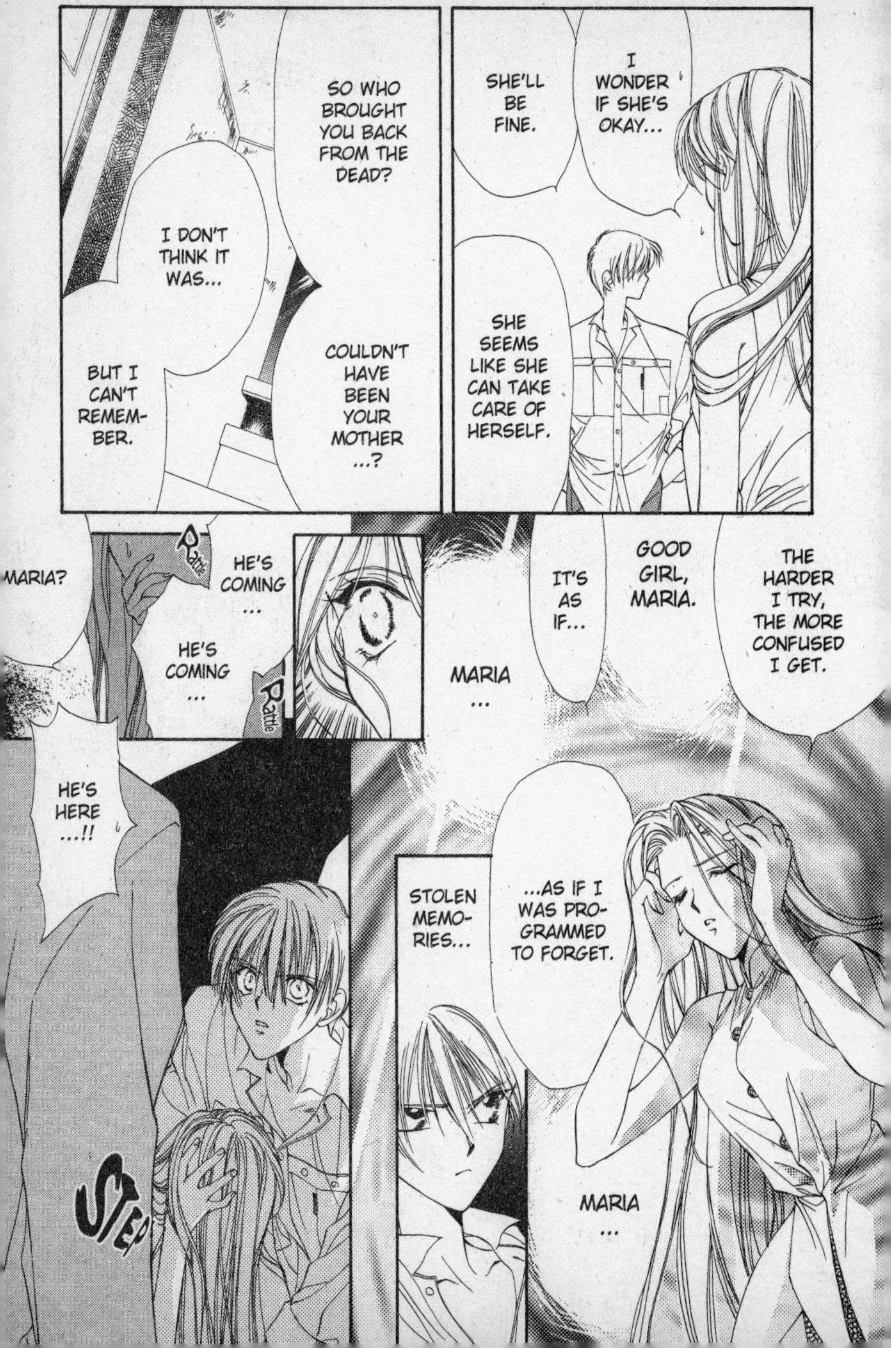

I WONDER IF SHE'S OKAY...
SHE'LL BE FINE.
SHE SEEMS LIKE SHE CAN TAKE CARE OF HERSELF.
SO WHO BROUGHT YOU BACK FROM THE DEAD?
COULDN'T HAVE BEEN YOUR MOTHER ...?
I DON'T THINK IT WAS...
BUT I CAN'T REMEMBER.
THE HARDER I TRY, THE MORE CONFUSED I GET.
GOOD GIRL, MARIA.
IT'S AS IF...
MARIA ...
Rattle
Rattle
HE'S COMING ...
HE'S COMING ...
MARIA?
...AS IF I WAS PROGRAMMED TO FORGET.
STOLEN MEMORIES...
MARIA ...
HE'S HERE ...!!
STEP

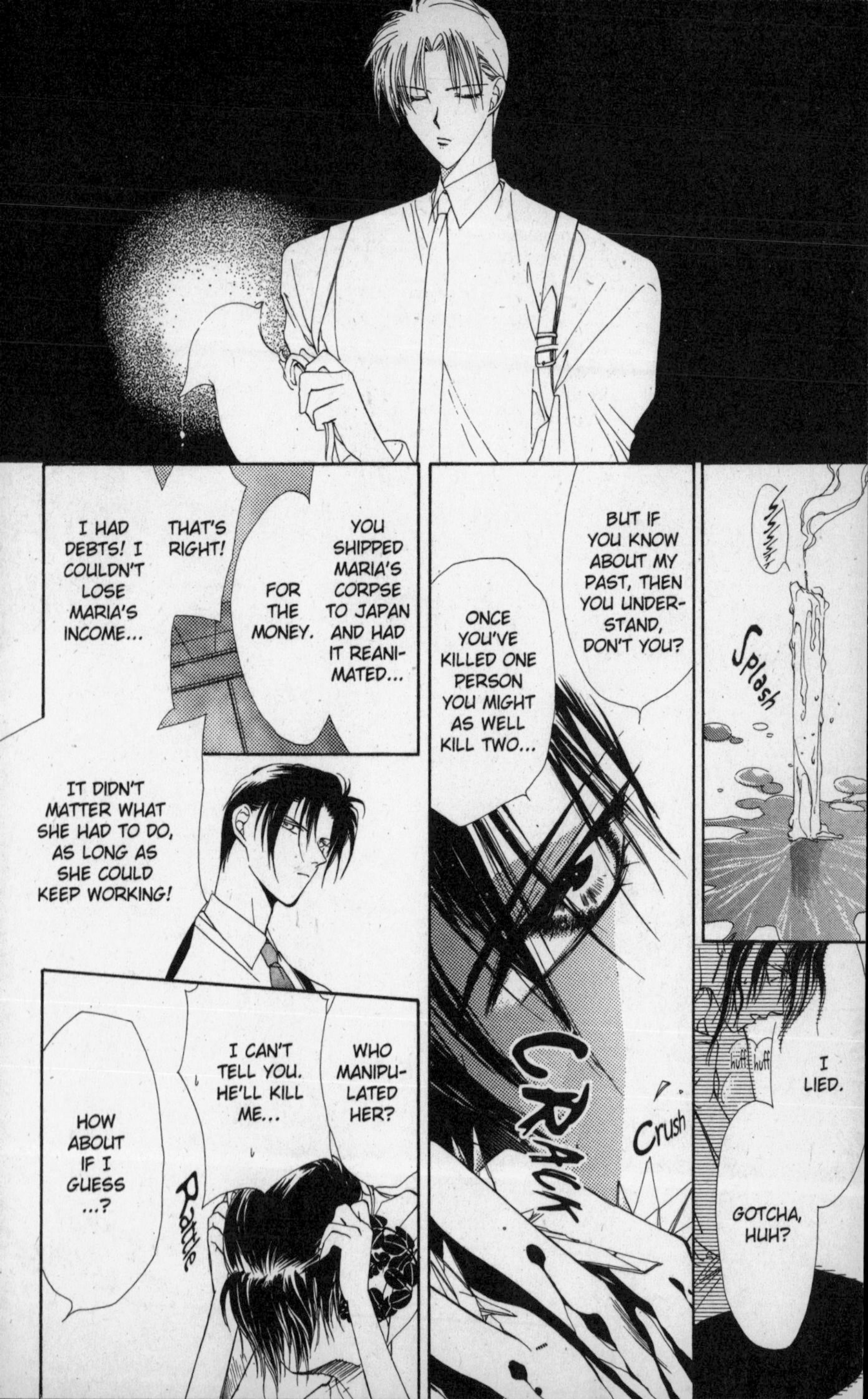

YOU SHIPPED MARIA'S CORPSE TO JAPAN AND HAD IT REANIMATED...
FOR THE MONEY.
THAT'S RIGHT!
I HAD DEBTS! I COULDN'T LOSE MARIA'S INCOME...
IT DIDN'T MATTER WHAT SHE HAD TO DO, AS LONG AS SHE COULD KEEP WORKING!
WHO MANIPULATED HER?
I CAN'T TELL YOU. HE'LL KILL ME...
HOW ABOUT IF I GUESS ...?
Rattle
BUT IF YOU KNOW ABOUT MY PAST, THEN YOU UNDERSTAND, DON'T YOU?
ONCE YOU'VE KILLED ONE PERSON YOU MIGHT AS WELL KILL TWO...
CRACK
Crush
Splash
huff huff
I LIED.
GOTCHA, HUH?

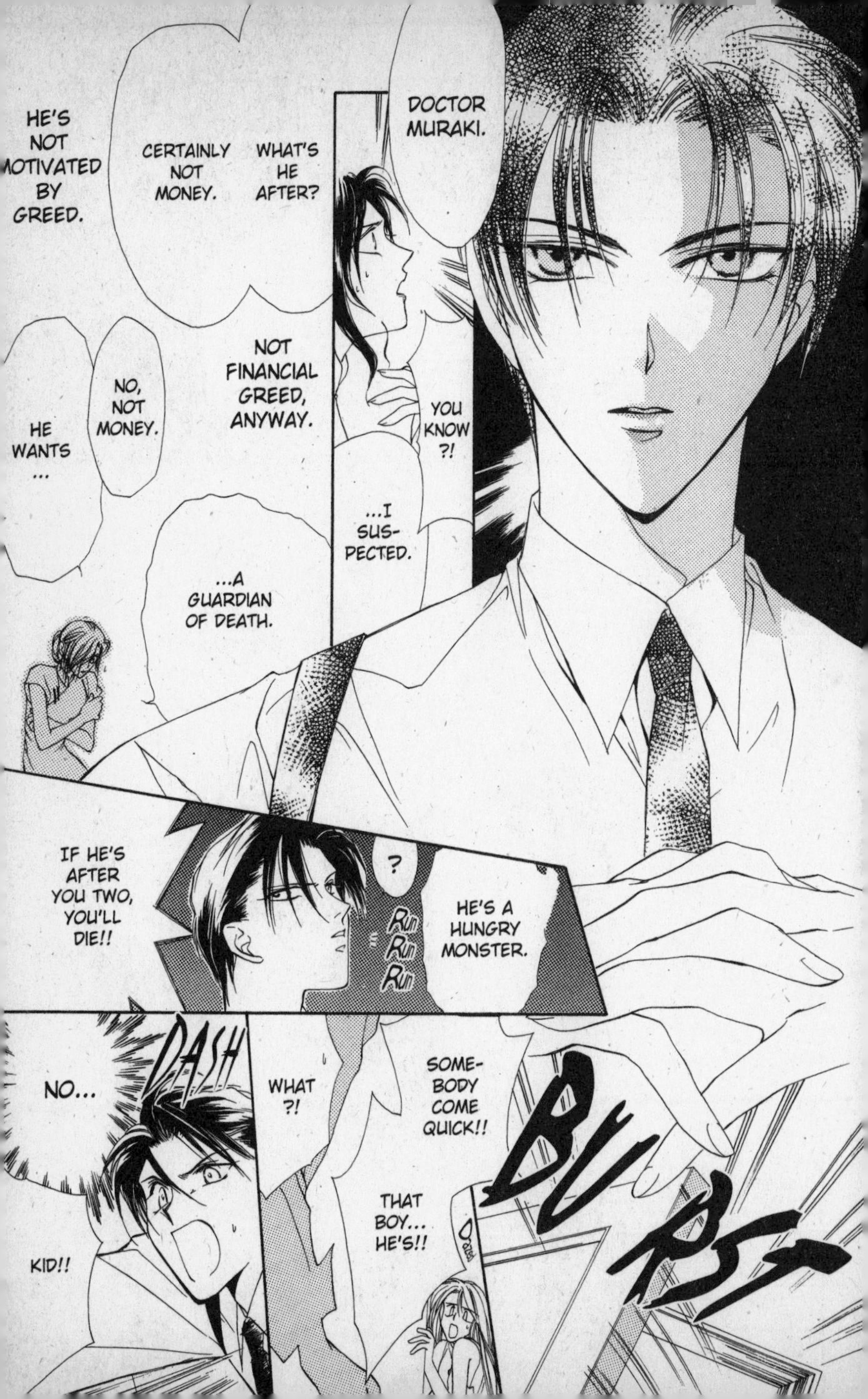
DOCTOR MURAKI.
YOU KNOW?!
...I SUSPECTED.
WHAT'S HE AFTER?
CERTAINLY NOT MONEY.
HE'S NOT MOTIVATED BY GREED.
NOT FINANCIAL GREED, ANYWAY.
NO, NOT MONEY.
HE WANTS...
...A GUARDIAN OF DEATH.
HE'S A HUNGRY MONSTER.
?
Run Run Run
IF HE'S AFTER YOU TWO, YOU'LL DIE!!
BURST
SOMEBODY COME QUICK!!
THAT BOY... HE'S!!
Dash
WHAT?!
DASH
NO...
KID!!

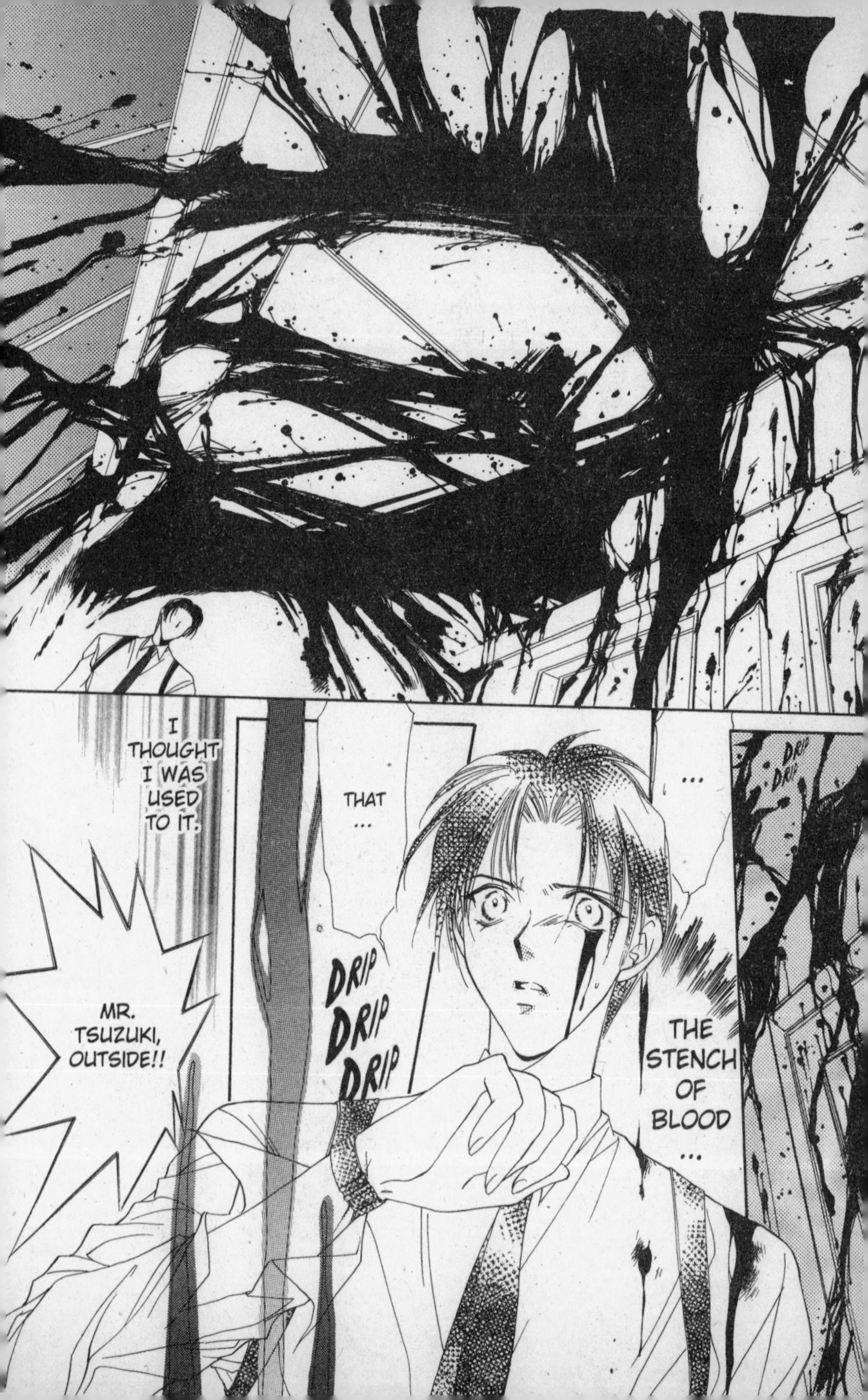
DRIP DRIP
...
THAT ...
I THOUGHT I WAS USED TO IT.
THE STENCH OF BLOOD ...
DRIP DRIP DRIP
MR. TSUZUKI, OUTSIDE!!

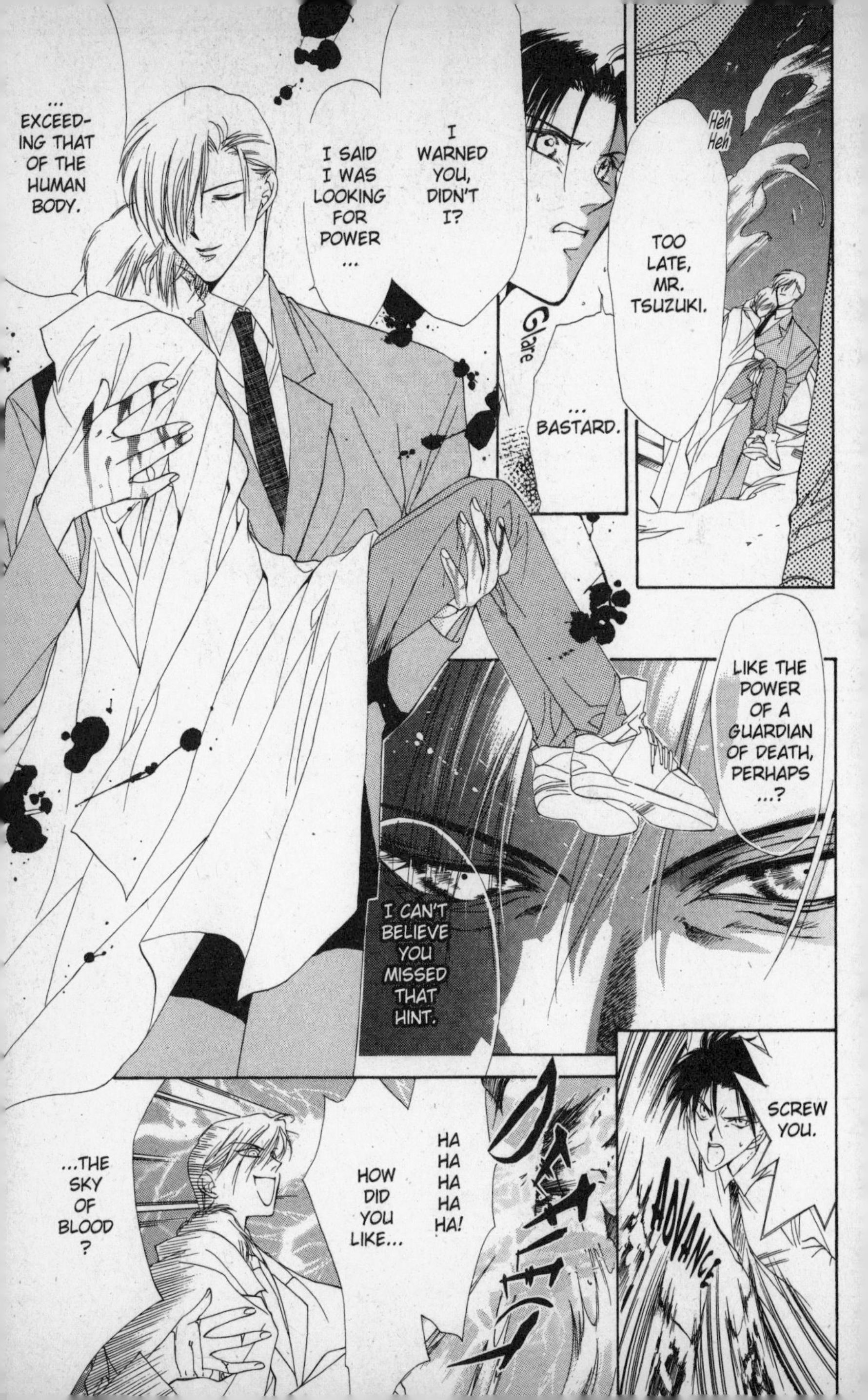
Heh Heh
TOO LATE, MR. TSUZUKI.
Glare
... BASTARD.
I WARNED YOU, DIDN'T I?
I SAID I WAS LOOKING FOR POWER ...
... EXCEEDING THAT OF THE HUMAN BODY.
LIKE THE POWER OF A GUARDIAN OF DEATH, PERHAPS ...?
I CAN'T BELIEVE YOU MISSED THAT HINT.
SCREW YOU.
ADVANCE
HA HA HA HA HA!
HOW DID YOU LIKE...
...THE SKY OF BLOOD ?

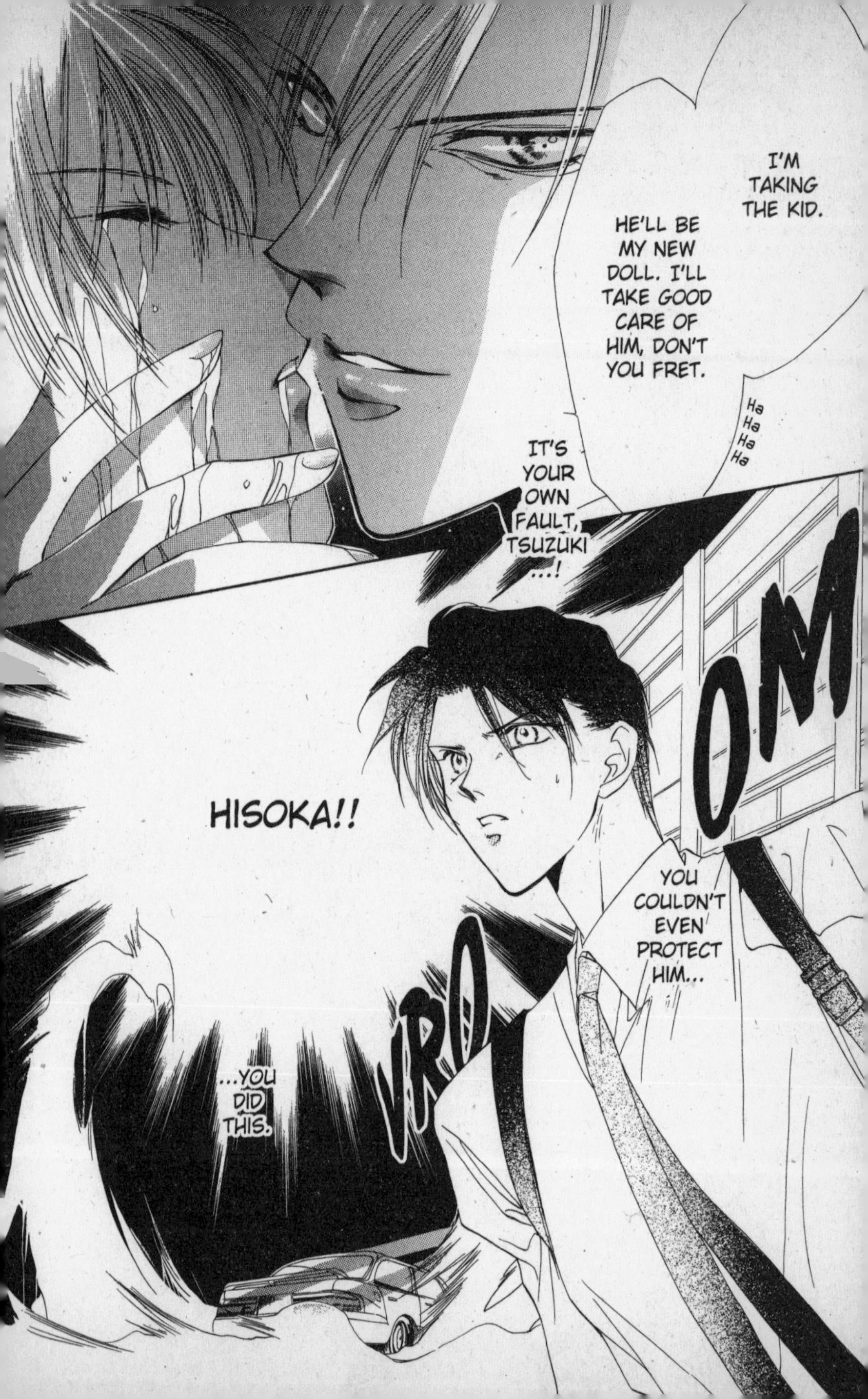
I'M TAKING THE KID.
HE'LL BE MY NEW DOLL. I'LL TAKE GOOD CARE OF HIM, DON'T YOU FRET.
Ha Ha Ha Ha
IT'S YOUR OWN FAULT, TSUZUKI ...!
OM
YOU COULDN'T EVEN PROTECT HIM...
HISOKA!!
VRO
...YOU DID THIS.

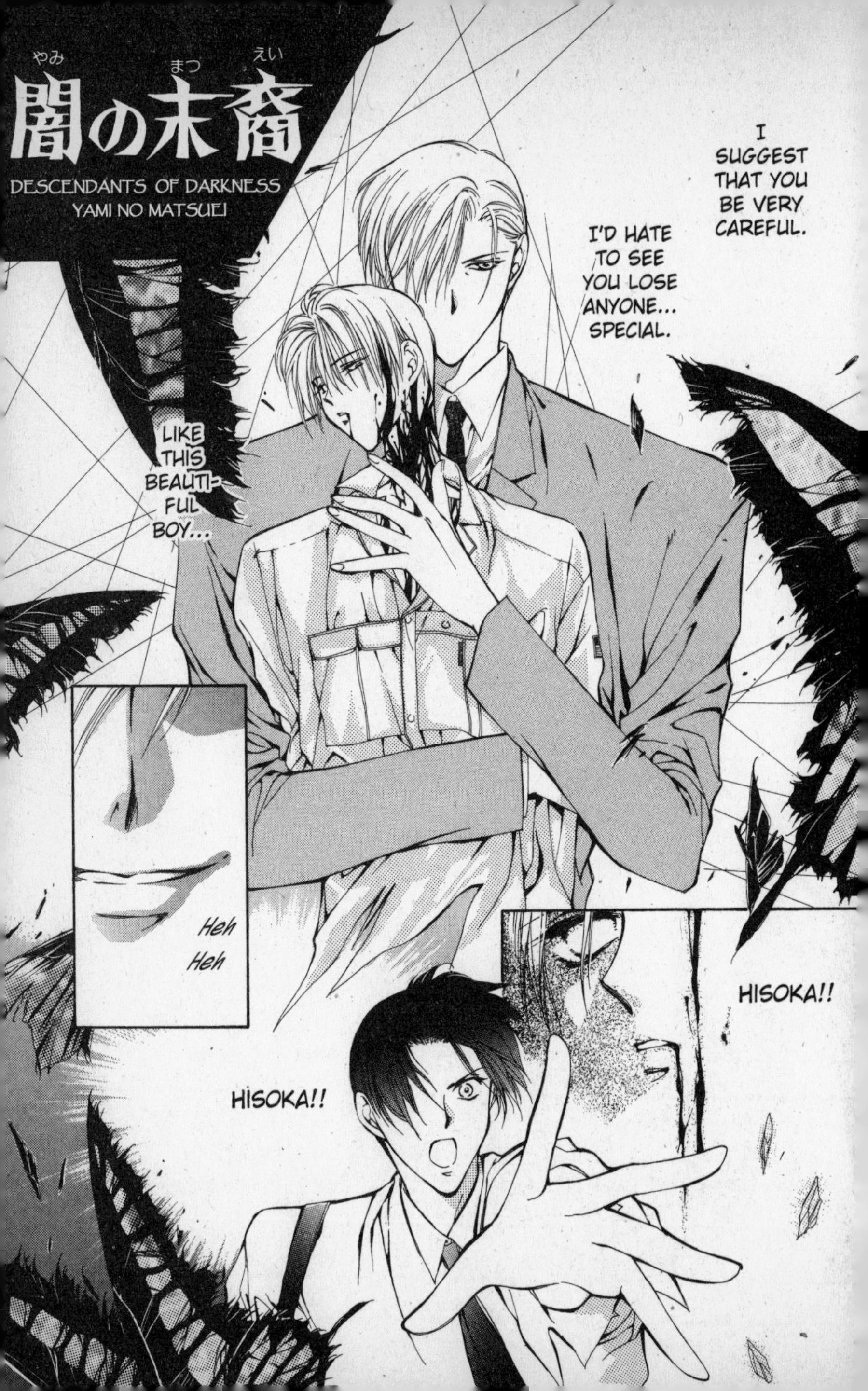
やみ まつ えい
闇の末裔
DESCENDANTS OF DARKNESS
YAMI NO MATSUEI
I SUGGEST THAT YOU BE VERY CAREFUL.
I'D HATE TO SEE YOU LOSE ANYONE... SPECIAL.
LIKE THIS BEAUTI-FUL BOY...
Heh Heh
HISOKA!!
HISOKA!!

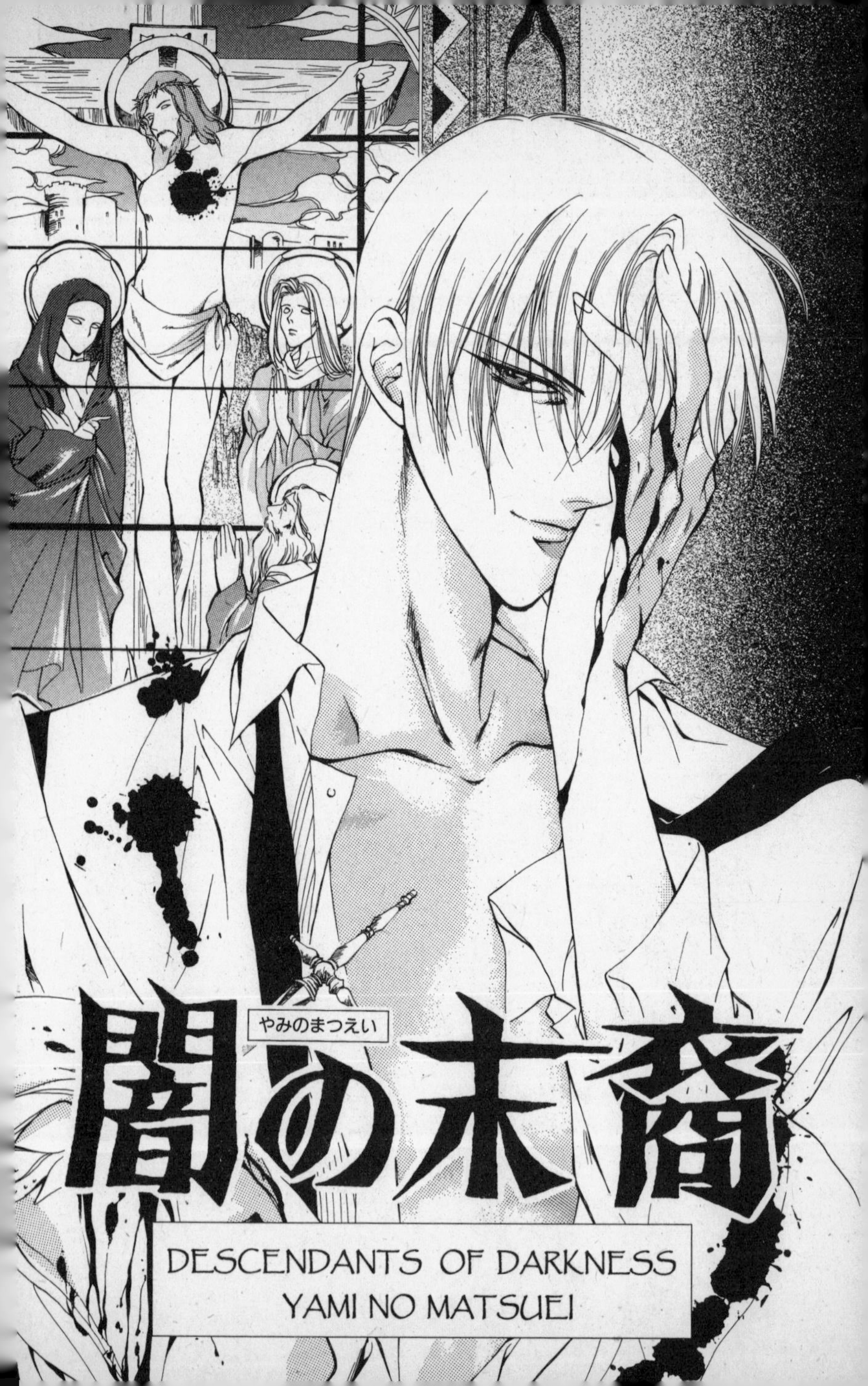
やみのまつえい
闇の末裔
DESCENDANTS OF DARKNESS
YAMI NO MATSUEI

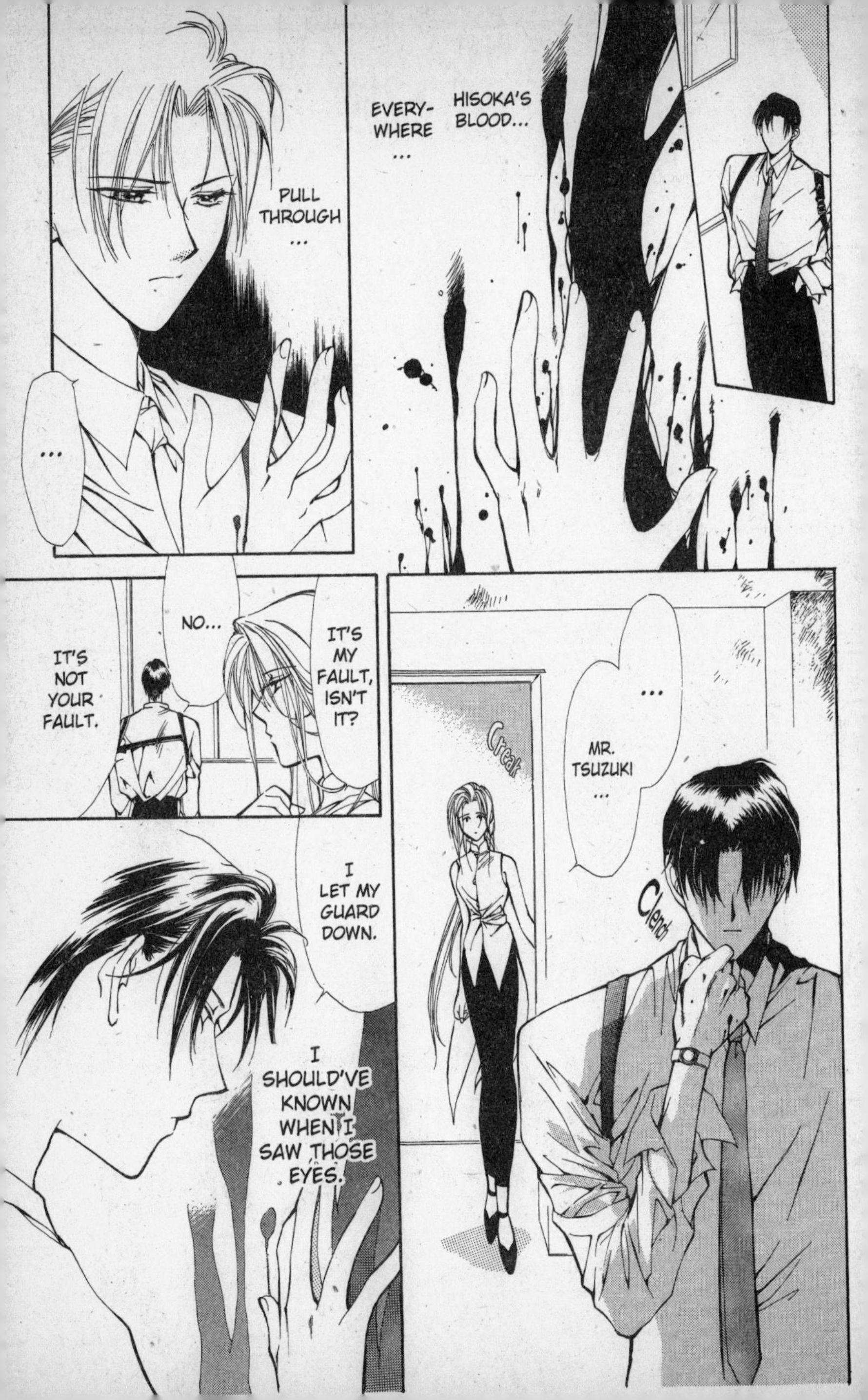
HISOKA'S BLOOD...
EVERY-WHERE ...
PULL THROUGH ...
...
... MR. TSUZUKI ...
Creak
Clench
IT'S MY FAULT, ISN'T IT?
NO...
IT'S NOT YOUR FAULT.
I LET MY GUARD DOWN.
I SHOULD'VE KNOWN WHEN I SAW THOSE EYES.

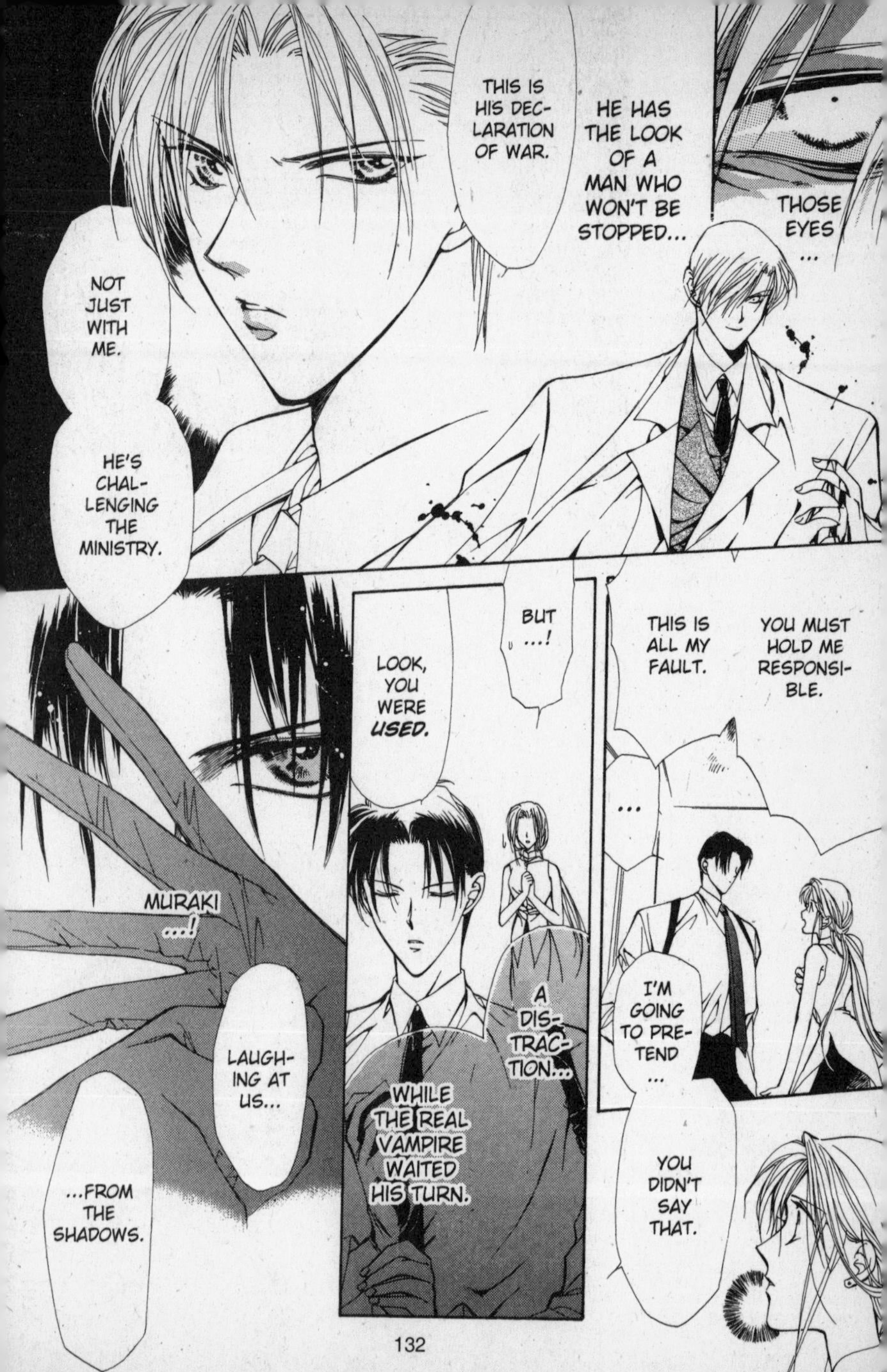
THOSE EYES...
HE HAS THE LOOK OF A MAN WHO WON'T BE STOPPED...
THIS IS HIS DECLARATION OF WAR.
NOT JUST WITH ME.
HE'S CHALLENGING THE MINISTRY.
YOU MUST HOLD ME RESPONSIBLE.
THIS IS ALL MY FAULT.
...
I'M GOING TO PRETEND...
YOU DIDN'T SAY THAT.
BUT...!
LOOK, YOU WERE *USED.*
A DISTRACTION...
WHILE THE REAL VAMPIRE WAITED HIS TURN.
MURAKI...!
LAUGHING AT US...
...FROM THE SHADOWS.

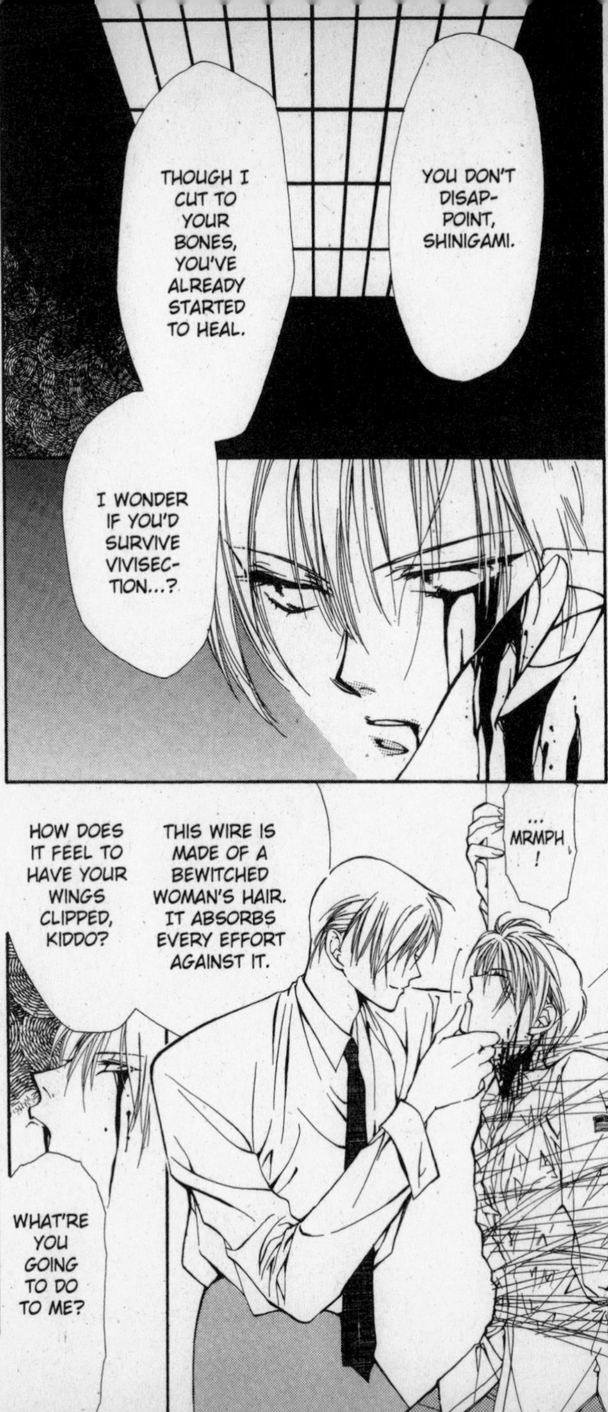

YOU DON'T DISAP-POINT, SHINIGAMI.
THOUGH I CUT TO YOUR BONES, YOU'VE ALREADY STARTED TO HEAL.
I WONDER IF YOU'D SURVIVE VIVISEC-TION...?
...MRMPH!
THIS WIRE IS MADE OF A BEWITCHED WOMAN'S HAIR. IT ABSORBS EVERY EFFORT AGAINST IT.
HOW DOES IT FEEL TO HAVE YOUR WINGS CLIPPED, KIDDO?
WHAT'RE YOU GOING TO DO TO ME?


Doctor Muraki is a completely different character now than he was when I first created him. First, his hair changed from black to white. Tsuzuki wears all black, so I thought I'd better put the doctor in white! For contrast, right? But that was just a superficial change, the most significant change was in his personality. Originally, he had a dark personality as well as dark hair. He was a loner, and as old as moss on a stone. (He's in his 30s now!) I kept making alterations until I settled on the strange Muraki we know today.

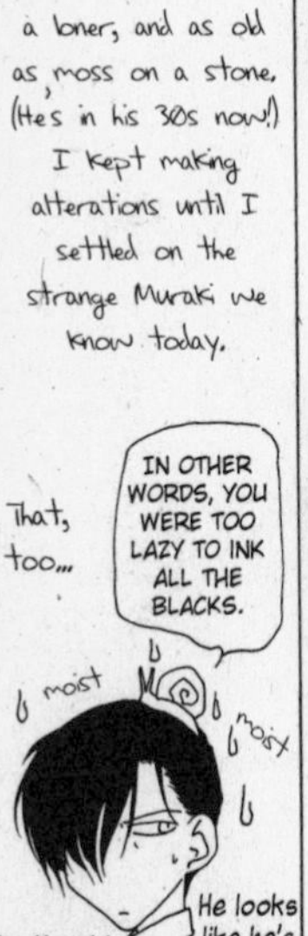

IN OTHER WORDS, YOU WERE TOO LAZY TO INK ALL THE BLACKS.
That, too...
moist
moist
He looks like he's moldy...
The Muraki Prototype

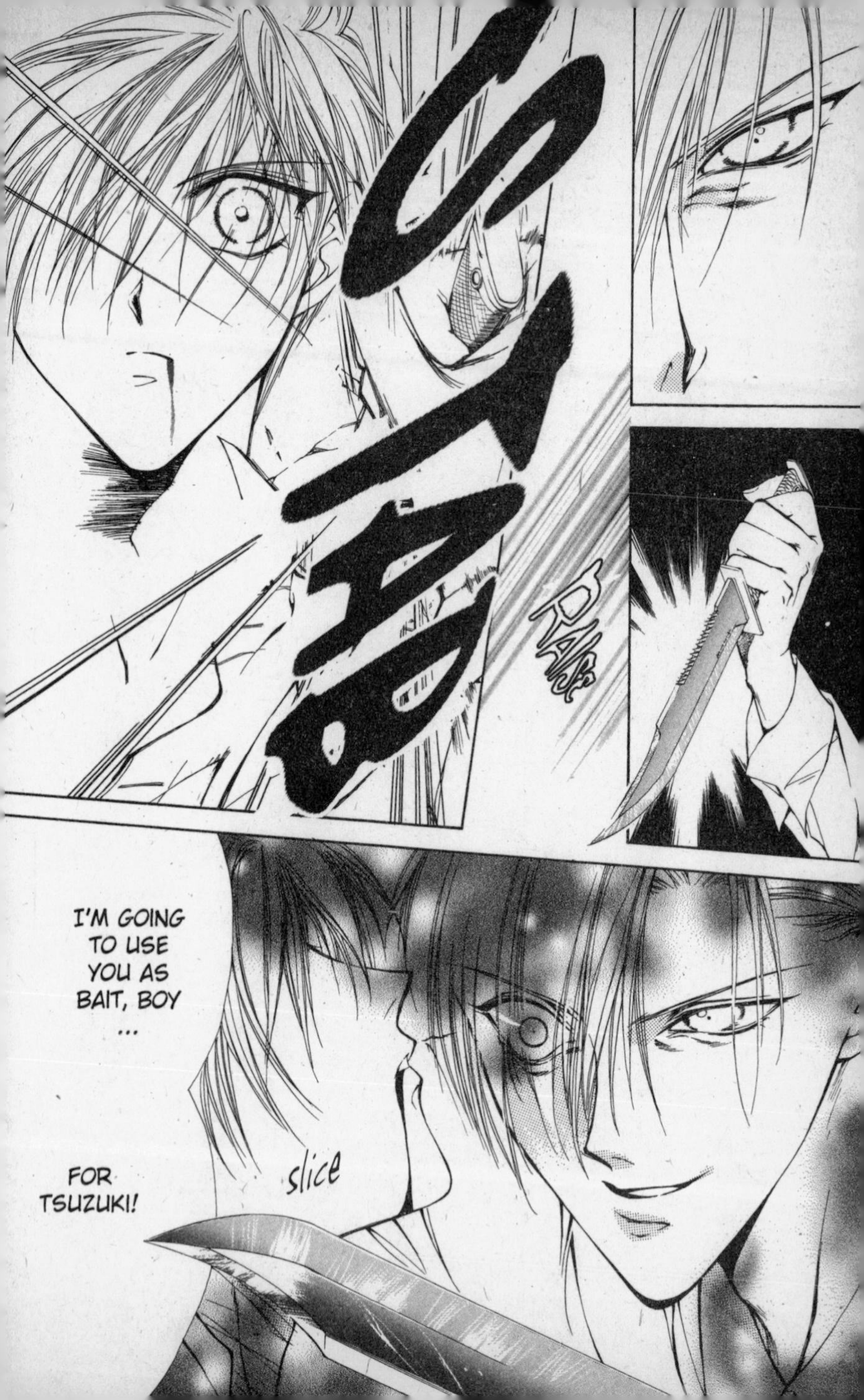
RAISE
I'M GOING TO USE YOU AS BAIT, BOY ...
slice
FOR TSUZUKI!

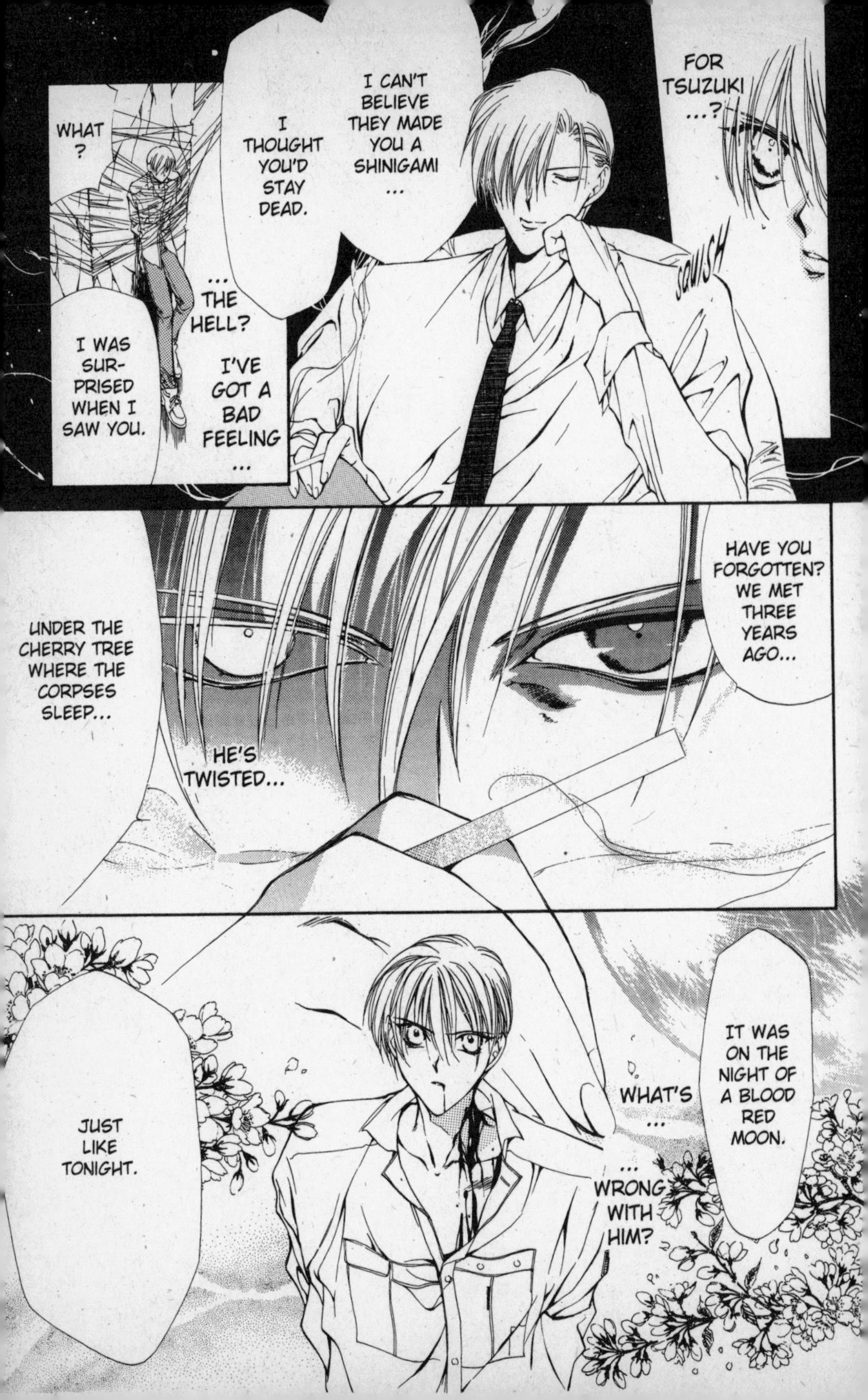
FOR TSUZUKI ...?
SQUISH
I CAN'T BELIEVE THEY MADE YOU A SHINIGAMI ...
I THOUGHT YOU'D STAY DEAD.
WHAT ?
... THE HELL?
I'VE GOT A BAD FEELING ...
I WAS SUR-PRISED WHEN I SAW YOU.
HAVE YOU FORGOTTEN? WE MET THREE YEARS AGO...
HE'S TWISTED...
UNDER THE CHERRY TREE WHERE THE CORPSES SLEEP...
IT WAS ON THE NIGHT OF A BLOOD RED MOON.
WHAT'S ...
... WRONG WITH HIM?
JUST LIKE TONIGHT.

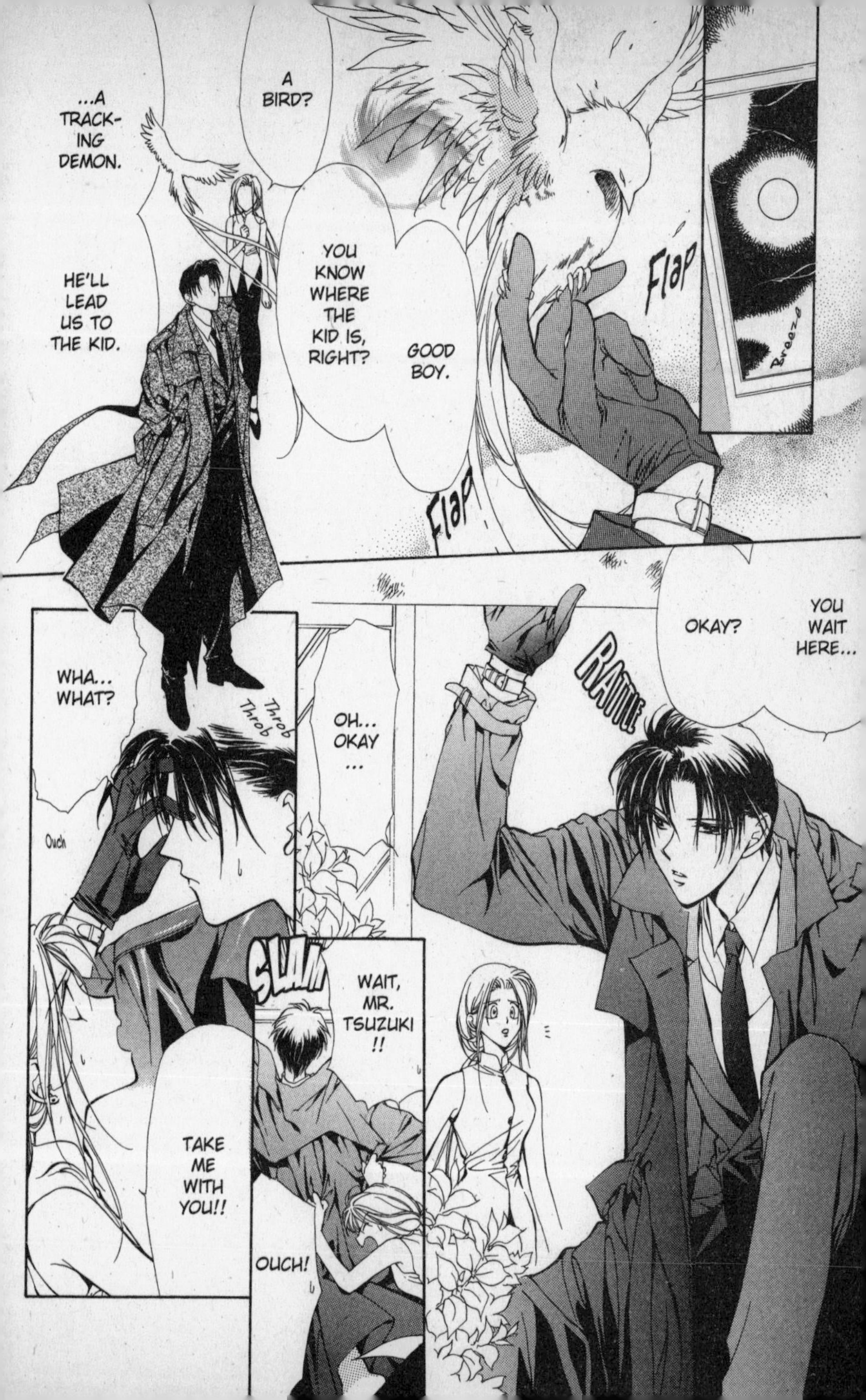
Flap
Breeze
A BIRD?
...A TRACKING DEMON.
HE'LL LEAD US TO THE KID.
YOU KNOW WHERE THE KID IS, RIGHT?
GOOD BOY.
Flap
YOU WAIT HERE...
OKAY?
RATTLE
OH... OKAY...
SLAM
WAIT, MR. TSUZUKI!!
OUCH!
WHA... WHAT?
Throb Throb
Ouch
TAKE ME WITH YOU!!

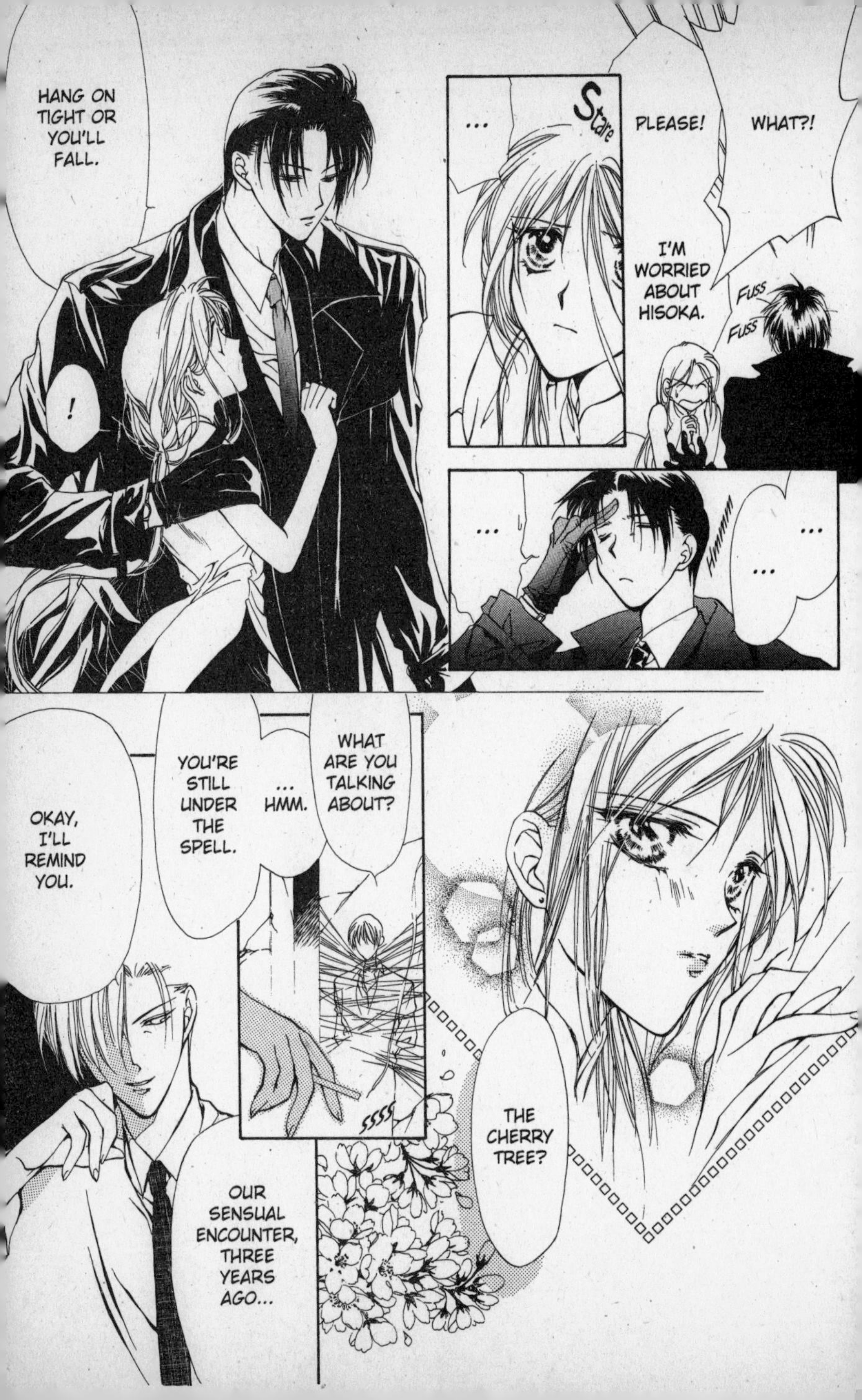
WHAT?!
PLEASE!
Stare
...
I'M WORRIED ABOUT HISOKA.
Fuss Fuss
... ...
Hmmm
...
HANG ON TIGHT OR YOU'LL FALL.
!
THE CHERRY TREE?
WHAT ARE YOU TALKING ABOUT?
... HMM.
YOU'RE STILL UNDER THE SPELL.
SSSS
OKAY, I'LL REMIND YOU.
OUR SENSUAL ENCOUNTER, THREE YEARS AGO...

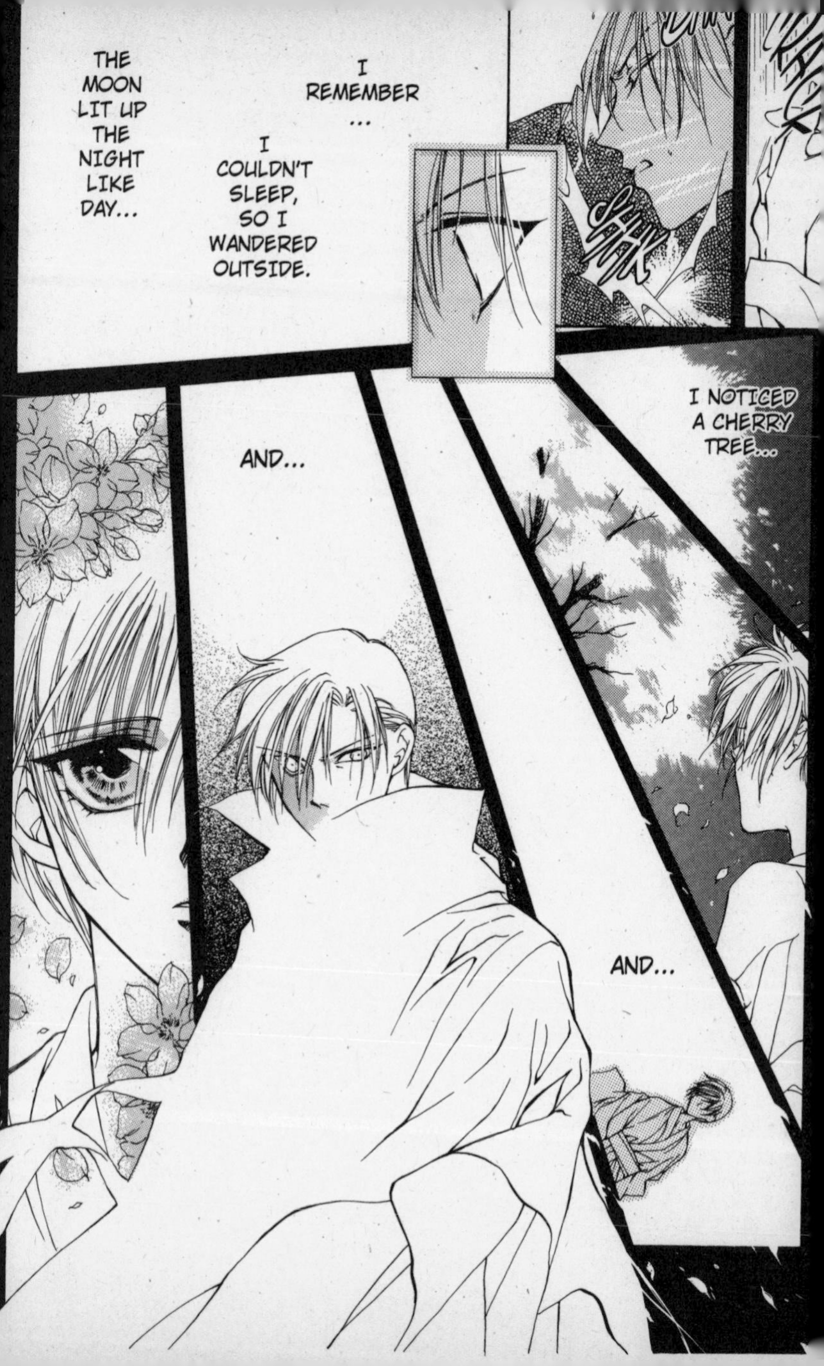
SHK
I REMEMBER ...
I COULDN'T SLEEP, SO I WANDERED OUTSIDE.
THE MOON LIT UP THE NIGHT LIKE DAY...
I NOTICED A CHERRY TREE...
AND...
AND...

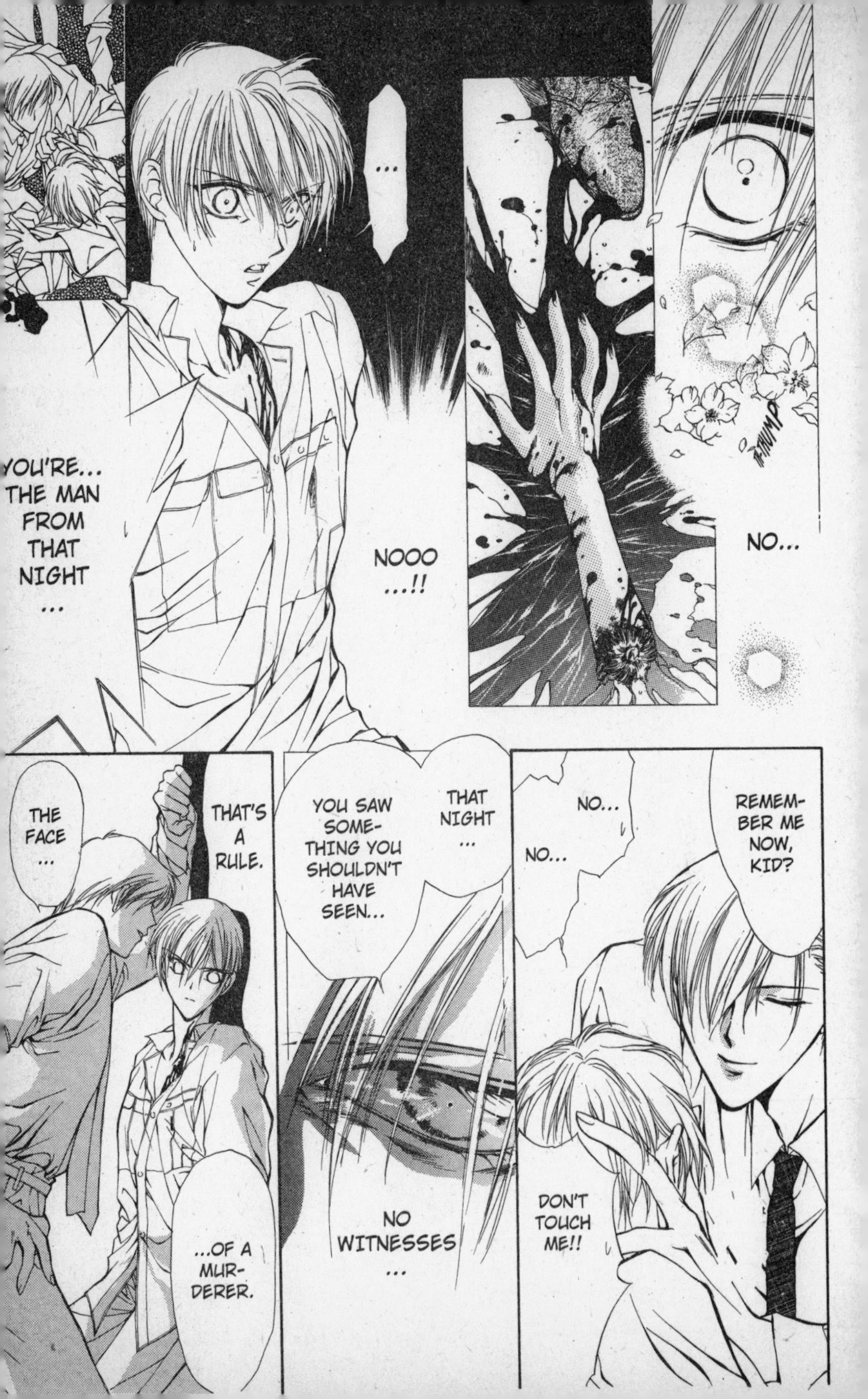
THUMP
NO...
NOOO...!!
!
...
YOU'RE... THE MAN FROM THAT NIGHT...
REMEMBER ME NOW, KID?
NO...
NO...
DON'T TOUCH ME!!
THAT NIGHT...
YOU SAW SOMETHING YOU SHOULDN'T HAVE SEEN...
NO WITNESSES...
THAT'S A RULE.
THE FACE...
...OF A MURDERER.

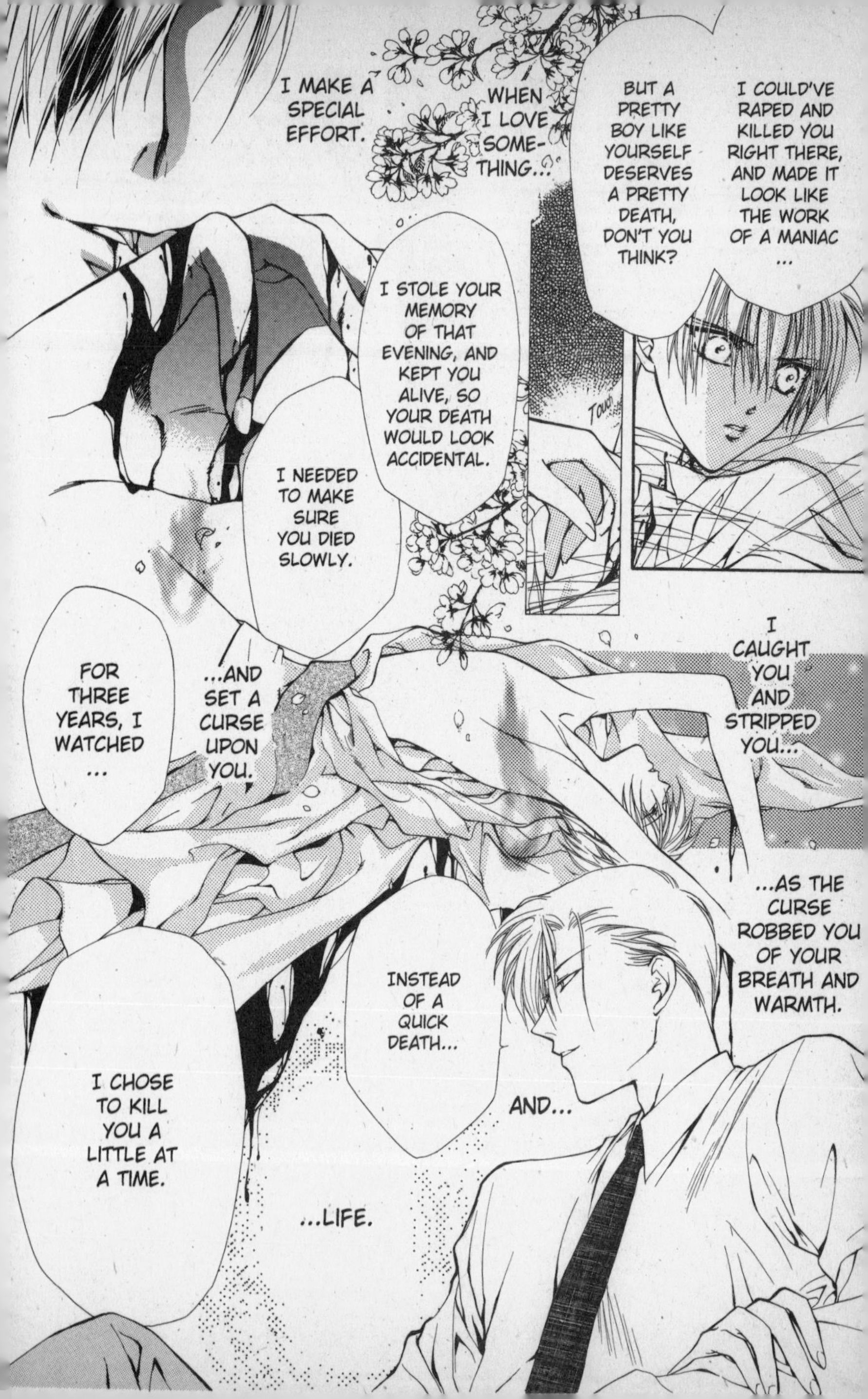
I COULD'VE RAPED AND KILLED YOU RIGHT THERE, AND MADE IT LOOK LIKE THE WORK OF A MANIAC ...
BUT A PRETTY BOY LIKE YOURSELF DESERVES A PRETTY DEATH, DON'T YOU THINK?
Touch
WHEN I LOVE SOME-THING...
I MAKE A SPECIAL EFFORT.
I STOLE YOUR MEMORY OF THAT EVENING, AND KEPT YOU ALIVE, SO YOUR DEATH WOULD LOOK ACCIDENTAL.
I NEEDED TO MAKE SURE YOU DIED SLOWLY.
I CAUGHT YOU AND STRIPPED YOU...
...AND SET A CURSE UPON YOU.
FOR THREE YEARS, I WATCHED ...
...AS THE CURSE ROBBED YOU OF YOUR BREATH AND WARMTH.
AND...
...LIFE.
INSTEAD OF A QUICK DEATH...
I CHOSE TO KILL YOU A LITTLE AT A TIME.

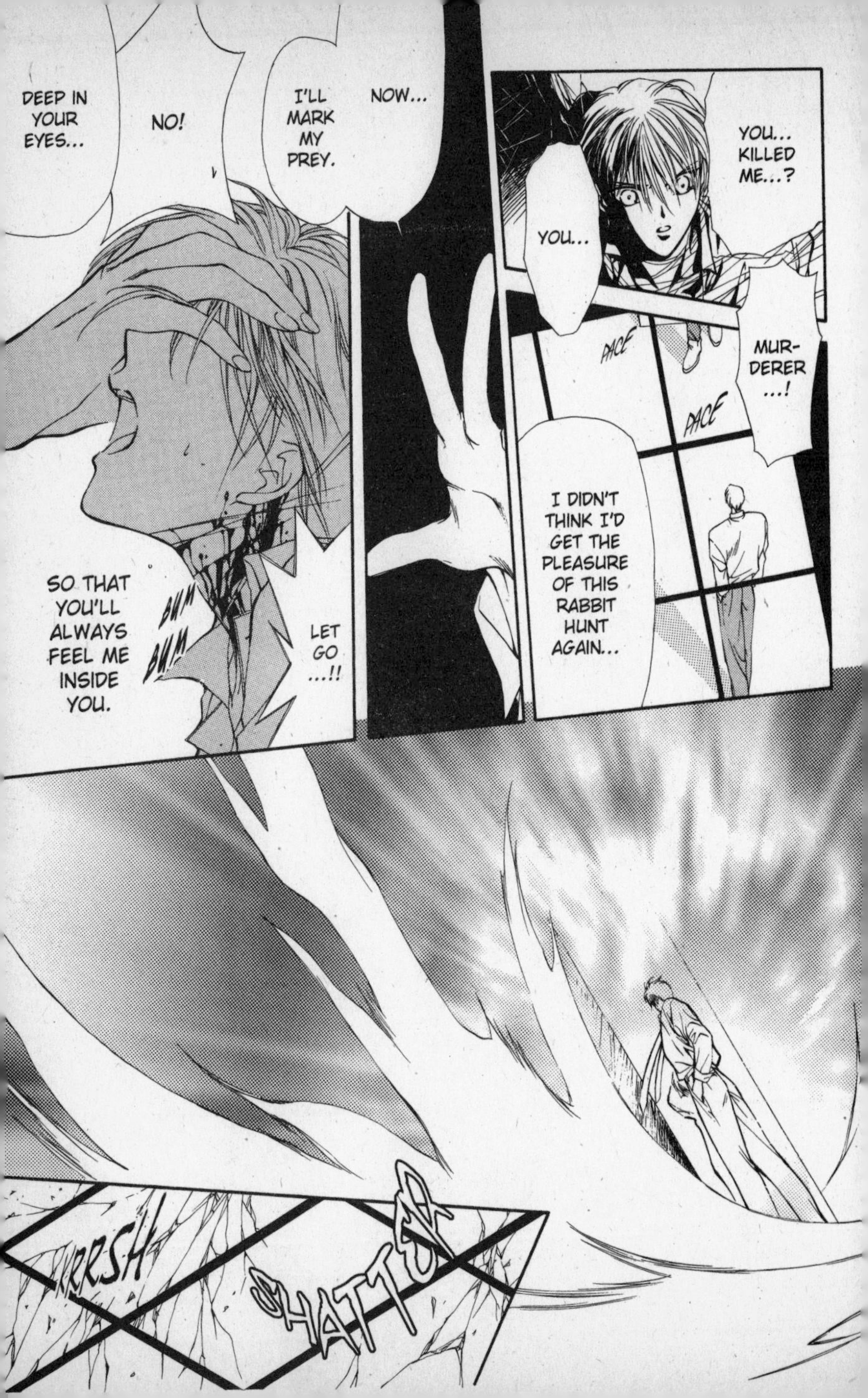

YOU... KILLED ME...?
YOU...
MURDERER...!
PACE
PACE
I DIDN'T THINK I'D GET THE PLEASURE OF THIS RABBIT HUNT AGAIN...
NOW...
I'LL MARK MY PREY.
NO!
DEEP IN YOUR EYES...
LET GO...!!
BUM BUM
SO THAT YOU'LL ALWAYS FEEL ME INSIDE YOU.
KRRSH
SHATTER

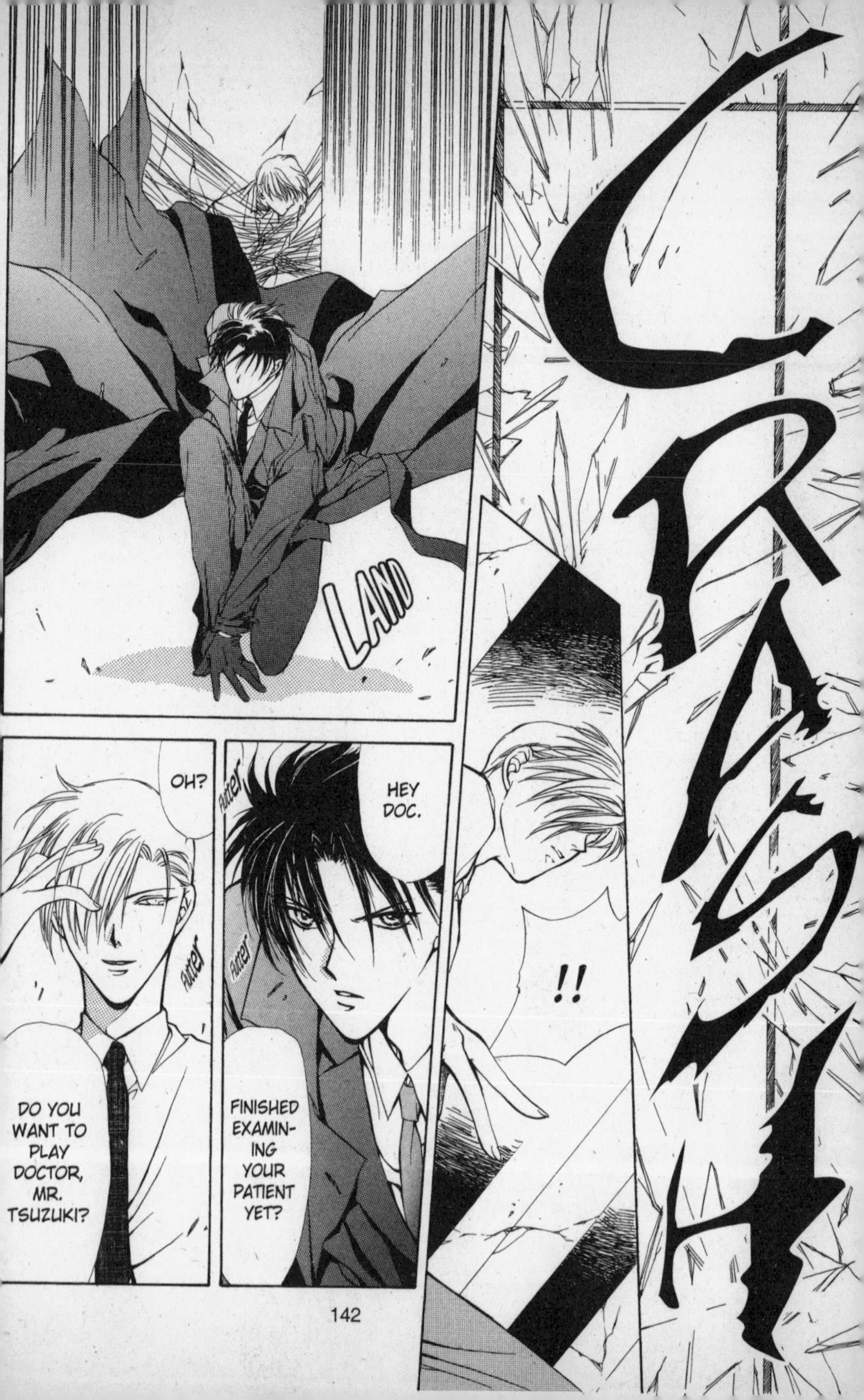
CRASH
!!
LAND
HEY DOC.
FINISHED EXAMINING YOUR PATIENT YET?
flutter
flutter
OH?
DO YOU WANT TO PLAY DOCTOR, MR. TSUZUKI?
flutter

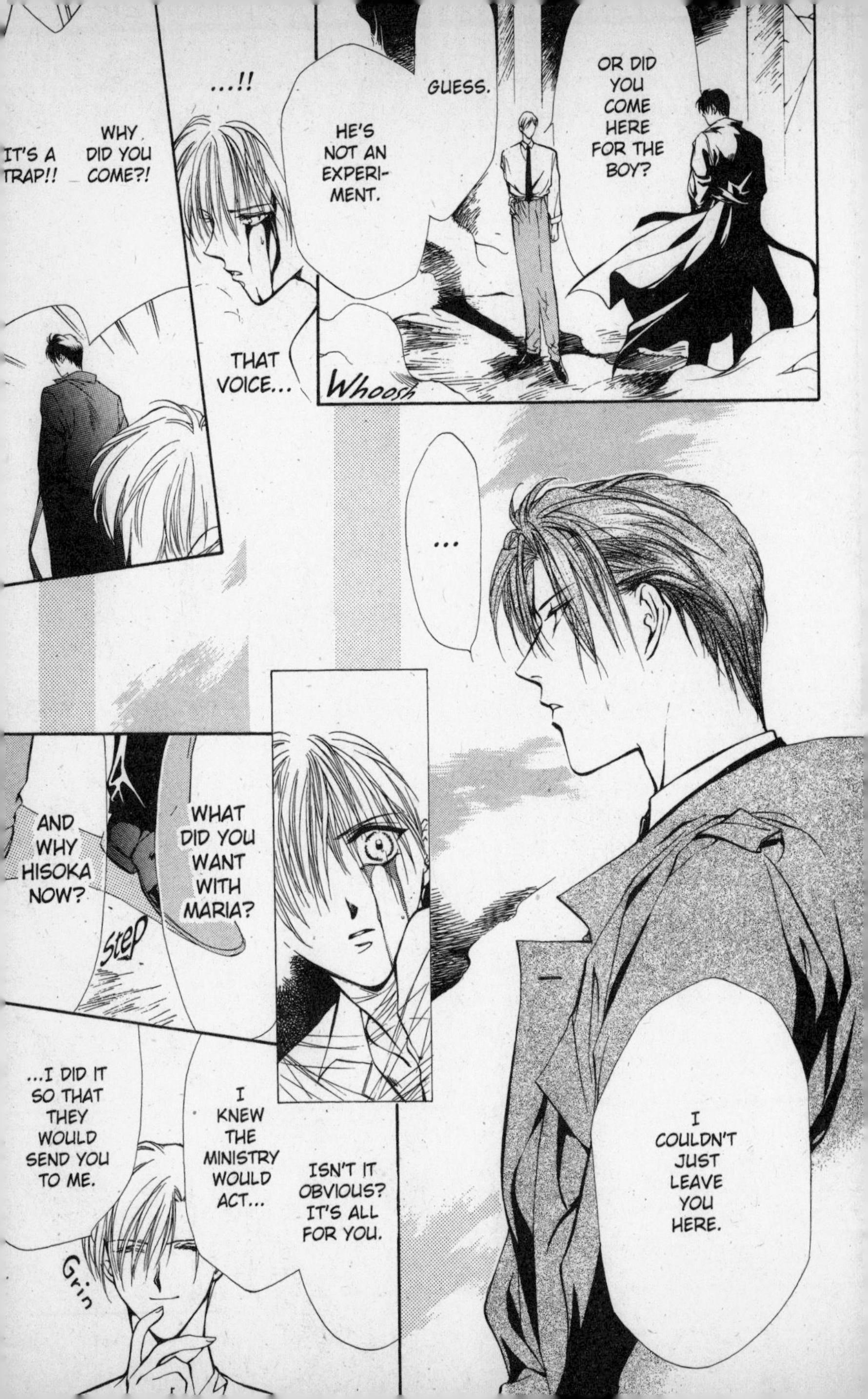
OR DID YOU COME HERE FOR THE BOY?
GUESS.
HE'S NOT AN EXPERIMENT.
Whoosh
...!!
WHY DID YOU COME?!
IT'S A TRAP!!
THAT VOICE...
...
I COULDN'T JUST LEAVE YOU HERE.
WHAT DID YOU WANT WITH MARIA?
AND WHY HISOKA NOW?
Step
ISN'T IT OBVIOUS? IT'S ALL FOR YOU.
I KNEW THE MINISTRY WOULD ACT...
...I DID IT SO THAT THEY WOULD SEND YOU TO ME.
Grin

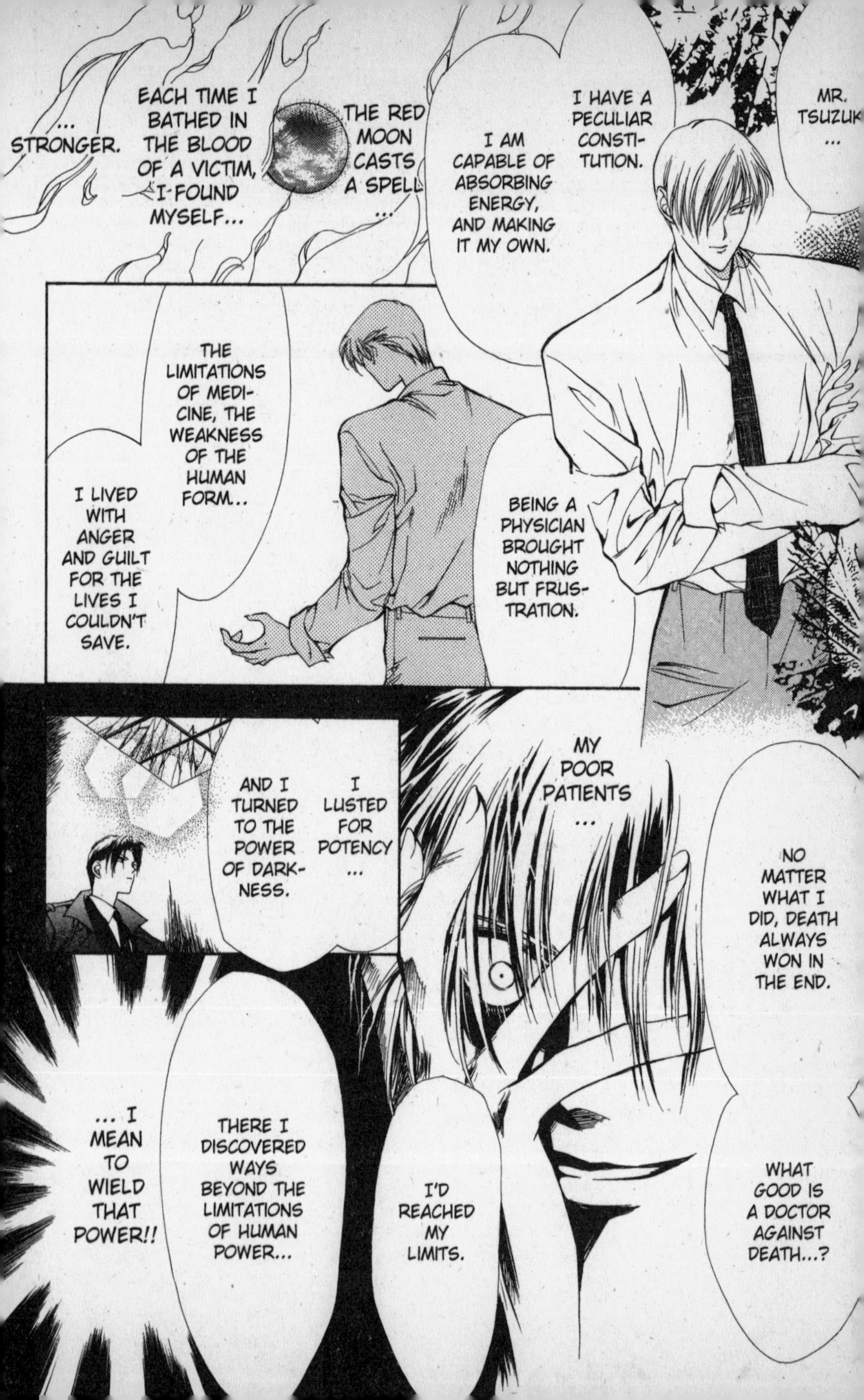
MR. TSUZUK ...
I HAVE A PECULIAR CONSTITUTION.
I AM CAPABLE OF ABSORBING ENERGY, AND MAKING IT MY OWN.
THE RED MOON CASTS A SPELL ...
EACH TIME I BATHED IN THE BLOOD OF A VICTIM, I FOUND MYSELF...
... STRONGER.
BEING A PHYSICIAN BROUGHT NOTHING BUT FRUSTRATION.
THE LIMITATIONS OF MEDICINE, THE WEAKNESS OF THE HUMAN FORM...
I LIVED WITH ANGER AND GUILT FOR THE LIVES I COULDN'T SAVE.
MY POOR PATIENTS ...
NO MATTER WHAT I DID, DEATH ALWAYS WON IN THE END.
WHAT GOOD IS A DOCTOR AGAINST DEATH...?
I'D REACHED MY LIMITS.
I LUSTED FOR POTENCY ...
AND I TURNED TO THE POWER OF DARKNESS.
THERE I DISCOVERED WAYS BEYOND THE LIMITATIONS OF HUMAN POWER...
... I MEAN TO WIELD THAT POWER!!

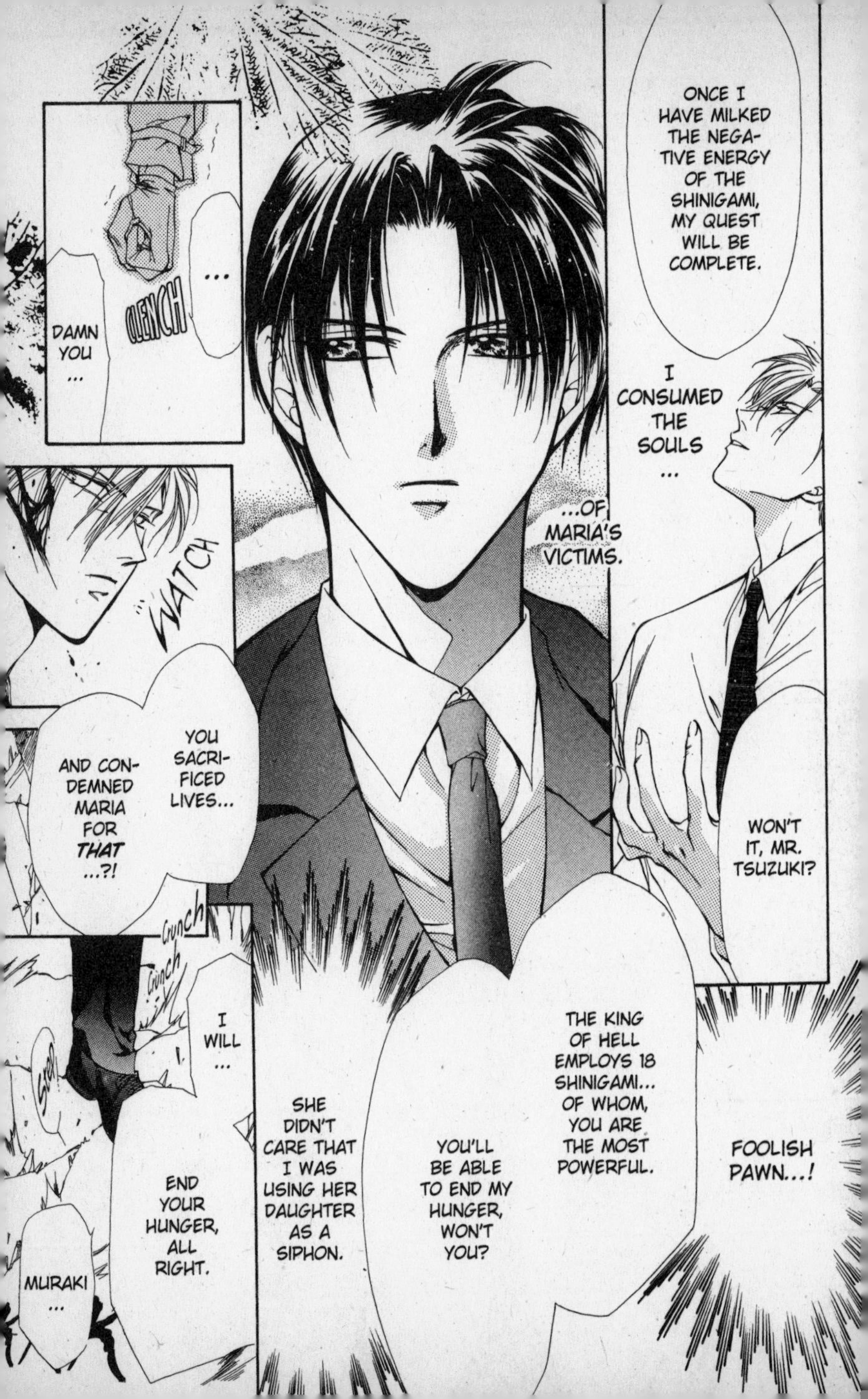

ONCE I HAVE MILKED THE NEGA-TIVE ENERGY OF THE SHINIGAMI, MY QUEST WILL BE COMPLETE.
I CONSUMED THE SOULS ...
...OF MARIA'S VICTIMS.
WON'T IT, MR. TSUZUKI?
FOOLISH PAWN...!
THE KING OF HELL EMPLOYS 18 SHINIGAMI... OF WHOM, YOU ARE THE MOST POWERFUL.
YOU'LL BE ABLE TO END MY HUNGER, WON'T YOU?
SHE DIDN'T CARE THAT I WAS USING HER DAUGHTER AS A SIPHON.
...
CLENCH
DAMN YOU ...
WATCH
YOU SACRI-FICED LIVES...
AND CON-DEMNED MARIA FOR *THAT* ...?!
Crunch
Crunch
STEP
I WILL ...
END YOUR HUNGER, ALL RIGHT.
MURAKI ...

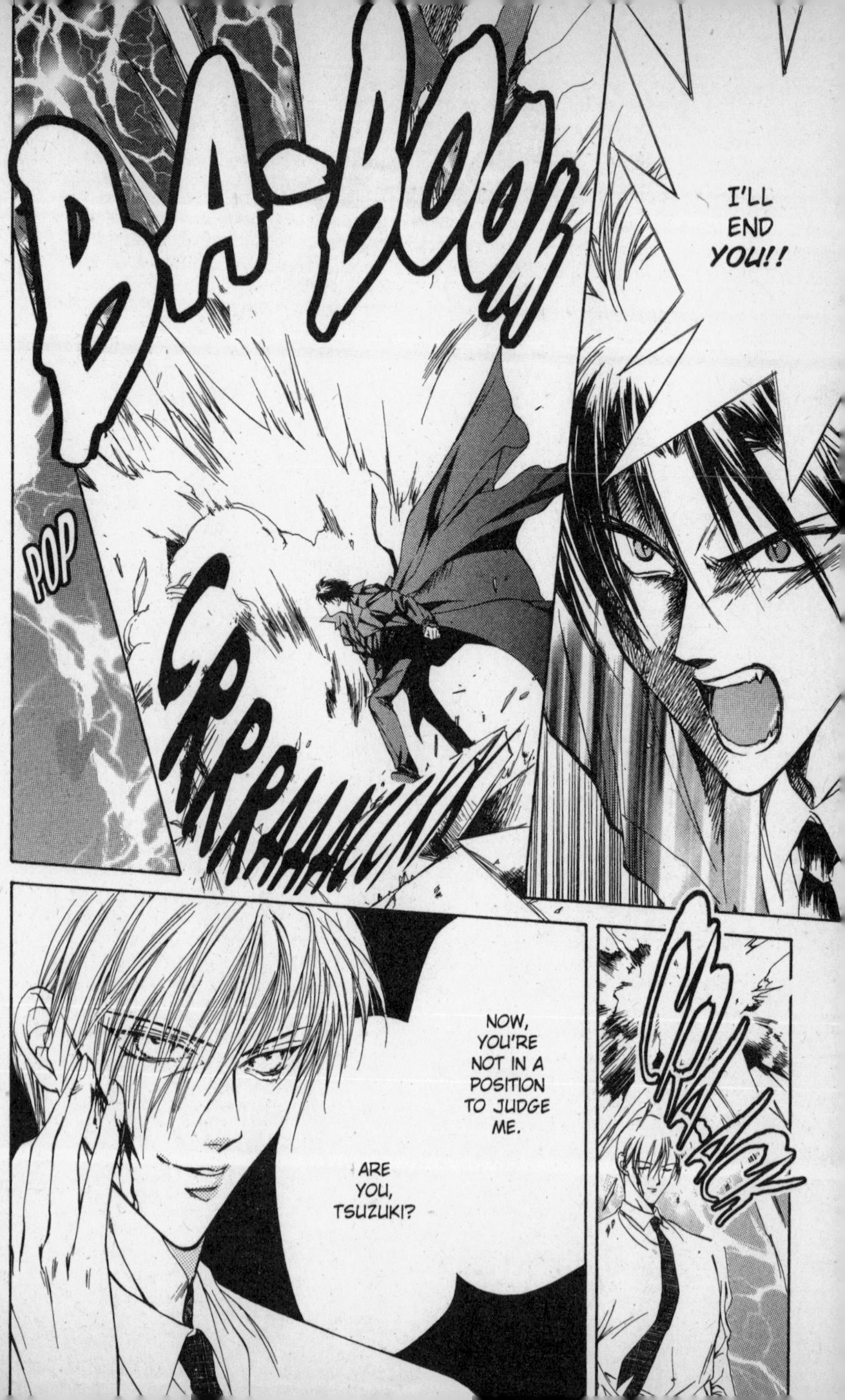
I'LL END YOU!!
BA-BOOM
POP
CRRAAACK
NOW, YOU'RE NOT IN A POSITION TO JUDGE ME.
ARE YOU, TSUZUKI?

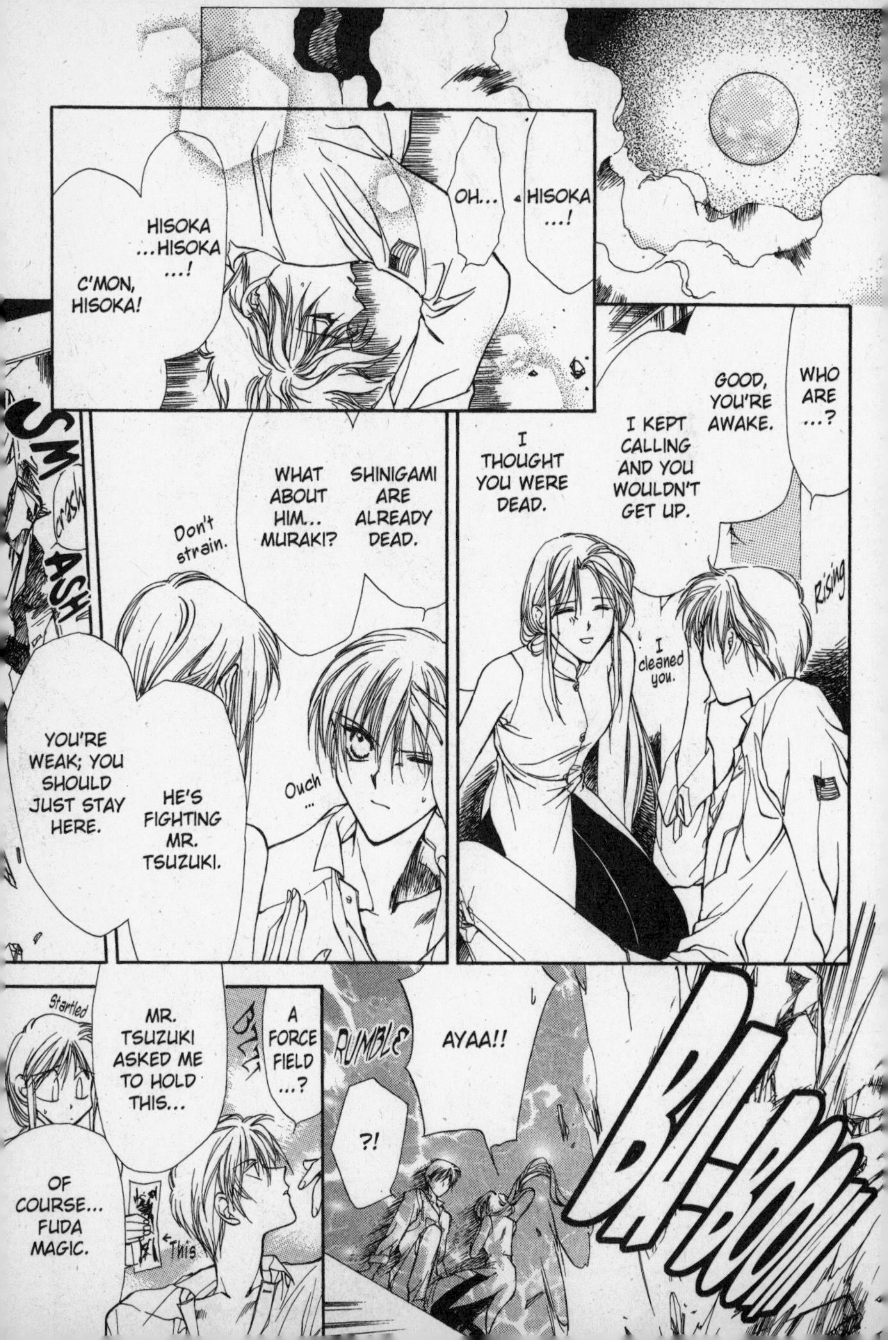

OH...
HISOKA ...!
HISOKA ...HISOKA ...!
C'MON, HISOKA!
WHO ARE ...?
GOOD, YOU'RE AWAKE.
I KEPT CALLING AND YOU WOULDN'T GET UP.
I THOUGHT YOU WERE DEAD.
Rising
I cleaned you.
SHINIGAMI ARE ALREADY DEAD.
WHAT ABOUT HIM... MURAKI?
Don't strain.
Ouch ...
HE'S FIGHTING MR. TSUZUKI.
YOU'RE WEAK; YOU SHOULD JUST STAY HERE.
crash
SMASH
BA-DOOM
AYAA!!
RUMBLE
?!
A FORCE FIELD ...?
MR. TSUZUKI ASKED ME TO HOLD THIS...
Startled
OF COURSE... FUDA MAGIC.
This

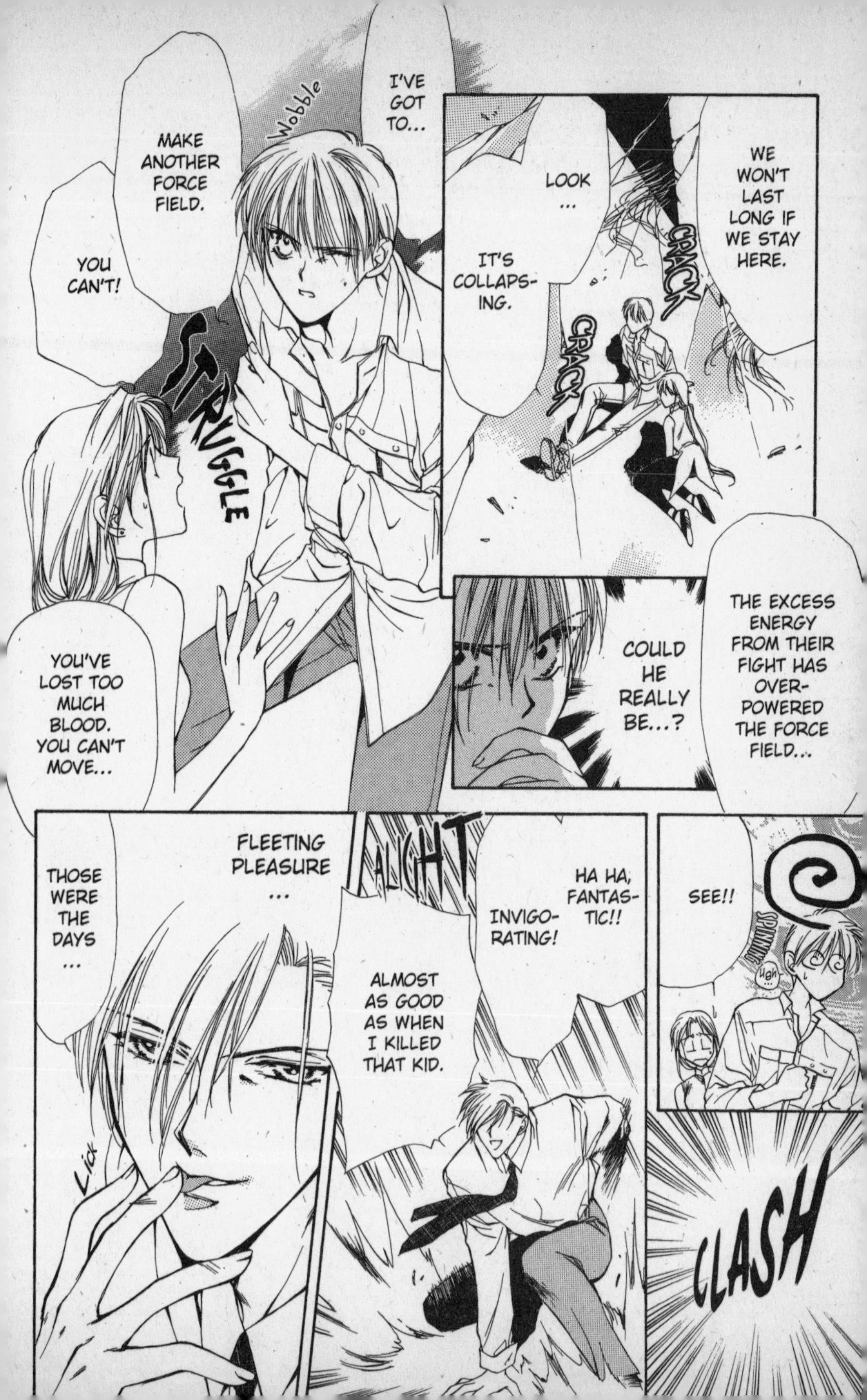
WE WON'T LAST LONG IF WE STAY HERE.
LOOK ...
IT'S COLLAPS- ING.
CRACK
CRACK
THE EXCESS ENERGY FROM THEIR FIGHT HAS OVER- POWERED THE FORCE FIELD...
COULD HE REALLY BE...?
I'VE GOT TO...
Wobble
MAKE ANOTHER FORCE FIELD.
YOU CAN'T!
STRUGGLE
YOU'VE LOST TOO MUCH BLOOD. YOU CAN'T MOVE...
SEE!!
SPINNING
Ugh
CLASH
HA HA, FANTAS- TIC!!
INVIGO- RATING!
ALMOST AS GOOD AS WHEN I KILLED THAT KID.
ALIGHT
FLEETING PLEASURE ...
THOSE WERE THE DAYS ...
Lick

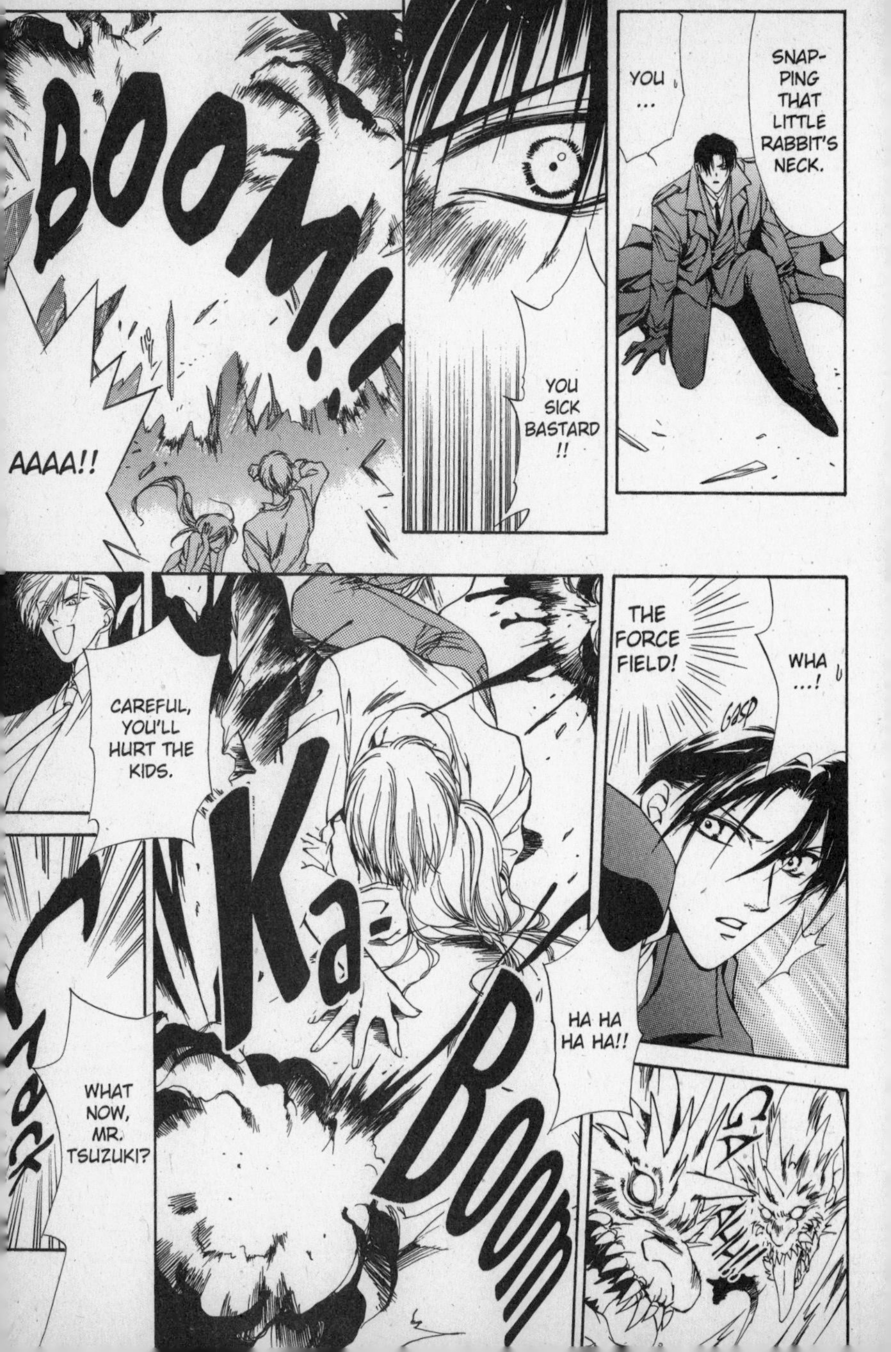
SNAP-PING THAT LITTLE RABBIT'S NECK.
YOU ...
YOU SICK BASTARD !!
BOOM!!
AAAA!!
WHA ...!
Gasp
THE FORCE FIELD!
HA HA HA HA!!
Ka-BOOM
CAREFUL, YOU'LL HURT THE KIDS.
Crack
WHAT NOW, MR. TSUZUKI?

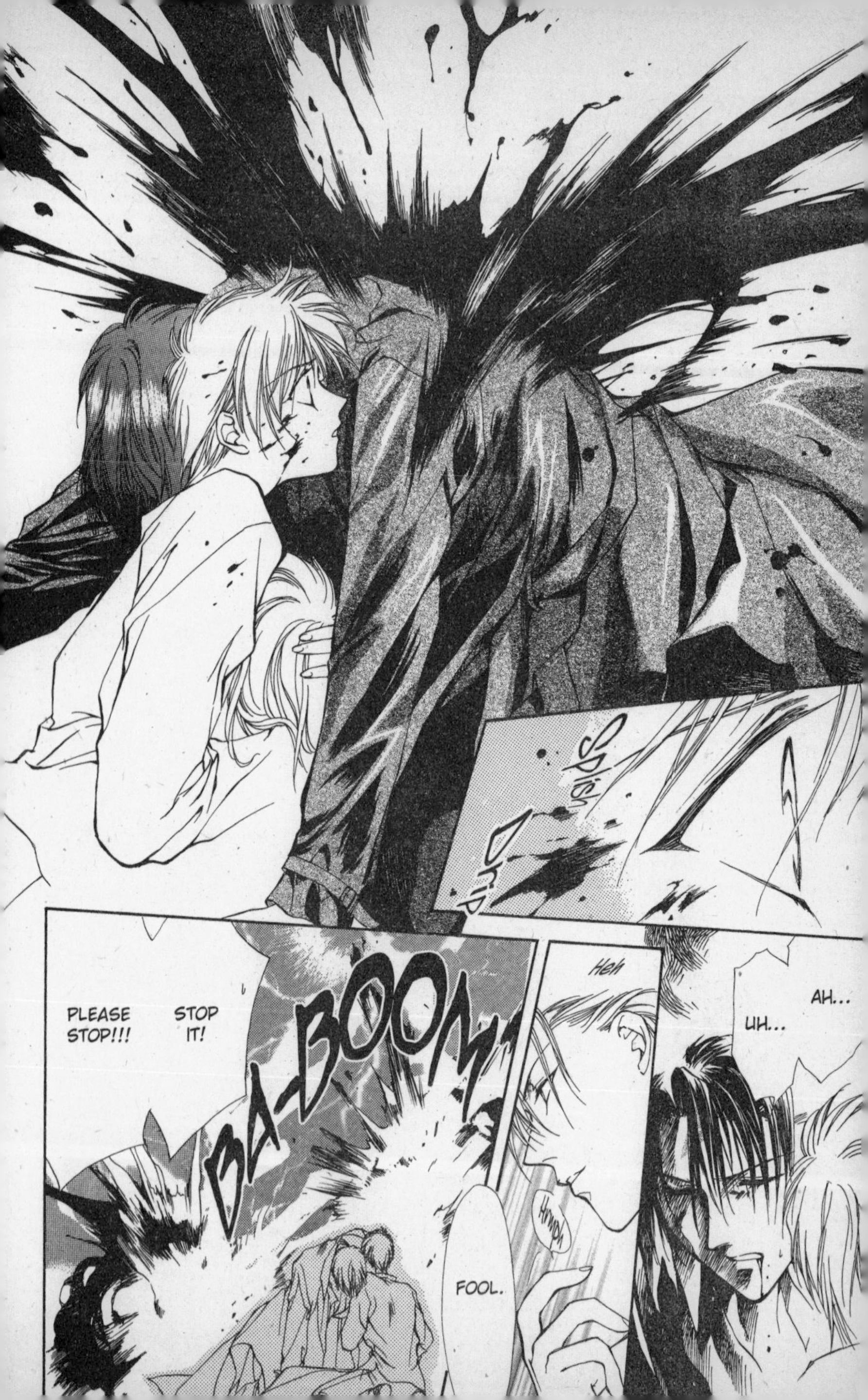
Splish
Drip
AH...
UH...
Heh
Hmph
FOOL.
STOP IT!
PLEASE STOP!!!
BA-BOOM

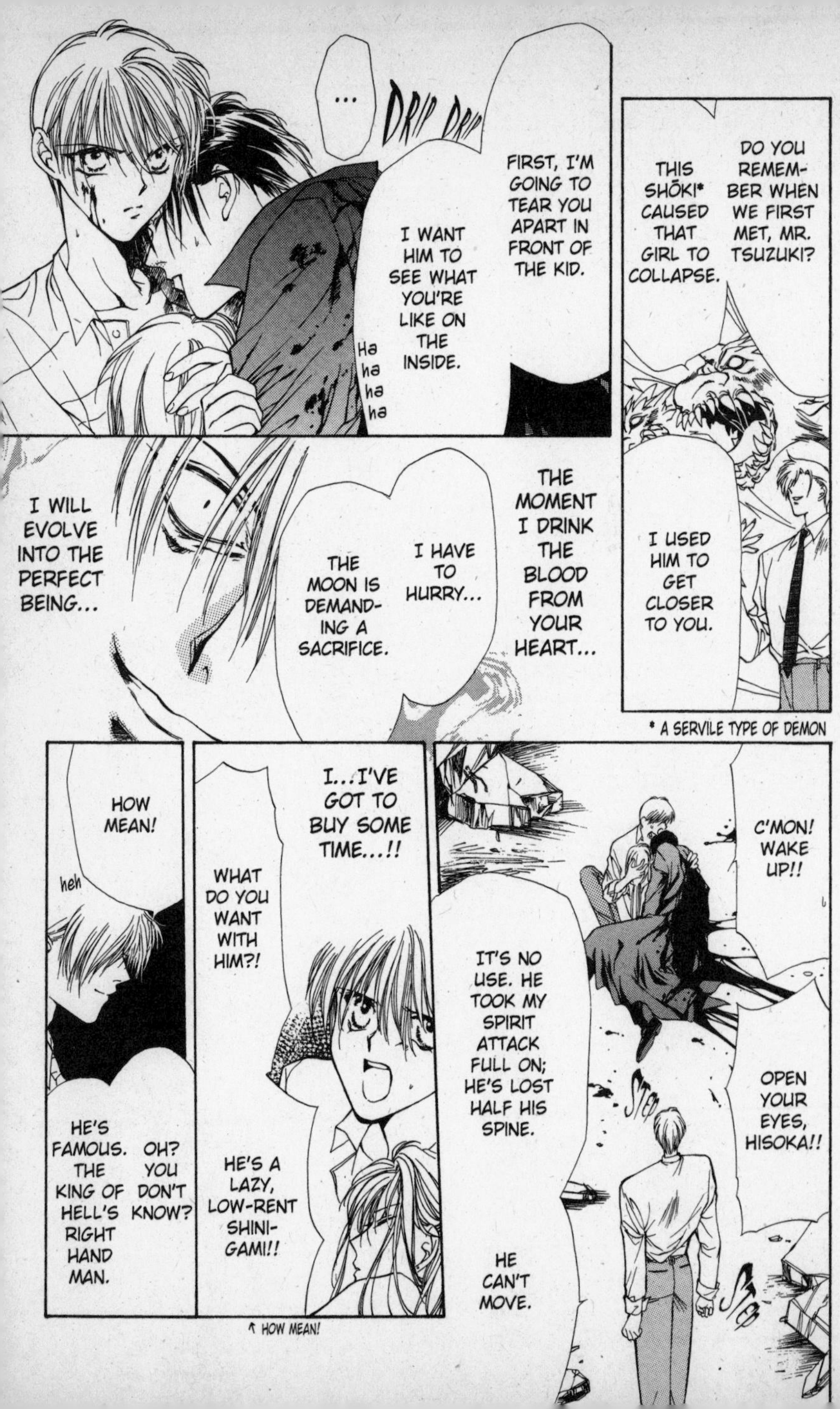
DO YOU REMEMBER WHEN WE FIRST MET, MR. TSUZUKI?
THIS SHŌKI* CAUSED THAT GIRL TO COLLAPSE.
I USED HIM TO GET CLOSER TO YOU.
...
DRIP DRIP
FIRST, I'M GOING TO TEAR YOU APART IN FRONT OF THE KID.
I WANT HIM TO SEE WHAT YOU'RE LIKE ON THE INSIDE.
Ha ha ha ha
THE MOMENT I DRINK THE BLOOD FROM YOUR HEART...
I HAVE TO HURRY...
THE MOON IS DEMANDING A SACRIFICE.
I WILL EVOLVE INTO THE PERFECT BEING...
C'MON! WAKE UP!!
OPEN YOUR EYES, HISOKA!!
STEP
STEP
IT'S NO USE. HE TOOK MY SPIRIT ATTACK FULL ON; HE'S LOST HALF HIS SPINE.
HE CAN'T MOVE.
I...I'VE GOT TO BUY SOME TIME...!!
WHAT DO YOU WANT WITH HIM?!
HE'S A LAZY, LOW-RENT SHINIGAMI!!
HOW MEAN!
heh
OH? YOU DON'T KNOW?
HE'S FAMOUS. THE KING OF HELL'S RIGHT HAND MAN.

* A SERVILE TYPE OF DEMON

↖ HOW MEAN!

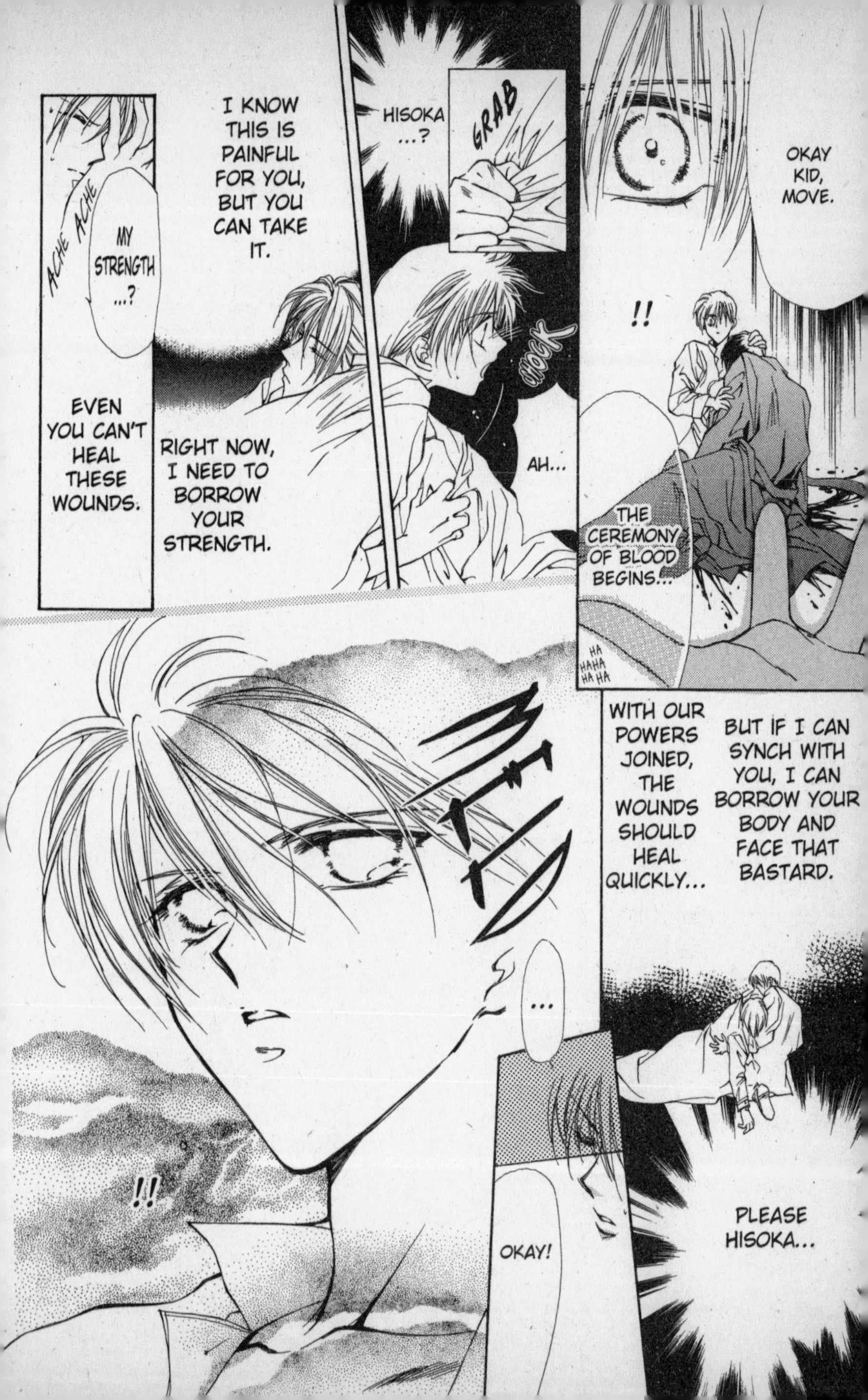
OKAY KID, MOVE.
!!
THE CEREMONY OF BLOOD BEGINS...
HA HAHA HA HA
HISOKA ...?
GRAB
SHOCK
AH...
I KNOW THIS IS PAINFUL FOR YOU, BUT YOU CAN TAKE IT.
RIGHT NOW, I NEED TO BORROW YOUR STRENGTH.
ACHE ACHE
MY STRENGTH ...?
EVEN YOU CAN'T HEAL THESE WOUNDS.
BUT IF I CAN SYNCH WITH YOU, I CAN BORROW YOUR BODY AND FACE THAT BASTARD.
WITH OUR POWERS JOINED, THE WOUNDS SHOULD HEAL QUICKLY...
PLEASE HISOKA...
...
OKAY!
!!

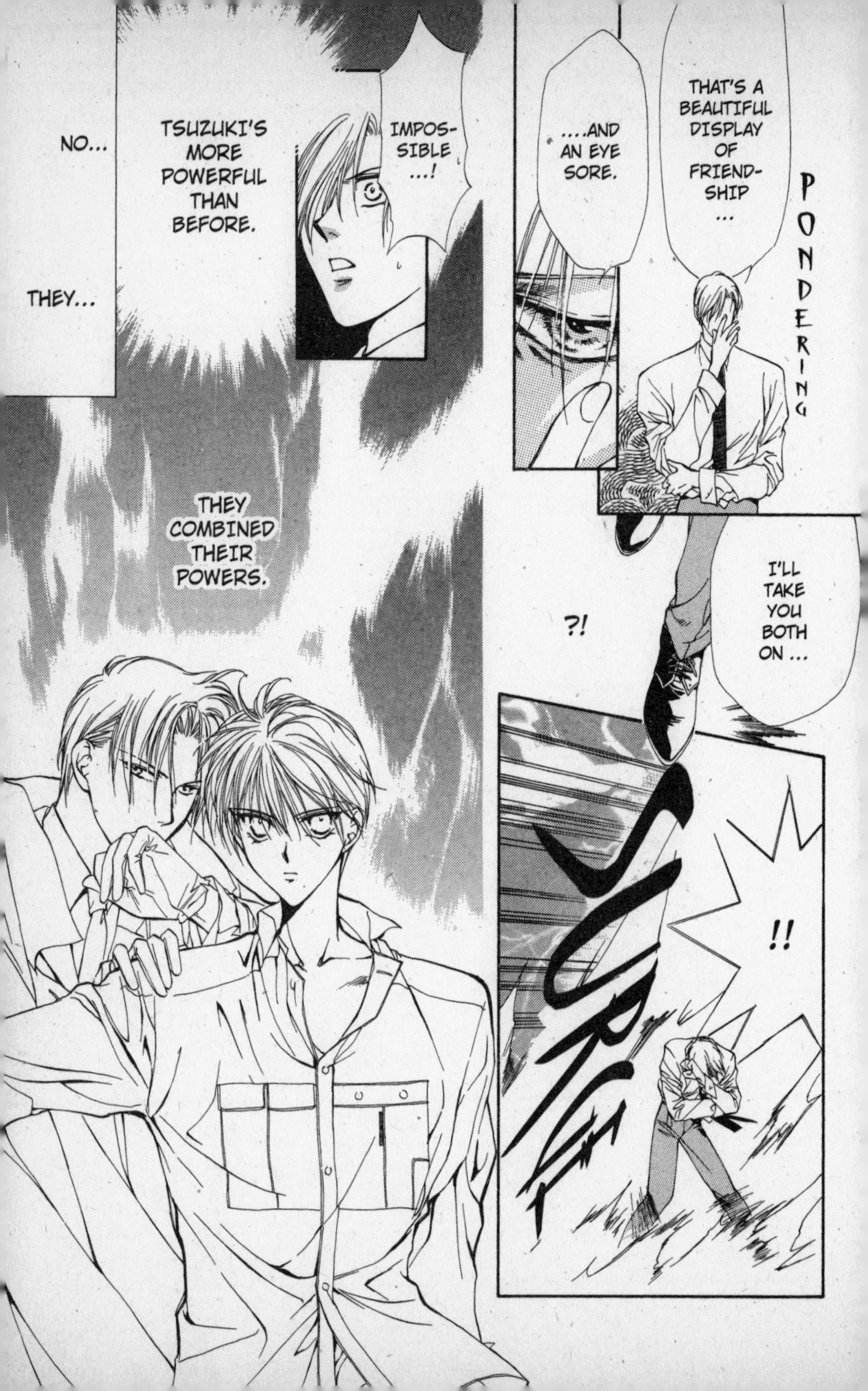
THAT'S A BEAUTIFUL DISPLAY OF FRIENDSHIP ...
....AND AN EYE SORE.
PONDERING
I'LL TAKE YOU BOTH ON ...
?!
!!
IMPOSSIBLE ...!
TSUZUKI'S MORE POWERFUL THAN BEFORE.
NO...
THEY...
THEY COMBINED THEIR POWERS.

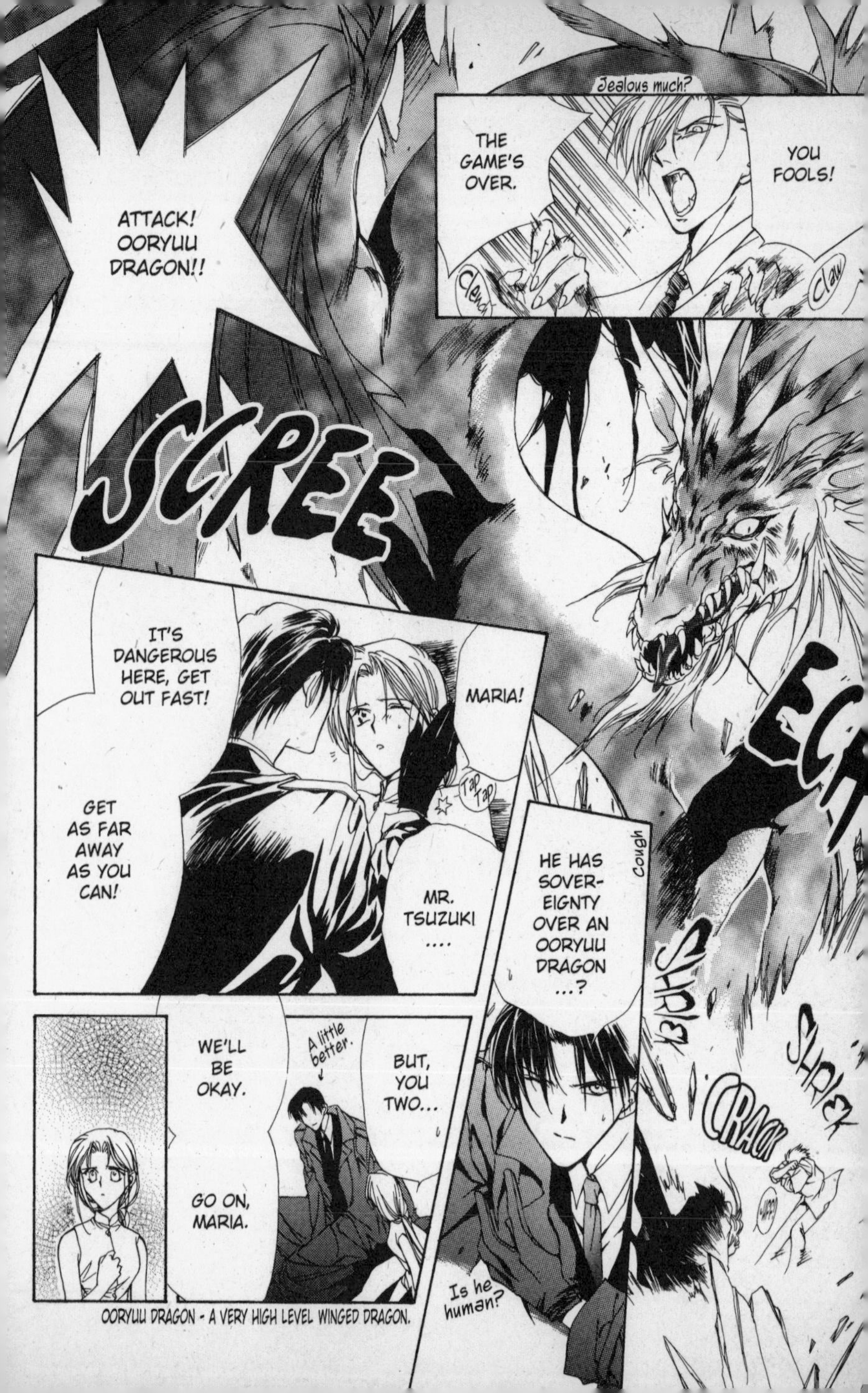
Jealous much?
YOU FOOLS!
THE GAME'S OVER.
Claw
Clench
ATTACK! OORYUU DRAGON!!
SCREE
ECH
HE HAS SOVEREIGNTY OVER AN OORYUU DRAGON ...?
Cough
SHRIEK
SHRIEK
CRACK
Is he human?
MARIA!
Tap Tap
MR. TSUZUKI ....
IT'S DANGEROUS HERE, GET OUT FAST!
GET AS FAR AWAY AS YOU CAN!
BUT, YOU TWO...
A little better.
WE'LL BE OKAY.
GO ON, MARIA.
OORYUU DRAGON - A VERY HIGH LEVEL WINGED DRAGON.

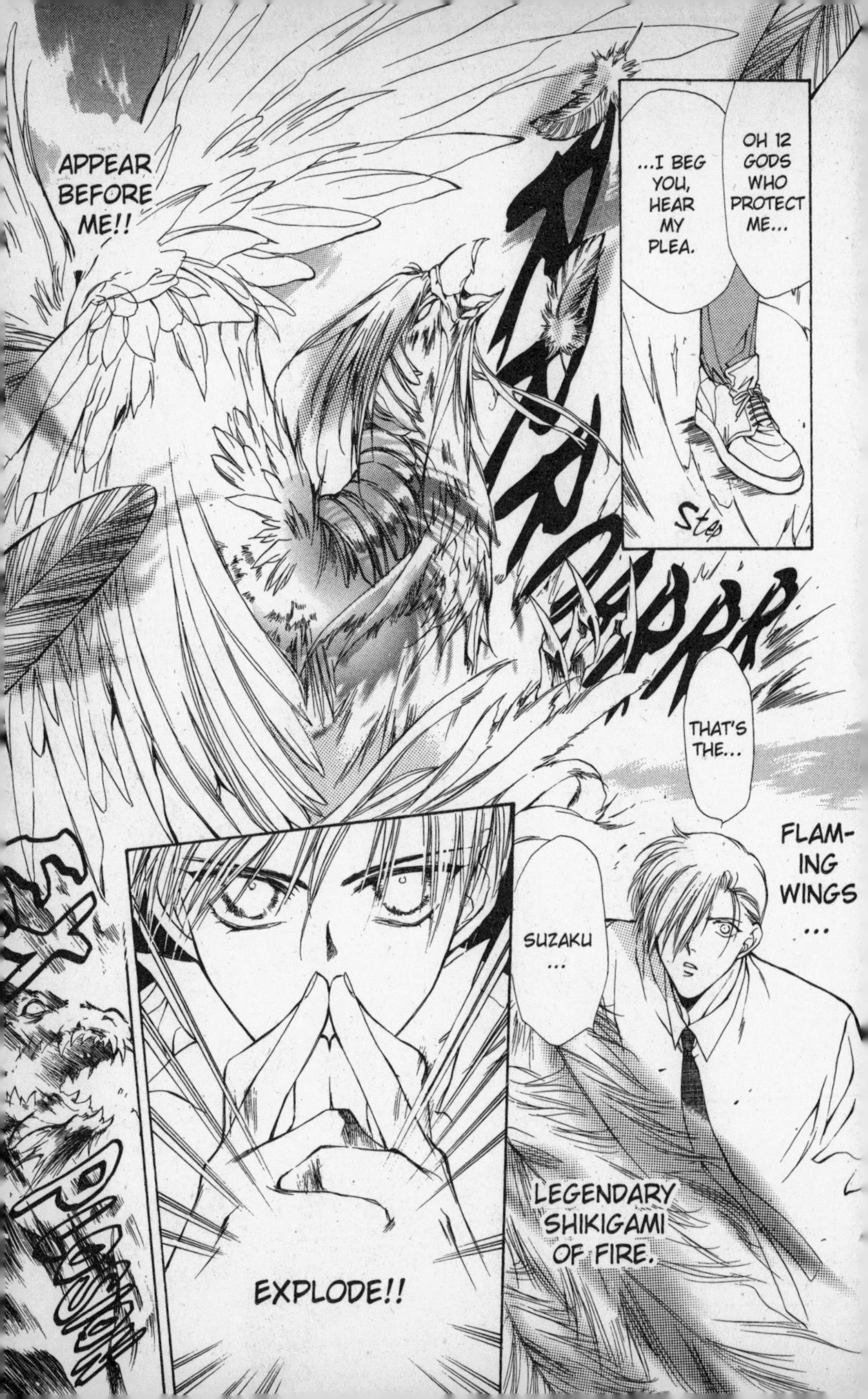

OH 12 GODS WHO PROTECT ME...
...I BEG YOU, HEAR MY PLEA.
Step
APPEAR BEFORE ME!!
THAT'S THE...
FLAM-ING WINGS...
SUZAKU...
LEGENDARY SHIKIGAMI OF FIRE.
EXPLODE!!

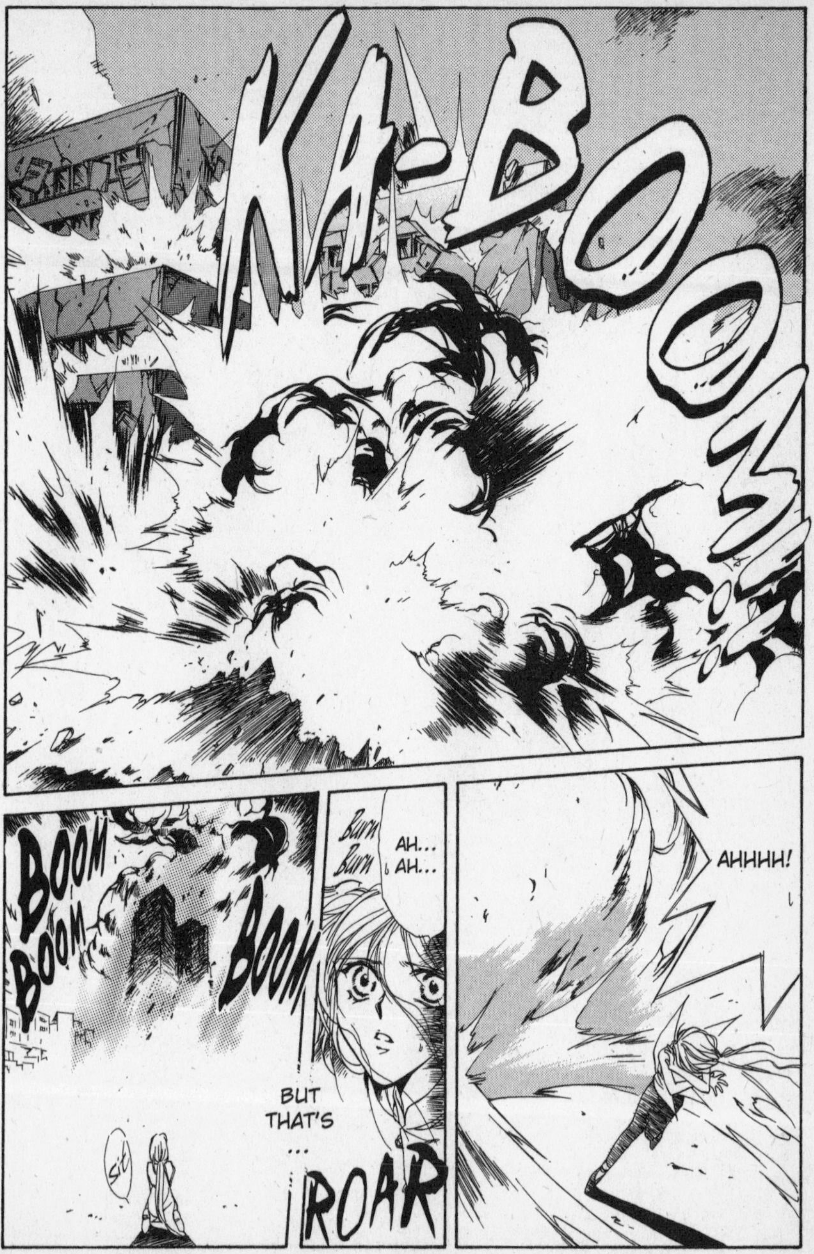
KA-BOOM
AHHHH!
Burn Burn
AH... AH...
BUT THAT'S ...
ROAR
BOOM BOOM
BOOM

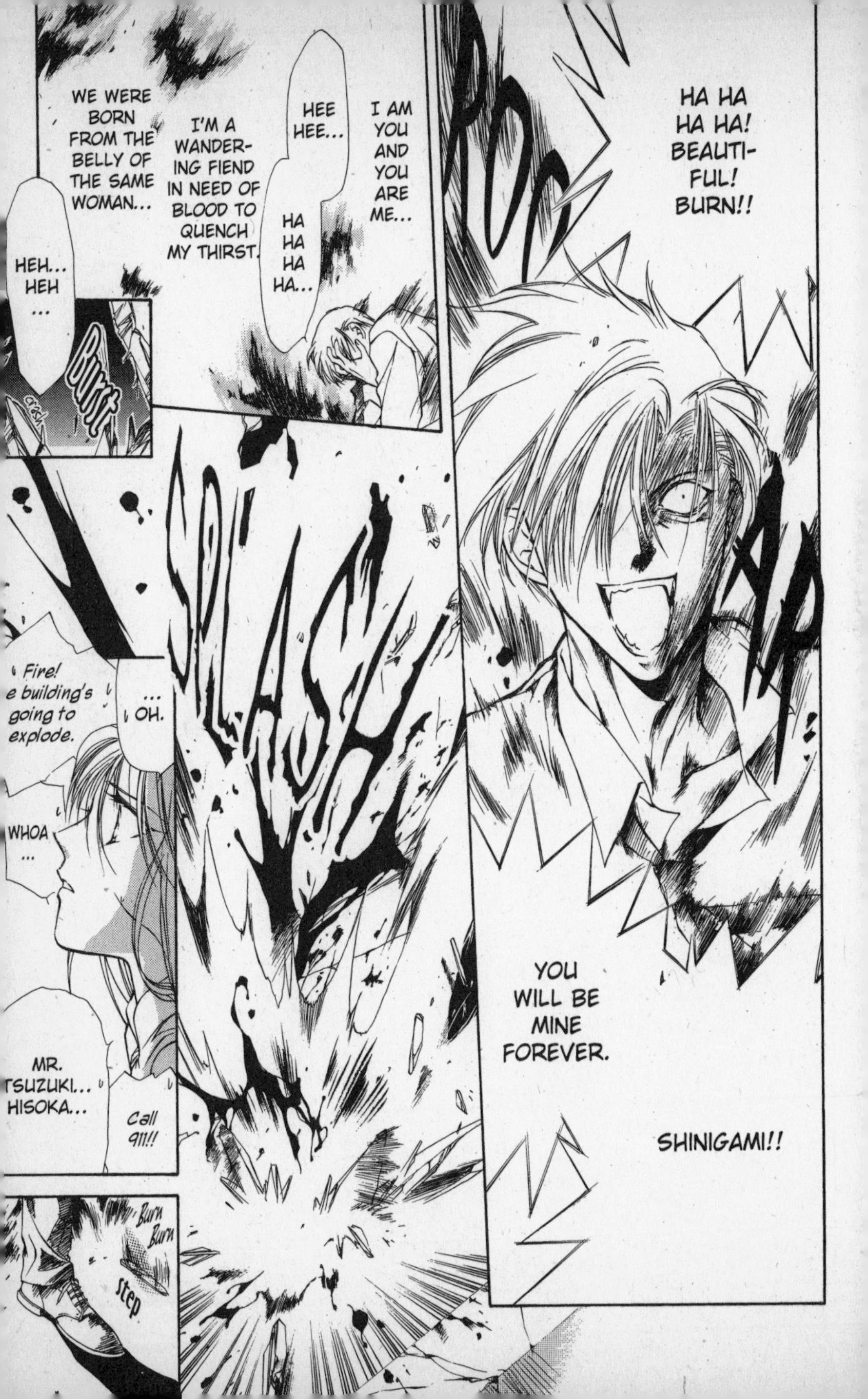
HA HA HA HA! BEAUTI-FUL! BURN!!
YOU WILL BE MINE FOREVER.
SHINIGAMI!!
I AM YOU AND YOU ARE ME...
HEE HEE...
HA HA HA HA...
I'M A WANDER-ING FIEND IN NEED OF BLOOD TO QUENCH MY THIRST.
WE WERE BORN FROM THE BELLY OF THE SAME WOMAN...
HEH... HEH ...
Burst
crash
SPLASH
... OH.
Fire! e building's going to explode.
WHOA ...
MR. TSUZUKI... HISOKA...
Call 911!!
Buru Buru
step

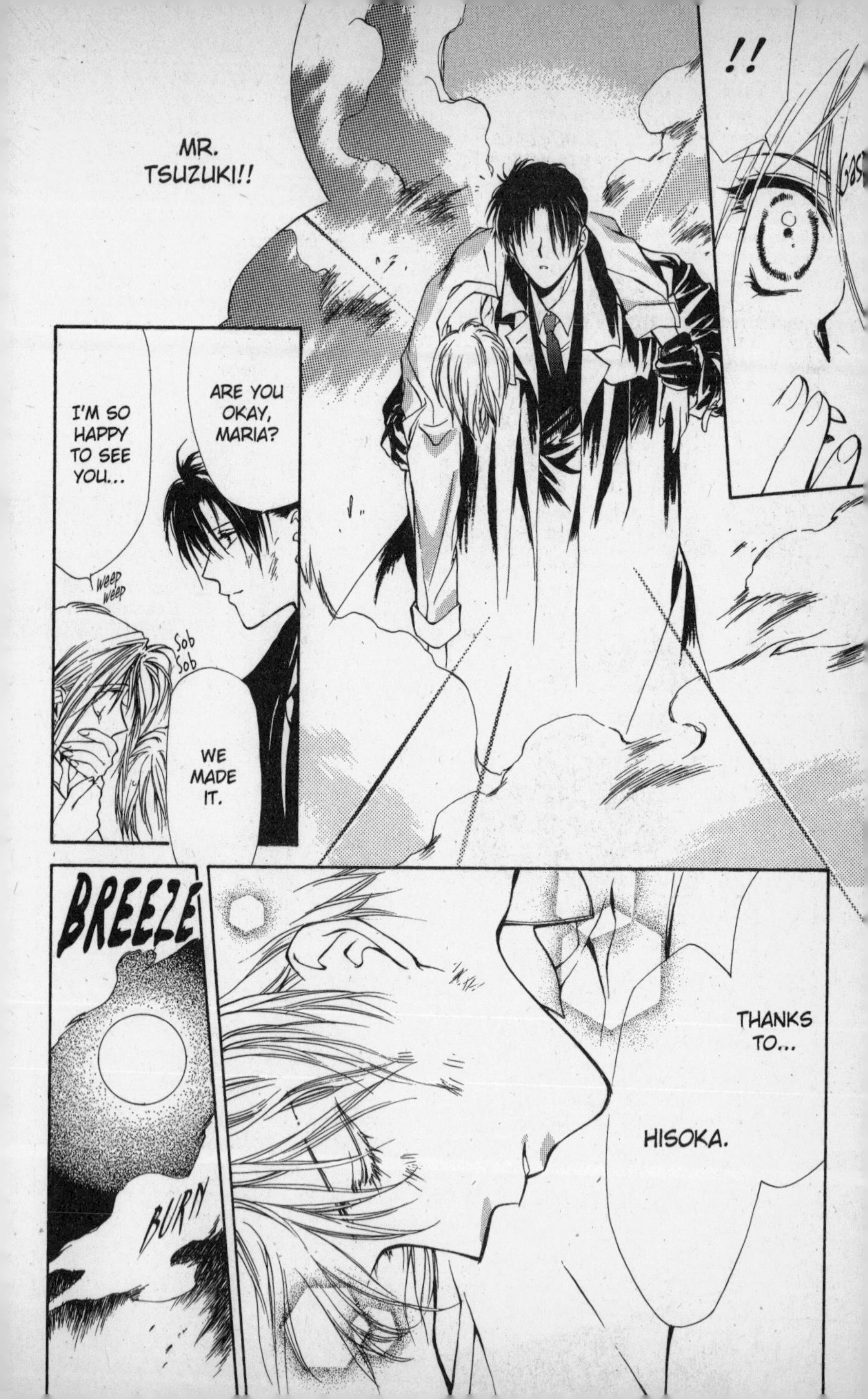
!!
MR. TSUZUKI!!
ARE YOU OKAY, MARIA?
I'M SO HAPPY TO SEE YOU...
weep weep
Sob Sob
WE MADE IT.
THANKS TO...
HISOKA.
BREEZE
BURN

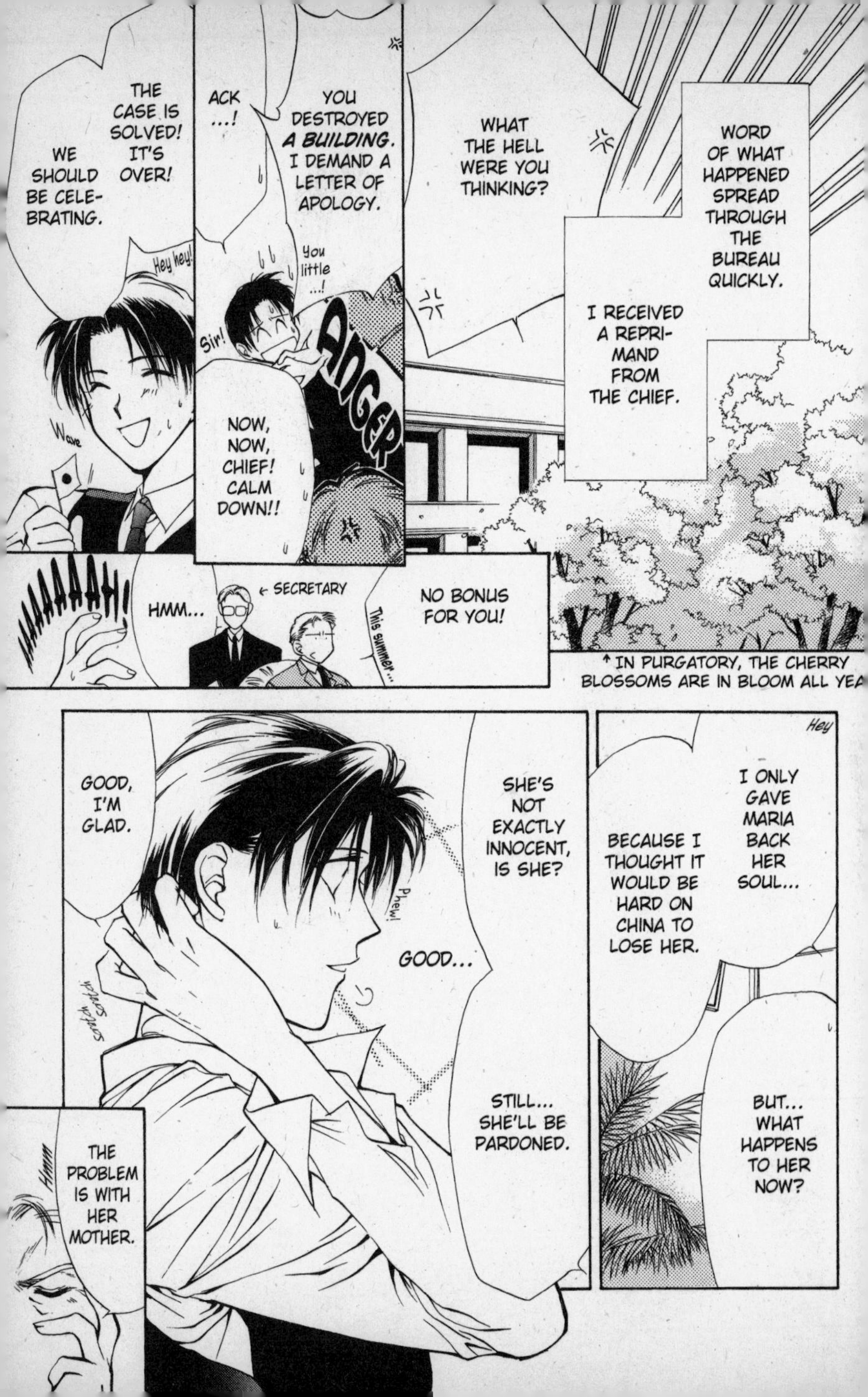
WORD OF WHAT HAPPENED SPREAD THROUGH THE BUREAU QUICKLY.
I RECEIVED A REPRIMAND FROM THE CHIEF.
↑IN PURGATORY, THE CHERRY BLOSSOMS ARE IN BLOOM ALL YEA
WHAT THE HELL WERE YOU THINKING?
YOU DESTROYED **A BUILDING**. I DEMAND A LETTER OF APOLOGY.
ACK ...!
You little ...!
ANGER
Sir!
NOW, NOW, CHIEF! CALM DOWN!!
THE CASE IS SOLVED! IT'S OVER!
WE SHOULD BE CELEBRATING.
Hey hey!
Wave
NO BONUS FOR YOU!
This summer...
← SECRETARY
HMM...
AAAAAAAAH!
Hey
I ONLY GAVE MARIA BACK HER SOUL...
BECAUSE I THOUGHT IT WOULD BE HARD ON CHINA TO LOSE HER.
BUT... WHAT HAPPENS TO HER NOW?
SHE'S NOT EXACTLY INNOCENT, IS SHE?
STILL... SHE'LL BE PARDONED.
Phew!
GOOD...
GOOD, I'M GLAD.
Scratch scratch
Hmm
THE PROBLEM IS WITH HER MOTHER.

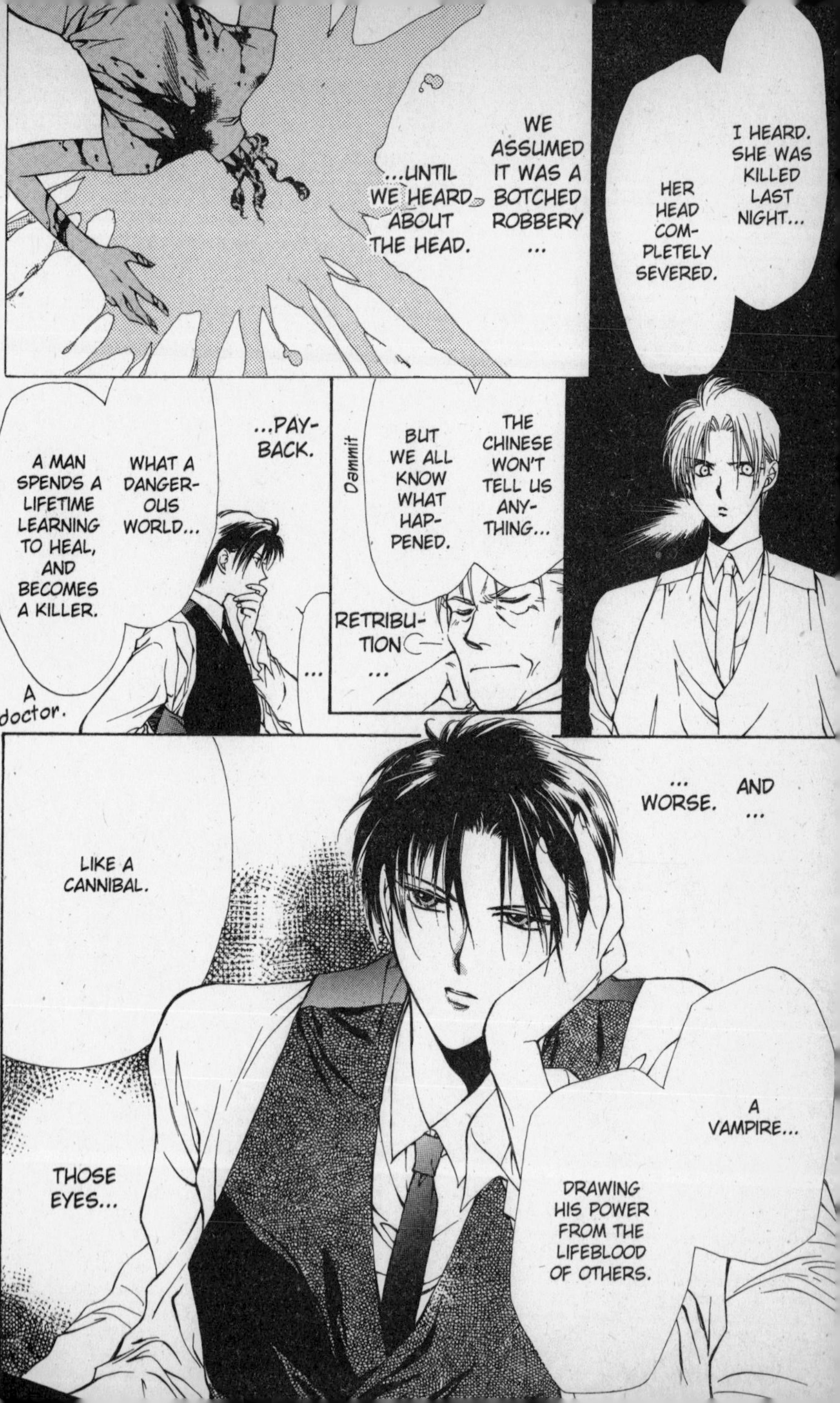
I HEARD. SHE WAS KILLED LAST NIGHT...
HER HEAD COMPLETELY SEVERED.
WE ASSUMED IT WAS A BOTCHED ROBBERY...
...UNTIL WE HEARD ABOUT THE HEAD.
THE CHINESE WON'T TELL US ANYTHING...
BUT WE ALL KNOW WHAT HAPPENED.
Dammit
RETRIBUTION...
...PAYBACK.
...
WHAT A DANGEROUS WORLD...
A MAN SPENDS A LIFETIME LEARNING TO HEAL, AND BECOMES A KILLER.
A doctor.
AND...
...WORSE.
LIKE A CANNIBAL.
A VAMPIRE...
DRAWING HIS POWER FROM THE LIFEBLOOD OF OTHERS.
THOSE EYES...

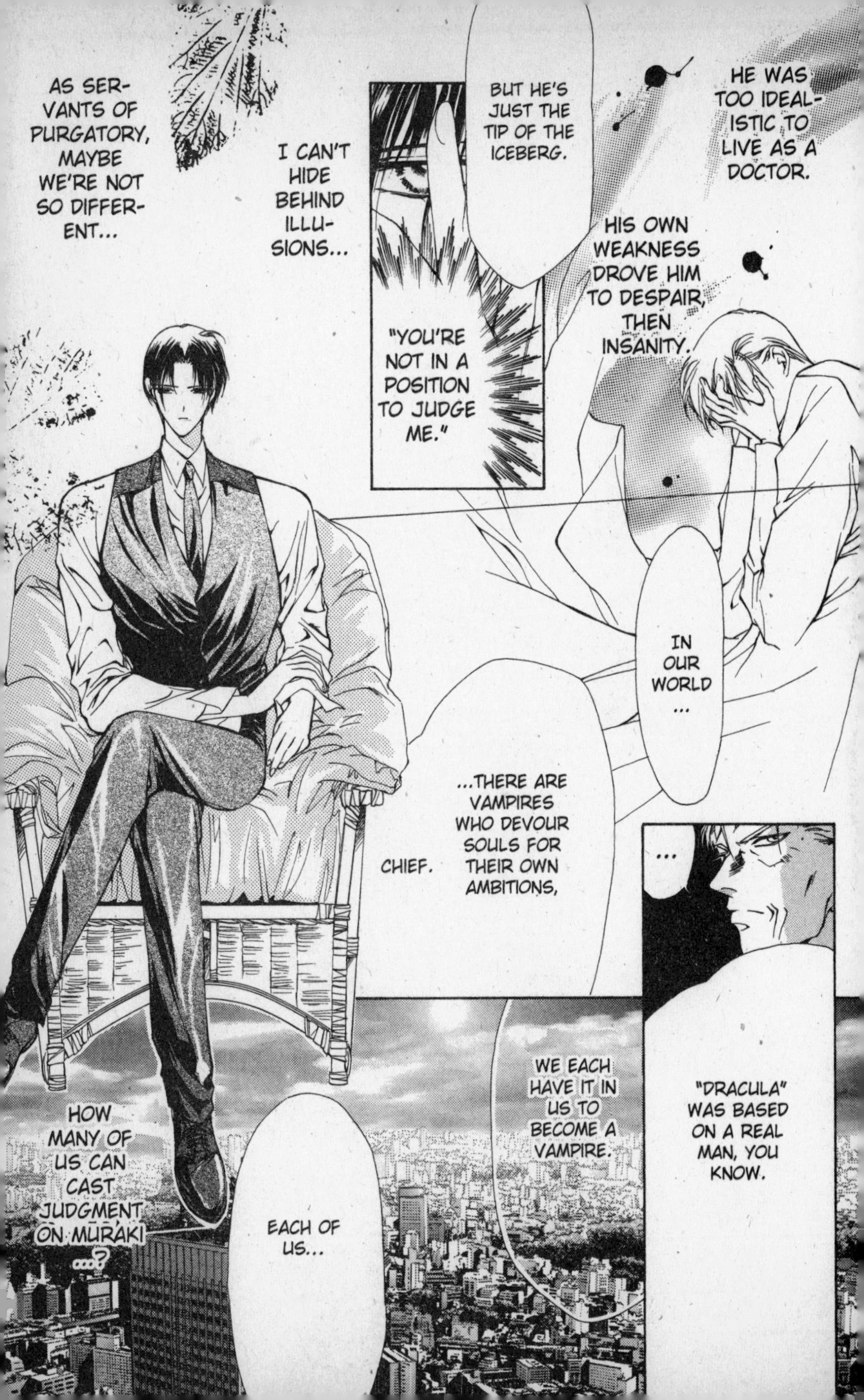
HE WAS TOO IDEAL-ISTIC TO LIVE AS A DOCTOR.
HIS OWN WEAKNESS DROVE HIM TO DESPAIR, THEN INSANITY.
BUT HE'S JUST THE TIP OF THE ICEBERG.
"YOU'RE NOT IN A POSITION TO JUDGE ME."
I CAN'T HIDE BEHIND ILLU-SIONS...
AS SER-VANTS OF PURGATORY, MAYBE WE'RE NOT SO DIFFER-ENT...
IN OUR WORLD ...
...THERE ARE VAMPIRES WHO DEVOUR SOULS FOR THEIR OWN AMBITIONS,
CHIEF.
...
"DRACULA" WAS BASED ON A REAL MAN, YOU KNOW.
WE EACH HAVE IT IN US TO BECOME A VAMPIRE.
EACH OF US...
HOW MANY OF US CAN CAST JUDGMENT ON MURAKI ...?

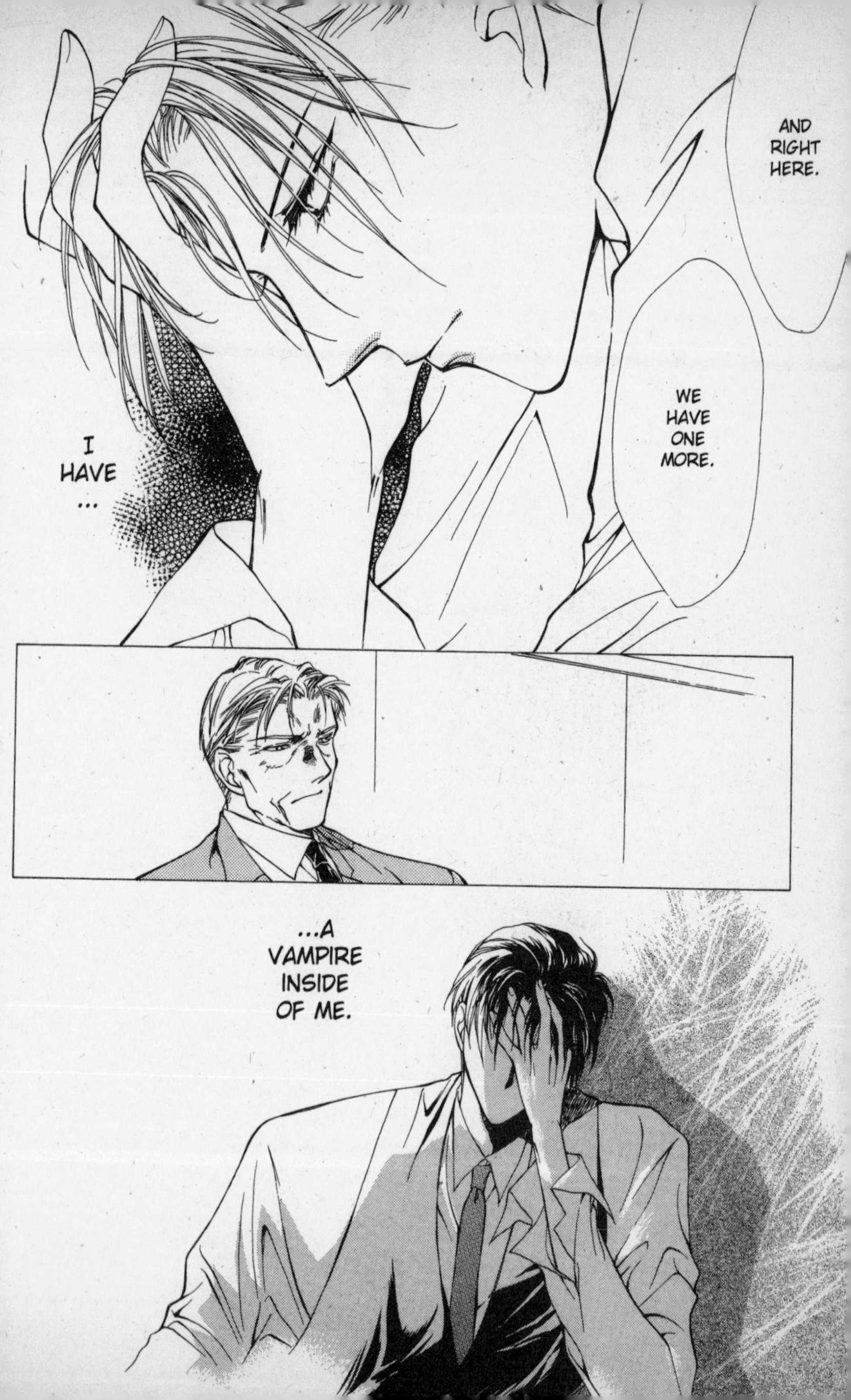
AND RIGHT HERE.
WE HAVE ONE MORE.
I HAVE ...
...A VAMPIRE INSIDE OF ME.

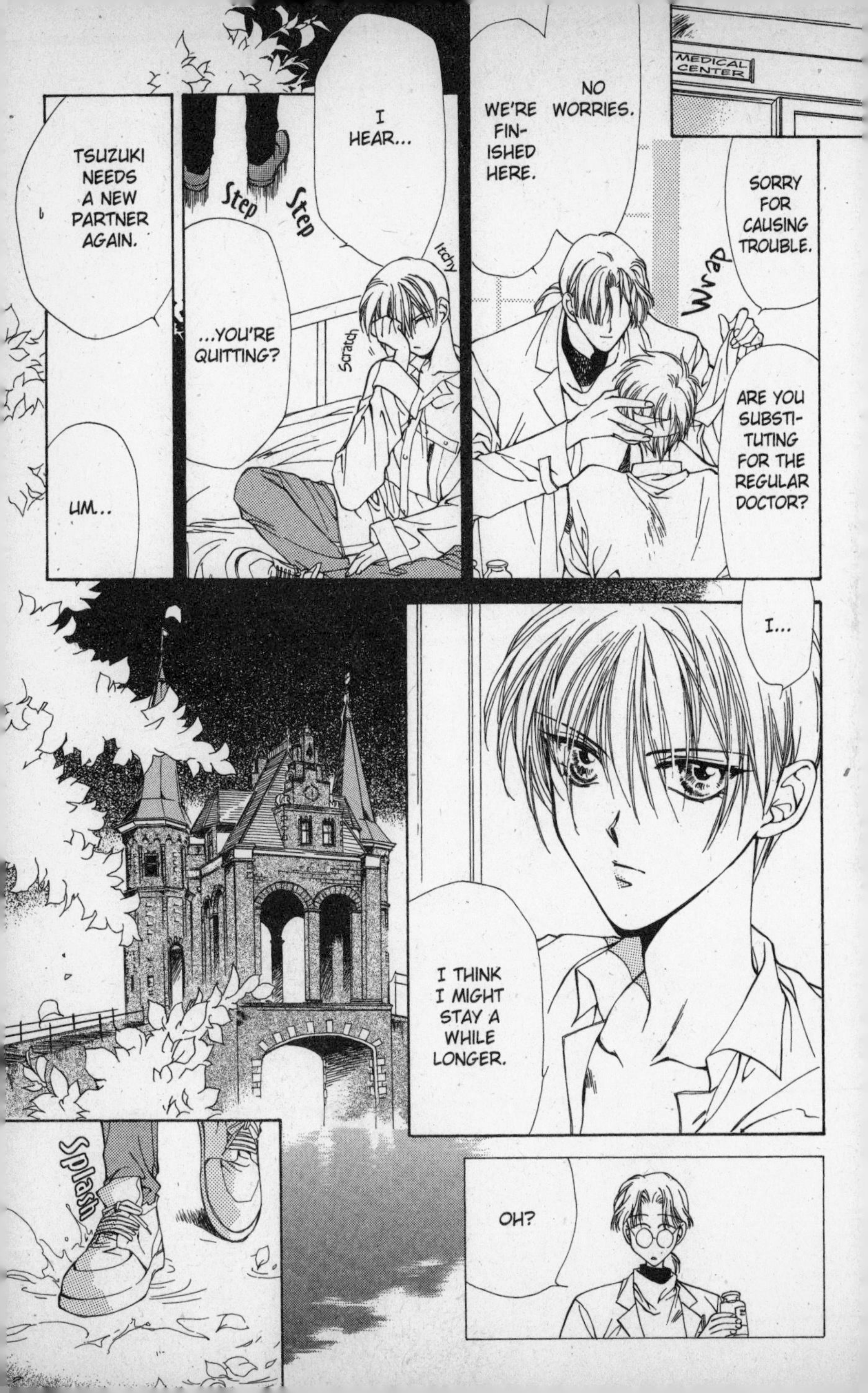
MEDICAL CENTER
SORRY FOR CAUSING TROUBLE.
Wrap
NO WORRIES.
WE'RE FIN-ISHED HERE.
ARE YOU SUBSTI-TUTING FOR THE REGULAR DOCTOR?
I HEAR...
Step
Step
Itchy
Scratch
...YOU'RE QUITTING?
TSUZUKI NEEDS A NEW PARTNER AGAIN.
UM..
I...
I THINK I MIGHT STAY A WHILE LONGER.
OH?
Splash

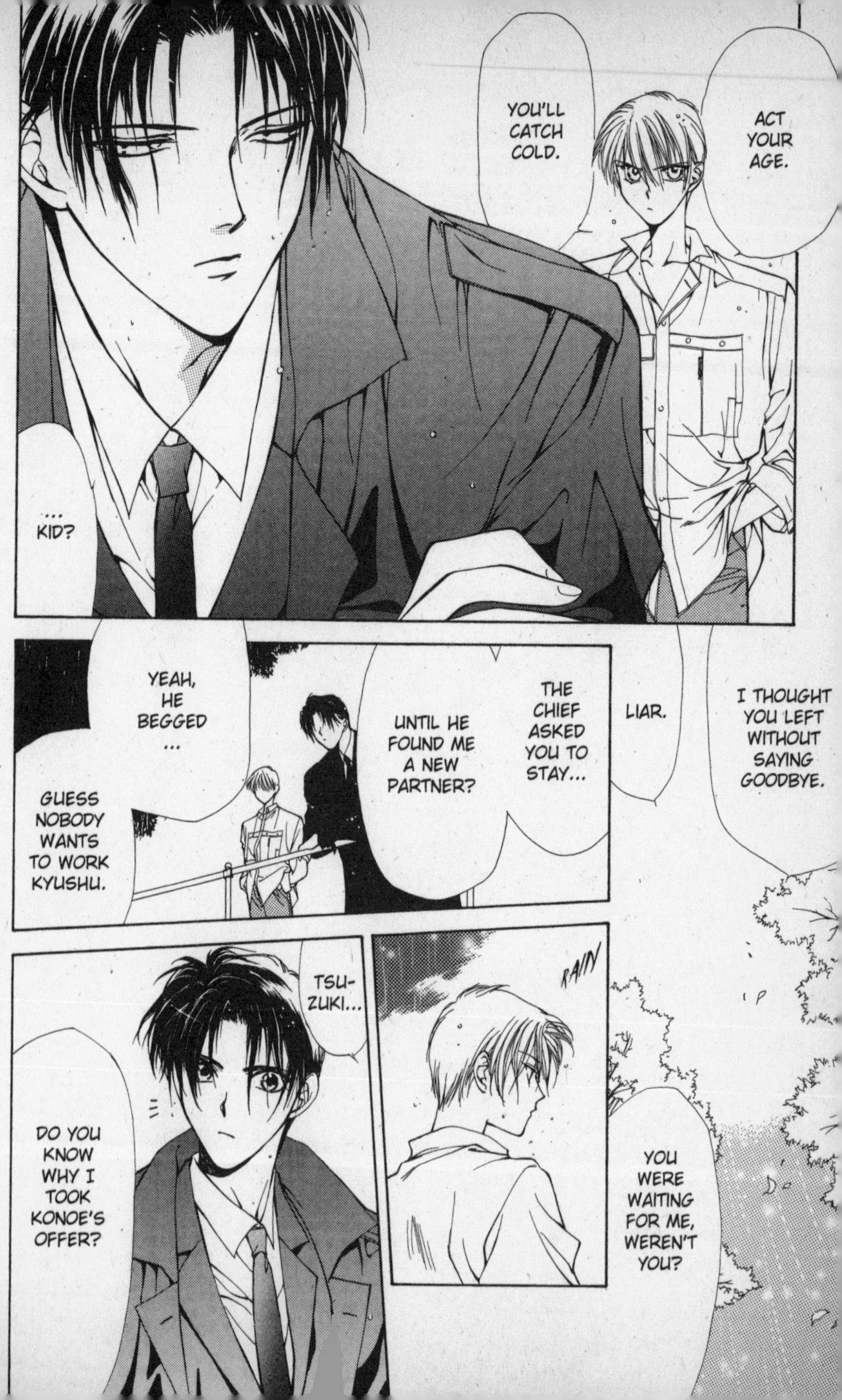
ACT YOUR AGE.
YOU'LL CATCH COLD.
... KID?
I THOUGHT YOU LEFT WITHOUT SAYING GOODBYE.
LIAR.
THE CHIEF ASKED YOU TO STAY...
UNTIL HE FOUND ME A NEW PARTNER?
YEAH, HE BEGGED ...
GUESS NOBODY WANTS TO WORK KYUSHU.
RAIN
YOU WERE WAITING FOR ME, WEREN'T YOU?
TSU-ZUKI...
DO YOU KNOW WHY I TOOK KONOE'S OFFER?

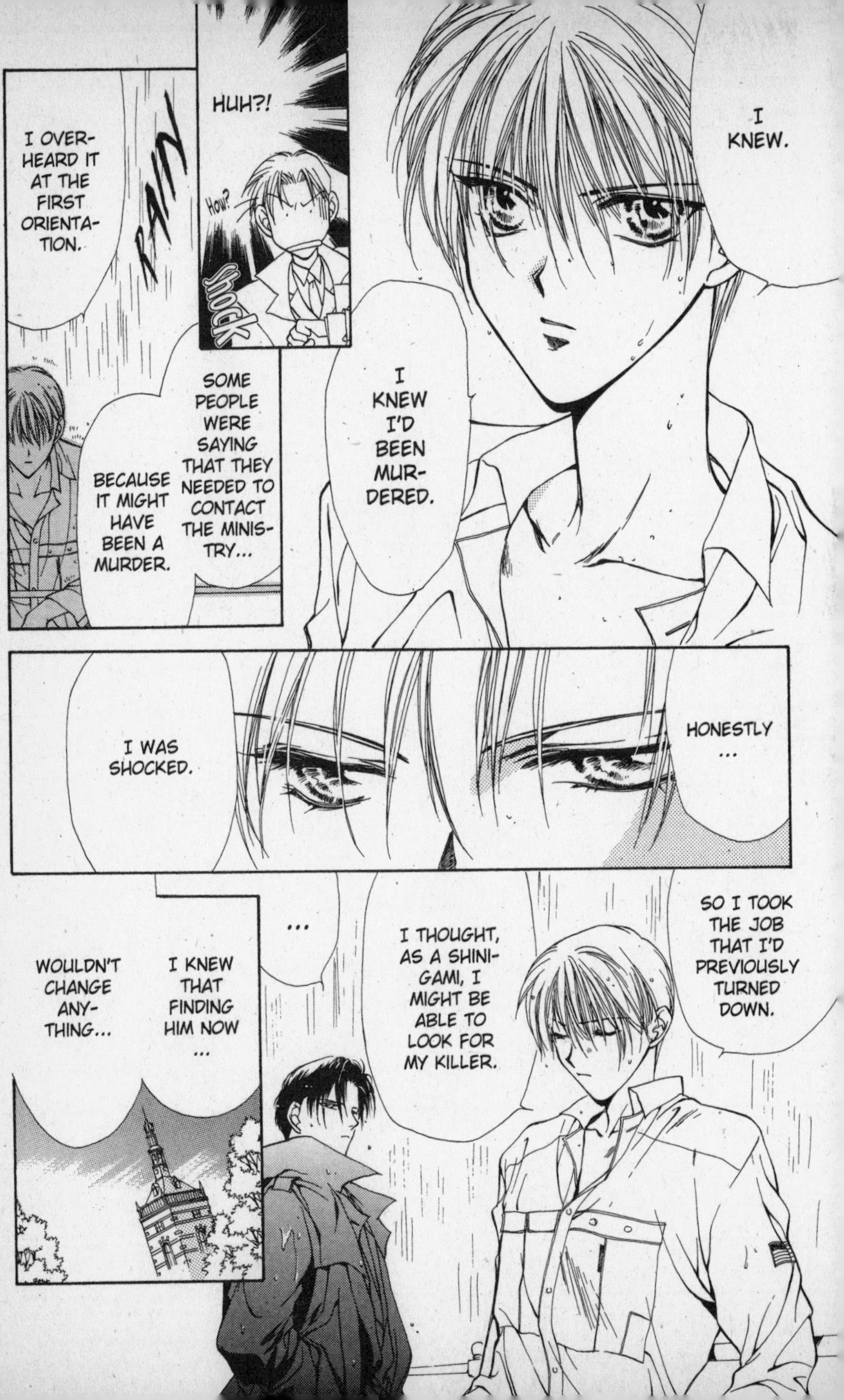
I KNEW.
I KNEW I'D BEEN MURDERED.
HUH?!
How?
shock
RAIN
I OVER-HEARD IT AT THE FIRST ORIENTA-TION.
SOME PEOPLE WERE SAYING THAT THEY NEEDED TO CONTACT THE MINIS-TRY...
BECAUSE IT MIGHT HAVE BEEN A MURDER.
HONESTLY ...
I WAS SHOCKED.
SO I TOOK THE JOB THAT I'D PREVIOUSLY TURNED DOWN.
I THOUGHT, AS A SHINI-GAMI, I MIGHT BE ABLE TO LOOK FOR MY KILLER.
...
I KNEW THAT FINDING HIM NOW ...
WOULDN'T CHANGE ANY-THING...

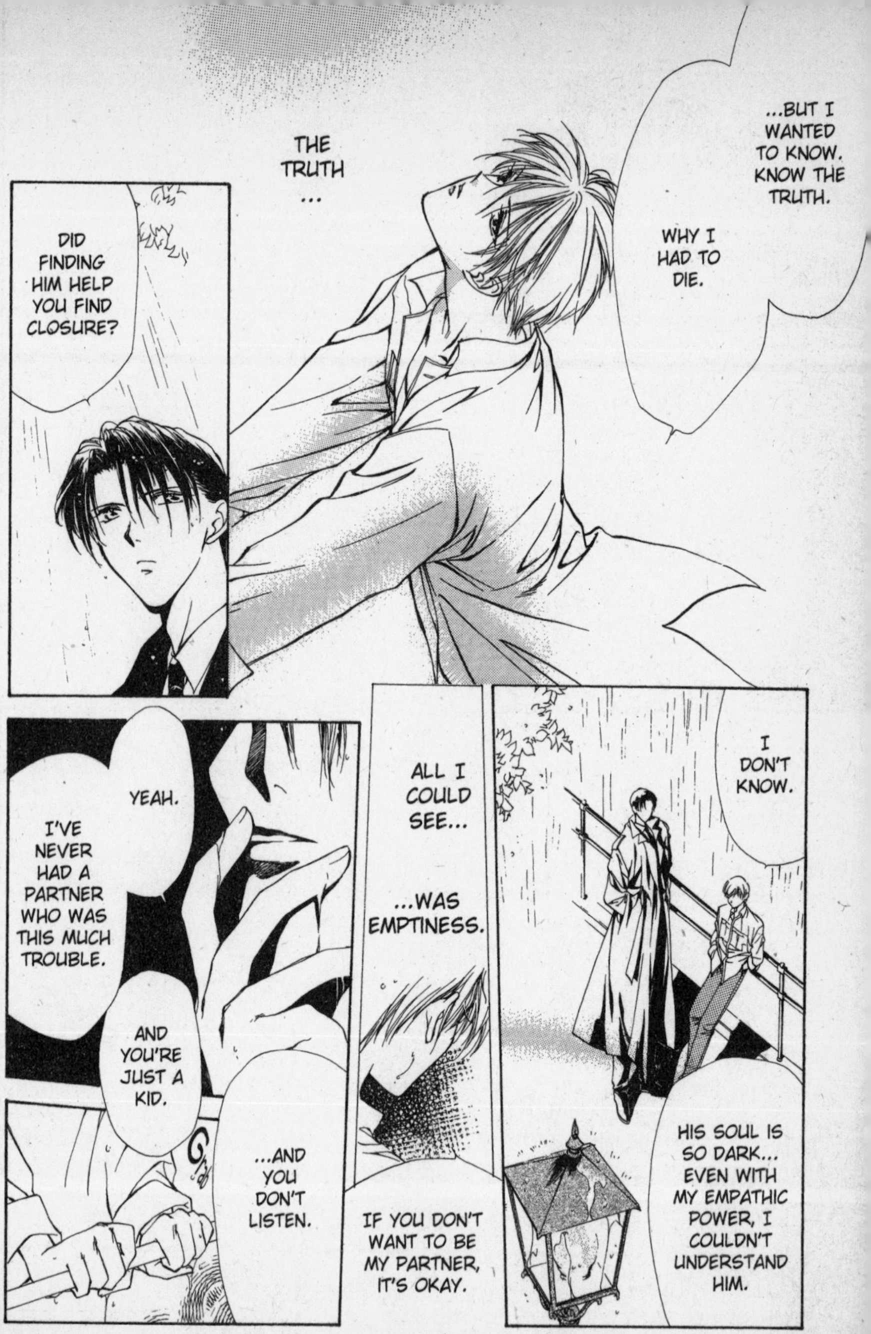
...BUT I WANTED TO KNOW. KNOW THE TRUTH.
WHY I HAD TO DIE.
THE TRUTH ...
DID FINDING HIM HELP YOU FIND CLOSURE?
I DON'T KNOW.
HIS SOUL IS SO DARK... EVEN WITH MY EMPATHIC POWER, I COULDN'T UNDERSTAND HIM.
ALL I COULD SEE...
...WAS EMPTINESS.
IF YOU DON'T WANT TO BE MY PARTNER, IT'S OKAY.
YEAH.
I'VE NEVER HAD A PARTNER WHO WAS THIS MUCH TROUBLE.
AND YOU'RE JUST A KID.
...AND YOU DON'T LISTEN.

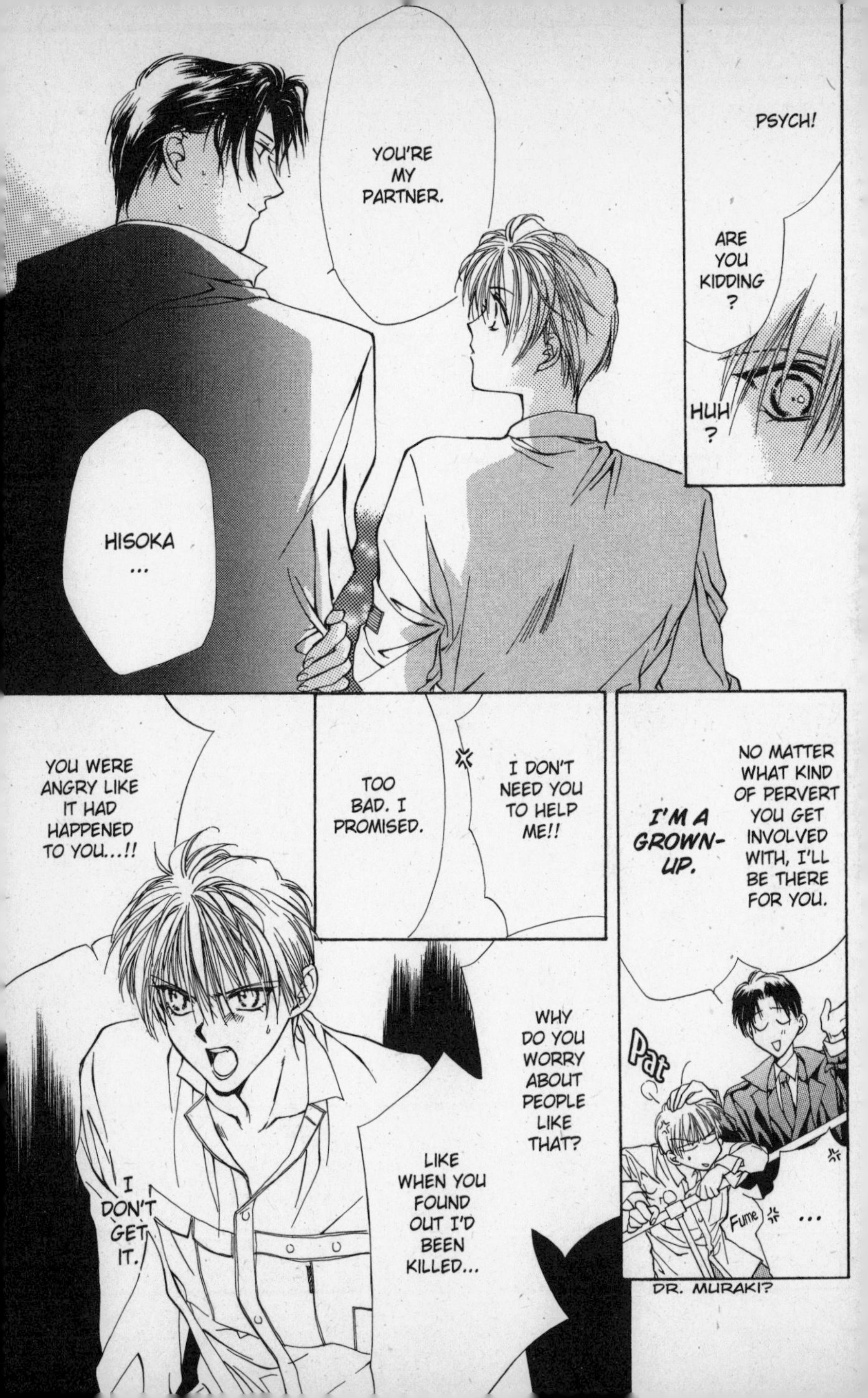
PSYCH!
ARE YOU KIDDING?
HUH?
YOU'RE MY PARTNER.
HISOKA...
NO MATTER WHAT KIND OF PERVERT YOU GET INVOLVED WITH, I'LL BE THERE FOR YOU.
I'M A GROWN-UP.
Pat
Fume
...
DR. MURAKI?
I DON'T NEED YOU TO HELP ME!!
TOO BAD. I PROMISED.
WHY DO YOU WORRY ABOUT PEOPLE LIKE THAT?
LIKE WHEN YOU FOUND OUT I'D BEEN KILLED...
YOU WERE ANGRY LIKE IT HAD HAPPENED TO YOU...!!
I DON'T GET IT.

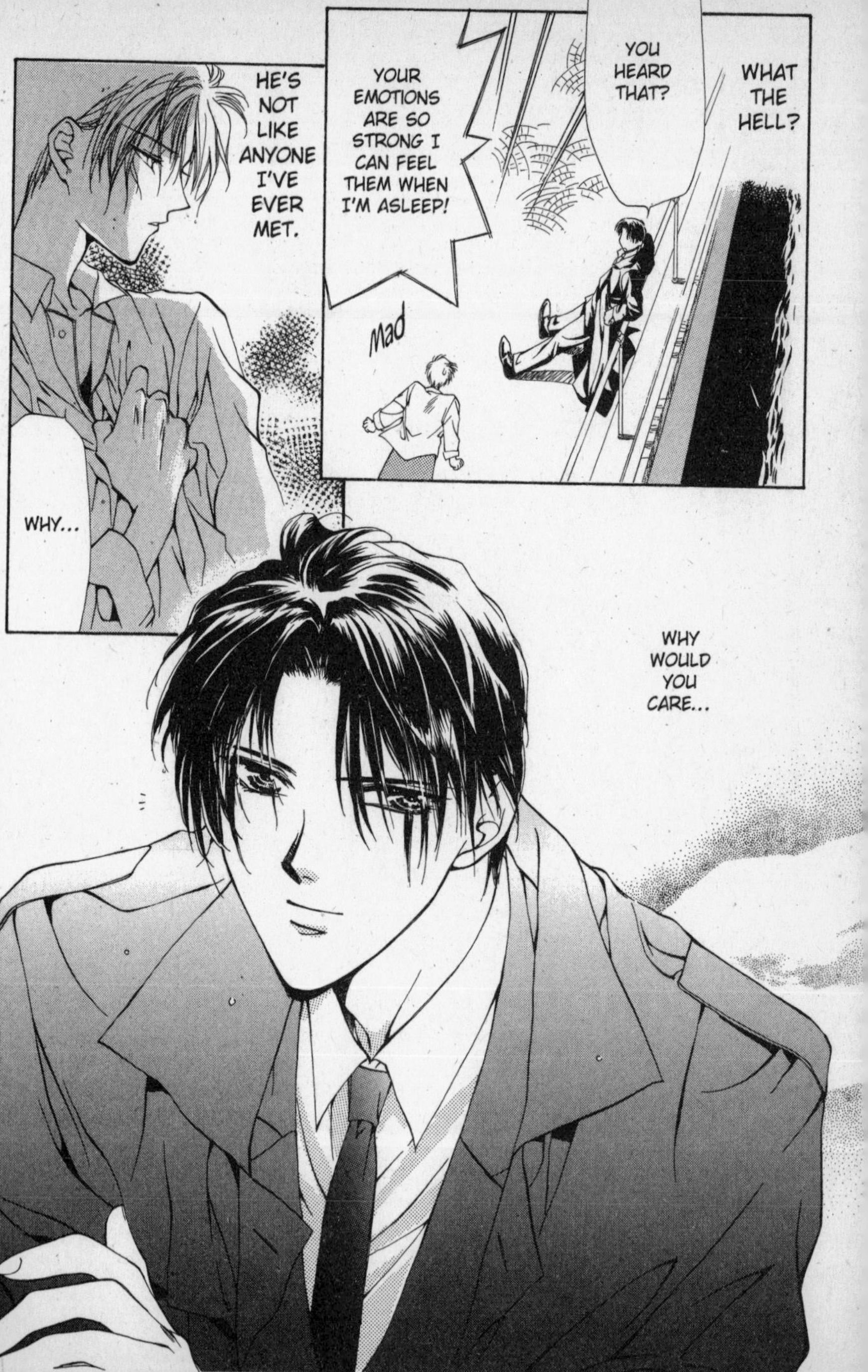
WHAT THE HELL?
YOU HEARD THAT?
YOUR EMOTIONS ARE SO STRONG I CAN FEEL THEM WHEN I'M ASLEEP!
Mad
HE'S NOT LIKE ANYONE I'VE EVER MET.
WHY...
WHY WOULD YOU CARE...

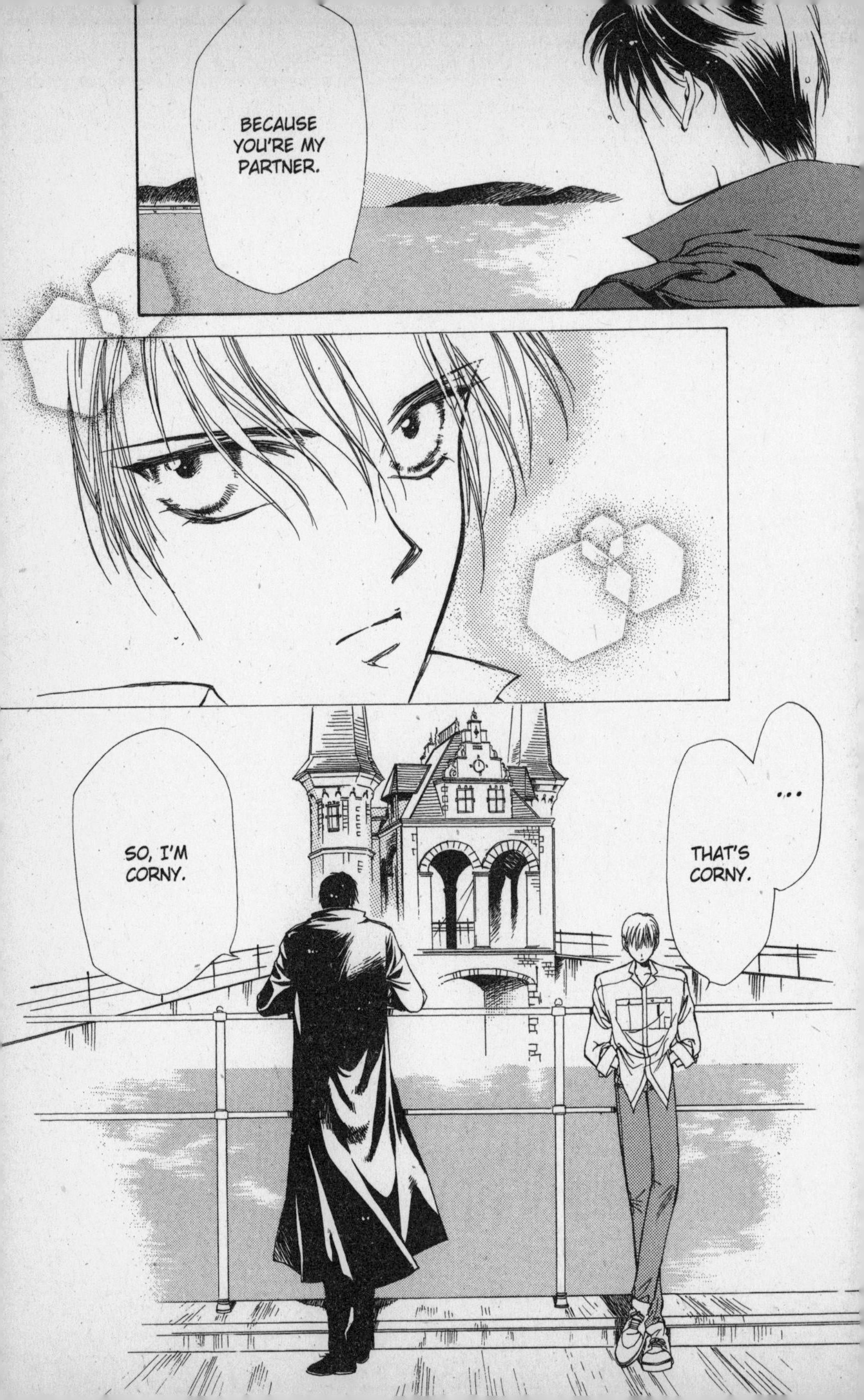
BECAUSE YOU'RE MY PARTNER.
... THAT'S CORNY.
SO, I'M CORNY.

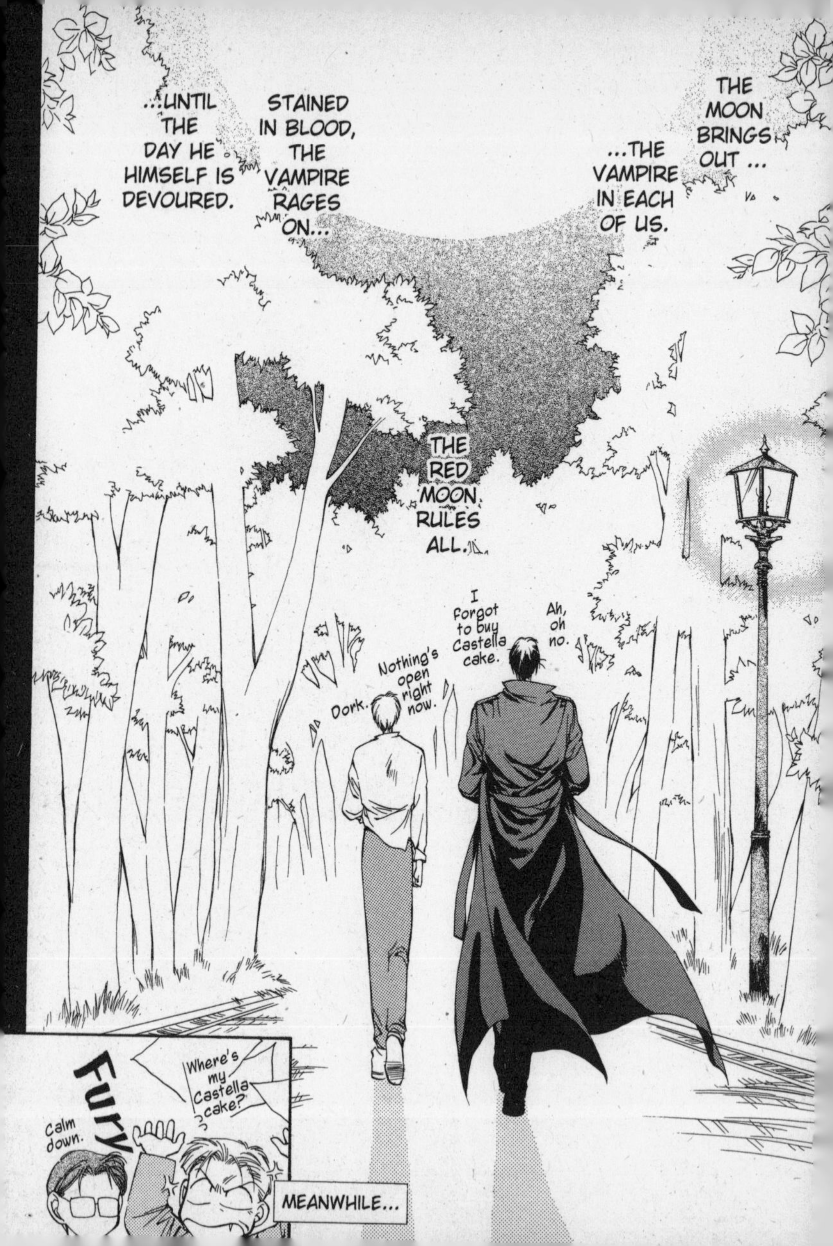
THE MOON BRINGS OUT ...
...THE VAMPIRE IN EACH OF US.
STAINED IN BLOOD, THE VAMPIRE RAGES ON...
...UNTIL THE DAY HE HIMSELF IS DEVOURED.
THE RED MOON RULES ALL.
Ah, oh no.
I forgot to buy Castella cake.
Nothing's open right now.
Dork.
MEANWHILE...
Where's my Castella cake?
Fury
Calm down.

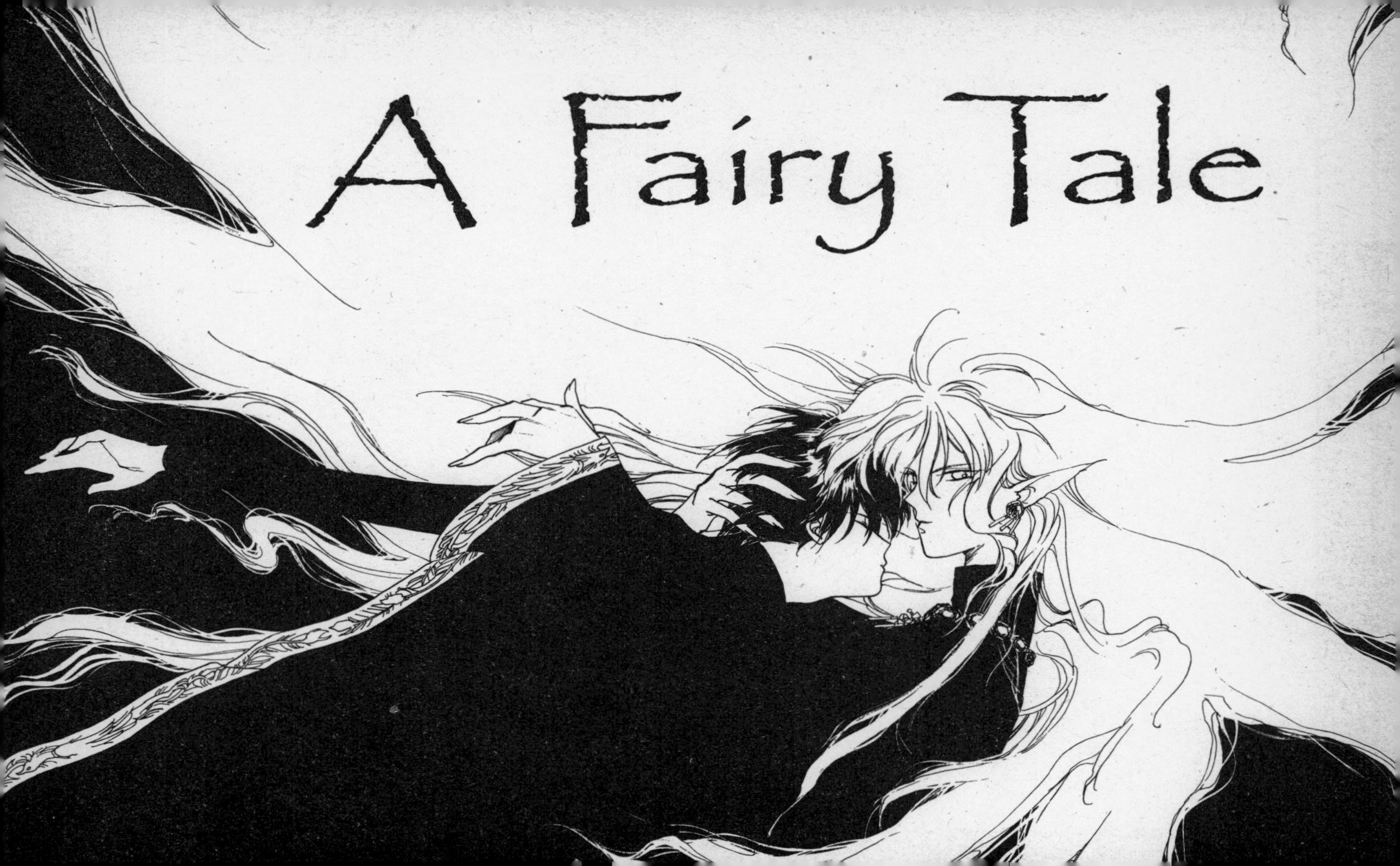
A Fairy Tale

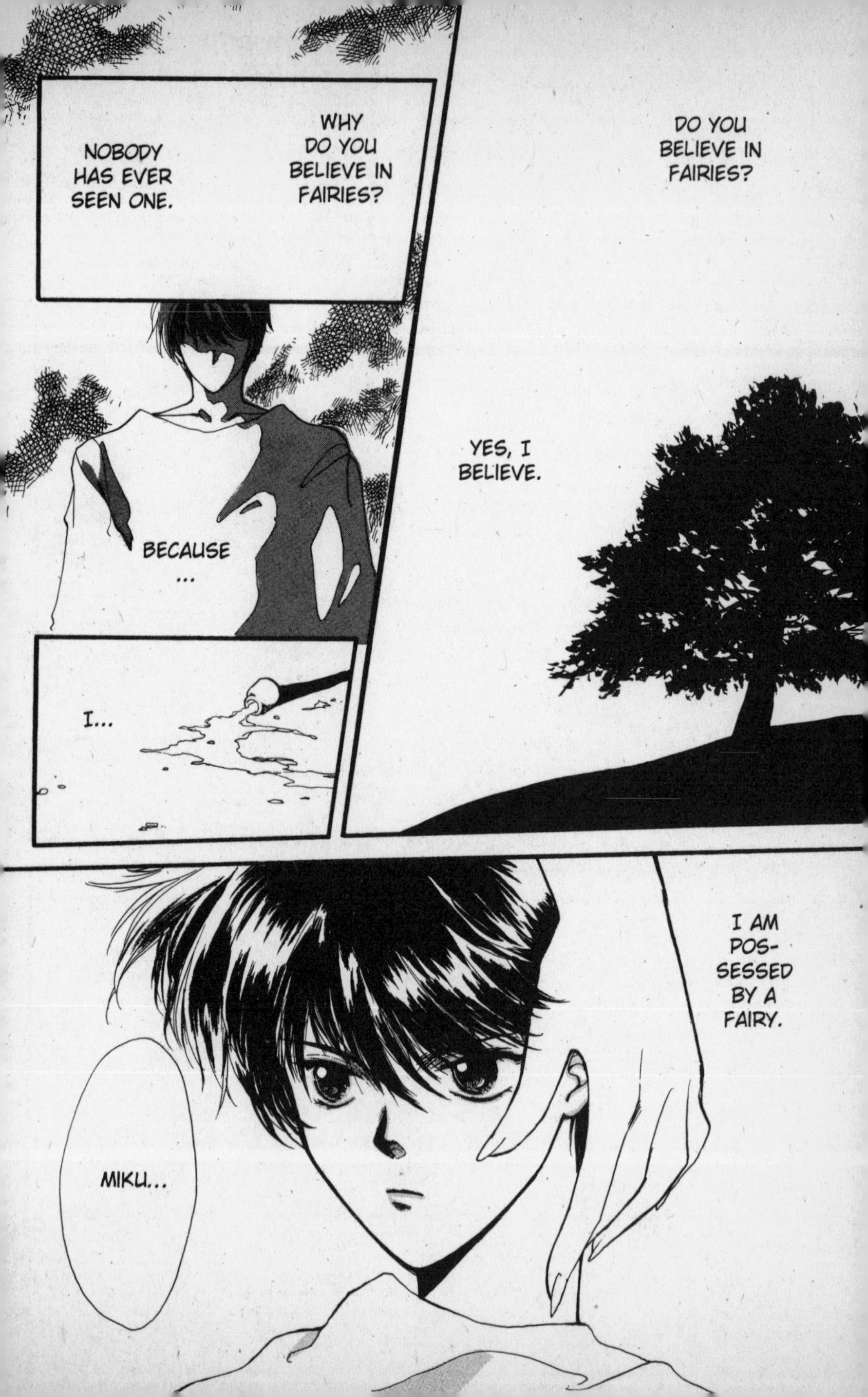
DO YOU BELIEVE IN FAIRIES?
YES, I BELIEVE.
WHY DO YOU BELIEVE IN FAIRIES?
NOBODY HAS EVER SEEN ONE.
BECAUSE ...
I...
I AM POS-SESSED BY A FAIRY.
MIKU...

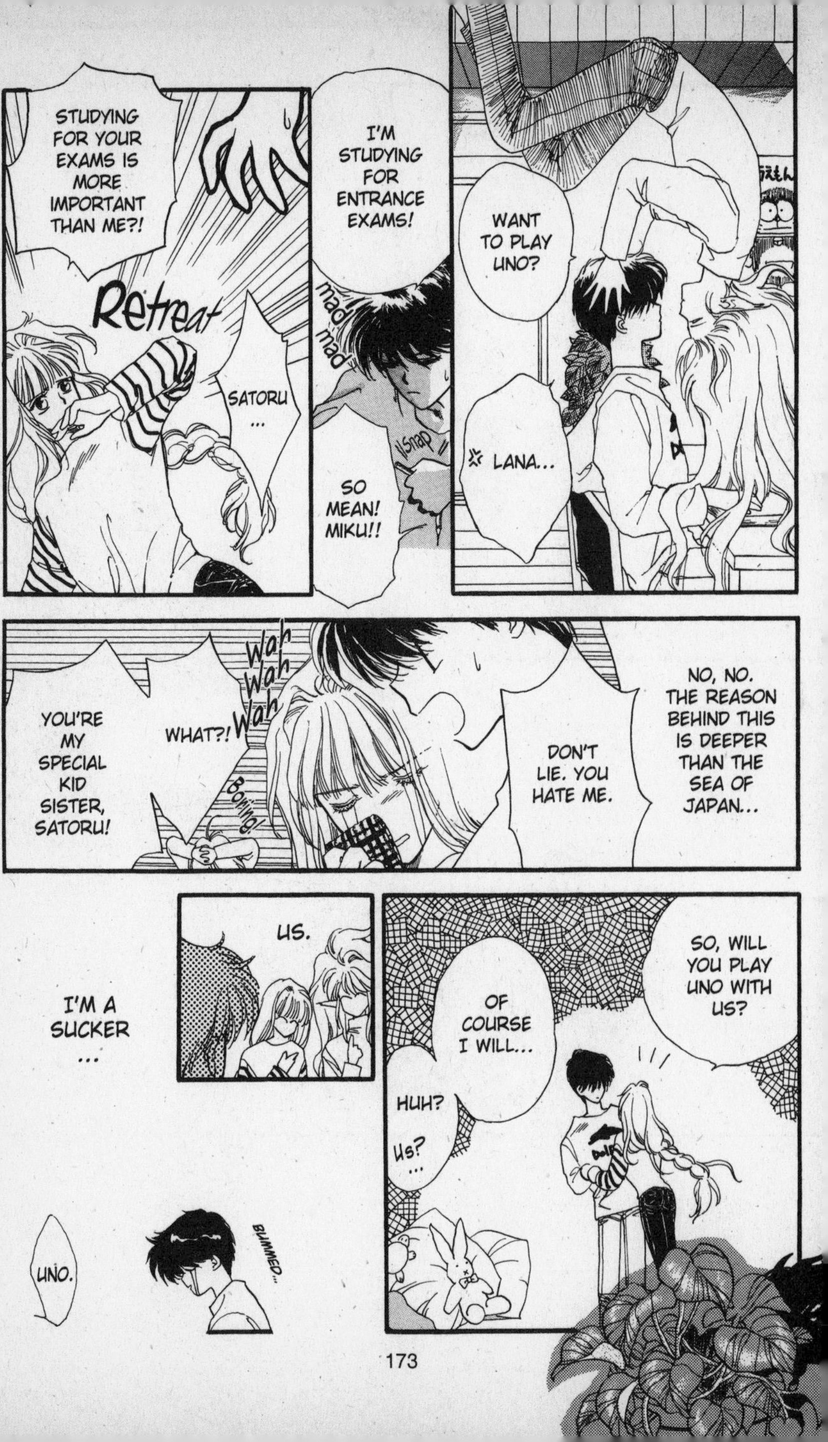
WANT TO PLAY UNO?
LANA...
I'M STUDYING FOR ENTRANCE EXAMS!
mad mad
Snap
SO MEAN! MIKU!!
STUDYING FOR YOUR EXAMS IS MORE IMPORTANT THAN ME?!
Retreat
SATORU ...
NO, NO. THE REASON BEHIND THIS IS DEEPER THAN THE SEA OF JAPAN...
DON'T LIE. YOU HATE ME.
Wah Wah Wah
Boing!
WHAT?!
YOU'RE MY SPECIAL KID SISTER, SATORU!
SO, WILL YOU PLAY UNO WITH US?
OF COURSE I WILL...
HUH? US? ...
US.
I'M A SUCKER ...
BUMMED...
UNO.

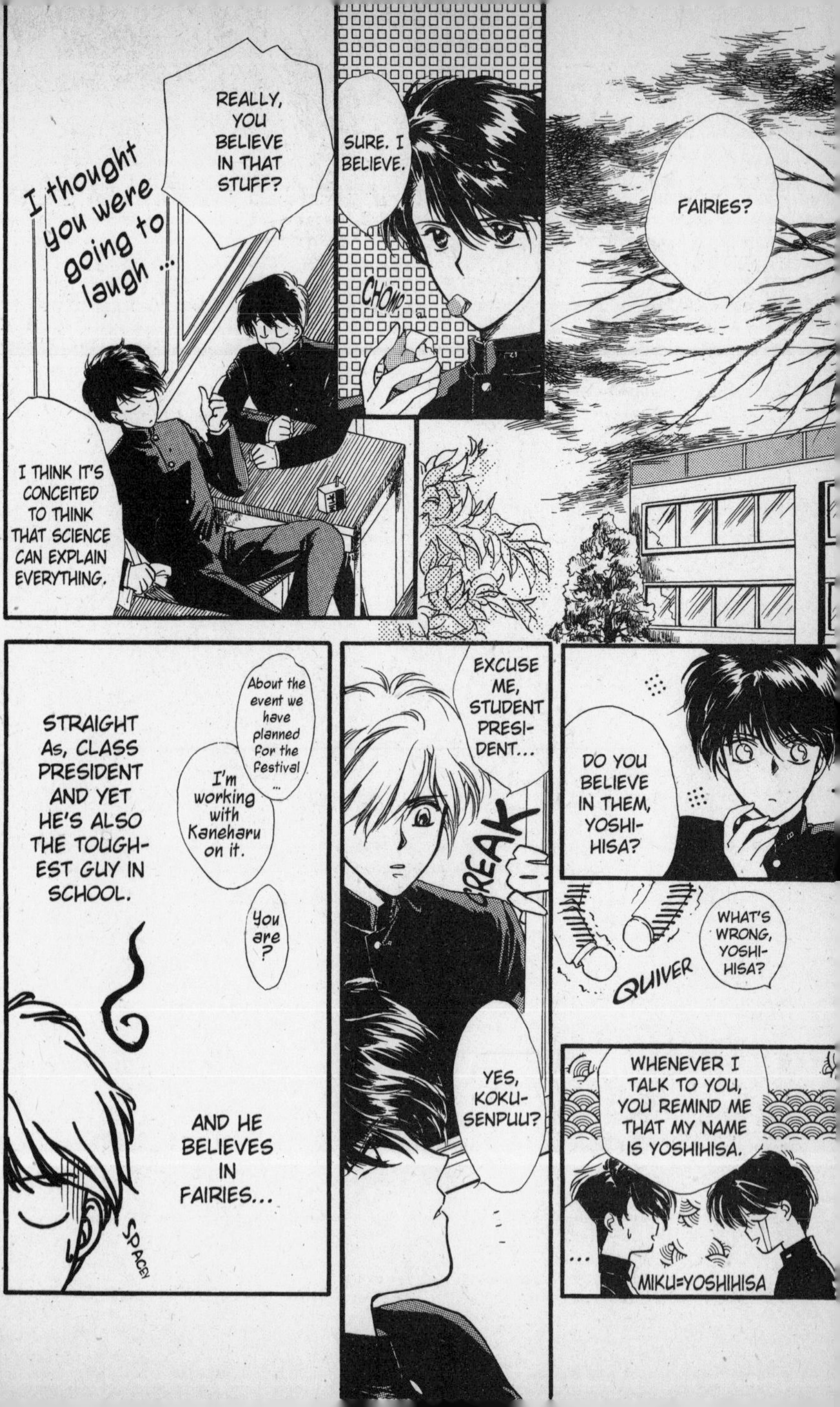
FAIRIES?
SURE. I BELIEVE.
CHOMP
REALLY, YOU BELIEVE IN THAT STUFF?
I thought you were going to laugh ...
I THINK IT'S CONCEITED TO THINK THAT SCIENCE CAN EXPLAIN EVERYTHING.
DO YOU BELIEVE IN THEM, YOSHI-HISA?
WHAT'S WRONG, YOSHI-HISA?
QUIVER
WHENEVER I TALK TO YOU, YOU REMIND ME THAT MY NAME IS YOSHIHISA.
...
MIKU=YOSHIHISA
EXCUSE ME, STUDENT PRESI-DENT...
CREAK
YES, KOKU-SENPUU?
About the event we have planned for the festival ...
I'm working with Kaneharu on it.
You are?
STRAIGHT As, CLASS PRESIDENT AND YET HE'S ALSO THE TOUGH-EST GUY IN SCHOOL.
AND HE BELIEVES IN FAIRIES...
SPACEY

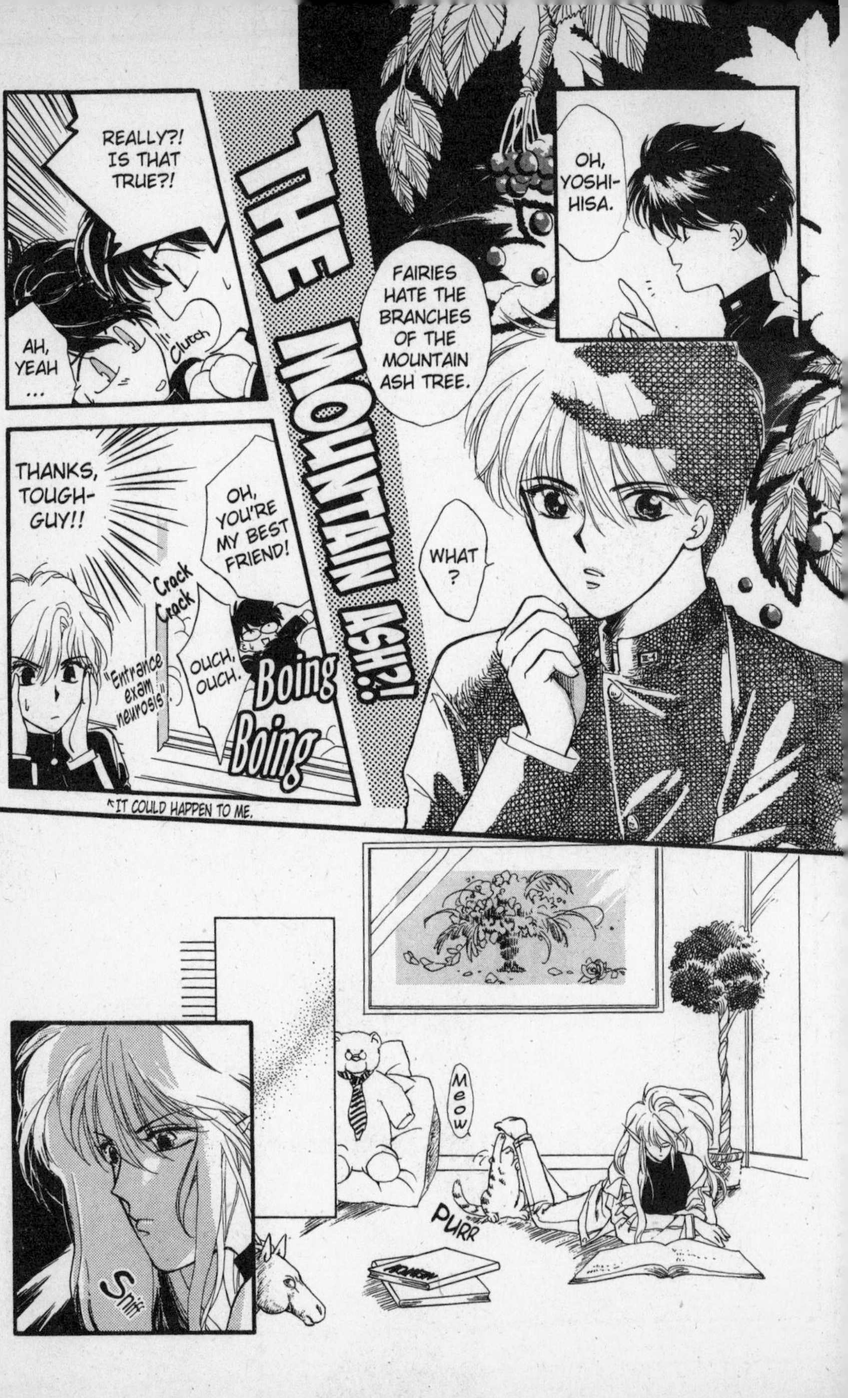
OH, YOSHI-HISA.
FAIRIES HATE THE BRANCHES OF THE MOUNTAIN ASH TREE.
WHAT?
THE MOUNTAIN ASH?!
REALLY?! IS THAT TRUE?!
Clutch
AH, YEAH ...
OH, YOU'RE MY BEST FRIEND!
THANKS, TOUGH-GUY!!
Crack Crack
Boing Boing
OUCH, OUCH.
"Entrance exam neurosis".
↖IT COULD HAPPEN TO ME.
Meow
PURR
Sniff

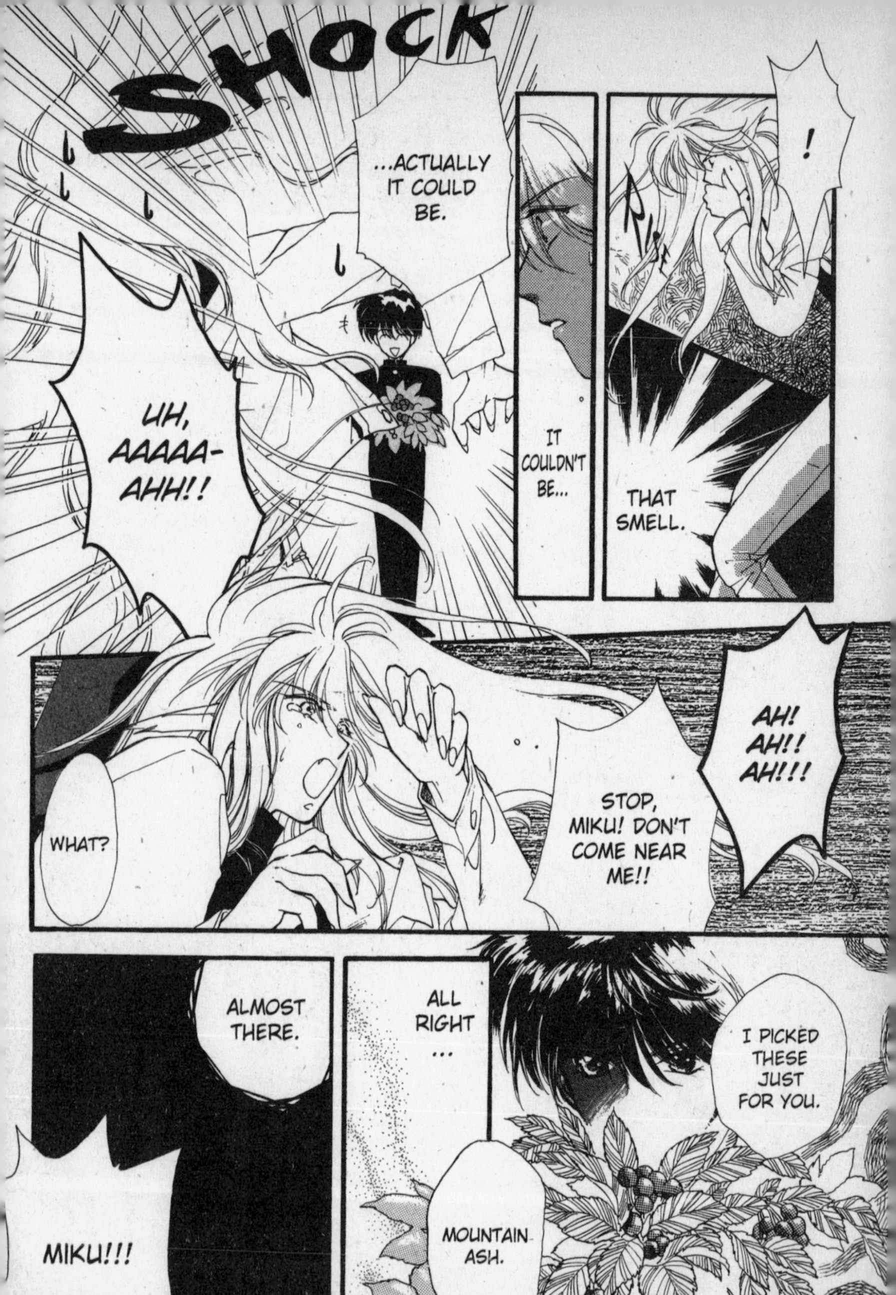
!
RISE
THAT SMELL.
IT COULDN'T BE...
...ACTUALLY IT COULD BE.
SHOCK
UH, AAAAA-AHH!!
AH! AH!! AH!!!
STOP, MIKU! DON'T COME NEAR ME!!
WHAT?
I PICKED THESE JUST FOR YOU.
MOUNTAIN ASH.
ALL RIGHT ...
ALMOST THERE.
MIKU!!!

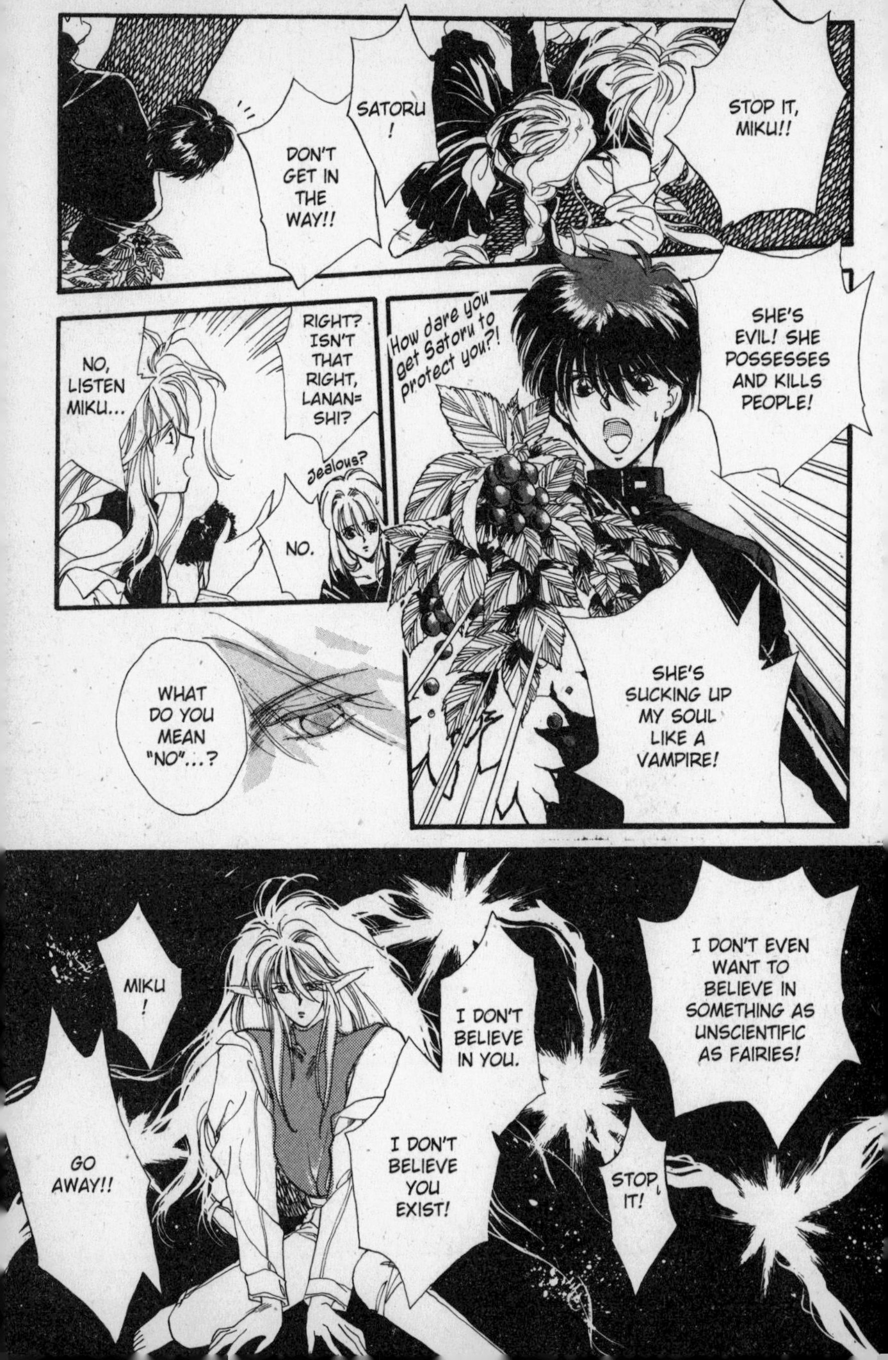
STOP IT, MIKU!!
SATORU!
DON'T GET IN THE WAY!!
SHE'S EVIL! SHE POSSESSES AND KILLS PEOPLE!
How dare you get Satoru to protect you?!
SHE'S SUCKING UP MY SOUL LIKE A VAMPIRE!
RIGHT? ISN'T THAT RIGHT, LANAN=SHI?
NO, LISTEN MIKU...
Jealous?
NO.
WHAT DO YOU MEAN "NO"...?
I DON'T EVEN WANT TO BELIEVE IN SOMETHING AS UNSCIENTIFIC AS FAIRIES!
I DON'T BELIEVE IN YOU.
MIKU!
STOP IT!
I DON'T BELIEVE YOU EXIST!
GO AWAY!!

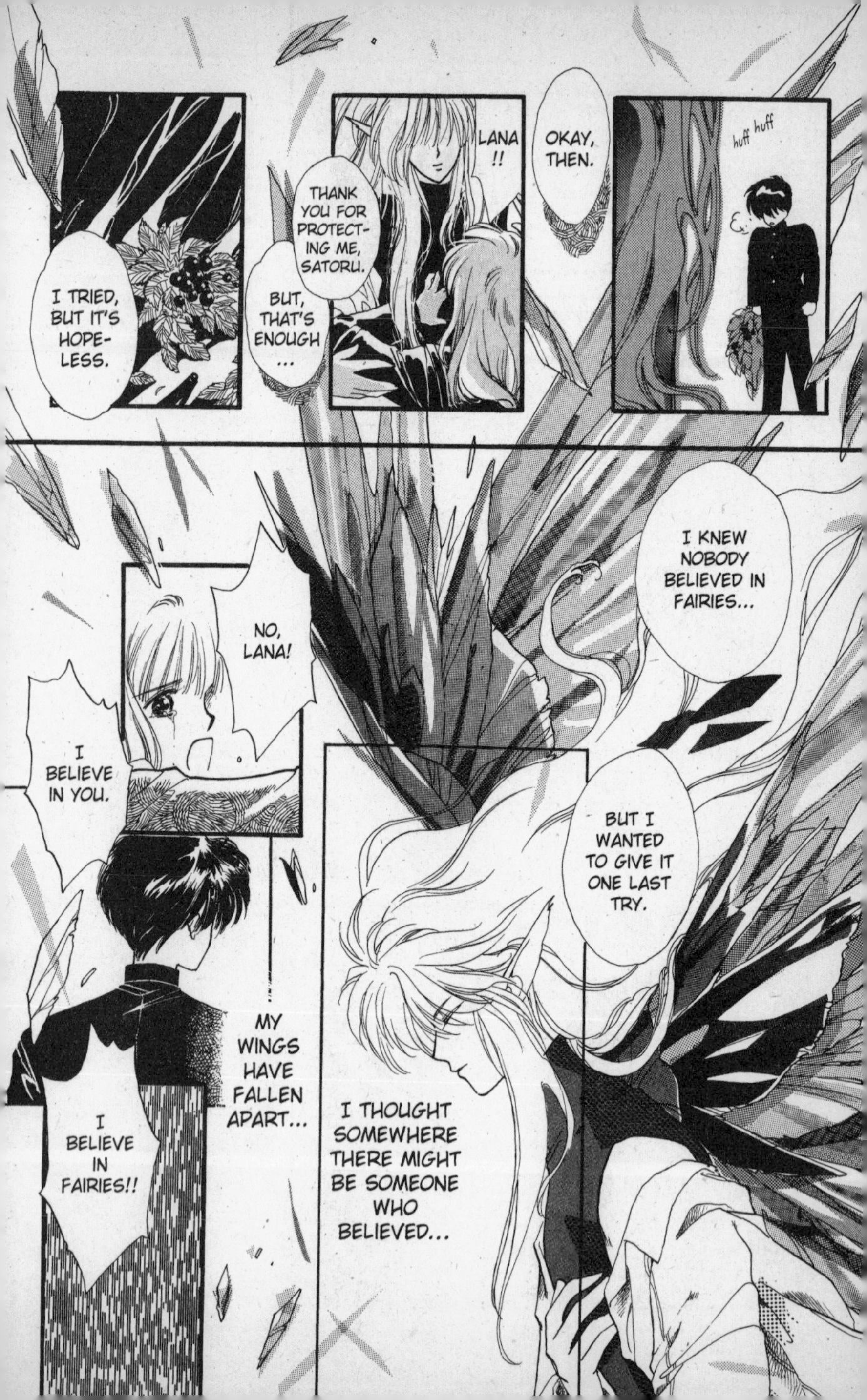
huff huff
OKAY, THEN.
LANA !!
THANK YOU FOR PROTECTING ME, SATORU.
BUT, THAT'S ENOUGH...
I TRIED, BUT IT'S HOPELESS.
I KNEW NOBODY BELIEVED IN FAIRIES...
BUT I WANTED TO GIVE IT ONE LAST TRY.
I THOUGHT SOMEWHERE THERE MIGHT BE SOMEONE WHO BELIEVED...
MY WINGS HAVE FALLEN APART...
NO, LANA!
I BELIEVE IN YOU.
I BELIEVE IN FAIRIES!!

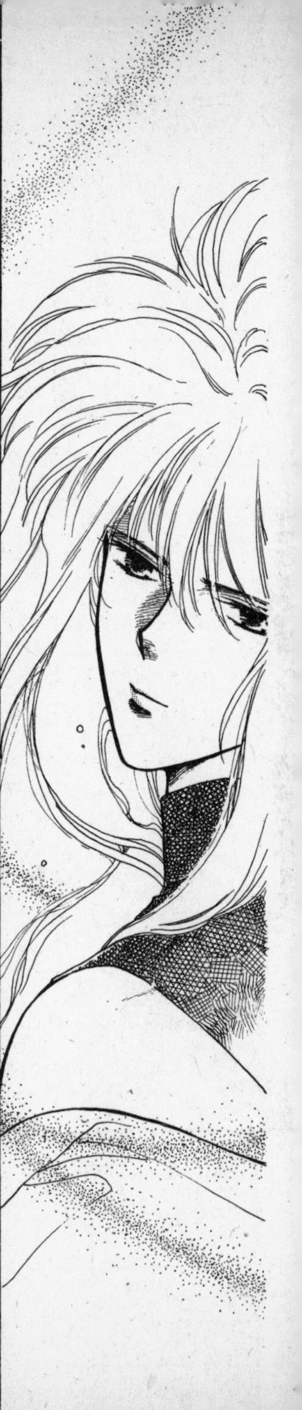

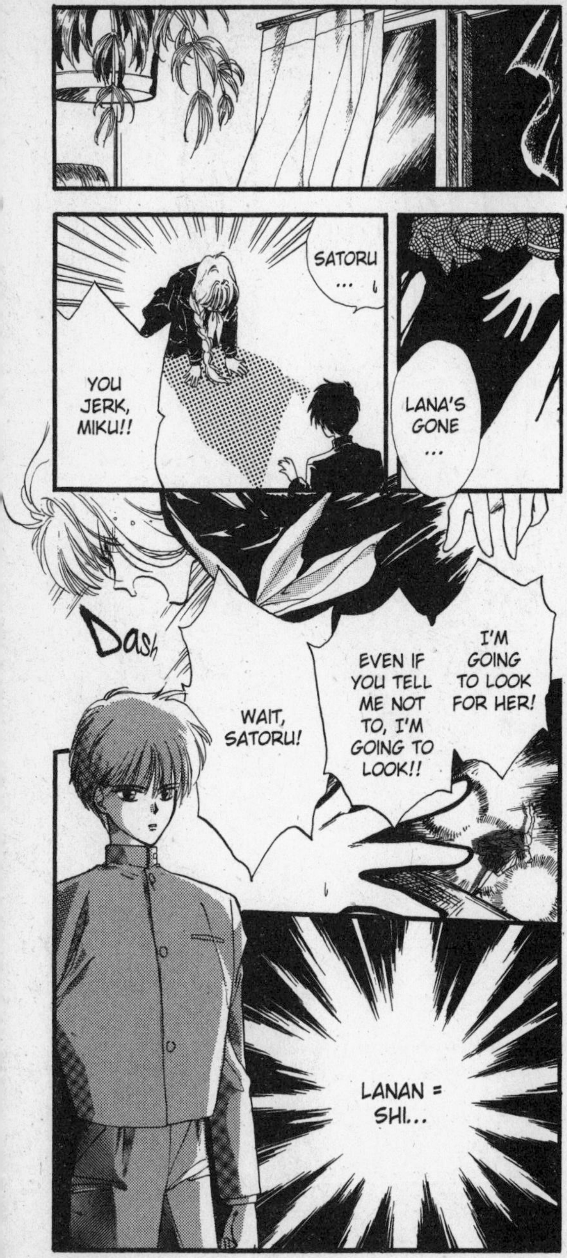
LANA'S GONE ...
SATORU ...
YOU JERK, MIKU!!
Dash
I'M GOING TO LOOK FOR HER!
EVEN IF YOU TELL ME NOT TO, I'M GOING TO LOOK!!
WAIT, SATORU!
LANAN = SHI...

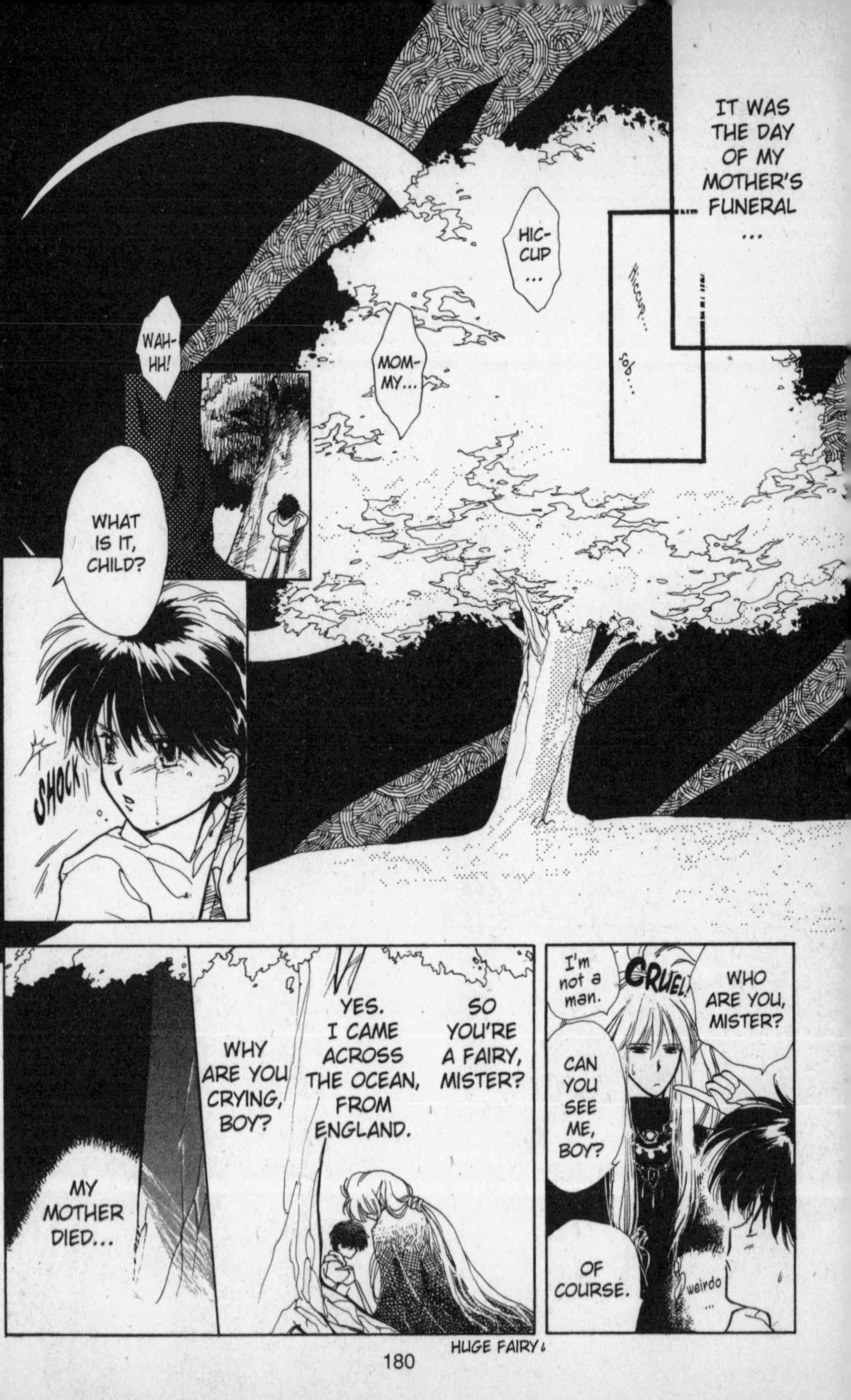
IT WAS THE DAY OF MY MOTHER'S FUNERAL...
Hiccup... sob...
HIC-CUP...
MOM-MY...
WAH-HH!
WHAT IS IT, CHILD?
SHOCK
WHO ARE YOU, MISTER?
CRUEL!
I'm not a man.
CAN YOU SEE ME, BOY?
OF COURSE.
weirdo...
SO YOU'RE A FAIRY, MISTER?
YES. I CAME ACROSS THE OCEAN, FROM ENGLAND.
WHY ARE YOU CRYING, BOY?
MY MOTHER DIED...
HUGE FAIRY

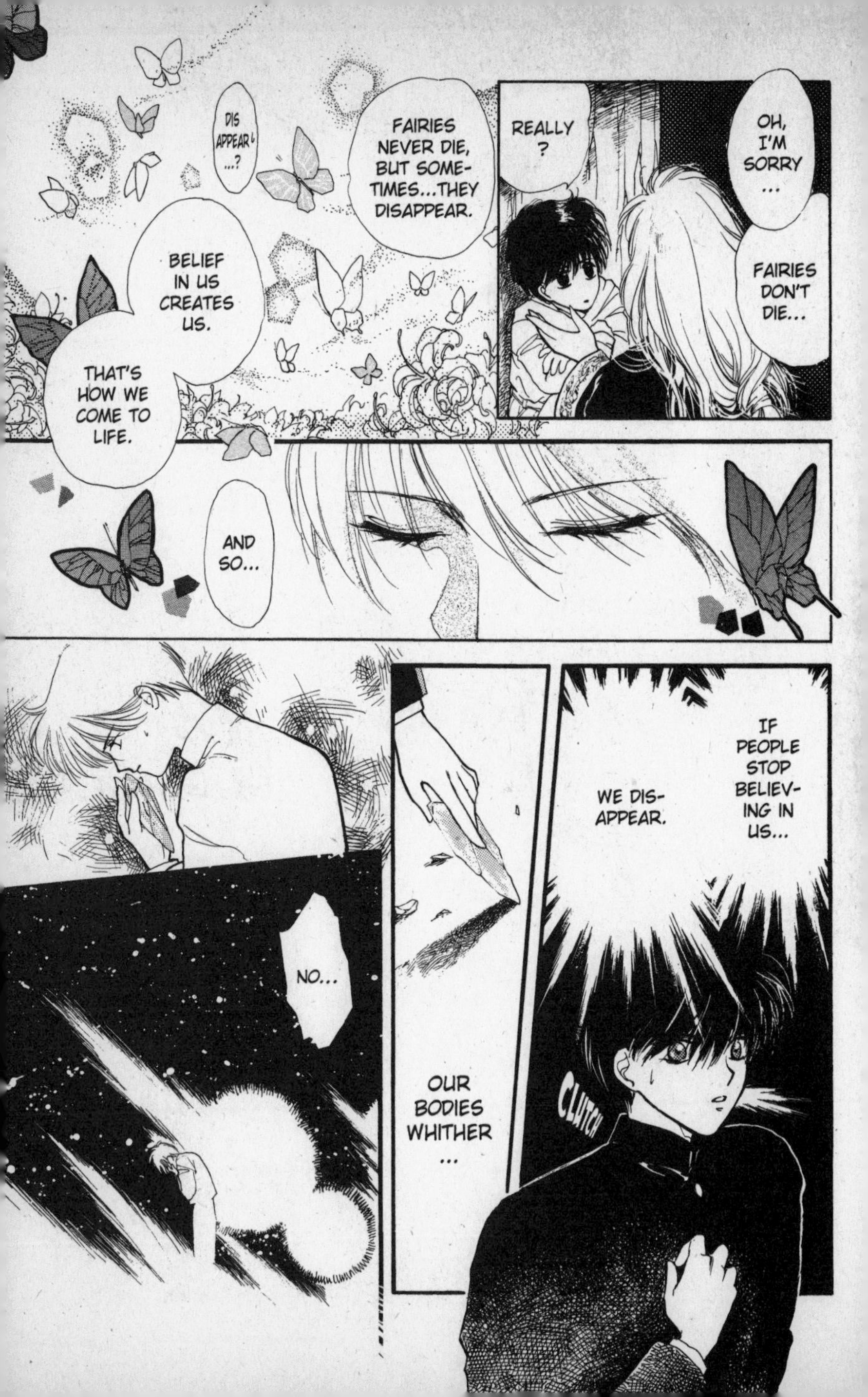

OH, I'M SORRY...
FAIRIES DON'T DIE...
REALLY?
FAIRIES NEVER DIE, BUT SOME-TIMES...THEY DISAPPEAR.
DIS APPEAR...?
BELIEF IN US CREATES US.
THAT'S HOW WE COME TO LIFE.
AND SO...
IF PEOPLE STOP BELIEV-ING IN US...
WE DIS-APPEAR.
CLUTCH
OUR BODIES WHITHER...
NO...

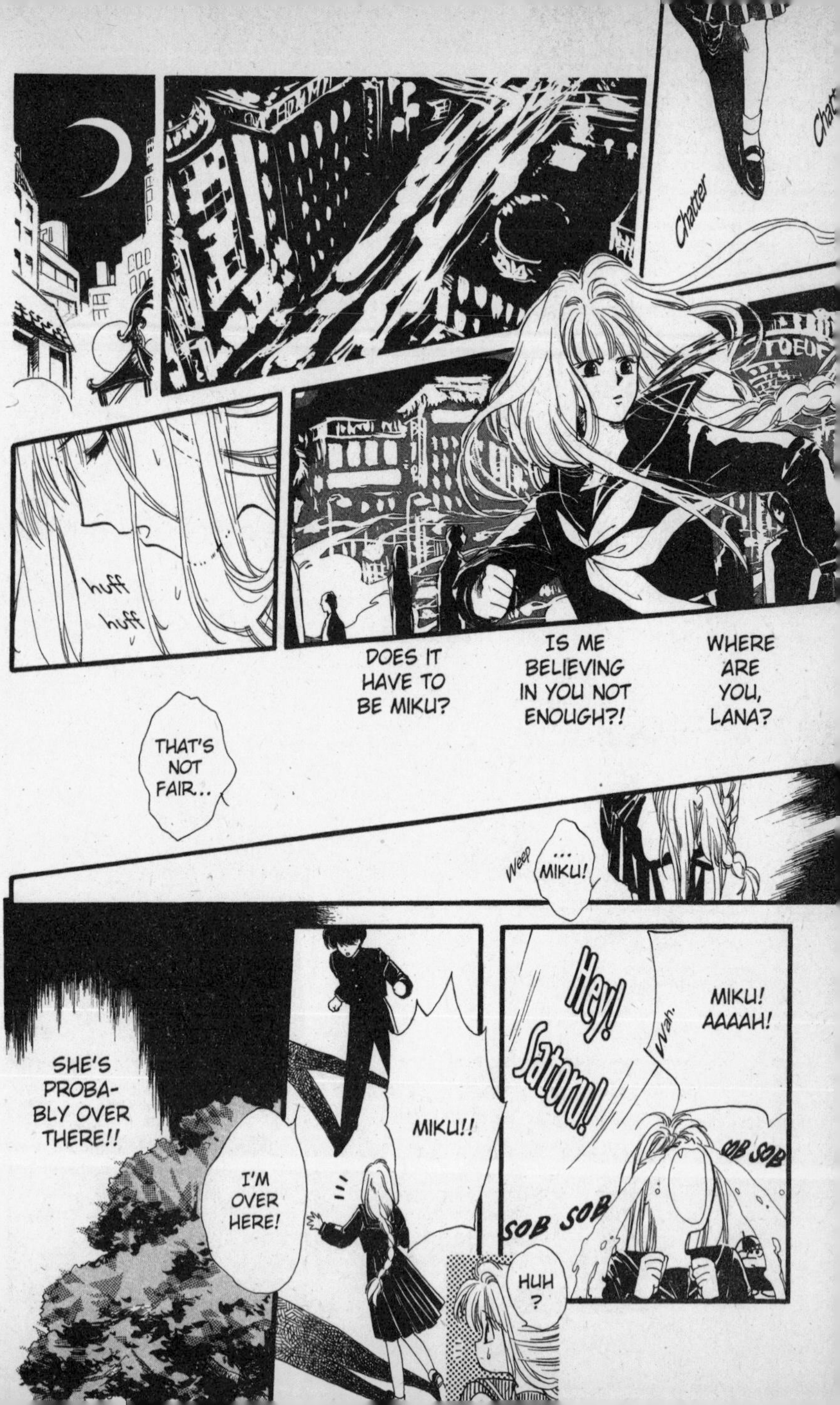
Chatt
Chatter
WHERE ARE YOU, LANA?
IS ME BELIEVING IN YOU NOT ENOUGH?!
DOES IT HAVE TO BE MIKU?
huff
huff
THAT'S NOT FAIR..
...MIKU!
Weep
MIKU! AAAAH!
Wah.
Hey! Satoru!
SOB SOB
SOB SOB
HUH?
MIKU!!
I'M OVER HERE!
SHE'S PROBA-BLY OVER THERE!!

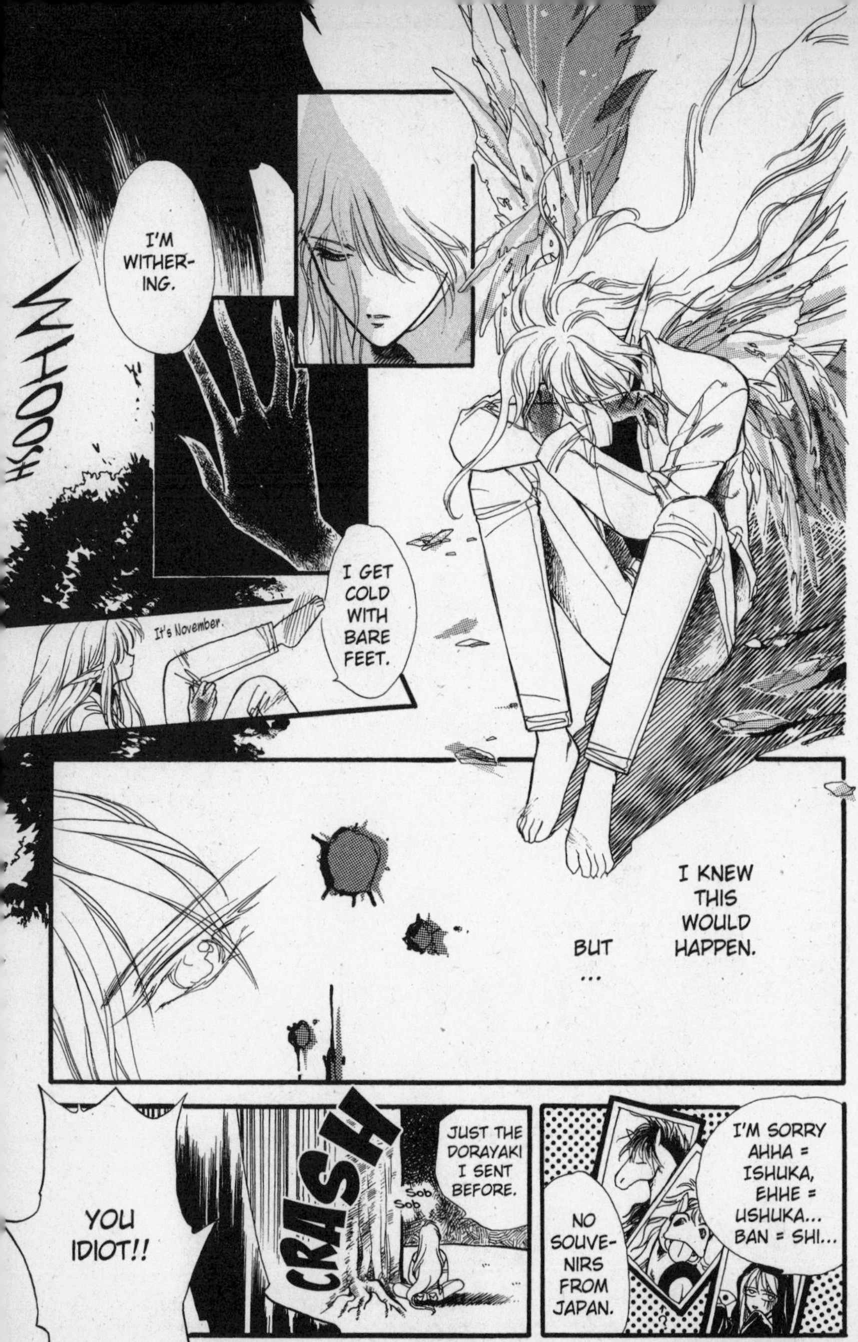
I KNEW THIS WOULD HAPPEN.
BUT ...
I'M WITHER-ING.
WHOOSH
I GET COLD WITH BARE FEET.
It's November.
I'M SORRY AHHA = ISHUKA, EHHE = USHUKA... BAN = SHI...
NO SOUVE-NIRS FROM JAPAN.
JUST THE DORAYAKI I SENT BEFORE.
Sob Sob
CRASH
YOU IDIOT!!
NO GOOD FRIENDS.

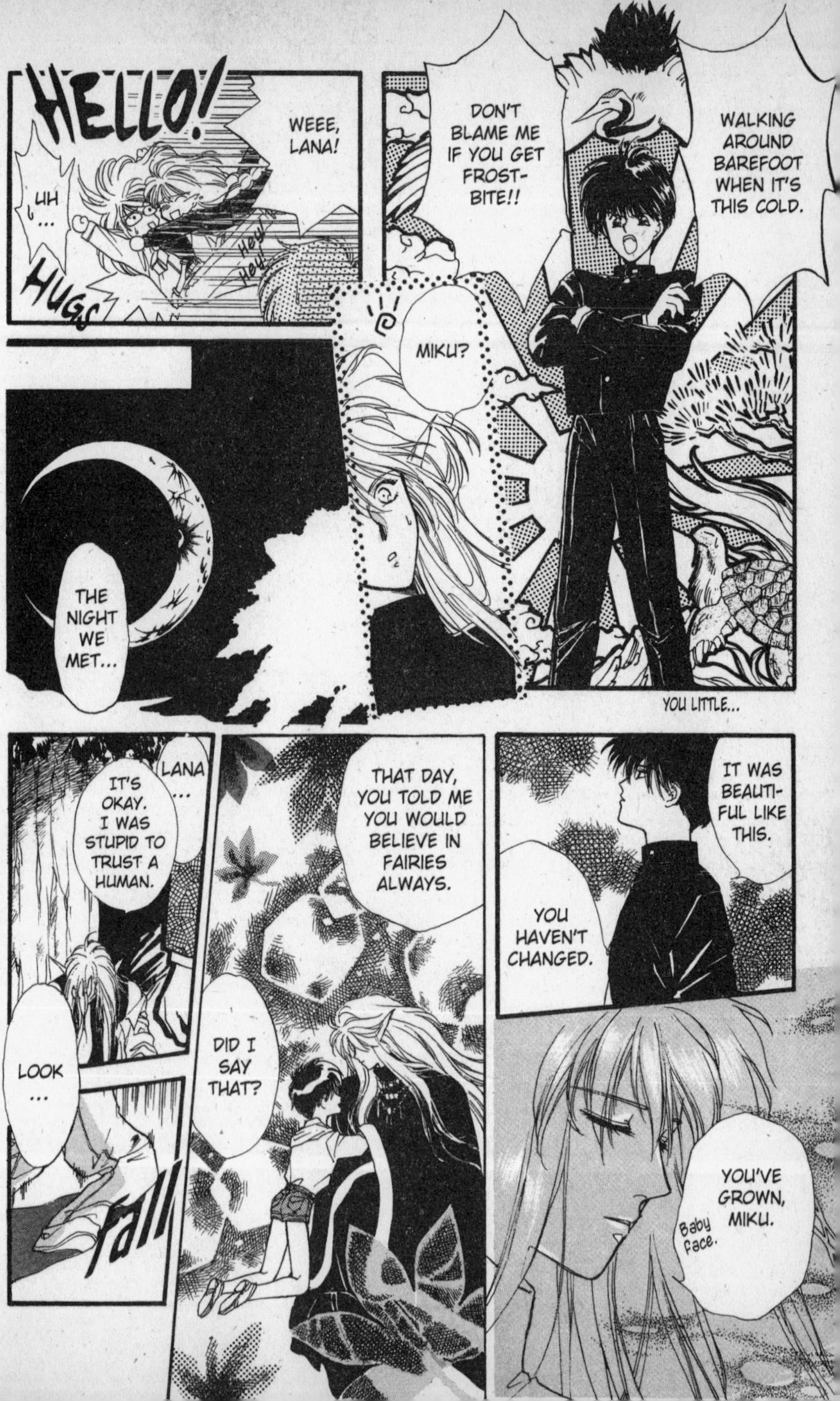
WALKING AROUND BAREFOOT WHEN IT'S THIS COLD.
DON'T BLAME ME IF YOU GET FROST-BITE!!
HELLO!
WEEE, LANA!
UH...
Hey Hey
HUGS
YOU LITTLE...
MIKU?
THE NIGHT WE MET...
IT WAS BEAUTI-FUL LIKE THIS.
YOU HAVEN'T CHANGED.
YOU'VE GROWN, MIKU.
Baby face.
THAT DAY, YOU TOLD ME YOU WOULD BELIEVE IN FAIRIES ALWAYS.
DID I SAY THAT?
LANA...
IT'S OKAY. I WAS STUPID TO TRUST A HUMAN.
LOOK...
fall

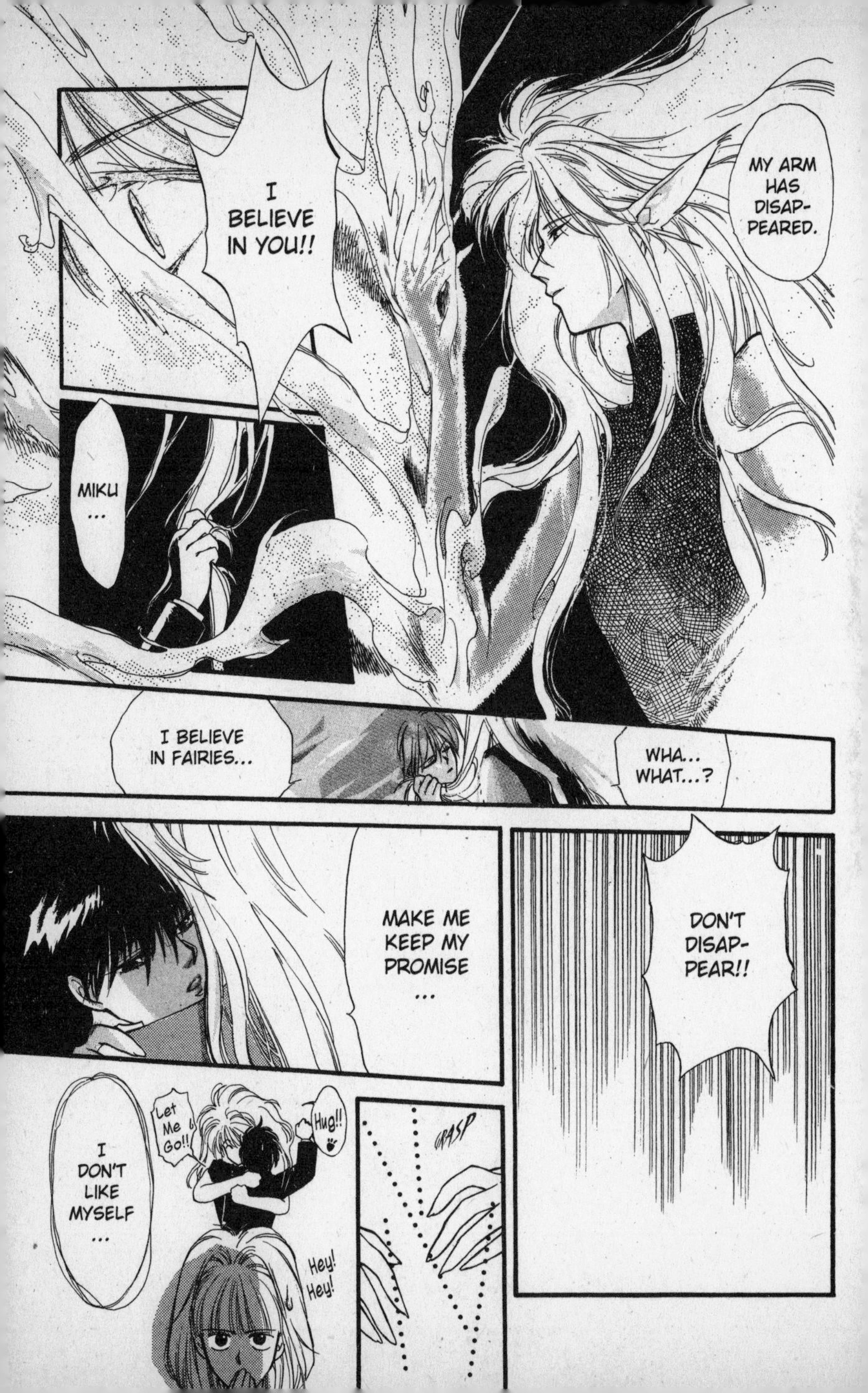
MY ARM HAS DISAP-PEARED.
I BELIEVE IN YOU!!
MIKU ...
WHA... WHAT...?
I BELIEVE IN FAIRIES...
DON'T DISAP-PEAR!!
MAKE ME KEEP MY PROMISE ...
GRASP
Hug!!
Let Me Go!!
I DON'T LIKE MYSELF ...
Hey! Hey!

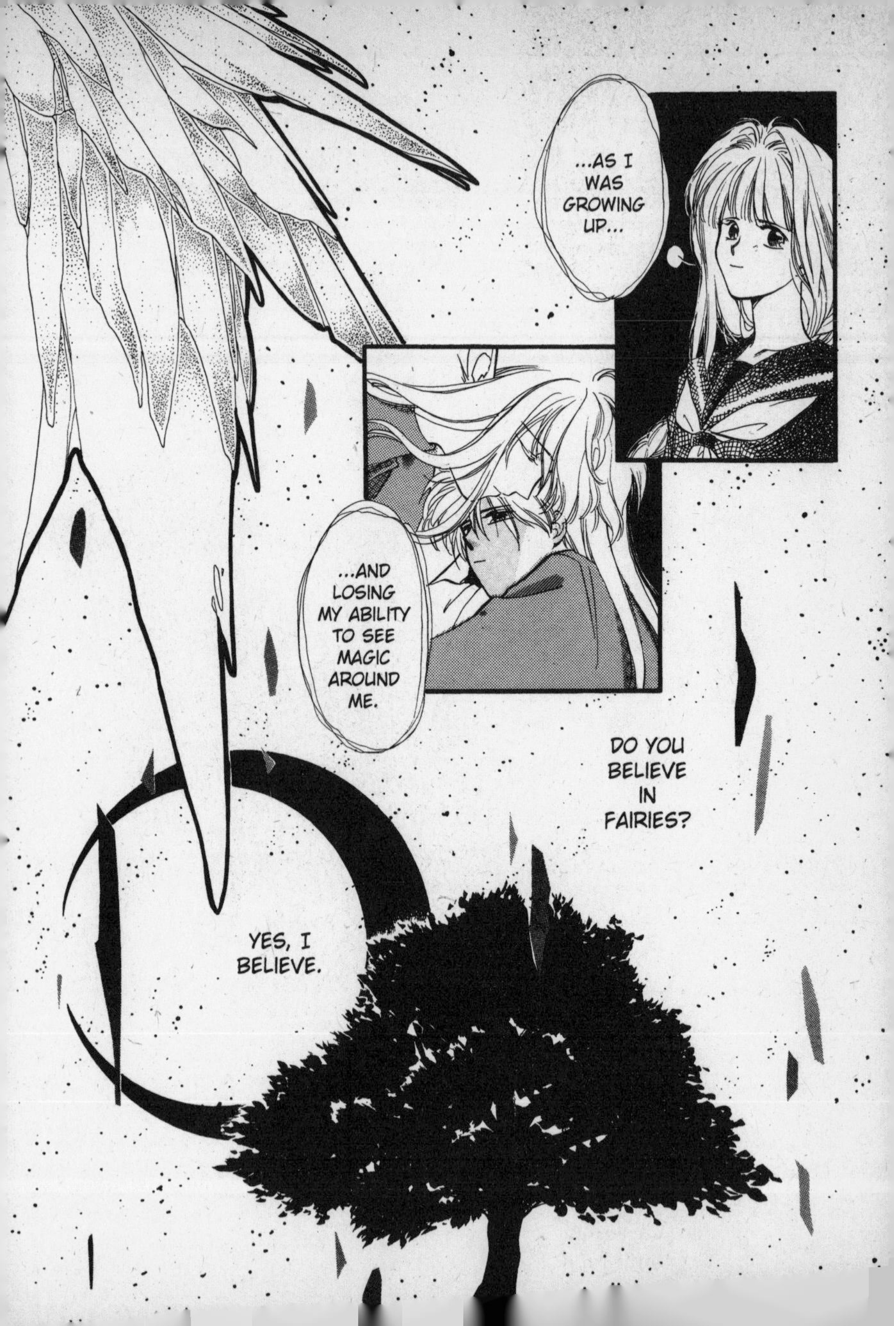
...AS I WAS GROWING UP...
...AND LOSING MY ABILITY TO SEE MAGIC AROUND ME.
DO YOU BELIEVE IN FAIRIES?
YES, I BELIEVE.

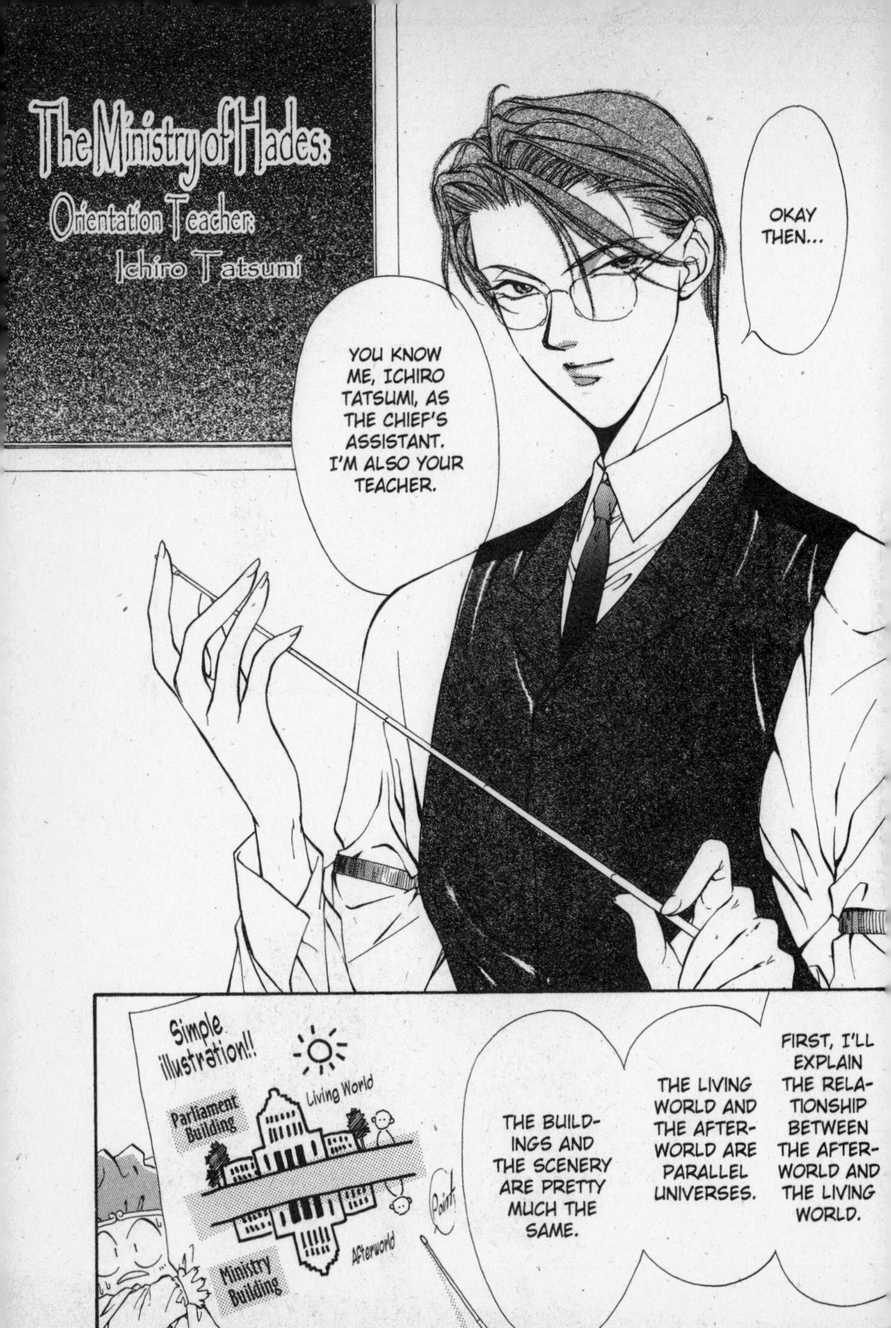
The Ministry of Hades:
Orientation Teacher:
Ichiro Tatsumi
OKAY THEN...
YOU KNOW ME, ICHIRO TATSUMI, AS THE CHIEF'S ASSISTANT. I'M ALSO YOUR TEACHER.
FIRST, I'LL EXPLAIN THE RELATIONSHIP BETWEEN THE AFTERWORLD AND THE LIVING WORLD.
THE LIVING WORLD AND THE AFTERWORLD ARE PARALLEL UNIVERSES.
THE BUILDINGS AND THE SCENERY ARE PRETTY MUCH THE SAME.
Point
Simple illustration!!
Living World
Parliament Building
Afterworld
Ministry Building

THE MINISTRY IS DIRECTLY BENEATH THE PARLIAMENT.

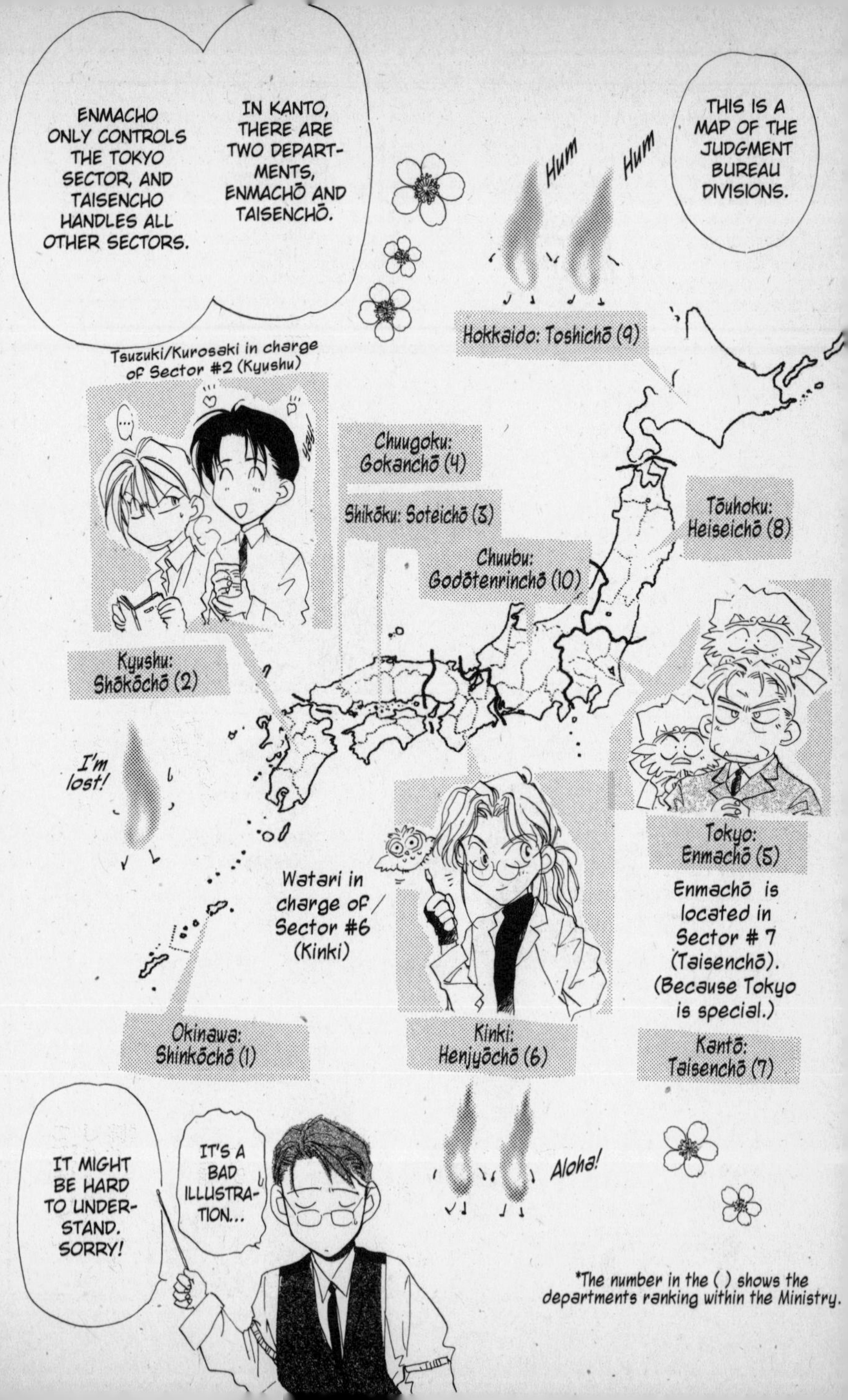
THIS IS A MAP OF THE JUDGMENT BUREAU DIVISIONS.
Hum Hum
IN KANTO, THERE ARE TWO DEPART-MENTS, ENMACHŌ AND TAISENCHŌ.
ENMACHO ONLY CONTROLS THE TOKYO SECTOR, AND TAISENCHO HANDLES ALL OTHER SECTORS.
Hokkaido: Toshichō (9)
Tsuzuki/Kurosaki in charge of Sector #2 (Kyushu)
...
Yay!
Chuugoku: Gokanchō (4)
Shikōku: Soteichō (3)
Tōuhoku: Heiseichō (8)
Chuubu: Godōtenrinchō (10)
Kyushu: Shōkōchō (2)
I'm lost!
Tokyo: Enmachō (5)
Enmachō is located in Sector # 7 (Taisenchō). (Because Tokyo is special.)
Watari in charge of Sector #6 (Kinki)
Okinawa: Shinkōchō (1)
Kinki: Henjyōchō (6)
Kantō: Taisenchō (7)
Aloha!
IT'S A BAD ILLUSTRA-TION...
IT MIGHT BE HARD TO UNDER-STAND. SORRY!
*The number in the ( ) shows the departments ranking within the Ministry.

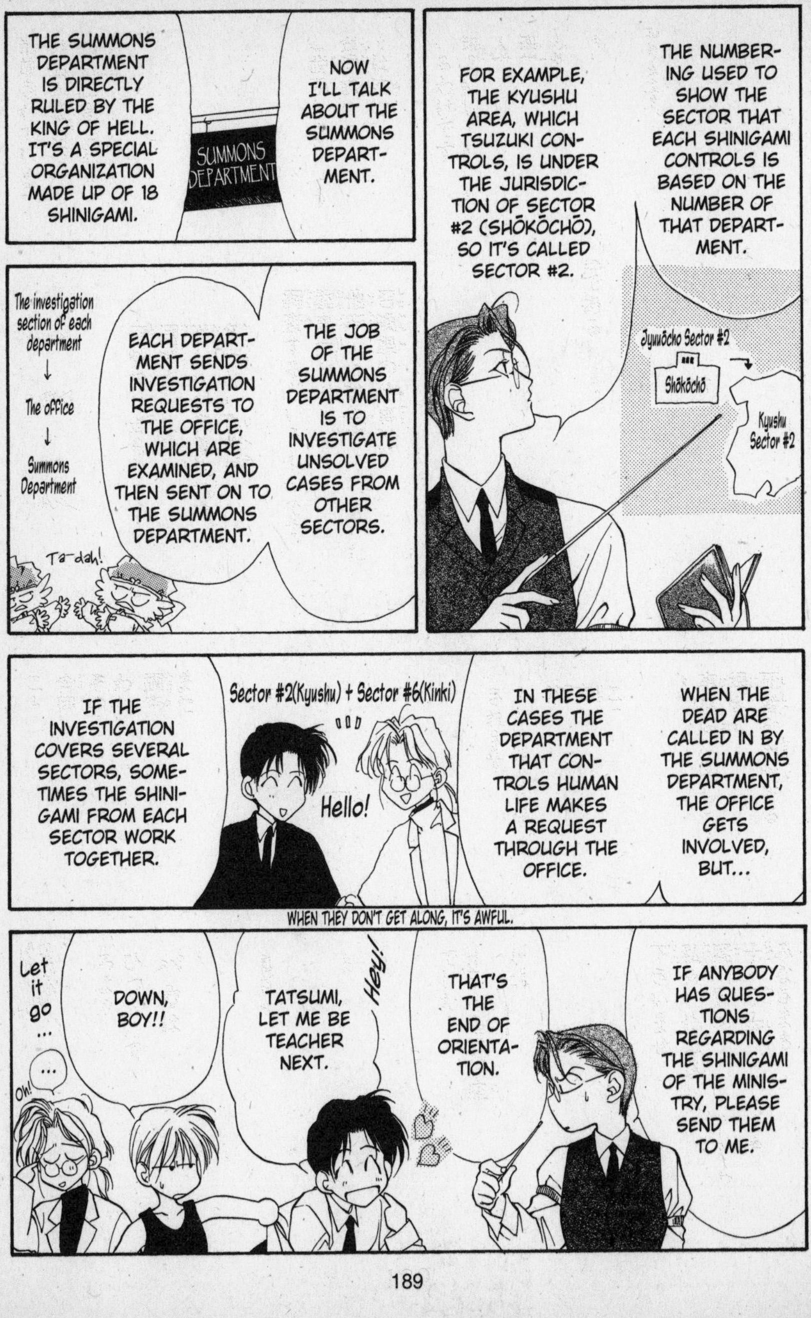
THE NUMBERING USED TO SHOW THE SECTOR THAT EACH SHINIGAMI CONTROLS IS BASED ON THE NUMBER OF THAT DEPARTMENT.
FOR EXAMPLE, THE KYUSHU AREA, WHICH TSUZUKI CONTROLS, IS UNDER THE JURISDICTION OF SECTOR #2 (SHŌKŌCHŌ), SO IT'S CALLED SECTOR #2.
Jyuuōcho Sector #2
Shōkōchō
Kyushu Sector #2
NOW I'LL TALK ABOUT THE SUMMONS DEPARTMENT.
SUMMONS DEPARTMENT
THE SUMMONS DEPARTMENT IS DIRECTLY RULED BY THE KING OF HELL. IT'S A SPECIAL ORGANIZATION MADE UP OF 18 SHINIGAMI.
THE JOB OF THE SUMMONS DEPARTMENT IS TO INVESTIGATE UNSOLVED CASES FROM OTHER SECTORS.
EACH DEPARTMENT SENDS INVESTIGATION REQUESTS TO THE OFFICE, WHICH ARE EXAMINED, AND THEN SENT ON TO THE SUMMONS DEPARTMENT.
The investigation section of each department ↓ The office ↓ Summons Department
Ta-dah!
WHEN THE DEAD ARE CALLED IN BY THE SUMMONS DEPARTMENT, THE OFFICE GETS INVOLVED, BUT...
IN THESE CASES THE DEPARTMENT THAT CONTROLS HUMAN LIFE MAKES A REQUEST THROUGH THE OFFICE.
Sector #2(Kyushu) + Sector #6(Kinki)
Hello!
IF THE INVESTIGATION COVERS SEVERAL SECTORS, SOMETIMES THE SHINIGAMI FROM EACH SECTOR WORK TOGETHER.
WHEN THEY DON'T GET ALONG, IT'S AWFUL.
IF ANYBODY HAS QUESTIONS REGARDING THE SHINIGAMI OF THE MINISTRY, PLEASE SEND THEM TO ME.
THAT'S THE END OF ORIENTATION.
Hey!
TATSUMI, LET ME BE TEACHER NEXT.
DOWN, BOY!!
Let it go...
...
Oh!

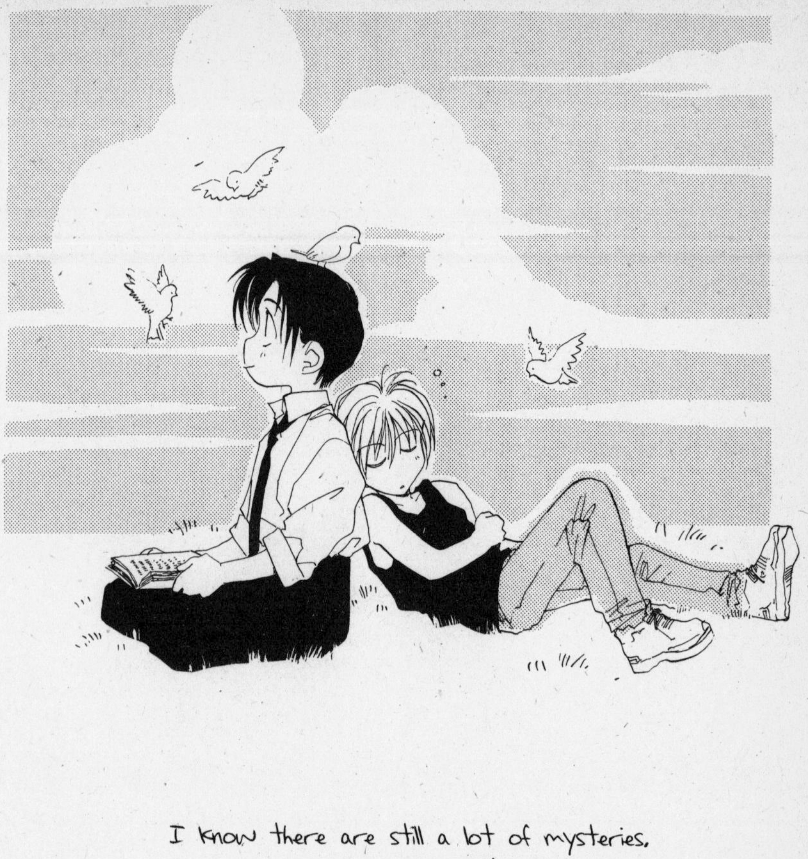

I know there are still a lot of mysteries. (Especially about Tsuzuki. You're all probably really annoyed. Oh, well.) Be patient and enjoy. Eventually the shinigami in your region will reveal themselves. When they do, don't get mad. Be nice to them.

—Yoko Matsushita.

Since food is a big part of Descendants of Darkness (Asato Tsuzuki loves his sweets, after all), we thought readers would be interested in a little bit more information about the foodstuffs mentioned in this particular volume. Space permitting, the book's scriptwriter has agreed to continue contributing a handy glossary of relevant miscellanea for each new book.

- Editor

# English Adaptation Notes
## by Kelly Sue DeConnick

**Castella Cake** – a light, sweet sponge cake popular in Nagasaki, where they claim it's been made since the 16th century. The name may come from the Spanish "Castile," though the recipe is apparently Portuguese.

**Chanpon** – a classic Nagasaki clear soup with meat, shellfish and vegetables. I found one Web site that claims the name is derived from "chapon" which, in Chinese, means "Have you eaten yet?" It would be like if we had a soup called "d'jeet yet" in English. (Did-ya-eat yet?) Someone should totally invent a soup called D'jeet Yet.

**Dorayaki** - Japanese pancakes, traditionally served sandwich fashion, with a scoop of sweet azuki bean paste between two cakes. Remember that cute little bunny with the pancake on his head who was Internet famous a while back? His name was Dorayaki.

**Sake** – Japanese rice wine.

**Shoronbô** – a small meat bun that you might eat at a ramen shop or a Chinese restaurant in Japan. Comes from the Chinese "xiaolong baozi." Pronounced "shourounpou."

**Toraya** – famous Japanese candy-making family. According to their site, the Toraya confectioners made candy for the Imperial Family in the 16th Century, as they do today.

**Yôkan** - a crystallized fruit made from soybean jam and sometimes mixed with hazel nuts (mushi yôkan) or sesame (goma yôkan).

# Dispatches of Darkness
## by Kelly Sue DeConnick

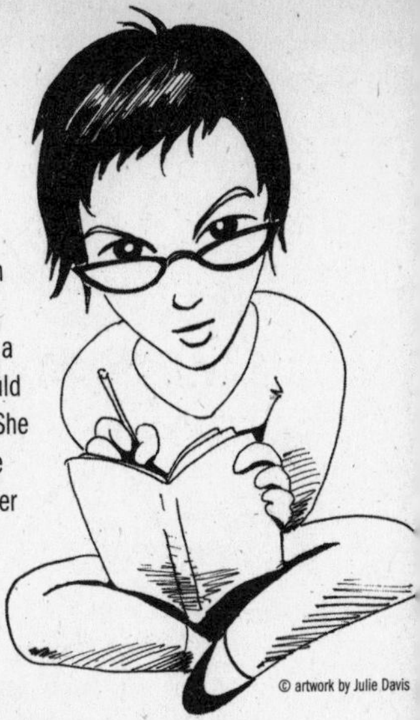
© artwork by Julie Davis

I just got off the phone with my grandmother, Mary. She was calling to thank me for some flowering quince branches I sent and to catch up on news of our new house, our new puppy, and the billion other this-es-and-thats-es that grandmothers call to catch up on. Mary is a beautiful and brilliant woman who, despite her many infirmities, could easily pass for being two decades younger than her near 80 years. She has a tremendous wit and there's usually a fire in her voice, but she hasn't been feeling well lately. She's got arthritis in her spine and her hip and swelling in her knee and, that most debilitating of human ailments, a broken heart. Her husband, Bob, my grandfather, has been gone just over a year now.

Bob's last few years were tough ones. Blood transfusions every two weeks and dialysis every other day. If the Ministry were real, Bob's name would have been on the kiseki for a long, long time before he passed. Years. For years, Mary managed their lives and their household around doctors' appointments and pharmacy visits and Bob continued to defy the odds. And everyone who knew him knows that he did it for her-- because, dammit, 55 years of laughing and crying just wasn't enough. So the summonses kept coming, not in the form of handsome men in trenchcoats, sadly, but in new diagnoses. First diabetes, then a stroke, then a rare blood condition, and so on. On April 9th, 2003, it was just too much. They found him and made him let go of her hand.

It's comforting to know that even outside of fiction, there are everyday love stories worth fighting for, vows that are somehow bigger than death.

My husband sent me a piece from Peter Johnson's USA Today column last month: "Marguerite Rooney, 85, wife of 60 Minutes commentator Andy Rooney, died Tuesday in New York. They met when they were both 14 at Mrs. Munson's dance class in Albany, N.Y., white gloves and all, and were married in 1942. Not a bad run. 'Not good enough,' Rooney says."

The bit about the white gloves hit me like a fist to the chest.

Here's to Bob and Marguerite and all the people on the list who wouldn't go when they were supposed to. They couldn't run forever, but I'm damned sure glad they tried.

Kelly Sue DeConnick is responsible for the English adaptation of Descendants of Darkness. She also works on the titles Sensual Phrase, Kare First Love and Blue Spring. She lives in Kansas City and can be contacted c/o VIZ.

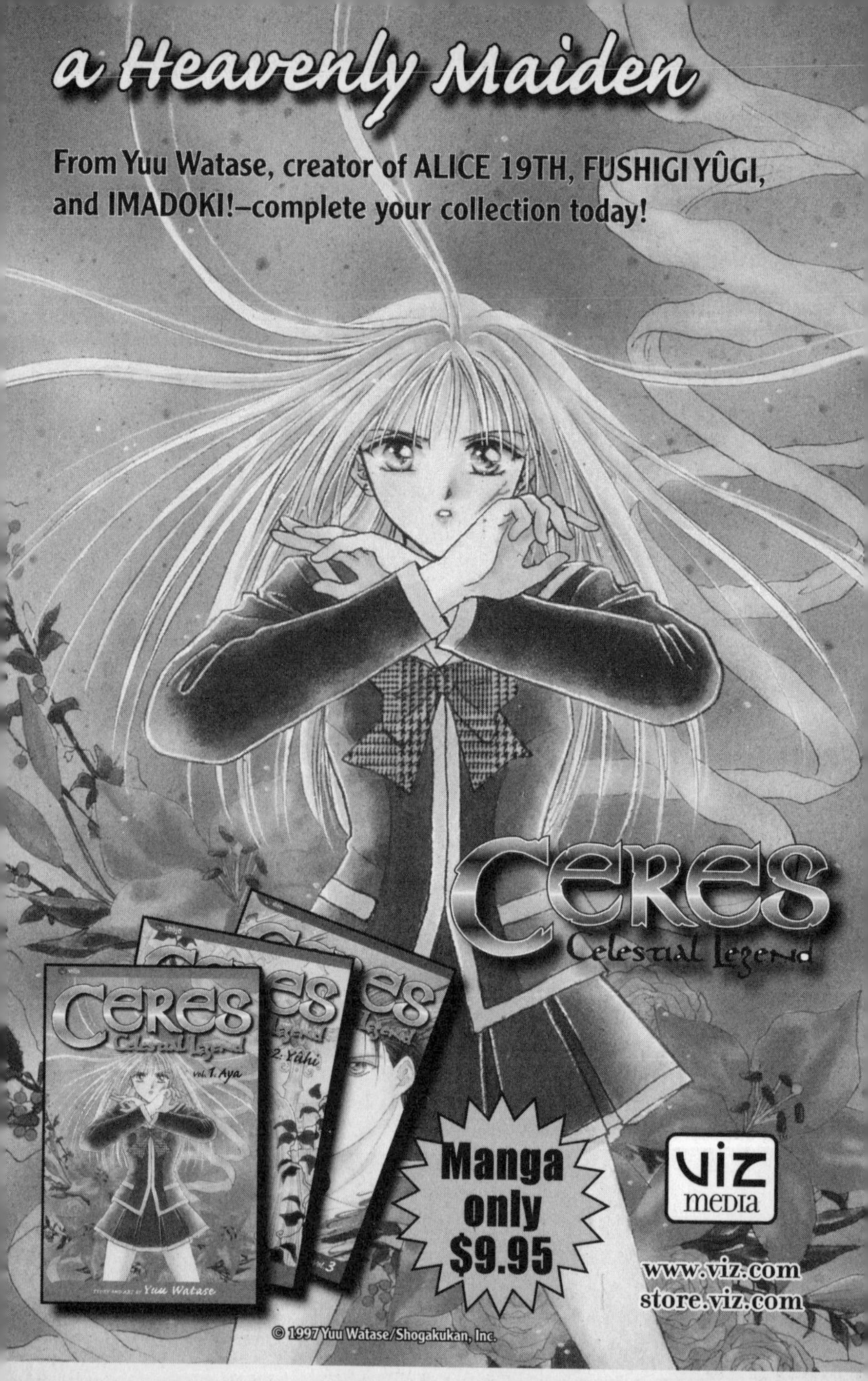
a Heavenly Maiden
From Yuu Watase, creator of ALICE 19TH, FUSHIGI YÛGI, and IMADOKI!–complete your collection today!
Ceres
Celestial Legend
Ceres Celestial Legend vol. 1 Aya
Yuu Watase
2 Yûhi
vol. 3
Manga only $9.95
viz media
www.viz.com
store.viz.com
© 1997 Yuu Watase/Shogakukan, Inc.